MW01118225

THE HOUSE OF
MORGAN

A SOCIAL BIOGRAPHY OF THE
MASTERS OF MONEY

BY

LEWIS COREY

GROSSET & DUNLAP
PUBLISHERS · NEW YORK

J. PIERPONT MORGAN

CONTENTS

LIST OF ILLUSTRATIONS

PART ONE

———————

BACKGROUNDS

CHAPTER I

ARISTOCRACY

> The Fish-Footman said in a solemn tone,
> "For the Duchess. An invitation from the
> Queen to play croquet." The Frog-Footman
> repeated, in the same solemn tone, only
> changing the order of the words a little,
> "From the Queen. An invitation for the
> Duchess to play croquet."
>
> ALICE IN WONDERLAND

IN 1901 Windsor Castle, hallowed by royalty, courtiers and men-at-arms, echoed to the tread of a score of American multi-millionaires. They composed a delegation of the New York Chamber of Commerce come to felicitate Edward VII, newly crowned King of Great Britain and Ireland (and Emperor of India). The King was curious to see the millionaires, particularly J. Pierpont Morgan and Andrew Carnegie.

Carnegie was not there but Morgan was—the uncrowned American money king who had just confirmed his mastery by organizing the United States Steel Corporation, the industrial giant which awed equally the man on the throne and the man in the street, and was now buying British ships to form an international shipping trust. "From the King down," according to contemporary report, "all concentrated their attention on Mr. Morgan, and their curiosity was not unmixed with awe." Court officers "trembled" (humorously but none the less suggestively, as Morgan had been actively buying British art treasures) "lest Mr. Morgan should take a fancy to Windsor and buy it."[1] Resenting the "American invasion," one British newspaper suggested Morgan's coronation.[2]

Wealthy Americans, seeking the accolade of royal recogni-

tion and presentation, flocked to the British court. Competing
with Britain in this, as in other things, Kaiser Wilhelm II
began a campaign to secure Americans for his own court, until
the honor of German presentation almost matched the British.
Morgan was one of Wilhelm's favorites. The Kaiser dined on
Morgan's yacht, the *Corsair,* decorated him with the Order of
the Red Eagle, sent him a marble bust of himself, and once
called Morgan "my mascot" because the only time His Majesty's yacht won in the Kiel races was when the American
financier was aboard.[3] Morgan himself cultivated the regal
temper, arrogant, arbitrary, massive, and its accompanying delight in splendor and magnificence, assuming the majesty of
Renaissance merchant princes. Among the English clergy,
whom he often entertained, Morgan was known as "Pierpontifex Maximus" (so named by an ironical archbishop).[4]
Behind the magnificence and regal temper towered the House
of Morgan, dominant financially in the world's mightiest industrial nation. The financial power of a new economic system
permitted Morgan to become magnificent, to mingle with
kings, and to say in royal strain after meeting Kaiser Wilhelm
II, "He pleases me."[5]

It was the new aristocracy of money accepting and being
accepted by the old aristocracy of blood in a world where aristocracy and money were combining and coming to mean the
same thing.

An aristocracy may perish but the aristocratic ideal survives.
... Although American colonization (particularly in New
England) was an expression of the revolt against aristocracy,
class and caste distinctions prevailed among the settlers. Each
stage of colonial development projected its own aristocracy.
The older colonial aristocracy bent to the storms of the Revolution and Jeffersonian democracy, assumed new forms and
pretensions in terms of commercial affluence. By 1850 a pane-
gyrist was crowing:

"There is no nobility in this country. There is a class of

princes...the princes of commerce, and such names are *good* in Asia, Africa, Europe, or in any part of America." [6]

This commercial aristocracy, however, yielded to the industrial and financial aristocracy arising after the Civil War out of the onward sweep of capitalist enterprise. Multi-millionaires now dominated the scene—Kings of Railways, Oil, Steel, Beef, Pork, Copper, Tin, Banking—developing the American aristocracy of money.

But this aristocracy was apparently tormented by an inferiority complex, in spite of adopting seignorial manners and trappings. Biting the hand that fed it, the new aristocracy began to consider American money as rather common and not quite distinctive. Amassers of illegitimate millions, whose methods would now land them in prison, started the sport of buying European titles for their daughters. (The sport is still on, although declining and cheapened by the competition of movie stars and Russian émigrés.) But since only women could marry titles and the opportunity, moreover, was limited, the aristocracy of money began to acquire ancestors (minus the prisons and the gallows). It helped socially, if one's immediate progenitors were pioneers or uncouth business pirates. That the original American Astor was a peddler and his brother a butcher didn't harmonize with Mrs. William Astor's queenly rule of New York's social élite. So they discovered Astors of seignorial lineage in the aristocracy of France and Castile. Genealogy went on a spree, seeking and finding the most astonishing lineages. John D. Rockefeller is a descendant of Henry I, King of France, and Calvin Coolidge of Charlemagne. J. Pierpont Morgan, according to one genealogist, descends from David I of Scotland, while another ignores the kingly strain and traces the Morgans to Norman robber barons who "received" large estates in England after the Conquest. [7]

This tracing of aristocratic lineage, however, was only a stage in the development of the aristocracy of money, and now is largely limited to its "genteel" fringe which has more blood than money. Research is democratizing aristocratic descent: every American family of English origin, it appears, stems from Alfred the Great, William the Conqueror or Robert Bruce.[8] Moreover, the Morgans and other masters of money can dispense with lineage in favor of the more substantial trappings of aristocracy which money provides—*their own* aristocracy.

Power and being are aristocracy's final justification. The aristocracy of money is supreme, and supremacy reconciles it to its lowly origins in the conquest of a continent by the sweat and blood and agony of ordinary men and women, particularly as origins recede in tradition and become ancestry. Aristocracy conforms to its age, developing its own ideals and trappings, which are more than snobbery: they are the manifestations of class supremacy and authority, insuring order, security and stability. Power is aristocracy, and money is the source of power in modern civilization and constitutes its aristocracy.

CHAPTER II

COLONIAL ORIGINS

*"When I used to read fairy tales, I fancied
that kind of thing never happened, and
now here I am in the middle of one!"*

ALICE IN WONDERLAND

MILES MORGAN, the American ancestor of the masters of the
House of Morgan, arrived in Boston in 1636, accompanied by
his brothers John and James. They came, as most immigrants
then and now, seeking economic betterment. The grandfather
was a Welsh saddler, the family originally of the minor gentry
come upon evil times.[1] The New World might mean fortune.

Colonial immigrants were plain people, in spite of the aristocratic pretensions of their successful descendants. The underlings of English society, they had least to lose and most to
gain from adventuring in the wilderness. Considered "rabble"
by the aristocracy, the settlers were merchants, yeomen, mechanics, indentured servants and imprisoned debtors—the
"despicables" in a system of privilege, yet destined to create
a finer civilization. Colonial immigration was an aspect of the
general movement of revolt against aristocracy, of the capitalist transformation of feudalism. The onward sweep of this
movement washed the Morgans ashore in New England.

John Morgan did not tarry in Boston. He was either a
skeptic or too merry, for an old chronicle reports that, "observing the bigotry and persecuting spirit of the *Godly Puritans*
... he quitted these *meek disciples* of *John Calvin* with disgust
and indignation," going to more congenial Virginia.[2] John's
brothers were of tougher (or more godly) fiber. James settled
peacefully in New London. The more adventurous Miles ac-

companied an expedition under Col. William Pynchon to build a new settlement in the wilderness.

The Pynchon party found the Indians "perfectly friendly" and for £30 bought a tract of land which now includes seven towns in Massachusetts and Connecticut. The settlement was at Springfield. Although under twenty-one years of age, Miles Morgan "suppressed the fact of his minority in the drawing for house lots, which minors were not privileged to do." [3] This was the first "business stroke" of the American Morgans. Being a soldierly youngster, Miles built a fortified blockhouse upon his property; enterprising and acquisitive, he secured grant after grant of land, was elected constable, selectman, member of the Committee to Grant Land, and became one of Springfield's three most substantial citizens. [4]

Miles Morgan thrived exceedingly in Springfield, married twice, had nine children and died at the patriarchal age of eighty-four. [5] But before his death he took part in King Philip's War, becoming a captain in the colonial militia.

Friendly relations between Indians and settlers in New England did not last long. At first "buying" their land, the settlers simply took it as they became stronger. They would pick a quarrel with the Indians, declare war and seize coveted lands. The courts assumed jurisdiction over the Indians even when they did not live in the settlements, and ordered Indians fined or whipped for "profaning the Sabbath" by hunting, fishing or other "misdemeanors"—the fines being usually paid in land. [6] The inconvenient questioning of the settlers' land titles brought Roger Williams into conflict with the governing oligarchy and his banishment from Massachusetts. Overmastered and expropriated, the Indians in 1675 flared up in general revolt. King Philip's War was a war of extermination in which the savagery of the Indians was matched by the savagery of the settlers.

The Indians attacked, sacked and burned Springfield, the survivors taking refuge in Miles Morgan's blockhouse and under his command beat back all attacks. It was a hopeless situation, however, unless reënforcements came; and the survivors would have been exterminated if a friendly Indian had not crept through the besieging lines and brought aid.[7] A statue in Springfield honors Morgan's services—but not the Indian's.

Captain Miles Morgan served throughout the war, as did three of his sons of whom an old chronicle reports that "they are said to have been perfect *Nimrods* at the *laudable business* of Indian hunting." [8]

Business was not neglected during the war. Two weeks after its start a Boston gentleman proudly announced in a letter that "the land already gained is worth £10,000." [9] The Connecticut Council gave soldiers, in addition to regular pay, "all such plunder as they shall seize, both of persons and corn or other estate, to be dissposed of by them in the way of sale, so as they may best advantage themselves, providing Authority shall have the first tender of theire disspose of captives, allowing them the market price; to be divided amongst them, to the private soldiers, each man alike, and to the commanders so much a better part as there is difference in theire wages." [10]

The offer of "all such plunder as they shall seize, both of persons and estate," apparently inflamed some soldiers to plunder friends and foes alike, as the Council subsequently decreed that "if so it shall appear that wampum and other goods that was taken as plunder, yet is said to belong to innocent persons not enemies, it ought to be restored, for we may not allow wrong doing nor disorder in the persuit of our just revenge." [11]

Urged by the Connecticut Council to encourage volunteers "as wee doe, who doe grant them all plunder and souldyers pay," the Massachusetts Council in declaring unprovoked war upon the Narragansetts offered its soldiers allotments of land seized from the Indians in addition to regular pay. Indian volunteers in the colonial militia, however, were not granted land for their services during the war.[12]

Immense tracts of land were seized and divided as spoils. Connecticut granted land to 180 volunteers, among them James and Joseph Morgan.[13] After the war Miles Morgan and three others received "all the Swamp against their meddow over Agawam River vizt the upper meddow there."[14] In addition to land seizures, hundreds of Indian captives were sold as slaves in the West Indies and others retained as "servants" by the settlers. Among the sales were "13 Squawes and papooses, 1 sick" for £20, "1 woman, 4 little children" for £5, and "41 captives" for £82.[15] The Morgans, apparently, did not participate in this slave traffic.

All of which was considered legitimate. The Puritans identified self-interest and religion, ascribing a godly origin to their actions and the consequences. Instead of realizing that King Philip's War might have been caused by their oppressive behavior toward the Indians, the arrogant clergy (the governing power) insisted in a long proclamation that God had let loose the war because of His displeasure at too much drinking among the settlers, their laxity in persecuting the Quakers, impatience in listening to sermons, women's "immodesty" in dress, and scores of similar "sins."[16] Moreover, dominant Puritanism justified the acquisitive, pecuniary vices, inspired by the Calvinist doctrines sanctifying business enterprise and accumulation (in contrast to aristocracy). God was manifest in "good works" and "good works" meant labor and property. Property being the manifestation of God's will and blessing, its acquisition was an ideal. The New England settlers interpreted Puritanism in terms of their immediate environment: land was the most important form of property, "one of the gods of New England," and it was doing God's work to expropriate the Indians of their land, the Indians being "children of the Devil." The Morgans, in acquiring their original stake, were serving God according to their lights ... and their interests.

But there were other than pecuniary ideals in Puritanism.

MILES MORGAN

JOHN PIERPONT

Forged in the revolt against the old feudal order, and formu-
lating ideals of individual and social freedom, the Puritan
movement was fundamentally progressive in spite of the limitations imposed upon it by theology and the requirements of
developing capitalism of which it was an ideological expression. There were many radical Puritan sects which broke
through the limitations and proposed drastic reforms and
equalitarian democracy, expressing the aspirations of common
men and women. These sects thrived upon a contradiction in
the new creed. Since being poor or rich were equally manifestations of God's will, an intolerant contempt of the poor was
bred among the rich. But a Puritan might be godly and still
unsuccessful in acquiring property: what then? This was unimportant in the early settlements where conditions were primitive, land abundant, measurable equality prevailed and the
clerical aristocracy ruled ruthlessly in God's name. But conditions changed. By 1680 there were already thirty Massachusetts merchants each worth between $50,000 and $100,000,[17]
and by 1700 there was a definite cleavage between rich and
poor. Theocracy was overthrown, government being by the
new aristocracy of wealth, which considered government a
prerogative of property, serving property (instead of God).
There were murmurs of protest among the poor, both of the
older stock and the newer immigration. The protest identified
itself with the more radical aspects of Puritanism, with equalitarian democracy and liberty—an ideology that definitely colored American developments. In isolated cases the protest
projected proposals of ownership of property in common, implicit in the Scriptural sanctions of the Puritan creed.

The Morgans did not participate in this protest of the poor
against the rich, not being inflamed by the ideology of liberty.
Nor were they poor, being substantial landowners, conservative, prosperous and God-fearing. One of them was an impas-
sioned fighter against the newer radical ideas on property.
This was the Rev. Joseph Morgan, a descendant of Miles Mor-

gan's brother James. The reverend gentleman, it appears, was
not precisely immaculate. He was on trial in one church for
"practising astrology, countenancing promiscuous dancing, and
transgressing in drink." The charges were not sustained, but the
Rev. Joseph found it expedient to resign. He was suspended
from the ministry in another church because of intemperance,
but reinstated two years later "on the intercession of many
good people." [18] The Rev. Joseph Morgan, however, was sound
as a bell on property. In a sermon delivered in 1732 he said: [19]

"Covetousness (which is Idolatry) must be the Support of the
World, and the misery of it both. Each man coveting to make
himself rich, carries on the Publick Good: Thus God in His
Wisdom and *Mercy* turns our Wickedness to Publick Benefit."

This identification of God and the accumulation of riches
is supplemented by an idealization of poverty:

"It were better for the most of People to be poor than to be
born rich. For such have in general, really a more comfortable
Life here and far less dangerous as to the next Life.....A Rich
Man has a *miserable* life: for he is always full of Fear and
Care....Whereas a Man that has but Food and Raiment with
honest labour, is free from these Fears and Cares....We *need*
to *pity* and *love* Rich Men."

Since the trend of this argument might conceivably discourage the accumulation of riches, the Rev. Joseph Morgan
exclaims:

"But what am I doing? If this discourage People from
seeking after Riches, it would be a great Detriment to the
Publick, if not the undoing of the World....A rich Man is a
great friend to the Publick, while he aims at nothing but
serving himself. God will have us live by helping one another;
and since *Love* will not do it, *Covetousness* shall."

There is in this sermon a social twist to the Puritan identification of religion and self-interest, of God and the pecuniary
motives. In the older creed riches and poverty were matters
of individual relations with Deity: poverty was a sign of God's

displeasure, the poor being ungodly outcasts. In that particular form the creed could not survive the coming of social protest and more liberal ideas. The Rev. Joseph Morgan's formulation retains the religious sanction, but "socializes" the old creed by identifying it with the "Publick Good." In this the reverend gentleman probably paraphrased Mandeville's theory that "private vices are public virtues"—an important aspect of the ideology of developing capitalism. By identifying self-interest and religion the Puritans imparted an irresistible moral passion to acquisition and accumulation which survived the decay of their theology.

CHAPTER III

JOSEPH MORGAN, INNKEEPER

> *"They were learning to draw," the Dor-*
> *mouse went on, yawning and rubbing its*
> *eyes; "and they drew all manner of things,*
> *everything that begins with an M—."*
>
> ALICE IN WONDERLAND

THE curious error persists that J. Pierpont Morgan's grandfather was a captain in the Continental Army.[1] It was the
great-grandfather, however, who fought in the Revolution, an
American Cincinnatus retiring after the war to the ancestral
farm near Springfield. The son, grandfather of J. Pierpont
Morgan, was more enterprising and successful. This Joseph
Morgan, born in 1780, is described in the family chronicles as
"a renowned hotel-keeper" who died in 1847 "leaving a very
large estate."[2] Very formal, these chronicles. Joseph Morgan
was an innkeeper, owner of stage-coach lines and stock speculator, a shrewd Yankee with one eye on the main chance and
the other eye on any stray chance lying about.

There were many chances for the enterprising. The Revolution liberated political and economic forces. In the midst of
class conflicts over the forms and purposes of the new government, industrial changes shaped the nation in the image of
capitalism. Dominant contemporary opinion interpreted the
Revolution in terms of larger commercial opportunity: "The
American Revolution was not so much a liberation from political as from commercial thralldom ... a commercial movement favored by the merchant, producer and manufacturer."[3]
Industry and commerce developed intensively, while the west-

ward migrations produced new wealth and larger markets. The chances of making money multiplied.

But one could not make much money as a farmer in New England, where farming was becoming unprofitable and farms being deserted. The enterprising Joseph Morgan decided to make a change. He became an innkeeper.

Commercial progress imparted new importance to taverns and stage-coach transportation. Taverns usually prospered exceedingly, our ancestors being heroic drinkers—"a man was not considered 'drunk' unless prostrate and unconscious." [4] But the tavern was more than a place patronized by the world, the flesh and the Devil. It was a social, political and business center, the stopping-place of the stage-coach and of businessmen on their travels. Being the chief means of transportation, stages earned high profits, and the high profits bred competition and rate wars. In one case a rate war ended in the competitors luring passengers with the offer of free fare plus free dinner and a bottle of wine. [5] Ownership of taverns and stage lines was often combined: it was "big business."

This flourishing business attracted Joseph Morgan. In 1817 he left the ancestral farm and, accompanied by his wife and their son, Junius Spencer Morgan, moved to Hartford. This city was the most important and prosperous trade center of the Connecticut River Valley, thriving upon the active movement of population and business. Taverns were probably not in the tradition of the Morgan ancestors, but man must often stoop to conquer, and Joseph Morgan's Inn set out its shield. [6]

The owner being a shrewd and ingratiating host, Joseph Morgan's Inn prospered immediately. Ye host was neither brusque nor reserved, but greeted the stages and their passengers and mingled with the guests, who consumed enormous meals including much wine and rum. Joseph Morgan's Inn bid for the patronage of Hartford's prosperous, substantial citizens, and got it.

This patronage gave Morgan his chance and was responsible

for his fortune. In 1819 a group of Hartford's most important businessmen met at the Inn and organized the Aetna Fire Insurance Company. Joseph Morgan was not among the organizers. Only a small part of the capital was paid in cash, the balance in promissory notes, it being anticipated that the profits would make unnecessary any more cash payments from stockholders. But progress was slow and discouraging, arousing the fear that assessments might become necessary to meet obligations. The price of stock declining disastrously, Joseph Morgan bought many shares for almost nothing, and possibly received shares outright from patrons of his Inn, there being "plenty of instances where stockholders boasted of having found some one who would take their shares off their hands, liabilities and all." Morgan's profit from a comparatively negligible investment must have been large, as within a few years Aetna's capital had become $3,000,000, of which only $196,000 was paid in by stockholders, the difference representing capitalized earnings and profits.[7] This stroke of speculation made Joseph Morgan a really rich man.

As the stages, impressive in their bright colors, showy animals and picturesque drivers, drove up to Joseph Morgan's Inn, ye host pondered the profits in the business. Tavern and stages could easily be combined in profitable joint enterprises. Hartford was a transportation center, one of the most important stage lines being the Middle Road line from Boston to New York via Hartford and New Haven, thence by steamboat to New York. Joseph Morgan acquired considerable interests in stage lines. There is a story that he "eventually rose to the control of the chief roads of transportation in the State," [8] but of this there is no proof. Morganized enterprise was still to come.

Then railroads appeared, and—

...a shrill whistle blew,
And the merciless age with its discord and din
Made wreck, as it passed, of the stage and the inn.[9]

The railway accelerated the industrial and commercial revolution which produced disturbing social changes. Identified with the factory system and other developments, the railway was unsparingly condemned by people who clung to the old system of things. It was "an invention of the Devil" encouraging "capitalist monopoly and, therefore, anti-republican," calculated to "introduce manufactures into the heart of the country, divert industry from the primitive and moral pursuits of agriculture, and bring on us the vices and miseries of manufacturing and commercial places." [10] This expressed the agrarian revolt against developing industrialism, the struggle between agriculture and industry which was to persist in one form or another until the end of the century.

Railroads drove the stages and their drivers out of business. The stage driver had been a flame of color in a generally drab life, a picturesque personage beloved of women and an ideal of youth. The populace sympathized with the stage driver in his downfall. Moreover, the new form of transportation also wrecked taverns which had depended largely upon the stagecoach for their business. Recognizing the irresistibility of the new form of travel and its consequences, Joseph Morgan prudently withdrew in time from the tavern and stage business, prosperously surviving a change which to others meant disaster.

Travel was now a prerogative of the railroads, traveling guests of the hotel, and drink of the saloon. Joseph Morgan opened a large hotel in Hartford, more in consonance with the times and his position as an affluent and important citizen.

Meanwhile the son, Junius Spencer Morgan, born in 1809, was becoming an active and successful businessman. Starting at sixteen as a bank clerk, Junius Morgan five years later entered independent business on his father's money, forming the New York City banking house of Ketchum, Morgan & Co.[11] Upon the dissolution of this partnership Junius Morgan went into the drygoods business as a junior partner in Howe,

Mather & Co., and in 1851 became a partner in J. M. Beebe & Co. of Boston.[12] Beebe, the son of a farmer, started in the retail business and then acquired undisputed leadership as a wholesale merchant. When a customer doubted his resources Beebe proudly answered, "This store is good for a million."[13] It was. The firm soon became J. M. Beebe, Morgan & Co., testifying to Junius Morgan's resources and business capacity. One of the junior partners in Beebe, Morgan & Co. was Levi P. Morton—the same Morton who in later years was first a financial ally and then subordinate of J. Pierpont Morgan (at this time still in high school). As most other affluent merchants, Morgan and Beebe engaged actively in banking and insurance, Beebe himself dabbling in railroad promotion.[14]

Neither the temperament nor the activity of Junius Spencer Morgan was dramatic. Perseverance and commercial rectitude constituted his most important characteristics. Particularly rectitude, in an age when the following mordant suggestion could appear in a business journal:

"The proper course for a merchant to pursue when he fails, is to go deliberately to work. When he finds he is to fail and cannot help it, if he owes half a million dollars, he should immediately buy to the extent of a million—then turn it into cash, say $800,000. Then report that his failure is an immensely bad one, and that the unfortunate merchant will never pay two cents on the dollar. In this way he will be able to purchase all his debts for ten cents on the dollar or $100,000. This leaves him clear in bank or United States stocks $700,000. All will join in saying: 'What an honest man!' Let him give up every dollar and not have enough to buy a morsel of victuals, and every one will say: 'What a damned scoundrel!' "[15]

Junius Spencer Morgan, on the contrary, maintained a high code of business morality. One indication of this was dissolution of the partnership of Ketchum, Morgan & Co. Morris Ketchum was an unscrupulous speculator, engaged in many shady business transactions,[16] an important reason for J. S. Morgan severing the partnership.

This rectitude of J. Pierpont Morgan's father mingled with a ruthlessly acquisitive temperament, grim-mouthed, pompously dignified, coldly conservative and antagonistic to democracy.

The anti-democratic bias was developed in Junius Morgan by the business and social aristocracy of Hartford. Federalist reaction after the Revolution conquered the democratic radicals among the farmers, small traders and mechanics, particularly in New England where the clergy united with the mercantile aristocracy and the newly rich created by speculation to usurp the government. This aristocracy believed in government by "the charmed circle of the rich or well-born" and used the words "rich, wise, good and able" interchangeably.[17] Thomas Jefferson was a viper, the democratic movement a menace to civilization. The most reactionary of the New England States was Connecticut, ruled by an aristocracy which also ruled Hartford— the city founded by Thomas Hooker and his followers as a democratic challenge to the theocratic oligarchy of Massachusetts. The mood of this aristocracy was expressed by the Hartford Wits, a group of merchants, lawyers, professors and ministers clinging to ancestral customs and the stakes of power, scorning progress, contemptuous of the plain men and women creating a more democratic society. The pioneers in the great westward migration which was to recast American civilization were excoriated by the president of Yale: "They are not fit to live in regular society. They are too idle; too talkative; too passionate; too prodigal, and too shiftless to acquire property or character. They are impatient at the restraints of law, religion or morality."[18] Another of the Wits, Dr. Lemuel Hopkins, expressed the aristocracy's mood in hysterical verse:

> Led by wild demagogues, the factious crowd,
> Mean, fierce, imperious, insolent and loud . . .

See, from the shades, on tiny pinions swell
And rise, the young DEMOCRACY *of* Hell! [19]

This was the mood in Hartford. Joseph Morgan the inn-keeper trimmed his sails to its wind, tolerated if not accepted. But Junius Morgan was of the aristocracy, born and bred in the purple. Contempt of democracy was in him an ingrained characteristic.

Aristocracy must conform to its age, and Junius Morgan interpreted the aristocratic mood in terms of the modern business aristocracy which recognizes *noblesse oblige* by assuming the "moral" and "philanthropic" responsibility of community life. Junius Morgan was a vestryman of Christ Church, advisor of the Orphan Asylum, an incorporator, trustee and vice president of the Young Men's Institute. This Institute was a primitive model of business civic and moral organizations, formed "for the moral and intellectual improvement of its members"—"the vain and frivolous pleasures of youth giving place to higher and more rational enjoyments." [20] The conservative Junius Morgan, however, was not in the least moved by progressive social ideals and movements. His interest in civic and moral endeavors was an expression of the Rev. Joseph Morgan's conviction that "rich Men carry on the Publick Good" transformed into civic endeavors justifying (and developing) the ideology and practice of acquisition. Junius Morgan's successors are legion.

CHAPTER IV

JOHN PIERPONT, REBEL

> *She knelt down and looked along the*
> *passage into the loveliest garden you ever*
> *saw. How she longed to get out of that*
> *dark hall, and wander among those beds*
> *of bright flowers and those cool fountains.*
>
> ALICE IN WONDERLAND

JUNIUS SPENCER MORGAN was the father of John Pierpont Morgan, born April 17, 1837. The mother was Julia Pierpont, daughter of John Pierpont the clergyman, poet and rebel. Disinterested opinion is that Pierpont "was the most striking character among all of Morgan's forebears." [1] The Morgans apparently prefer the shrewd, acquisitive innkeeper, one biographer saying: "Joseph Morgan was altogether less distinguished than Pierpont, but he has the credit of founding the Morgan fortune, while the other, after a stormy, brilliant but disappointing career, died as the holder of an obscure government post at Washington." [2]

In his own words, Pierpont was animated by "love of right, freedom and men, and corresponding hatred of everything that is at war with them." The "meanness and crime which he saw about him in high places" aroused flaming protest. Pierpont's political inspiration was Samuel Adams, professional agitator and rebel, relentless organizer of colonial revolutionary activity, antagonist of British and American aristocracy, the enemy of Alexander Hamilton and friend of Thomas Jefferson and Tom Paine. [3]

Born in 1785, John Pierpont was successively academy teacher, private tutor, lawyer and merchant. Urged to the church, he was ordained minister in 1819, accepting a call to become pastor of the Hollis Street Church, Boston. Pierpont was a vital force in the Unitarian Church and one of the most active organizers of the American Unitarian Association.[4]

But the man was more than a minister, he was a social rebel. Compact of scriptural austerity, righteous indignation and moral passion, John Pierpont's religion was warmed by humanitarian aspirations for social betterment. "It is upon the great, breathing mass of the community," Pierpont insisted, "that the Christian minister is to act."[5] Although couched in terms of "Thus saith the Lord," his revolt was determined by contemporary social conditions and aspirations, an expression of the libertarian enthusiasm which swept New England prior to the Civil War.

This movement of social and humanitarian protest was a product of the industrial revolution which was particularly active in New England. Old institutions, class privileges and ideas crumbled under the impact of capitalist development. The old commercial aristocracy declined, and by 1834 about 85 per cent of Boston's merchants were identified with manufacturing enterprises.[6] The advances in well-being of farmers and workers were trifling compared with the accumulation of riches by the factory owners and their merchandising allies, intensifying economic and social inequality. Labor was industrially oppressed and socially degraded, the workers complaining of "the low estimation in which useful labor is held" by the prosperous.[7] Unions appeared, strikes and independent labor political action, shocking the aristocracy of money and culture, securing universal suffrage and free public schools (which were condemned as "un-American" and a threat to the Republic). Agriculture was becoming unprofitable, farms being abandoned, and the westward migration almost depopulated New England of its old stock, while immigrants flocked in as raw material for the factory system. These immigrants, mostly Irish and German, were despised in much the same manner as their descendants later despised the immigrants from Southern Europe, their radical ideas of equalitarian democracy sharpening the hatred. On the frontier clamored the new pioneer democracy, independent, scornful of privilege, and in control of the presidency under Andrew Jackson. The old order was breaking down, the new still a confusing chaos.

The sufferings, resentments and instability produced by social change aroused protest, humanitarianism, millennial aspirations. In the twilight zone between the old and the new order reform movements and romantic enthusiasms flourished. It was a mixed crop, mingling reactionary and progressive protest against the new state of things. Gentle Unitarian melancholy mourning the old familiar order and then merging with the new, flaming protest against social injustice, dreams of utopian socialism, hopes of restoring the old social equilibrium, Transcendentalist philosophy, labor organization and action, the strident anti-slavery movement of William Lloyd Garrison and other agitators. James Russell Lowell expressed the rebel mood: "Truth forever on the scaffold, Wrong forever on the throne, Yet that scaffold sways the future." The social sap was stirring, stirring—in John Pierpont among many others.

But that was not the mood of the majority, which felt that the misery of the industrial revolution was justified by its profits. Conditions in the factories were bad, very bad, but contemporary opinion persisted in sentimentalizing the situation, as in the following apology:

· "The principles of our holy religion are too deeply implanted in the soil to further that course of policy which might lead either to vice or ignorance; and it is well-known that in no other part of the globe are moral principles more widely diffused than in that particular section of the republic where the manufacturing system most extensively prevails." [8]

This complacent, sentimental indifference infuriated Pierpont. He did not yearn for the past, but was concerned with the present and the future. Flamingly, unyieldingly he preached the word of God in terms of social action. The pulpit was his forum. "So many," said Pierpont, "even of the professed disciples of Jesus, have lived after the flesh, minding things of the flesh, and so few, comparatively, after the spirit, minding things of the spirit.... Dare we state the amount that shall exhibit fairly the relative amount of our service to God, and to Mammon?" [9]

In a sermon comprising an imaginary discussion between an Apostle and a new convert who objected to the burning of the Ephesian books, John Pierpont categorically rejected the idea that the rights of property are supreme over life and progress:

"The fashions of this world pass away, and with them must pass away the employments that depend upon those fashions. ... All those who are connected, at any time, with the existing order of things, when that order gives place to a better, must give place to those who bring in the better, or must themselves take hold of that which *is* better.... Will even Roman righteousness consider the claims of the Druid minister *to be left alone in his business?* ... When the merchants of the earth shall weep because no man buyeth any more merchandise of slaves, and the souls of men—what will become of those, or of their vocation, who now so curiously braid the slave-driver's thong? ... And well may the craftsmen tremble for their trade, when the gods are falling whom it is their trade to serve!... The *scenes of human duty and trial change* with the ever-changing circumstances of human life. The *principles of the moral government of God,* and the rules by which duty is measured, are as unchangeable as God himself." [10]

The social creed in these scriptural images is simple and direct: You can't be let alone in your business if it doesn't serve humanity. The opposite of Junius Morgan's creed (and of his son, J. Pierpont Morgan)....

One of the reforms urged by John Pierpont was the abolition of imprisonment for debt. This atrocious law, which weighed most heavily upon the poor, was condemned by labor organizations as "a law that makes poverty a crime" and "a remnant of the feudal system." An average of 75,000 persons were imprisoned for debt yearly in the United States, 1,400 in Boston alone. One-half of these imprisonments were for debts of less than $20. In Boston, a blind man with a dependent family was imprisoned for a debt of $6; in Salem, a veteran of Bunker Hill for a few dollars; in Providence, a widow for 68 cents, imprisoned by the man to save whose property from fire her husband had lost his life.[11] The indecency of the law aroused Pierpont, and his denunciations were frequent and savage.

Temperance was another issue. Pierpont's approach was more social than individual, his invective being directed primarily against business exploitation of drink. He urged temperance (not prohibition), serving wine at his table. Drink being morally, economically and politically a definite power in New England, Pierpont's agitation aroused the hostility of powerful vested interests.

But the great issue was slavery and John Pierpont was an ardent abolitionist, active in organizing the New England Anti-Slavery Society, a comrade of Garrison and a frequent contributor to *The Liberator*. The slavery issue was now inflaming the nation and Pierpont unflinchingly preached resistance to the great wrong. New England preferred slavery to disturbance, in spite of its finest representatives favoring abolition. The aristocracy of money and culture was prosperous, comfortable: let us alone! Slaving, moreover, had contributed immensely to colonial New England's wealth, and many a merchant still reaped riches from smuggling black ivory, while the aristocrats of Cambridge built their mansions on proceeds of West Indian slave plantations.[12] Still more important, the textile mills depended upon Southern cotton, and the manufacturers, eager not to antagonize the slavocracy, were almost solid against the agitators. The irrepressible conflict as yet was irrepressible only in the minds of farseeing radicals.

Uncompromising as Garrison, John Pierpont identified abolition with the struggle against reaction in general. His mood is expressed in the following stanzas from one of his poems:

> *Ay, slaves of slaves! What, sleep ye yet,*
> *And dream of freedom while ye sleep?*
> *Ay, dream while Slavery's foot is set*
> *So firmly on your necks, while deep*
> *The chains her quivering flesh endures*
> *Gnaw, like a cancer, into yours?*
>
> *Ha! say ye that I've falsely spoken,*
> *Calling you slaves? Then prove ye're not.*
> *Work a free press!—ye'll see it broken;*
> *Stand to defend it!—ye'll be shot.*
> *Oh, yes, but people should not dare*
> *Print what "the brotherhood" won't bear!* [13]

Pierpont condemned the Fugitive Slave Law as "a covenant with Judas," and his answer to the argument that it was constitutional was this:

"What if it is? If the Constitution justifies wrong, I am *bound* to transgress the Constitution.... If I see even the Constitution of the United States in my path...it shall not hinder —it shall help me on my way; for I will mount upward by treading it under my feet." [14]

These utterances, barbed with indignation, invective and logic, exceedingly disturbed Pierpont's congregation. The "Sunday-go-meeting" mood was of gentle meditation on the hereafter, communing comfortably with Deity, and reconciling religion and self-interest; but this madman insisted on identifying Christ's teachings with everyday life, and proposed disturbingly radical intervention in social struggles! The congregation was indignant—at least, the majority was. Why shouldn't Pierpont conform to the advice of the Rev. Francis Parkman (acted upon by the overwhelming majority of ministers) to avoid "certain vexed and complicated questions," such as slavery? Dr. Parkman imposed comfortable limits on the task of the clergyman:

"To preach the unchangeable word; to offer up with a pure heart the prayers of the people; to maintain in their simplicity and sanctity the ordinances of our faith; to watch for souls ...maintaining the quiet tenor of his way, not entangling himself with the passing interests of this life—such an one will approve himself to God as a good minister."[15]

But to John Pierpont this was a paltering with the faith and compromise with evil, an evasion of the social tasks of religion. The Christian minister was to act "upon the great, breathing mass of the community," religion being the sword of social justice. The prophets of the Old Testament did not avoid "vexed and complicated questions" nor "maintain the quiet tenor of their way." That was the way of peace, undoubtedly, but not of righteousness. And so Pierpont in the pulpit thundered against social wrongs—particularly against the wrong of slavery—and justified his procedure by scriptural authority.

Part of the congregation protested, but Pierpont was implacable. In 1838 the friction broke into war. A committee of the congregation, representing a bare majority, asked the pastor to avoid "exciting" subjects, "above all, the abolition of slavery," to which Pierpont answered: "If I could consent that *any* topic should be taken out of the cognizance of my pulpit, it should be some one that is *not* exciting."[16] The struggle becoming more bitter, the opposition accused Pierpont of "interfering with the laws of the land," of commercial dishonesty and moral impurity (the "moral impurity" consisting of using the word "whore" in a lecture!), and demanded his resignation. The pastor refused to resign, insisting on a trial before a church court: "To me it is fatal if your charges are true: to you, if they are false and malicious. Either meet me upon them, or retract them." [17] Apparently afraid of a trial, the opposition insisted on resignation and refused to pay the pastor's salary.

Unyielding, John Pierpont secured the trial he insisted upon. The formal complaint to the Ecclesiastical Council comprised a series of charges impeaching Pierpont's moral character, but the burden of the complaint was the pastor's "too busy interference with questions of legislation on the subject of prohibiting the sale of ardent spirits; too busy interference with questions of legislation on the subject of imprisonment for debt; too busy interference with the popular controversy on the subject of the abolition of slavery." [18]

The trial was held in 1841 and lasted six months, arousing large public interest. Pierpont retracted nothing and was triumphantly sustained by the Council, which dismissed the moral charges and, while disapproving of some phases of Pierpont's controversial activities, decided there was nothing to justify his removal. On appeal, the Supreme Judicial Court sustained the decision. Having received vindication, John Pierpont resigned his pastorate. [19] The resignation was accepted.

While as uncompromising as Garrison on slavery, Pierpont favored the Abolitionists who broke with Garrison on the issue of independent political action. He was active in organizing the Liberty Party and its candidate for governor of Massachusetts. Appreciating that slavery was interwoven with other social problems—labor, government corruption, the seizure of the public lands by Northern speculators and Southern slaveholders—Pierpont accepted the merger of the Liberty Party with the Free Soil Party and was one of its Congressional candidates. [20] Although not Abolitionist, the Free Soil Party was against the extension of slavery to new States and pledged itself to "maintain the rights of free labor against the aggression of the slave power, and secure a free soil to a free people." The new party, moreover, favored granting public lands free to settlers, a popular demand which culminated in the Homestead Act of 1862, and was supported by labor groups which recognized that "the influence of slavery is against labor and reform." [21] The Free Soil Party was assailed by the Whigs and Democrats (who dodged the slavery issue) as violently revolutionary, but it was unflinchingly accepted by John Pierpont and directly contributed to organization of the Republican Party.

Then—civil war! The 76-year-old rebel, still a fighter, enlisted as chaplain in the army that was to end slavery. In April, 1865, Pierpont's eightieth birthday was celebrated in Washington, becoming a celebration of the final victory of the anti-slavery cause. William Lloyd Garrison greeted the old rebel as "distinguished for independence of thought, boldness of speech, fearlessness of investigation, and an untiring interest in the cause of progress and reform on the broadest scale." [22] John Pierpont was of the breed of the scriptural prophets, to whom religion was not the salvation of miserly souls but the flaming sword of righteous social struggle—expressing the deeper, finer nature of Puritanism.

CHAPTER V

FINANCE: GEORGE PEABODY AND JUNIUS MORGAN

> *"How puzzling all these changes are! I'm never sure what I'm going to be, from one minute to another!"*
>
> *So many out-of-the-way things had happened lately, that Alice had begun to think that very few things indeed were really impossible.*
>
> ALICE IN WONDERLAND

JOHN PIERPONT's rebel mood was not the mood of a nation being shaped by developing industrialism, simply an accompaniment and complement of that development.

It was distinctively an age of material progress, preparing the conquest of a continent of unlimited natural resources and potential wealth. Like all elemental forces, this upthrust of material progress was ruthless, impatient of restraint, and often terrifying in its immediate consequences. But it was dynamic, irresistible and progressive in the larger final meanings. While John Pierpont's flaming rebellion was magnificent, the movement of material progress determined issues and decisions.

Out in the Western plains pioneers built up a new agrarian nation, producing an agricultural surplus and an insistent demand for manufactured goods. In the East, in New York, Pennsylvania and New England, the factory system established itself firmly, stimulated and sustained by widening markets. Manufactures grew quickly after the Revolution, but their growth was now positively feverish, particularly the textile industry and iron and steel.[1] Railroad construction was still more feverish. In 1828 there were three miles of railroads,

1,417 miles in 1837, and 24,476 in 1857.[2] Exploitation and acquisition, regardless of means and purposes, dominated men's ideas and actions, opportunity was interpreted in terms of the small businessman's ideal of "making one's pile" in a régime of free and equal competition, and business enterprise moved irresistibly onward.

While accepting the ideal of *laissez faire* (in making and retaining profits) developing capitalism was not in the least doctrinaire and modified the ideal by proposing that a paternalistic government benevolently aid industry and commerce by legislation and direct money grants. This was the American Plan, which agrarians opposed on the ground that it neglected their interests. The independent, embattled pioneers, sensing their power, transformed the philosophical agrarianism of Thomas Jefferson into the practical politics of Andrew Jackson's homespun democracy, captured the government and temporarily smashed the American Plan. Jacksonian democracy was violently antagonistic to aristocracy, but the conquest of the West was to develop its own middle-class aristocracy out of speculation, the rise in realty values and commercial growth. This aristocracy united with Eastern industrialists and financiers and reintroduced the American Plan under other forms.

The struggle between agrarianism and industrialism, then as later, was waged upon financial issues. As capitalist industry developed, money became the dominant form of expression of economic activity. In the primitive Colonial economy money was scarce and banks still scarcer. As settlements and trade grew, money multiplied, but banks did not become important until after the Revolution. The widening and specialization of markets, arising out of the transfer of manufactures from the home to the factory, the development of production for profit instead of use, and the consequent rapid growth of trade required money and banks. Under the impact of these economic changes, banks and their capitalization increased swiftly.[3] Money and the banks were becoming the decisive factor in bringing together land, labor and capital for purposes of production, annihilating the former independence of agrarians and artisans, who now developed a struggle against the banks.

There were two aspects of this struggle. One was the protest of people clinging to the older primitive economy and who, appreciating that the banks constituted the heart of capitalism, opposed banks as insuring the supremacy of the new capitalist economy. In 1819 an economist identified banks with corporations, the object of which, he insisted, was to create artificial power, cause a more unequal division of property and decrease the national wealth, concluding: "A bank is able to put almost any man down, who shall attempt to do business without their agency, and swallow up the proceeds of years of laborious industry." [4]

But there was another and more important aspect. Mismanagement, fraud and failures flourished. The banks were often speculative, wild-cat enterprises, which multiplied overnight, garnered profits for the organizers, and crashed.[5] Bank failures often produced riots and bloodshed. Moreover, the banks issued millions of worthless paper currency which constituted a fraud upon the public, and were usually more interested in speculation than in the legitimate requirements of industry and trade. These conditions bred corruption, bankers' cliques manipulating State governments, until the Philadelphia *Public Ledger* exclaimed: "Our corruption is excessive, and the banking system is the corrupter." [6] In a memorial to Congress in 1833 labor organizations in New York protested against the banks' manufacture of paper currency as tending "to diminish the value of money by increasing the price of all the fruits of labor." [7]

The homespun Jacksonian democracy identified the banks with the new capitalist forces oppressing farmers, pioneers and artisans, and in denying a charter to the United States Bank tried to strike a blow at all banks. But banks multiplied, since capitalism functions through a network of complex financial relations, and the struggle was to become one for the governmental control of the banking system instead of its annihilation. The pioneers and artisans, themselves inflamed with the ideal of individualism, could not see that the problem was one of social control—a problem that was to agitate, and still agitates, American life.

While the struggle over banks and currency was being waged, there was another important financial development out of which arose the House of Morgan. This was the rapid growth of imports of European capital to finance American industry and trade. European capital had played a considerable rôle in Colonial enterprises, while large amounts of money were borrowed abroad by the Continental Congress during the Revolution. By 1812, however, the national government's foreign debt was wiped out. But the immense expansion of agriculture, industry and trade encouraged new borrowings of foreign capital by State governments and business enterprises. The United States was predominantly an agricultural economy and its demand for goods and capital exceeded the domestic supply. Foreign trade increased four-fold between 1820 and 1860 and the import of manufactured goods almost six-fold.[8] There was an unfavorable balance of trade which increased steadily, our excess of imports over exports being paid for largely by the sale of American securities in Europe. State governments sold bonds abroad in order to finance canals and other improvements under the American Plan, while corporate enterprises (particularly railroads) sold large amounts of their securities to foreign investors. By 1856 foreign investors owned $203,000,000 out of an aggregate of $1,407,-000,000 of American national, State, city and corporate bonds and stocks.[9]

There was much popular opposition to these imports of foreign capital, a phase of the struggle against the new industrial and financial system, on the ground that foreign debts constituted an onerous burden upon the nation, encouraged speculation and the formation of corporations. But the opposition was futile.

These international financial relations produced a number of investment banking houses specializing in foreign exchange and the sale of American securities to European investors, the most important being George Peabody & Co., American investment bankers in London. In 1853 Junius Spencer Morgan became a partner in Peabody & Co., and upon George Peabody's retirement in 1863 the firm became J. S. Morgan & Co. This was the origin of the House of Morgan.

George Peabody was an original. Shrewd Yankee and money-maker, he moved urbanely in British society, retained his republican simplicity and declined Queen Victoria's offer of a baronetcy. Unlike Junius Morgan, Peabody was a humanitarian, interested in philanthropic social reform and a friend of Robert Owen the socialist-businessman. Most of Peabody's fortune was spent in philanthropy—$2,500,000 to build "model homes" for the London poor, $3,500,000 for Negro education in the South (after the Civil War) and $2,000,000 to American scientific and educational foundations.[10] This was unusual and startling in an age which insisted that John Jacob Astor "had at heart the culture and elevation of the laboring class" because he gave $20,000 to the Society for Aged Females and $25,000 to the German Society for an office in New York City to give "advice and information, without charge, to all immigrants."[11] Louis Blanc considered George Peabody "a friend of the poor," and Victor Hugo "a rich man who would feel the cold, the hunger and the thirst of the poor."[12] Philanthropy is an evasion and not the solution of social problems. But where grim-mouthed Junius Morgan pompously engaged in forms of "social and moral welfare" constituting the defensive *noblesse oblige* of business aristocracy, George Peabody was moved by human misery and aspirations, a fine humanitarian with all the nobility (and limitations) of the humanitarian.

Originally a grocery clerk and storekeeper, George Peabody soon became a prosperous merchant. The merchant capitalist was still the most important factor in business life—not the industrial or financial capitalist. Production being small-scale and isolated, merchants dominated producers in the movement of goods from producer to consumer. But as industry became larger and banking more important, many prosperous merchants, possessing abundant money resources, began to finance the production of goods as well as their distribution until they became exclusively investment bankers. Most of the important investment houses originated in the mercantile business—the House of Morgan, Brown Bros., Kuhn, Loeb & Co., J. & W. Seligman & Co., Lazard Frères; and James Stillman, who built up the great National City Bank, started in the cotton merchandising business.[13] The merchants Junius Morgan and Levi Morton ended as investment bankers, and so did George Peabody. Developing capitalism dethroned the merchant as the aristocrat of business.

While still a merchant George Peabody sensed the importance of new industrial and financial developments. He was a railroad pioneer, one of the incorporators and president of the Eastern Railroad, a road of sixty miles built in 1836. By amalgamation and lease the Eastern became one of the most important New England railroads, paying higher dividends than most other railroads.[14] Peabody not only appreciated the importance of railroads in "giving every aid to commerce and manufactures," but also their political importance in strengthening "the bonds of the Union" and offsetting "the evils to be apprehended from a too extended territory."[15]

Railroad financing revealed to Peabody the significance and profitable character of capital importation. In 1835 he organized George Peabody & Co. in London, specializing in foreign exchange and American securities; and in 1843 Peabody severed all his mercantile affiliations in order to devote himself exclusively to international banking.[16] Peabody's large fortune was acquired in the banking business between 1844 and

1864. "Everything I touched within that time," he said in after years, "seemed to turn to gold." [17] The American demand for foreign capital was almost insatiable, most of it being supplied by British investors who, in spite (or because) of the depressed well-being of the masses during the "Hungry Forties" and after, managed to accumulate enough money to buy all sorts of foreign securities. Peabody & Co. competed with the Rothschilds and the Barings for American financial business—and got it.

The panic of 1837 shook American credit in Europe. George Peabody had foreseen this panic in 1836, writing to a friend that "the rage for speculation which characterized the last two or three years, must produce disastrous results. . . . I have written to my partners to keep everything *snug,* and be prepared for the emergency." [18] The industrial and financial interests accused the Jacksonian democracy of causing a panic by its attack upon the United States Bank in particular and financial institutions in general, but in reality the panic was caused by frenzied speculation, unregulated industrial development, incompetent (and often dishonest) banking, and, according to a contemporary business journal, the "desire of gain at the expense of individuals and the public." [19] Wild-cat banks multiplied, speculation dangerously inflated all sorts of values, and the inevitable crash came, producing a large crop of business failures, wiping out savings, creating general unemployment and acute distress among the workers, particularly in manufacturing districts. [20] The panic spread to London where three American houses were compelled to suspend payments owing to "enormous and extravagant" speculative engagements. [21] There was considerable liquidation of American securities and the rejection of new offerings. The situation was made still worse by several American States repudiating their foreign debts.

State debts had increased from $12,790,000 in 1820 to $170,-000,000 in 1838, [22] most of the bonds being owned in Europe—

the basis for the development of American foreign investment banking on which George Peabody & Co. thrived. The American Plan actively encouraged industry by tariff protection and the grant of public money to aid private enterprise, particularly transportation improvements. By 1836 canals and railroads had absorbed more than $90,000,000, of which 50 per cent was represented by State bonds mostly owned by British investors.[23] There was considerable corruption in securing State money, many of the enterprises were unscrupulously speculative and mismanaged, and some of the State governments did not make definite provisions to meet debt charges. Mismanaged speculative enterprises crashed in the 1837 panic, the situation progressively became worse, and in 1841 nine States suspended interest payments and three repudiated their debts.

This action shocked European investors and threatened the business of foreign investment banking. George Peabody called upon the States "to preserve their commercial honor" and "pledged his word that they would soon resume payment of interest and fully redeem their obligations."[24] Peabody devoted himself to the task of restoring confidence in American credit and, according to Edward Everett, "performed the miracle by which an honest man turns paper into gold" by buying "largely of depreciated State bonds and while thus relieving the financial embarrassment of the States, by raising their credit, he greatly increased his own fortune when these securities advanced in price owing to restored confidence."[25]

Among the mismanaged enterprises largely financed by public money was the Chesapeake & Ohio Canal Co., the fiscal agents of which in England were Peabody & Co. This canal was the joint enterprise of Maryland, Virginia and the national government to connect the Potomac and Ohio Rivers. It was started in spite of the appearance of railroads, "prudent" and "farseeing" businessmen insisting that railroads would not become practicable for years to come. Chartered at about the same time, the Chesapeake & Ohio Canal and the Baltimore

& Ohio Railroad engaged in a struggle for public and governmental support. The struggle flared up in Congress, where a speaker said that the Chesapeake Canal must give way to the superior improvement of railroads, while Chesapeake's president denounced the Congressional "delusion in favor of the railroad." [26] It was apparent that railroads were more practicable than canals, but Chesapeake & Ohio persisted, securing more money from the national government and the State of Maryland.[27] Although this money was larger than the original estimate of construction costs, the canal was still uncompleted owing to mismanagement and waste.* The money crisis in 1839 almost wrecked the enterprise, the directors complaining that its debt, secured by Maryland State bonds, permitted "the banks and bankers to prescribe and enforce the time of payment and enrich themselves at the expense of the company, by causing immediate sale of the bonds." This was apparently true, but the directors were seeking a scapegoat for their own mismanagement and persistence in an enterprise which should have yielded to the railroad. Of Chesapeake's debt $1,250,000 was held in Europe, the security being bonds pledged with Peabody & Co. Owing to the impairment of Maryland's credit these bonds depreciated considerably, but the directors complained that the sacrifices in Peabody's sales were excessive and that he "has placed us in a most painful situation" by refusing to accept the company's bills.[28] Peabody thereupon resigned as agent, refusing to become further involved in the affairs of a mismanaged corporation.

Between 1840 and 1857 railroad construction developed feverishly and American railroad securities became favorites of

* In order to lower construction costs the Chesapeake & Ohio Canal Co. imported much indentured labor from Ireland and Holland. Illness decimated the workers, they revolted at the low wages and conditions of labor, and scores ran away. Some of the runaways were arrested in Baltimore, but a sympathetic mob freed them. These imported workers were stigmatized as "plagues" by the company's secretary and their importation discontinued. (George F. Ward, *The Early Development of the Chesapeake & Ohio Canal Project,* pp. 90-2.)

European investors, the rapid development of our rail transportation system being immensely facilitated by the import of foreign capital. Among the many railroad issues disposed of by Peabody & Co. were stocks and bonds of the Ohio & Mississippi Railroad in 1853, which was unable to raise additional capital in the United States.[29]

While grants of public money by State governments aided the construction of railroads, such aid was not given by the national government until after 1850. Congress aided the railroads indirectly, however, by lower tariff rates on rails and other iron imports for railroad use (against the iron manufacturers' protests), banking privileges and tax exemptions.[30] Speculation, mismanagement and corruption appeared in the railroads, although not assuming catastrophic proportions until after the Civil War. But already the Erie Railroad was infamous for its mismanagement and demoralization, coming into the clutches first of Jacob Little and then of Daniel Drew as the plaything of business buccaneers.

Being a debtor nation, the United States pursued an almost consistently liberal foreign policy, usual in the case of debtor nations. There was an appetite for territorial aggrandizement, but it expressed itself in settlement of the American wilderness, not imperialistic expansion (except for the Southern slavocracy's desire to annex Latin-American lands in order to create a slave empire and offset the power of the Northern "free labor" States). Manifest Destiny was not to become an issue until the development of monopolistic industry and finance. Cornelius Vanderbilt, rising from ferryboats to steamships and master of unscrupulous competition, was mixed up in transportation enterprises in Nicaragua out of which developed the first foreign American railroad. His franchise being confiscated by an American filibuster and resold to others, Vanderbilt resorted to the characteristic predatory methods of concessionaires to regain his property.[31] It was an anticipation of imperialism (mildly), but it bore no immediate fruit. Internal development absorbed the United States.

Developing swiftly, American industry astonished other nations at the London industrial exhibition in 1851, participation in which by the United States was made possible by the financial aid of George Peabody, Congress making no appropriation.[32] The exhibit of American manufactures aroused enormous interest. The British marveled at one hundred power tools being used to shape the parts of a Springfield rifle, and one journal declared that England had received more real benefit from the American exhibit than any other.[33] Owing to its exceptionally large crop of inventors (most of whom received little from their inventions) the United States was improving rapidly upon industrial technique, being much in advance of other nations in the use of interchangeable mechanism, automatic machinery and standardization. Between 1850 and 1860 iron and textile manufactures increased 65 per cent, and there was a substantial development of locomotive, machinery and other iron and steel exports.[34]

But this progress was interrupted by alternate periods of prosperity and depression in industry and trade, culminating in the panic of 1857 which almost wrecked Peabody & Co. It was worse than 1837: the distress in all manufacturing towns was "absolutely sickening." [35] Again unregulated industrial development, over-building of railroads, frenzied speculation in Western lands and financial mismanagement reaped the whirlwind of business disaster. Peabody's American representatives, Duncan, Sherman & Co., were barely saved from bankruptcy. The crisis severely affected British industry and finance, and particularly the American houses there whose representatives in the United States could not remit. Peabody & Co. were pressed for funds, their acceptances amounting to £2,300,-000, at a time when money could be secured only through the Bank of England. Junius Morgan (who in 1853 had become a partner in Peabody & Co.) negotiated with the Bank for a loan of £800,000 and was crushed by the answer: the Bank would make the loan providing Peabody & Co. agreed to cease business in London after 1858. But George Peabody was a fighter; he dared the Bank to cause his failure, mobilized powerful British support, received the loan and survived the crisis.[36] Peabody practically retired after this, Junius Morgan becoming dominant in the firm.

At this time John Pierpont Morgan, twenty years old, was employed as a clerk by Duncan, Sherman & Co. The firm having been saved from bankruptcy by Peabody & Co., Junius Morgan seized the opportunity to ask them to make his son a partner. Upon this being refused the younger Morgan was set up independently in the banking business by his father, gradually assuming the functions of American representative of Peabody & Co.[37]

J. Pierpont Morgan was almost the only one of the captains of industry and finance coming to power after the Civil War who was not self-made but a rich man's son—Junius Morgan being a millionaire. It meant much in his rise to power.

The young Morgan lived in Hartford until he was twelve, was under the care of a physician for a few years owing to lung trouble, and at fourteen entered the English High School in Boston. He did not mingle much with the other sons of wealth, being reserved, silent and antagonistic. Morgan was average in school, slow, dignified and ponderous, not brilliant but painstaking and plodding, mathematics being the one subject in which he showed decided talent. After graduation, his health still a source of worry, Morgan spent some time in the Azores and then made the Grand Tour of Europe, ending with two years at the University of Göttingen, where he distinguished himself in mathematics (but in nothing else).[38]

His son worried Junius Morgan. "What shall I do with him?" The father was worried by the young man's ingrowing reserve, his abrupt, domineering almost morose manner (only

partly the result of an inbred arrogance of caste) and apparent
lack of talent. No spark, no urge to work, which particularly
worried old Junius, his dynastic impulse being to make a
banker out of the only son to carry on the business of the
House of Morgan. Junius Morgan succeeded, but only after
another interval of worry.

Beneath young Morgan's gruff, arrogant reserve was something sentimental, almost romantic, probably the Pierpont influence of his mother. He held it down but it did mysterious
things to him, flaring up in overwhelming love of a woman
who was consumptive and approaching death. Amelia Sturges,
the beloved, declined Morgan's offer of marriage. But the
youngster, twenty-two years old, insisted—the man who was
to command now begged, who was to defy antagonists and
public opinion now defied death. The beloved was in Paris
and there Morgan went, abandoning his business. (More worry
for old Junius: "What *shall* I do with him?") They married,
and within three months she died, in spite of love's defiance
of death.[39] Romance!...It never happened again. Morgan
overwhelmed his sentimental, almost romantic quality in the
gruff masculinity of the strong, silent man wrapt in the ecstasy
of business. It survived in his love of medieval splendor and
magnificence: the quality itself Morgan repressed as weakness.
Power was to be his ideal, its pursuit his romance, love becoming the conquest of women as an appanage of power.

Thereafter J. Pierpont Morgan concentrated on banking,
and old Junius ceased worrying. He took hold and never let
go, energized by his will to power—never let go until three
months before his death. Finance was becoming the dominant
force in economic life, assuming new forms and functions.
By identifying himself with finance and its crucial changes,
Morgan was to rise to supreme power in the American scene.
The story of the House of Morgan is the story of the transformation of American capitalism, in the midst of an economic civil war, by the centralization of industry and finance.

Men may be significant as the multiplied expression of common men and common things, usually the case with preachers and politicians; Morgan was significant in being the multiplied, concentrated expression of fundamental changes in industrial and financial institutions, of the power, splendor and magnificence of the American aristocracy of money.

PART TWO

CIVIL WAR

CHAPTER VI

WAR—AND CARBINES

> *"What do you mean by that?" said the*
> *Caterpillar sternly. "Explain yourself!"*
> *"I can't explain myself, I'm afraid, sir,"*
> *said Alice, "because I'm not myself, you*
> *see."*
> *"I don't see," said the Caterpillar.*
> *"I'm afraid I can't put it more clearly,"*
> *Alice replied very politely.*
>
> ALICE IN WONDERLAND

MORAL issues are ordinarily helpless against the force of economic institutions unless they express and serve competing institutions. The moral agitation of Garrison, Pierpont and others against slavery was a declining force until it assumed new vigor by definitely becoming the ideology of an irrepressible social and political conflict.

Industrial transformation developed a struggle between agrarianism and industrialism, which was complicated by slavery, the slavocracy being itself agrarian. Industrialism shaped economic and political institutions antagonistic equally to agrarian democracy and slavocracy. But Northern agriculture, by its free and individualistic character, fostered capitalist enterprise, which was hampered by static and reactionary slavocracy. Compromise as Northern capitalism might, and persecute slavery agitators, its progressive economics compelled struggle against slavocratic economics. Driven desperate by the growing economic and political power of the North and its own inescapable alternative of expansion or downfall, the slavocracy during its control of the national government fatedly emphasized the irreconcilability of free labor and slave labor, of business enterprise and slavocratic agriculture. The Southern statesmen infuriated industry and finance by rejecting important legislative measures fostering industrial development, and they infuriated labor and frontiersmen by rejecting "free soil" proposals in their campaign to seize the Western lands for slavocracy.

An uncompromisable struggle for power developed, the struggle for power of competing economic and political systems and institutions. Transformed by the logic of events from a moral issue into an issue of practical politics, the struggle over slavery flared up in war. Liberation of the Negro (decided upon as a measure of war) constituted the ideology of the inexorable necessity of capitalism to crush slavocracy. The war was a social war.

Upon the opening of the war John Pierpont, now seventy-six years old, enlisted as chaplain in the Union army.* His grandson of twenty-four, J. Pierpont Morgan, was neither volunteer nor conscript, although a widower who did not remarry until 1865 (marrying Frances Louisa Tracy, the issue being three daughters and one son, John Pierpont Morgan, Jr., born September 7, 1867). Rich men avoided the draft by hiring substitutes for $300, the providing of which was an organized profitable business. Advertisements offering to provide substitutes appeared frequently: "Gentlemen will be furnished promptly with substitutes by forwarding their orders to the office of the Merchants, Bankers and General Volunteer Association."[1]

Other potential captains of industry and finance besides Morgan did not fight during the Civil War, "pacifism" being rather common among them. Jay Gould was meditating, husky Jim Fisk selling blankets to the government at substantial

---

* Ill health compelled Pierpont to resign from the army. Secretary Salmon P. Chase gave him a job in the Treasury Department compiling a digest of decisions. Apparently there was a break between John Pierpont and his millionaire daughter, son-in-law and grandson. He died in 1868 in poverty; among his papers was a promissory note for $1500 endorsed by a Boston publisher. (James Grant Wilson, *Bryant and His Friends*, pp. 381-2.)

profit, William H. Vanderbilt farming, John D. Rockefeller investing savings in an oil refinery, Andrew Carnegie in civilian service, and Philip Armour speculating in pork (which he sold "short" on the approach of Union victory, clearing $2,000,000).[2] The call "to make men free" did not thrill these men, calculating the chances of becoming rich: others might die but they must amass.

The son of Junius Morgan concentrated on business during the war under the firm name of J. Pierpont Morgan & Co., private bankers. On Exchange Place, in the shadow of the Wall Street he was later to rule, the arrogant, massive youngster plied his business, mostly foreign exchange. Nothing about him attracted attention or indicated the coming master of money (unless it was his concentration on business). Men later tried to create an aura for the young Morgan, attributing to him an "impressive" utterance: "We are going some day to show ourselves to be the richest country in the world in natural resources. It will be necessary to go to work, and to work hard, to turn our resources into money to pay the cost of the war just as soon as it is ended."[3] Which was neither impressive nor original, being the common talk of the day. Morgan was an up-and-coming youngster ploddingly engaged in the banking business in a comparatively small way and pursuing the ordinary routine of making money, of which the war was simply an aspect. In doing this and while awaiting the rich future, J. Pierpont Morgan participated in a transaction characterized by a committee of the House of Representatives as fraudulent—"an effort to obtain from the government some $49,000 over and above the value of the property sold" and "a crime against the public safety."[4]

This transaction of Morgan's was included among the war-contract frauds revealing an extraordinarily low level of business morality. Six weeks after the war started the New York *Times* declared that "very general and, we fear, well-grounded complaints and apprehensions exist of great corruption and

wastefulness in contracts for our Army and Navy." [5] The
House of Representatives immediately appointed a select committee to investigate, the chairman of which wrote privately
to Secretary of the Treasury Salmon P. Chase of an "organized
system of pillage . . . robbery, fraud, extravagance, peculation." [6]

The charges were amply proven by the facts. In the business
world speculation and profiteering flourished menacingly and
unashamed, multiplying the burdens of war and the chances
of disaster. While the lonely man in the White House (the
practical politician becoming great under tragic pressure) tried
to impose his dreams upon events and soldiers yielded their
full measure of devotion to the music of "As He died to make
men holy let us die to make men free," buccaneers in the
business community interpreted the mighty events of an epic
age in terms of profit and loss. The soul of the nation was not
in them but in the men who answered the call for volunteers,
singing as they marched, "We are coming, Father Abraham,
300,000 more"—in these men and in the man who aroused
their devotion.

Profiteers swooped upon the government (in the North and
in the South). Systematic customs frauds prevailed, which
Secretary Chase reported had "been successfully carried on for
a series of years." [7] A legion of traders in government patronage sprang up who, by corrupt political influence, secured
contracts which they sold to manufacturers at a large profit:
the manufacturers raised their prices accordingly, and a trifle
more. Fraud tainted much of the money paid by the government on contracts and the balance was tainted by excessive
profits. The committee of the House of Representatives in
1862 reported large frauds in the purchase of ordnance and
stores, Treasury and War Department employees, contractors,
politicians and bankers conspiring to swindle the government.
"Profits from the sales of arms to the government have been
enormous," said the investigating committee, "and realized
by a system of brokerage as unprincipled and dishonest, as

unfriendly to the success of the nation, as the plottings of actual treason." [8] Neither the investigation nor ousting of the Secretary of War improved matters much, leading one Representative in 1863 to say: "After the lapse of two years we find the same system of extortion, frauds and peculation prevailing." [9] The cry went up: "Corruption will ruin us!"

The investigating committee reported frauds in 104 cases and refused payment of $17,000,000 out of $50,000,000 on contracts. J. Pierpont Morgan appeared in a case as financing the sale to the government of the government's own arms at an extortionate profit. The facts are in the Congressional Reports, "Case No. 97. J. Pierpont Morgan. Claim for payment of ordnance stores.... Referred by special direction of the Secretary of War.... Claimed, $58,175." [10]

In 1852 certain unserviceable ordnance stores were condemned by inspecting officers of the army, among them a batch of Hall's carbines, which were thereafter sold from time to time at prices ranging from $1 to $2 apiece. Upon the outbreak of war an adventurer, Arthur Eastman, negotiated for the purchase of these carbines. After haggling over price and terms the War Department issued instructions to sell Eastman 5,000 carbines at $3.50, "to be paid for at once." The prospective buyer, having no money of his own, tried to buy the carbines 1,000 at a time payable in ninety days, and was refused. Eastman was unable to raise the necessary money until a corrupt speculator, Simon Stevens, agreed to make a loan of $20,000 in return for a lien on the carbines (which Eastman had not purchased and which were still government property) and an agreement to sell them to Stevens at $12.50 apiece. All Eastman offered in this transaction was a letter from the War Department which magically produced a profit of $20,000. It was not Stevens' money which Eastman received, but a draft issued by J. Pierpont Morgan & Co. which was sold by Eastman to Ketchum, Son & Co. who, according to Morris Ketchum's testimony, expected "to get their money out of Mr. Morgan when he gets it." (Ketchum refused to tell the investigating committee what his profit was on the deal, that "being my private business which the government has no right to inquire into.")[11]

Although desperately in need of arms the government was not using any of the Hall carbines, condemned as unfit and dangerous for military use. Simon Stevens offered the carbines for sale in a telegram to General J. C. Frémont, saying "I *have* 5,000 carbines for sale," which was untrue, no purchase having been made and the carbines being still government property stored in a government arsenal. Frémont, needing arms badly and "in business as gentle as a girl and confiding as a woman,"[12] accepted Stevens' offer, the price being $22. The day *after* the receipt of Frémont's telegraphic acceptance Arthur Eastman bought the 5,000 carbines at $3.50 apiece from the War Department, payment of $17,486 being made by J. Pierpont Morgan. When the "sale" was made to General Frémont "the arms were still the property of the government," reported the investigating committee, "the proposal being to sell the government its own arms. . . . The government not only sold, one day, for $17,486 arms which it had agreed the day before to repurchase for $109,912, making a loss to the United States on the transaction of $92,426, but virtually furnished the money to pay itself the $17,486 which it received."[13] Moreover, the arms were more dangerous to the Union troops than to the Confederates.

The conspirators shipped 2,500 carbines. Apparently apprehensive, they did not ship the other carbines until payment of $55,550 for the first batch had been received by J. Pierpont Morgan—that is, forty days after the "sale," although General Frémont had urged "hurry." Their apprehensions were justified. Payment for the second batch of carbines was refused and Morgan's bill for $58,175 turned over to the Secretary of War who referred it to the committee investigating government contracts. After severely castigating the participants in the transaction, the committee allowed $9,678 on Morgan's claim plus brokerage of $1,330. The claim for payment, Morgan insisted, was justified because his House had "made advances in good faith to Mr. Stevens on the security of his agreement with General Frémont." This claim of "good faith" was dismissed by the committee since Morgan "declined to disclose the terms" upon which the advances were made to Stevens. The committee said:

"Nor is it an unfair inference, from the unwillingness evidenced by the House in question [J. Pierpont Morgan & Co.] to state the terms on which their advances were made, that if these terms were disclosed they might supply evidence that, during the negotiations for funds, doubts as to the sufficiency of the security had actually presented themselves, and that the confidence claimed to have been felt by them was largely mingled with distrust." [14]

The committee included in its decision a discourse to Stevens, Morgan, Ketchum and Eastman on equity and good citizenship:

"It is impossible to regard such a transaction as having been entered upon in good faith, and as having, for such reason, an equitable claim to be confirmed. In France, during periods of civil commotion, may often be seen inscribed on the bridges, monuments and other public structures the words '*committed to the guardianship of the citizens of France.*' In our country it should not be regarded as a romantic stretch of political morality to declare that all public interests ought to be regarded as under similar guardianship, more especially in time of trial and need like the present. He cannot be looked upon as a good citizen, entitled to favorable consideration of his claim, who seeks to augment the vast burdens, daily increasing, that are to weigh on the future industry of the country, by demands on the Treasury for which nothing entitled to the name of an equivalent has been rendered." [15]

The carbine scandal assumed considerable political importance, being one of many frauds reported in General Frémont's army. Although the frauds were many (General Grant complained of bad muskets, unfit beef, poor hay and extortionate prices)[16] there was proof of incompetence in Frémont's case and the investigating committee proposed to oust him. But Frémont was an implacable enemy of slavery and there was an immediate rally to his defense by men who considered the proposed ouster a move against the anti-slavery forces (and of men who despised Abraham Lincoln). Thaddeus Stevens interpreted the issue in terms of Frémont's "honesty, integrity and patriotism," and said that while "Simon Stevens' speculation may not be very pleasant to look at, it was a legitimate business transaction."[17] The implacable old man, wrapt in the struggle to crush the slavocracy by any and all means, cynically brushed aside the issue of corruption—as he did in the post-war struggle against the South. Nevertheless, General Frémont was ousted on charges of incompetence.

The investigating committee's castigation was wasted on Simon Stevens.* While Morgan withdrew from the case, Stevens persisted in his claim and it was granted in 1866 by the Court of Claims on a strictly technical decision. The Court, four against one, decided there was "no proof of fraud" and accepted Stevens' contention that he was the legal owner of the carbines at the time of their sale to Frémont, in spite of their being still government property and stored in a government arsenal. "It was General Frémont's duty to buy those arms," declared the Court. "Should he leave his troops unarmed and suffer rebellion to rush in unresisted?" Since Frémont did buy the carbines, "the government must abide the responsibility and pay."[18] This decision assured payment of

* Simon Stevens was mixed up in the customs frauds in New York City. He refused to answer an investigating committee's questions about his profits on a "labor contract" he had secured, insisting that "the government has no right to inquire into my private affairs." Under pressure, however, Stevens revealed having paid $20,000 for the contract, another $42,000 in bribes and making a profit of $60,000. (*Reports of Committees,* House of Representatives, 3rd Sess., 67th Cong., Court of Claims, 1862-3, pp. 83, 123.)

all the "dead-horse claims" against the government held by a horde of fraudulent contractors.[19] It was a decision, moreover, in accord with the mood of cynical corruption which flourished in the national government after the Civil War, unscrupulous, pervasive and appalling.

CHAPTER VII

SPECULATING IN GOLD

> *"And the moral of that is," said the Duch-
> ess, " 'The more there is of mine, the less
> there is of yours.' "*
>
> ALICE IN WONDERLAND

DURING the Civil War J. Pierpont Morgan was a financial fledgling. He revealed modest money-making talent, report-ing in 1864 for tax purposes an income of $53,286 (compared with William B. Astor's $1,300,000 and Cornelius Vanderbilt's $576,000),[1] which was neither bad nor exciting for a man of twenty-seven after four years in business.

Speculation interested the financial fledgling, an interest which did not persist in later years. While still a youth in London he heard discussion about coffee being a "good specu-lation." Morgan bought a shipload and told one of the Pea-body partners:

MORGAN: I've bought a shipload of coffee—it's a good specu-lation.

PARTNER: Why, it's absurd to buy all that coffee. Where will you get the money?

MORGAN (*stares angrily, silently, walks out, returns with a draft for the money signed by Junius Morgan*): There it is (*bruskly*).[2]

The story reveals Morgan's arrogance, and his speculative bent. He speculated considerably during the Civil War. Specu-lation was general and feverish, although condemned by press and pulpit in terms of morality and of disloyalty to the Union. But war breeds speculation, thriving on the nation's needs, the upset in economic equilibrium and the changing level of prices.

Almost everything assumes a speculative character, including life itself. "This riotous speculation in army contracts, oil wells, stocks and gold," according to a contemporary observer, "naturally fostered reckless extravagance, on the principle of 'easy come, easy go,' accompanied by display of diamonds, equipages, stately mansions, purple and fine linen." [3]

Gold was the speculative favorite, owing to the large range in its price movements. Objectively a rise in the price of gold was unavoidable, paper money forcing up the price, aggravated by the increased demand for gold for purposes of foreign trade and for the payment of customs duties and the interest on government bonds (which was payable in gold). But the price of gold was also manipulated and consciously forced up. Speculative dealings exceeded legitimate business purchases, the mercantile community and foreign bankers buying beyond their actual needs, while the public speculated as much in gold as in securities. Unscrupulous speculators bribed employees in the Department of War and in the Executive Mansion itself to secure advance information on military events, and often originated or magnified rumors for speculative purposes. The price of gold was intimately affected by military events, since continuation of the war meant more issues of paper money and more need of gold, with consequent higher prices. Confederate victory, therefore, meant an upward movement in the price of gold, Union victory movement downward. The struggle between bulls and bears in gold was identified with the agonizing military struggle. Clearly the upward movement in the price of gold, originally determined by objective economic conditions, was forced still higher by the unscrupulous manipulations of men intent on making money regardless of consequences to the Union—men whom Jay Cooke called "evil geniuses." Gold speculation was discouraged by the New York Stock Exchange, where it was considered the "patriotic and gentlemanly thing" to sell gold. The confirmed speculators thereupon met in the Coal Hole, "a dark, repulsive basement."

Business flourishing, an organization was formed which moved to larger quarters, where bulls forced up the price of gold to the strains of "Dixie." [4]

The price of gold being identified with the military struggle, if Union defeat forced up the price of gold the bulls sang:

> *Den I wish I was in Dixie,*
> *Hooray! Hooray!*
> *In Dixie land I'll take my stand*
> *To live an' die for Dixie!*

If Union victory forced down the price of gold the bears sang:

> *The stars of heaven are looking kindly down,*
> *The stars of heaven are looking kindly down,*
> *The stars of heaven are looking kindly down*
> *On the body of old John Brown.*

Only in this case the stars were looking down on profits garnered by speculators. Or the bears might sing, "We'll hang Jeff Davis on a sour apple tree"—speculators being more vengeful than soldiers at the front. The songs with which soldiers eased their souls were also sung by the patrioteering soldiers of speculation.

Most of the dealers in foreign exchange speculated heavily in gold, the fluctuations yielding immense profits. Morgan, owing to his foreign affiliations, was in an excellent position to exploit the situation. In one spectacular coup forcing up the price of gold, Morgan and an accomplice reaped a profit of $160,000—"which was big business in those days." [5] Morgan, too, was a bull on gold; but we don't know whether, in garnering the profits, he sang "Hooray! Hooray! I'll live an' die for Dixie!" Probably not, considering his habitual and temperamental reserve....

Morgan's accomplice in this particular speculative coup was a man of his own age, Edward B. Ketchum, an unscrupulous speculator and junior partner in Ketchum, Son & Co. Edward's father, Morris Ketchum, had been a partner of Junius Morgan in the banking business and associated with J. Pierpont Morgan in the scandalous sale of carbines to the government. The Ketchums engaged in all sorts of shady speculative enterprises * and were among the most active speculators in gold, their "gold bullings" being stigmatized as "embarrassing to the government." Although Morris Ketchum was Secretary Chase's loan representative in New York City, his operations were considered as "not always in the government interest." [6]

Edward Ketchum proposed a speculative coup in gold to Morgan shrewdly calculated to capitalize recent military events and the gold requirements of importers.

Early in 1863 gold was selling at 163. A series of Union victories produced considerable price declines. The Gettysburg victory sent the price down five points in one day, and the capture of Vicksburg down another five points. These events and conviction of the coming capture of Charleston resulted in gold falling to 125, the gold price range in September being 126-29. Importers and other buyers of foreign exchange expected the price to go still lower (the war might even end) and postponed buying to meet maturing bills. Then the onrushing Union troops met bloody reverses, Charleston was not captured, and the agonizing military struggle settled down to a war of attrition. Clearly, although Union victory was assured, the end was still far off. Slowly the price of gold began to rise. [7] The demand for gold by importers who had postponed buying foreign exchange was increased by active imports and moderate exports. By creating an artificial scarcity of

---

* In 1863 Morris Ketchum floated another of his characteristic enterprises. This was the incorporation of General J. C. Frémont's Mariposa estate in California, from which millions in gold had been taken. The corporation issued 100,000 shares of stock priced at $100, but without one cent of working capital. Ketchum received 75,000 shares which he easily disposed of to a get-rich-quick public. In 1865 the shares sold at 8c. Frémont was victimized. (New York *Times*, August 21, 1865.)

gold the price could be forced up and the buyers who *had to have* gold would be at the speculators' mercy.

After outlining the situation to Morgan, young Ketchum proposed that they buy $4,000,000 or $5,000,000 in gold on joint account with Peabody & Co., ship half abroad and resell the remainder at home.[8] Considering the scarcity of available gold the move would create and the active demand for foreign exchange, they could sell at practically their own price. The profits would be large and sure, since the buyers of foreign exchange would be helpless to resist under the prevailing conditions. After being approved by Morris Ketchum the speculation got under way, conspiratorially.

Gold was purchased secretly, being maneuvered to appear as ordinary business transactions. Covered up and timed perfectly, the operation conquered its immediate objectives. Gold rose to 143. "There is no special cause for the rise," said the New York *Times,* "other than a disposition to speculate on the current demand of customs and export."[9] The Morgan-Ketchum conspiracy was still unknown.

Although the speculators covered up their tracks, the scarcity of gold and the rising price indicated the engineering of a coup. This was clear on Saturday, October 10, when $1,150,000 of an unexpectedly large shipment of gold to England was identified as shipped "by a young House in Exchange Place [J. Pierpont Morgan & Co.] respectably connected on the other side, but whose regular business in exchange would be called large at 10 per cent of the sum," the New York *Times* adding: "This maneuver is not wholly new to the market, having been tried, but with no satisfactory result, last spring. It may succeed better in the present instance, as there is an active demand for bills."[10] The successful speculative coup created almost a corner in gold, the regular dealers were caught unawares, and the buyers of gold and foreign exchange were desperate. The price of gold went to 149. Brokers tried to break the price by selling gold, but Ketchum, who was not known as

Morgan's associate, bought all the gold offered and bid the price higher. By October 16 gold was selling at 156, exchange on London rising sympathetically to 171. Not only were the buyers of foreign exchange helpless but also a considerable short interest which had bought at 145-47. The conspirators reaped the large joint profit of $160,000. One week after the Morgan-Ketchum coup the price of gold declined to 145.[11]

This speculation of Morgan's disorganized the foreign exchange market temporarily and made still more difficult the carrying on of foreign trade. It was not the necessary expression of economic forces but wilful and predatory manipulation. A whole series of such manipulations interfered with trade and forced the high prices of all goods still higher—for while speculation was not the cause of high prices it was an important contributory factor.

Contemporary opinion of the gold speculators was scorching. The New York *Times* ascribed "the enormous and unprincipled speculation in gold" to "a knot of unscrupulous gamblers who care nothing for the credit of the country."[12] At a Union League meeting it was urged that "Congress at once order the erection of scaffolds for hanging" the speculators.[13]

It was the fact of its objective disloyalty that particularly inflamed the people against speculation. "The love of gain was fed by sacrificing the national credit and encouraging disloyalty," declared a contemporary observer. "How would an undertaker be regarded who, acquiring his wealth in burying the dead, rejoiced in the sufferings of those around him? Yet the gold brokers rejoiced over human slaughter and national defeat because their gains were thereby increased."[14] The speculators were bulls on gold and bears on the Union. "Men stand in groups upon the floor of the exchange," complained the New York *Post,* "and openly manifest their sympathy with the rebels."[15] Speculation *was* disloyal in fact if not intention: cornering gold in order to force up its price, as Morgan did, was not economic necessity but speculative malignancy.

Gold speculation harassed the government in financing the war and was dangerous in its influence on public opinion. Negro emancipation had been decreed by the practical dreamer in the White House, final victory was assured, but the immediate military situation was still agonizingly indefinite. Congress decided to act and in 1864 passed the Gold Bill to crush gold speculation.

At once there was a blast against the Bill. It was characterized by a group of bankers, among them J. Pierpont Morgan, as "only one more instance of the utter lawlessness of Congress." [16] A meeting was called in New York City "for the purpose of urging the repeal or modification of the Gold Bill, which has paralyzed business and forced honest men either to abandon their business or do what is repugnant to them—resort to expedients to evade the law." [17]

Among the group calling the meeting, of which Morgan was secretary, were some of the most active and hardened gold speculators. Their inflammatory sentiments were not shared generally by the business community, however, and they were rebuked by most of the participants in the discussion. S. B. Chittenden denied "that Congress had interfered with legitimate business" and urged "every loyal banker and merchant to submit unmurmuringly for a time to all the inconveniences until the Bill could be carefully amended or modified." Most of the private and State bankers opposing the Gold Bill were also opposed to the National Bank Act: it was an opportunity to strike the enemy. "So far from taking the back track," said John Thompson of the First National Bank, "Congress will compel Wall Street to use the government currency and show the gold speculators that there is a power in the land superior to their machinations." The meeting adopted the compromise of a committee to discuss modifying the bill with Secretary Chase. [18]

But Congress did take the back track. It had to. The Gold Bill was a loose measure utterly unable to accomplish its pur-

pose. Legitimate and speculative transactions in gold were not
clearly separated, and the closing of the Gold Room produced
bootleg speculation which shot the price of gold up to 198
and then 250. Speculation could not be suppressed simply by
making it illegal, since it was inherent in the prevailing organization of industry and finance. The suppression of speculation involved a whole series of measures in terms of the social
control of business for which neither Congress nor the nation
was prepared. Speculation proceeded in spite of its illegality.
The bulls, among them Ketchum, Son & Co., virtually cornered
gold and forced the price up. Business was being demoralized,
protests multiplied, and within two weeks a frightened Congress repealed the Gold Bill. Then a clique of bulls, who had
"cornered" gold, forced the price up to 285 and plundered
legitimate business of more millions.[19]

The Ketchums, particularly Edward, continued bulling gold.
The profits were still good. But in 1865 the approaching final
victory of the Union produced a decline in the price of gold.
Edward Ketchum persisted in bulling gold, however, and his
large speculative profits melted away. In desperation he stole
$2,800,000 in funds and securities from his father's firm and
forged $1,500,000 of gold checks which he put in circulation
as collateral for loans. The price of gold now definitely downward, the stolen millions went the way of the others, and
Ketchum was arrested after absconding. Revelation of this
enterprising speculator's swindles produced many failures,
Ketchum, Son & Co. crashing into bankruptcy. Edward
Ketchum, formerly considered (while successful) "a model
young man, discreet, just, sober," was now branded "the greatest defaulter of the age." [20]

In this swindle Morgan was mulcted out of $85,000—about
equal to his share of the profits from the Morgan-Ketchum
gold speculation of 1863. Among the eleven indictments against
Edward Ketchum were two sworn by Morgan's firm involving
seventeen forged gold checks, and a Morgan employee testi-

fied at the trial.[21] In spite of efforts to screen the swindler, Ketchum was convicted and sentenced to four years and six months imprisonment.[22] The speculative market in gold was broken, and speculation no longer flourished on the agony of military struggle: it turned to other channels.

In Morgan's activity during the Civil War one fact emerges clearly: he manifested little (if any) of the solidity and force of later years. Financing the scandalous carbine sale and speculating in gold constituted essentially "small-time" stuff. The petty money-maker was to become the master of money to whom money meant power, the mastery over men and things; but there was, at the time, scarcely any indication of the coming transformation. His aptitudes matured slowly, accretively, and his arrogant, antagonistic personality, together with the lack of brilliance, prevented rapid progress. After being elected to the board of directors of a corporation by his father's influence, Morgan was gently but ingloriously dropped because the other directors considered him dull: all his associates got out of him at board meetings was "yes" or "no" on roll-calls, and they objected to "dummy directors." [23] Neither dull nor a dummy, Morgan's aptitudes matured slowly, while he had another and probably more important characteristic: Morgan was uncomfortable among equals and repressed among superiors, his impulse being to issue orders and rule, an impulse which simply creates antagonism and enmity where it cannot compel obedience. Ideas and decisions formed in his mind, silently, issuing as orders and not as contributions to discussion. Unfit to be one among many, Morgan was driven to being one over many. This is the quality of dictatorship and usually disadvantageous (unless offset by brilliance or an ingratiating nature) until the moment of dictatorship comes. Morgan's rise was necessarily slow, in which the power and prestige of his father's firm largely offset temperamental defects until these merged in the sacrosanctity of power.

But the arrogant, silent financial fledgling made progress

surely, if slowly. In 1864 J. Pierpont Morgan & Co. became
Dabney, Morgan & Co., marking a distinct upward movement
in Morgan's development.[24] Charles H. Dabney had been a
partner in Duncan, Sherman & Co., where Morgan formerly
worked as a clerk. The firm's importance, which decided Dabney in his choice of partner, lay in being the American representatives of J. S. Morgan & Co. (the new style of Peabody &
Co. since 1864, George Peabody retiring). Dabney contributed
much in experience and affiliations: Morgan moved upward by
acquiring and discarding partners. In the seven years of the
partnership, Dabney, Morgan & Co. accumulated profits of
$1,000,000—an excellent showing, all things considered.[25] More
decisive, it meant an accumulation of power indispensable to
the development of J. Pierpont Morgan's personality.

CHAPTER VIII

ECONOMIC AND POLITICAL CHANGES

> *"Dear, dear! How queer everything is to-day! I wonder if I've changed during the night? Let me think: was I the same when I got up this morning? I almost think I can remember feeling a little different. But if I'm not the same, the next question is, who in the world am I? Ah, that's the great puzzle!"*
>
> ALICE IN WONDERLAND.

THE British branch of the House of Morgan during the war was limited to general European business, foreign exchange and particularly the resale of American securities owned abroad. Believing in Confederate victory, European investors almost completely disposed of their American holdings: it was not until 1864, upon definite assurance of Union victory, that foreign capital again began to flow into the United States. Most of the resales of American securities were through Peabody & Co., who dominated the field. The firm was in a difficult position, sentiment in British ruling circles favoring the Confederacy and manufacturers resenting the scarcity of cotton, although Liberals and popular feeling were with the Union. In spite of severe unemployment and distress caused by the war, the textile workers of Manchester sent an address to the American president expressing their solidarity, to which Abraham Lincoln replied that their action was "an instance of sublime Christian heroism which has not been surpassed in any age or country." [1] Peabody & Co., apparently, trimmed their sails to opinion in ruling British circles, arousing considerable American criticism. In 1866 the New York *Post* said:

"What was Mr. Peabody doing? He was making money by

the war. He was watching the ups and downs of the money market, the fluctuations of public credit, and was piling up his profits. In a time of war—especially such a terrible war as we were engaged in—a war in which the greatest interests, commercially speaking, are subject to great and sudden changes, a shrewd dealer in public securities has vast advantages. Mr. Peabody added largely to his princely fortune in this manner." This criticism was amplified by the Springfield *Republican* which insisted that George Peabody and Junius Morgan "gave us no faith and no help in our struggle for national existence.... Through no house were so many American securities sent home for sale as by them. No individuals contributed so much to flooding the money markets with the evidences of our debts to Europe, and breaking down their prices and weakening financial confidence in our nationality, and none made more money by the operation." [2]

Answers in the New York *Times* insisted the charges were "cruelly unjust" and that Peabody and Morgan simply did "what we all did" making money in the war, adding: "They could not refuse to 'send home' the securities of their correspondents. Such, indeed, was the 'distrust' at home that many of our capitalists sent their money abroad for safekeeping." [3] Speculation and profits are legitimate in terms of business morality, yet they may be objectively disloyal. Business identifies itself with the nation but the two are not synonymous: they may clash under certain conditions, particularly as there are divergent social groups in the nation.

George Peabody denied the charge of disloyalty in an address in 1868, just before his death:

"I wish publicly to avow that, during the terrible contest through which the nation has passed, my sympathies were still and always will be with the Union; that my uniform course tended to assist, but never to injure, the credit of the government of the Union." [4]

The sincerity of Peabody's disclaimer is unquestionable. Liberal and humanitarian, George Peabody appreciated the progressive issues involved in the Civil War, and his approval of Emancipation is proven by the gift of $3,500,000 to promote Negro education. Moreover, Peabody was old, inactive, and retired during the war, the firm becoming J. S. Morgan & Co. While favoring the Union, Junius Morgan was swayed neither by liberal nor humanitarian impulses, calculatingly businesslike. Business transcends national ideals. The House of Morgan "could not refuse to send home the securities of correspondents." Banking is banking and business is business. The unemployed, hungry textile workers of Manchester might tighten their belts and send resolutions of sympathy to Abraham Lincoln, but a banking house must serve its clients, maintain its credit or crash. In 1917 the then master of the House of Morgan, J. Pierpont Morgan, Jr., expressed the readiness "to be commandeered by the government," and said: "We will do anything that is right, honorable *and not to the injury of our credit.*" [5] In the choice between credit and the national interest, credit comes first. Junius Morgan was simply carrying on "business as usual" and making money. Money-making is as legitimate in war as in peace.

During the war Junius Morgan's sustained interest in American developments was curiously illustrated by his connection with the importation of indentured labor into the United States. Labor and frontiersmen had waged an unrelenting struggle against the seizure of the public lands by capitalist speculators and slavocrats, insisting on their free use by the people. Congress recognized the importance of this issue in 1862 by passage of the Homestead Act opening the Western lands to free settlement. Manufacturers had always opposed free land, fearful it would draw workers to the West, create labor scarcity, make the workers independent and increase wages. They combined with speculators to circumvent the Homestead Act. One means was the grant of millions of acres of public lands to speculators through fraudulent entry and other millions to railroad corporations. Another was the Immigration Act of 1864 authorizing the importation of foreign labor under conditions amounting to indentured servitude and the grant of lands to corporations engaged in the business of importing labor. One of these corporations was the American Emigrant Co., acting as the direct agent of employers by means of a system of indentured labor. Among its sponsors were J. S. Morgan & Co. The American Emigrant Co. was investigated by the Canadian Ministry of Agriculture, the report of 1865 emphasizing the company's "very considerable" profits and giving the sources: Fees from all applicants, graded charges to emigrants who were shipped to the United States, commissions on tickets from ships and railroads, taking the emigrant's fare in gold and paying same in American paper currency, loans to emigrants on pledge of wages, and participation in the profits of speculative land companies.[6] American labor opposed the emigrant companies, declaring they constituted "a direct attempt to control the price of home labor," but not until twenty years later did Congress initiate legislation against contract labor.[7]

There was no particular importance in Junius Morgan's sponsorship of the American Emigrant Co. (he received none of the profits, apparently) except as indicating the drift of class forces.

The Immigration Act of 1864 was an expression of aggressive capitalism, the power of which was consolidated by the Civil War, objectively waged to insure the supremacy of the industrial and financial interests of the North. Profiteering, speculation and corruption flourished during the war, but they were simply scum on the surface of fundamental economic and political changes. Slavocracy was crushed (crushing at the same time the agrarian democracy of Jefferson and Jackson). Economic mastery moved from farm to factory, from the country to the city—climaxing pre-war developments. Within thirty years capitalist enterprise converted the United

States into the mightiest of industrial nations—in the midst of which the House of Morgan conquered supreme power in industry and finance.

Business prospered during the Civil War, failures almost disappearing. By increasing prices the depreciated paper currency lowered the workers' real wages and the farmers' income while favoring business profits. Wealth concentrated among manufacturers, merchants, financiers and speculators, producing a large accumulation of investment capital available for new business enterprises. The war, moreover, accelerated industrial development. Inventions and technological improvements multiplied, plants becoming larger and more efficient. Iron and steel manufactures, the basis of modern industry, developed swiftly under pressure of the war's requirements for munitions; and after the war the expanded metallurgical industry increased its production of peace goods. The heavy demands upon war industries compelled more efficiency, larger plants and consolidation of scattered plants, a development emphasized by the general growth in standardization, quantity production and corporate enterprise. Petty industry was yielding to large-scale industry. Corporations combined in order to fix prices, evade taxation and profit from speculative opportunities (including large promoters' profits). Industry emerged from the Civil War larger, more efficient, "protected" by higher tariffs[8] and with an immense amount of investment capital for new enterprises, while consolidation and combination began their conquest of American business.

Although in control of the national government, triumphant industrialism politically was still insecure. In terms of all Americans the Republican Party was a minority party, and would have been swept out of the government had Northern and Southern Democrats been allowed to unite. But the Republican Party, by military force and under cover of Negro liberation, disfranchised the South, smashed political opposi-

JUNIUS SPENCER MORGAN

CORNELIUS VANDERBILT

tion as industrialists and financiers smashed economic opposition, and consolidated capitalist control of the national government. The implacable measures of Reconstruction, originally conceived by Thaddeus Stevens and others primarily and
in all sincerity to insure the Negro's rights, were soon transformed into a struggle of triumphant, unscrupulous capitalism
to retain control of government, a struggle directed equally
against Northern labor, agriculture and the middle class. Once
this capitalist control was accomplished the Republican Party
shamelessly deserted the Negro. The South was the anvil upon
which capitalism forged its political power—violently, often
illegally and always ruthlessly, Reconstruction being the Civil
War in other forms.

It was during the ten years of Reconstruction, when the Republican Party maintained itself in power largely by military
force and corruption, that politics itself became a business,
the source of many a fortune. National and State governments
showered favors lavishly upon industrialists, financiers and
speculators—nor was this aid the result of a definite social
policy to encourage business enterprise, but usually corrupt
favors secured by one set of businessmen at the expense of
other businessmen and society. The tariff, determined almost
exclusively by the interests of particular manufacturers and
not industry in general, was a source of much corruption. Most
railroad legislation was secured by corrupt practices, and the
Northern Pacific Railroad was stigmatized as "a gang of
plunderers." [9] By 1872 Congress had granted 150,000,000 acres
of public lands and millions in money to railroads, nearly all
of which went to enrich speculators.[10]

When investigations revealed corruption and plundering,
nobody was punished. Chicanery in politics expressed chicanery
in business. The dominant mood of the nation was itself corrupt. "Get rich!" was the universal cry, and becoming rich
legitimized the means, whether fair or foul. In the pulpit of

God Henry Ward Beecher preached variations on the theme, It is good to get rich. Money was the holy water of life. The finer aspects of Puritanism, expressed in pre-war humanitarian movements and culture, were crushed; the more ignoble aspects, identifying godliness and acquisition, survived and conquered. Amassing riches, regardless of the means, was justified by riches and by the old philosophy of the Rev. Joseph Morgan, "Each man coveting to make himself rich, carries on the Publick Good: thus God in His *Wisdom* and *Mercy* turns our Wickedness to Publick Benefit."

There was an illuminating secular expression of this curious philosophy of riches at a testimonial dinner to Junius Morgan in 1877, given in his honor for upholding American credit and honor in Europe "when disasters have swept over our enterprises and the public faith has been exposed to reproach." Among those present were prominent bankers, manufacturers, merchants, railroad men and speculators, including John Jacob Astor and Theodore Roosevelt (the elder), representing aggregate wealth of $1,000,000,000. Samuel J. Tilden, the chairman, said in his introductory remarks:

"The men I see before me are owners and managers of colossal capitals. You are, doubtless in some degree, clinging to the illusion that you are working for yourselves, but it is my pleasure to claim that you are working for the public. [Applause.] While you are scheming for your own selfish ends, there is an over-ruling and wise Providence directing that the most of all you do should inure to the benefit of the people. Men of colossal fortunes are in effect, if not in fact, trustees for the public." [11]

It was a comforting and inspiring philosophy, sanctifying not only riches but the *means* used to acquire riches. The exploitation of men, women and children, the violent crushing of competitors, fraud, thievery and corruption—they were all justified if they made one rich, since becoming rich meant "working for the public." Acquisitive and predatory impulses were universal: people were all brothers under their skins, big buccaneers being the concentrated expression of millions of little buccaneers all trying to get rich in exactly the same way.

The feverish years after the Civil War were economically and politically an age of buccaneering and of unprecedented economic civil war. It was an almost unbelievably fantastic amalgam of ruthless speculation, savage competition, political and business corruption, and of illegality cynically manipulating Law in its predatory operations. Business buccaneers swooped upon and seized the nation's resources and industry, plundered each other and society. Corporation clashed against corporation in the onward sweep of consolidation and combination. War was waged upon natural resources, against labor and the farmers, upon government. Often it was physical war, more often it was the war of intrigue, corporate manipulation, intimidating and crushing competitors, stock jugglery and corruption. Always the economic civil war was unscrupulous. The buccaneers corrupted legislators, judges and newspapers; and often businessmen were *blackmailed* by political threats: "If I had my way," said one politician, "I would put the manufacturers over the fire and fry all the fat out of them." [12] In this buccaneer age unscrupulous weaklings and scrupulous strong men were equally beaten down.

But beneath all the buccaneering, exploitation and shameless corruption there were irresistible constructive forces, and it was by levying tribute upon these constructive forces that the buccaneers acquired their fortunes and power. Industry and agriculture were transformed by more efficient machinery, multiplying the production of goods, developing the new economic system of large-scale production, of concentrated capitalism. A decisive aspect of this development was the increasing dependence of industry upon finance, the masters of money becoming the masters of industry. As industry assumed larger dimensions and functioned through an increasingly complex network of corporate and financial relationships, finance created an institutionalized technique for the regulation and control of industry. It was by means of this technique, expressing important economic changes, that the House of Morgan conquered power.

PART THREE

———

EMERGENCE

CHAPTER IX

INTERNATIONAL FINANCE

"No room! No room!" they cried out
when they saw Alice coming. "There's
plenty of room!" said Alice indignantly,
and she sat down in a large arm-chair at
one end of the table.

ALICE IN WONDERLAND

OVERSHADOWED during the Civil War by his father's English firm and his own immaturity, J. Pierpont Morgan slowly but steadily acquired an independent identity and reputation. In spite of intense competition, Dabney, Morgan & Co. by 1869 were considered among the important banking houses in New York City, "a House of high repute" doing an "immense" business.[1] The basis of this business was still largely foreign banking, comparatively neglected by other American bankers and mostly carried on by agents of European houses, in which J. P. Morgan specialized.

But J. S. Morgan & Co. were the dominant factor in the House of Morgan at this time. Old Junius Morgan, the most important American banker in London, in addition actively participated in British international financial operations, his firm identifying itself with the British export of capital and imperialism. The larger scope and power of J. S. Morgan & Co. were signalized in 1870 when they organized a syndicate to float a French loan of 750,000,000 francs. At the moment the Prussians were besieging Paris, that malignant ghost Louis Napoleon was a prisoner, and Junius Morgan's authorization issued by the new provisional government. The loan was risky and profitable. Taken at 80 the bonds were offered to

the public at 85, the syndicate clearing $5,000,000 in profits.[2]
One of the largest syndicate operations ever organized in London, the French loan broadened the influence of J. S. Morgan
& Co. independent of their American business.

This American business, however, was still the chief interest of Junius Morgan, the export of British capital to the United
States becoming again active. Among the many American
issues sold in Europe by J. S. Morgan & Co. was one of $4,000,-
000 6 per cent Erie bonds. The Erie Railroad's credit was low
(being in the stifling clutch of Daniel Drew) and its bonds
priced at 75 to yield 10 per cent.[3] A few years later Junius Morgan took from Andrew Carnegie $5,000,000 of American railroad bonds which neither American bankers nor the Barings
would take. Carnegie at the time was "on the make" and cannily using every opportunity, as he himself illustrates in this
report of a conversation with old Junius:

CARNEGIE: I will give you an idea and help you to carry it
forward if you will give me one-quarter of all the money you
make by acting upon it.

MORGAN (*smilingly*): That seems fair, we ought to be willing to pay you a quarter of the profit.[4] ...

The confidence of British investors in Peabody & Co. was
retained and strengthened by J. S. Morgan & Co., who never,
according to contemporary opinion, took part in the "speculative schemes which, originating (to put it very mildly) in the
brains of our over-sanguine countrymen" led the British victims
to speak "of America as a land of speculators and adventurers." [5] The majority of British investments in American
securities were through the House of Morgan, and these investments were large.

The very large purchases of American securities by
British (and other European) investors was not simply due
to this country's growing wealth and high investment returns.
Investors were in the grip of larger forces. The world was

being industrialized and production, markets and finance becoming more international. Capitalist industry depends upon
widening markets to sustain an increasing production of goods
and profits. Industrialized nations (particularly England) developed surplus goods and capital, and searched everywhere
(in the United States, Asia, Africa and Latin America) for new
markets and new sources of raw materials, as well as larger
yields on invested money. In the forefront of the movement was
the export of capital, precursing trade, railroads, factories,
mines, international antagonisms, colonial conquest and wars.

In the United States, a strong, independent nation, the import of foreign capital simply accelerated industrialization.
Transforming what was still partly a wilderness into a complex
industrial nation, this country developed an insatiable appetite for new capital and goods. American foreign trade expanded swiftly after the Civil War. Business was on the upsurge, eager for new capital. American corporate enterprises
secured large amounts of foreign capital, while after the Civil
War government bonds again became popular with European
investors. This steady import of capital was interrupted in
1866 by the London money panic and by the Franco-Prussian
War in 1871, but the interruptions were minor and temporary.
In 1869 Europeans owned $1,000,000,000 of American govern-
ment bonds (out of a total of $2,750,000,000) and $465,000,000
of American corporate securities.[6]

Contemporary business opinion considered this import of
European capital of prime importance, in spite of political
spread-eagleism and contemptuous flings by politicians about
"What have we to do with abroad?" When the London & San
Francisco Bank (financed by English investors, of which Dabney, Morgan & Co. were the agents in New York and J. S.
Morgan & Co. in London) increased its capital, the action was
greeted as an expression of the "confidence of European capitalists in our future," whose purchase of railroad bonds and

other securities was necessary "for carrying out our larger enterprises." [7] This import of capital constituted a business in which power was potential.*

Railroad construction absorbed more foreign capital than all other industrial enterprises. Immigrants flowed in by the millions, pioneers pressed against the Western wilderness, manufacturers sought new markets, speculators were attracted by large profits, and railroads multiplied almost overnight. These railroads opened up new lands, widened markets, and facilitated the geographic and corporate concentration of industry, constituting the most important factor in prosperity and industrial progress after the Civil War. Railroad construction projects tapped the reservoirs of capital accumulated during the War, Congress generously subsidized the Western roads, and foreign investors were impressed by the yields on American railroad stocks and bonds of which in 1869 they owned $243,000,-000. Between 1865 and 1869, 12,000 miles of new railroads were constructed, and by 1871, $500,000,000 had been invested in the transcontinental railroads alone.[8]

The Morgans, singly and in combination, sold millions of railroad securities to foreign investors. Among the issues floated by Dabney, Morgan & Co. was one in 1869 of $6,500,000 7 per cent gold mortgage bonds for the Kansas Pacific Railway, of which they were the New York bankers. Most of these bonds were sold in Europe (particularly Germany) and the balance advertised for sale to American investors. Dabney, Morgan & Co. engaged in an unusually large newspaper advertising campaign, one-column and half-column advertisements appearing frequently. The bonds were described as "a first-class investment," tax-free, and "even better than gov-

* At this time J. P. Morgan was already interested in the export of capital, Dabney, Morgan & Co. floating a Peruvian Government loan of $2,000,000 7 per cent gold bonds, $500,000 of which were redeemed in 1871. (New York Times, April 9, 1871.)

ernment securities," * guaranteed by Kansas Pacific's high earnings and its government land grants.[9]

In spite of the heavy advertising and its superlatives, the sale of Kansas Pacific bonds moved slowly in the United States. The confidence of American investors in railroad securities was being shaken by the manipulations of financial buccaneers. In 1868 the *North American Review* had said: "In many instances railroad managers have neither the ability nor the honesty—or if one, not the other—needed to give confidence to persons who seek security as well as a good percentage for their capital." [10] Jay Gould and Jim Fisk, busily plundering the Erie Railroad, notoriously justified the criticism and frightened investors. The railroad buccaneers interfered with the orderly business of investment banking. In 1869 Morgan was to clash with Gould and Fisk and decisively defeat them.

At every important stage in the development of the House of Morgan there is the shaping influence of international finance. They are almost inseparable. Activity in international finance first helped the Morgans secure American financial power and then the world financial power they now possess. The earlier stage expressed the immaturity of American capitalism, the later stage its maturity, while the whole period expresses the development of world capitalism and of financial imperialism. There is a complex interplay of national and international forces the dynamic movement of which decisively influenced the rise to power of the House of Morgan.

* The Kansas Pacific in 1873 defaulted on its bond issue. (*Commercial and Financial Chronicle*, November 15, 1873, p. 648.)

CHAPTER. X

MORGAN, GOULD, FISK

*"But do cats eat bats, I wonder?" And
here Alice began to get rather sleepy, and
went on saying to herself, in a dreamy sort
of way, "Do cats eat bats?" and sometimes, "Do bats eat cats?"*

ALICE IN WONDERLAND

THE railroads dominated economic activity after the Civil War.
While expressing constructive economic progress, railroads
were at the same time characteristic of the worst buccaneer
practices. The plundering of corporations by speculators and
managements was most active among the railroads, aggravated by financial and political corruption. Directors despoiled
stockholders, depressed values and forced railroads into bankruptcy, in spite of which, said the New York *Tribune,* "the
directors are still wealthy, and—out of prison."[1] The public
was oppressed, scorned, helpless, but sneakingly admired the
buccaneers and their profitable skullduggery.

J. Pierpont Morgan did not participate in this saturnalia of
manipulation, corruption and plunder, which was not the
least of the factors in the rise to power of himself and the
House of Morgan. Neither men nor events can be separated
from their age. Morgan developed in the midst of economic
civil war, of an age of buccaneering. He was measurably animated by the *spirit* of the buccaneers (whom he met on their
own terms, and conquered), but his *practice* was much higher.
Morgan was an organizer, an essentially integrating force
where others were customarily disintegrating, his activity being
identified with the more constructive forces of developing in-

dustry and finance, and their class expression. While capitalism produced savage competition and buccaneering, it also
produced the necessity of stabilization, of unity and order, the
antitheses of unrestrained competition. Morgan responded
to the necessity: the banker is usually a stabilizing force, and
Morgan's temperament insisted on unity and order, which
give the opportunity *to rule*. Objective conditions and temperament united to induce Morgan to wage war upon the buccaneers where their practices threatened the developing unity
of industrial and financial interests.

In 1869, when he was thirty-two years old, Morgan engaged in a struggle with Jay Gould and Jim Fisk, then plundering the Erie Railroad. The clash marked an important stage
in the financier's development. Morgan met the buccaneers
on their own terms, using manipulation against manipulation,
guile against guile, force against force—all their tricks—and
conquered.

The plundering of Erie was characteristic of the prevailing
buccaneer practices. Erie was an important transportation
project largely built by public money, the New York State
Legislature and local governments contributing generously to
the construction costs.[2] After which the Erie Railroad was allowed to come under the unregulated control of men like
Jacob Little, the speculator, who used the road for speculative
profit instead of public service. Its stock was manipulated by
Daniel Drew, an unscrupulous, pious old fraud whose machinations are still a revelation in duplicity. Drew was as spidery
as John D. Rockefeller without John D.'s supreme organizing
talent. While a drover he made the cattle drink immense
amounts of water in order that they might weigh more—and
yield more money: the term "watered stock" was used subsequently to describe his "watering" of railroad stocks. Drew
loved to manipulate stocks as other men love to fondle women,
and his penchant for short sales inspired the juicy couplet:

He who sells what isn't his'n,
Must buy it back or go to pris'n.

Drew's methods are revealed by one of his coups in 1866.
Erie stock was selling at 95. Drew had his agents sell stock
at current prices for future delivery; and when the price rose
the agents sold still more stock short. Meanwhile Drew, as
Erie's treasurer, made the company a loan of $3,500,000 (much
of the money being Erie plunder), receiving as security 28,000
shares of unissued stock and $3,500,000 of convertible bonds.
When the time approached to make good on his short sales
Drew took his collateral, converted the bonds into stock, and
threw all into the market. Prices declined swiftly and disastrously, Drew made delivery on his short sales and reaped
millions in profits.[3]

The depredations of Daniel Drew produced howls of anguish
from his victims, and demoralized Erie financially and in
terms of operating efficiency. Businessmen complained of poor
service and discrimination, the stockholders agonizingly observed the wrecking of their property, and labor growled at
low wages and overwork. But what of it? Drew accumulated
riches and unrestrained accumulation was the prevailing ideal.

The Erie Railroad now became an object of Cornelius
Vanderbilt's desire. This picturesque old pirate, who by
manipulation, driving energy and organizing force had become the largest shipowner (whence the honorary title "Commodore") and third richest man of his generation, suggested
the original John Jacob Astor: uncouth, predatory, indifferent
to things other than money and power. "Law?" cried the
Commodore. "What do I care for law? Hain't I got the
power?" In this spirit, when told certain plans conflicted with
a statute, he said: "You don't suppose you can run a railroad
in accordance with the statutes, do you?" Vanderbilt was master of all the buccaneering practices of the age—legislative and
judicial corruption, corporate manipulation, financial jugglery

and stock watering. He was an unscrupulous, savage competitor. To some men who cheated him Vanderbilt wrote: "I won't sue you, for law is too slow. I will ruin you." And he did.[4]

In 1865 Vanderbilt, by refusing the New York Central Railroad connections with his Hudson River Railroad, demoralized Central's traffic, depressed the price of its stock and acquired control. After "watering" the stock by doubling it, the Commodore proceeded to develop New York Central into one of the dominant railroad systems, and engaged in a struggle for control of Erie to monopolize New England business. In the preliminary clash for control, in 1867, Vanderbilt apparently won, and then decided to co-operate with Daniel Drew. The Commodore prepared to consolidate Erie and Central, dominate the northeastern railroad situation, and march triumphantly westward. But Drew prepared a treacherous stroke.

On the Erie board of directors were Jay Gould and Jim Fisk, preparing their partnership in financial crime. Shrinkingly quiet, foxlike in stealth and morally irreproachable, Gould was master of the "methods of acquiring control and possession of other people's property" which he "raised to the dignity of a fine art."[5] Fisk was a flamboyant blatherskite and voluptuary, formerly a mountebank peddler who began to acquire wealth rapidly after becoming an Erie director and the accomplice of Drew and Gould.

In spite of the agreement to co-operate with Vanderbilt, Drew united with Gould and Fisk to trick the Commodore. Vanderbilt kept on buying Erie stock for control, but the more he bought the more there was to buy, the three conspirators issuing secretly more and more stock and throwing it on the market. "If this printing press don't break down," said Jim Fisk, "I'll be damned if I don't give the old hog all he wants of Erie."[6] When Vanderbilt awoke to Drew's treachery he immediately secured an injunction against Erie issuing new stock. But Drew and his accomplices flung another block of stock on the market, which Vanderbilt bought, never suspecting they would risk contempt of court. Contempt of the courts, however, was ingrained in the buccaneers. This final outrage infuriated Vanderbilt. Threatened with arrest for contempt, Drew, Gould and Fisk fled to New Jersey under cover of night, beyond the New York courts' jurisdiction, carrying with them in a coach plunder amounting to $7,000,000 in currency.[7] In Jersey City the conspirators were guarded by a standing army of employees, the Vanderbilt party sent a gang of toughs to capture the Erie depot and kidnap Drew, Gould and Fisk, stores closed, citizens armed, and the militia prepared to intervene.[8] The situation suggested barons waging war on each other.

Jay Gould now started to work in characteristic fashion. The State Legislature was "prevailed" upon to make Erie a New Jersey corporation beyond the reach of litigation in New York City. Then Gould went to Albany, "Erie money poured out like water" among the New York legislators, and the acts of Drew, Gould and Fisk were legalized by a Legislature "shamelessly corrupt, hopelessly beyond the reach of public opinion."[9] Cornelius Vanderbilt waged a war of litigation (in the course of which two judges were implicated in charges of bribery, one being impeached and the other resigning) to compel restitution of the money the conspirators had plundered him of, and although forcing a settlement of $4,750,000 (paid out of Erie's treasury) Vanderbilt was the loser by $2,000,000 and Erie's control.[10] Jay Gould, the broad basis of his fortune originating in Erie plunder, was now definitely on the way to his sinister, unscrupulous amassing of millions, death in the midst of respectability and a funeral in which prominent multi-millionaires (including J. Pierpont Morgan) deferentially participated. . . .

Old Commodore Vanderbilt's defeat in the Erie struggle was unprecedented: always he had smashed opposition. Gould and Fisk now proceeded to consolidate their control of Erie

by ousting treacherous Daniel Drew, distrusted by all.* Erie
had an empty treasury but the conspirators demonstrated there
were still millions to be made out of the wreck. Jim Fisk, himself an unmitigated thief, broke the "systematic thieving"
among Erie employees, many being dismissed and others compelled to make restitution.[11] Gould made William "Boss"
Tweed a member of Erie's board of directors, securing the
support of Tammany Hall, New York City's corrupt, undisputed masters, and their venal judiciary. Then the plundering
began. In a few months Erie stock was "watered" from 165,-
000 shares to 700,000, and, the price falling to 35, the conspirators used Erie's money to "bull" the price to 62, cleaning
up millions.[12] There were other sources of plunder besides
manipulating the stock, Gould being subsequently sued for
$9,000,000 stolen from Erie and compelled to settle.

It was against these apparently irresistible buccaneers that
J. Pierpont Morgan now waged a victorious struggle for control of the Albany & Susquehanna Railroad, coveted by President Jay Gould of the Erie. For the first time Morgan participated directly in railroad affairs.

In January, 1869 the Albany & Susquehanna was completed,
consisting of 142 miles from Albany to Binghamton, and con-
necting with both the Erie and New York Central. Gould and
Fisk determined to get control of Albany & Susquehanna
and consolidate it with Erie. The consolidation would unite
Erie with a network of roads running to New England and
make Erie a formidable competitor of the New York Central
in those regions. Erie, moreover, had acquired coal mines in
Pennsylvania, actively competing for coal transportation business, and control of Albany & Susquehanna offered direct
connections with the anthracite regions and immense power

* In 1867 this pious old fraud endowed the Drew Theological Seminary
and the clerical recipient of the money said: "Oh, that we had one more
Daniel Drew! The church needs the money of its wealthy friends. Nothing
can be nobler than to give the funds and moneys which God himself has
bestowed." (Meade Minnegerode, *Certain Rich Men,* p. 95.)

over competitors. The consolidation, finally, would facilitate Jay Gould's plans for control of the Atlantic & Great Western Railroad and competitive penetration of the West.[13] Instead of the consolidation being motivated by economic and public considerations, it was inspired simply by Gould's ambition to build up a railroad empire for himself.

As in the case of Erie, Albany & Susquehanna had been constructed largely with public money, contributed by the State Legislature in cash while twenty-two towns subscribed for stock payable in bonds which the corporation sold in the market.[14] This enterprise now became the object of economic civil war.

The declaration of war was issued by Jay Gould and Jim Fisk in the form of Erie purchasing Albany & Susquehanna stock. Two large coal companies, competing for mastery in the Northern Pennsylvania coal regions, projected their rivalry into the situation. One of them, the Delaware & Hudson Canal Company, having advanced money to Albany & Susquehanna while under construction, was represented on the Albany & Susquehanna board of directors and constituted an opposition to President Joseph H. Ramsey. Erie allying itself with this opposition, Ramsey secured the support of Delaware & Hudson's competitor, the Delaware, Lackawanna & Western Coal Company. Gould and Fisk retaliated by withdrawing the Lackawanna's "privilege" to transport coal over Erie.[15] Meanwhile, Erie was buying Albany & Susquehanna stock, Jim Fisk issuing blustering declarations, and Jay Gould conspiring in the shadows.

A directors' meeting approaching and half the board being against him, President Ramsey was frightened and called upon J. P. Morgan for help, not only to beat off Erie but to maintain his own control. Morgan, it appears, directed the subsequent campaign against the Erie-Gould-Fisk offensive.

Morgan at this time was thirty-two years old, becoming a substantial financier, but still unknown beyond the inner

DANIEL DREW

JIM FISK

circle of bankers: a write-up of Dabney, Morgan & Co. in 1869 stressed Dabney's career but said nothing of Morgan.[16] He was, however, master in his own house, in spite of being still in the shadows.

Prepared to meet guile with guile and force with force, Morgan and Ramsey mapped out a campaign. Ramsey issued 3,000 shares of Albany & Susquehanna stock to Morgan, Dabney and seven others, Morgan and Dabney becoming members of the board of directors.[17] It was an indication of the importance attached to the new affiliation, and precipitated open war.

The Gould-Fisk party resorted to the courts. "Boss" Tweed on the Erie directorate was an asset and the Tammany judiciary favorable. Suit was brought against Albany & Susquehanna to declare "unauthorized and void" the 3000 shares issued to Morgan and Dabney and prevent their being voted in the coming elections. The necessary injunction was issued by Judge Barnard, who in the Vanderbilt war had issued orders of arrest against Drew, Gould and Fisk. Then the complaisant judge issued some more injunctions, all within fifteen minutes. One suspended Ramsey from the presidency of Albany & Susquehanna and another appointed Jim Fisk and Charles Couter receivers.[18] Learning of the receivership proceedings, the Ramsey-Morgan party in Albany the same evening had a judge of their own appoint another receiver in the person of Robert H. Pruyn.[19] The Gould-Fisk party retaliated by securing an injunction restraining Receiver Pruyn, the county sheriff and Albany police and all Albany & Susquehanna employees from interfering with Receiver Fisk taking possession of the railroad.[20]

Each party had its own pliant judges and the war became one of judge against judge, the judiciary participating actively in the civil war of competing corporations. Injunctions multiplied (about twenty-two in all), the orders of one judge nullifying another judge's orders. Unscrupulous lawyers thrived exceedingly. The legal profession itself was outraged, while the press scored "the indecencies" and "system of judicial abuse" producing "a series of decisions made on both sides with an utter disregard of judicial proprieties." [21]

In the midst of this litigation the struggle went on for control of Albany & Susquehanna stock in preparation for the directors' meeting. Much of this stock was owned by towns served by the railroad, which legally could not be sold except at par, but was selling at 18 in the market. The Gould-Fisk party negotiated a "purchase" of $450,000 stock owned by towns, on the basis of an agreement to buy the stock if it was voted for Gould and Fisk. This stroke the Morgan-Ramsey party answered by issuing 9,500 shares of stock to Ramsey's friends, only 10 per cent cash being paid with money borrowed by Ramsey himself on the security of Albany & Susquehanna bonds in the company's treasury. Receivers of the new shares obligingly gave Ramsey a proxy to vote them at the directors' meeting.[22] The transaction was an abuse of authority, wholly illegal. Duplicity against duplicity!

Two corporations (Gould and Fisk acted in Erie's name) now proceeded to wage war with armed force, each party acting through a receiver legally appointed by complaisant judges.

Receiver Jim Fisk, the man of action carrying out Jay Gould's conspiratorial combinations, forcibly took possession of the Albany & Susquehanna depot at Binghamton with Erie employees assisted by the local sheriff upon order of Judge Barnard. Fisk then proceeded to Albany, accompanied by a bodyguard of toughs, to seize possession of the Albany & Susquehanna offices there. Excited and abusive, Jim Fisk marched in and shouted to his men:

"Rush in, boys, and take possession."

The Albany & Susquehanna superintendent ordered the invaders to get out.

FISK: This is the twenty-seventh raid I've made and I propose to take you men.

SUPERINTENDENT: I hope you'll have a good time doing it.

FISK: I'll take possession of the road if it costs millions and takes any number of men.

SUPERINTENDENT: I am here by order of Mr. Pruyn, who has been appointed receiver by Judge Peckham. Get out!

FISK: I don't give a damn! Boys, throw that gang out! [23]

But the Morgan-Ramsey party was prepared to meet force with force. After a lively tussle, in which furniture was smashed and heads cracked, the invaders beat a hasty retreat. A Ramsey-Morgan man, masquerading as a policeman, "arrested" Jim Fisk, brought him to a police station, shoved him in a door, and disappeared.[24] After being "freed," Fisk returned to the Albany & Susquehanna offices and there met Ramsey, who had been arrested for contempt of court on order of Judge Barnard and immediately released on order of a Ramsey-Morgan judge. Flippantly and characteristically Fisk offered Ramsey to play seven-up for possession of the Albany & Susquehanna Railroad.[25]

Two armed groups were now in possession of the Albany & Susquehanna, Receiver Fisk operating the Binghamton end of the road and Receiver Pruyn the Albany end. The Morgan-Ramsey superintendent determined upon an offensive, and with 450 men marched upon Binghamton while an Erie-Fisk-Gould army prepared to invade Albany. Tracks were pulled up, trestles destroyed and "frogs" put down to derail engines. The marching armies met and clashed at a tunnel fifteen miles from Binghamton. An Erie engine approached an Albany & Susquehanna engine, each refusing to stop. There was a crash, two smashed engines, and a short but bloody battle. The Gould-Fisk party retreated to their entrenchments in the Binghamton depot, while the Morgan-Ramsey men tore up tracks, severed connections, entrenched themselves in the tunnel and prepared for a new battle. The arrival of State troops prevented further strife.[26]

Complete demoralization prevailed on the Albany & Susquehanna, businessmen protested and the press fulminated. Economic civil war was becoming a trifle unpleasant. The Governor issued an ultimatum that the riotous operations must cease until the courts decided the issue of control, and threatened to take military possession of the railroad.[27]

J. P. Morgan now executed a clever maneuver. He prevailed on the Erie-Gould-Fisk party to agree on a joint petition asking the Governor to take possession of, and operate, the road, as "it has become and is impracticable to operate the Albany & Susquehanna, either under the management of the directors, or the persons claiming to be receivers." [28] Jay Gould and Jim Fisk agreed, since the Governor owed his political preferment to their allies, Tammany Hall and "Boss" Tweed. But they miscalculated, as the move was simply a part of Morgan's larger strategy to throw the case into the up-State courts beyond the Tammany-Gould-Fisk judiciary's jurisdiction in New York City.

Acting as an umpire in the contest of competitive business enterprise, the Governor appointed a superintendent to operate the railroad and protect the rights of neutrals (business and the public).[29] The belligerents meanwhile prepared for the September meeting to elect the board of directors of the Albany & Susquehanna Railroad... and another war of litigation.

CHAPTER XI

OVERTONES: 1869

*And then—she found herself at last in the
beautiful garden, among the bright flower-
beds and the cool fountains.*

ALICE IN WONDERLAND

IN May two armies of workmen (mostly Irish immigrants and
Chinese coolies) constructing the Union Pacific Railroad met
at Ogden, Utah, the last spike was driven in and the rails
united. Ceremoniously two locomotives chug-chugged on their
way, completing one of man's great achievements while the
wires thrilled with the story of spanning a continent. . . . Manufacturers dreamed glowingly of conquering Asiatic markets
and ultimate control of the Pacific. . . . Pioneers pressed onward
in their terrible, demoralizing, magnificent struggle against
nature, triumphing over deserts and mountains, exterminat-
ing Indians, making two blades of grass grow where none
grew before. "Clever" men exploited the working pioneers
and acquired enormous estates by plundering the government,
the titles of scarcely any of the great Western estates being
untainted by fraud. . . . Technicians were revolutionizing industry, production multiplying, more goods and services becoming available to increasingly larger groups of the population,
and small-scale industry threatened by the onward sweep of
corporate enterprise. . . . The National Labor Union suggested
organizing Negro workers, while garment workers in Philadelphia started the Knights of Labor—proposing one class
organization of all workers and a new social order. The New
York *World* commented sympathetically on labor's new ideal

of unionizing skilled and unskilled workers regardless of craft.[1]

In the midst of the war for control of the Albany & Susquehanna Railroad, Jay Gould and Jim Fisk actively engaged in other enterprises. In September they engineered a corner in gold (in the interest of the farmers' crops, Gould blandly affirmed) after corrupting men high in the national government and smirching President Grant himself. The price of gold shot up disastrously and Black Friday brought panic and ruin. At the height of the panic Fisk and two of his lights o' love drove in a carriage through Wall Street. There were threats to hang Gould and Fisk, and of Fisk one broker said: "I'll buy a revolver and blow hell out of him." [2] The conspirators barricaded themselves in the Erie offices, protected by thugs and police against hostile crowds. Then government intervened, the Treasury selling gold and breaking the corner. But Gould, realizing the collapse of the conspiracy, secretly sold gold short and cleaned up millions in spite of the failure of the original plans (cheating his own partner, Fisk).[3]

Jay Gould and Jim Fisk, however, were still accepted as honorable and substantial citizens, participating some weeks later in the public ceremony unveiling a statue to Cornelius Vanderbilt. Among other notables were Daniel Drew, the Tammany Mayor Oakey Hall, Admiral Stringham, U.S.N., accompanied by his officers, United States District Attorney Pierrepont, the Right Rev. Bishop Janes, August Belmont, Henry Clews, Chauncey M. Depew and Col. F. A. Conkling. Bishop Janes prayed that the "authorities may be a terror to evil-doers," and "supplicated God that, as riches and honors in this world had been heaped on Vanderbilt, he might devote all his ability to the cause of humanity, and to seek to lay up treasures in heaven." Mayor Hall compared Vanderbilt to Franklin, Jackson and Lincoln—"a remarkable prototype of that rough-hewn American character ... which can carve the way of every humbly born boy to national eminence." [4]

Simultaneously another ceremony was being staged by irreverent brokers in the New York Stock Exchange. Amid uproarious laughter the brokers unveiled a "statue" to Commodore Vanderbilt—"a tall figure draped in white, with a face expressive of little but idiocy," carrying a well-worn watering pot symbolizing the Commodore's tendency to "water" corporation stocks. Then an "injunction" staying further proceedings in the ceremony was served signed "G. Bennerdo" (satirizing Judge Barnard who complaisantly issued the injunctions asked for by Vanderbilt, Gould and Fisk). Jeeringly the meeting decided to ignore the injunction. The chairman delivered an eulogistic speech: "It is the use of water, not as a beverage but as an element of public wealth, which has been the distinguishing characteristic of the achievements of Commodore Vanderbilt's later years." [5] Of the participants in this mock ceremony the New York *World* said: "The Commodore is the realized ideal of every one of them.... He has done what they all admire and envy him for doing, and what they would all do if they could." [6]

A few blocks away from Cornelius Vanderbilt's statue (which cost $500,000) were New York City's worst slums, "the squalid want, criminal woe, wretchedness and suffering of which no pen can describe." In one block lived 382 families— 1,266 persons, including 614 children.[7] ... The New York *Times* conservatively estimated there were 10,000 completely homeless children in the city, "exposed to incessant and overwhelming temptation, who suffer severely in winter and stormy weather—a fearful mass of childish misery and crime." [8] ... Horatio Alger was writing his "Pluck and Luck" stories of "rags to riches." ... An investigation in New York City revealed that the evil of child labor "is as great as in England." Paper-collar factories alone employed 1,500 to 2,000 children under fifteen years of age, and some who were only four years old: one little girl tending a machine was so small she had to stand on a box eighteen inches high to reach her work. Many of these children, after toiling ten hours, attended night school.[9]

The "élite" of New York, "coarse, vulgar, with whom money is the principal thing,"[10] cynically flaunted their riches in the form of conspicuous consumption.

Daniel Drew and J. Pierpont Morgan served as vice-presidents of an association organized to build a memorial statue of George Peabody, who had just died.[11]

In Pennsylvania there was a terrible disaster in a coal mine operated by the Delaware, Lackawanna & Western Coal Company (which was mixed up in the war for control of the Albany & Susquehanna Railroad). "The women sit, with stifled cry, waiting the arrival of their dead.... Fathers lay stiff in death, with arms about their sons. Some were kneeling, as if in prayer; strong men were hand in hand with their fellows. Little notes of tenderness and affection, written upon old fragments of paper to sweetheart, wife or child, are frequently found." There were 110 dead miners: some bodies, "badly bloated, are not recognizable."[12] Insisting that "it is a mockery of justice to term this disaster an accident," the New York *Times* declared "the leave-alone principle may be pushed too far" and demanded protective labor legislation, as did the New York *World*.[13] The business community raised a relief fund of $15,000; neither Drew, Gould, Fisk nor Morgan was among the contributors.[14]

New York City writhed under the exploitation of Tammany Hall—"the rule of a dozen sordid men of selfish hearts and narrow brains who have plundered us of millions, made our elections a farce and sold injustice at a price."[15] Many businessmen were intimately and corruptly identified with Tammany, but others (among them Dabney, Morgan & Co.) were preparing a call for action to investigate Tammany misrule.[16]

"Hideous suffering, horrible barbarity, abuses and degradation" flourished in the New York almshouses. Men and women were "bound with ropes and chains in dark, filthy, verminous cells" and "a strange, abnormal, hideous race of children is springing up" owing to promiscuity among inmates and guards.[17]

Investigations revealed income-tax frauds measured at 70 per cent and corruption again rampant in the New York customs-house.[18] ... The Northern Pacific Railroad lobby in Washington was stigmatized as "a gang of plunderers and beasts of prey."[19] Jay Cooke distributed Northern Pacific stock among influential people, and the Crédit Mobilier scandal was in the making.... The Whisky Ring frauds were mulcting the government of millions in revenue—

> *While Grant eats clams,*
> *And don't care two damns.*[20]

President Grant did care for some things, however, proposing the purchase of Santo Domingo for $1,500,000 and dreaming of annexing Cuba, which Senator Charles Sumner opposed while himself maneuvering to force England to cede Canada to the United States.[21] ... Former Secretary of State William H. Seward, who had purchased Alaska but had been foiled by Congress in his designs upon Santo Domingo, the Virgin Islands and the Isthmus of Panama, busily preached the doctrine of Manifest Destiny—expansion in the Caribbeans and the Pacific.... Egypt celebrated completion of the Suez Canal, which Disraeli in a few years was to buy from a bankrupt Khedive—accelerating the onward sweep of British imperialism.

John D. Rockefeller prepared plans for the creation of an empire in oil by ruthlessly crushing competition, the Standard Oil Co. being organized in 1870.

In October and November strikes broke out on the Erie Railroad against wage decreases, arbitrary discharges, etc. "Admiral Fisk declares he will not submit to dictation" by the Erie workers and, gathering together 1,000 armed men, prepared to "put down" the revolt, although, said the New York *Times*, the strikers "have not manifested the slightest desire to disturb persons or property." [22] ... In October the Gould-Fisk directors of Erie were re-elected, and in November 50,000 shares of new stock issued. [23] ... Accidents on the Erie were so numerous and terrible that newspapers appeared repeatedly with the headline, "Erie Massacre." ... And a wag was composing a song to be sung by Jay Gould to his confederate:

> O Jimmy Fisk, my Jo, Jim,
>   We'll never, never weary
> Of squeezing every penny from
>   The stockholders of Erie.
> And if by any chance, Jim,
>   We to the gallows go,
> We'll sleep together at the foot,
>   O Jimmy Fisk, my Jo. [24]

CHAPTER XII

THE BUCCANEERS BEATEN

Speak roughly to your little boy,
And beat him when he sneezes.
ALICE IN WONDERLAND

THE war for control of the Albany & Susquehanna Railroad flared up again at the stockholders' meeting in September, 1869. Each party came with half a dozen lawyers, Jim Fisk "with a whole carpet-bag full of injunctions," and the Ramsey-Morgan party equally prepared.[1] Neither Gould nor Morgan was present, but theirs was the strategy.

This stockholders' meeting developed aspects of a circus. Crowds. Police. Blustering lawyers. Injunctions. Alarms. Life in the mass was drab and the crowds thrilled to the war businessmen waged upon each other. Flamboyant Jim Fisk, "arrayed in his usual fancy style, gay and frisky," was the crowds' particular delight, the sentimentalized buccaneer of whom later they sang, "He never went back on the poor." (As they sang of Jesse James, "Jesse was a man—a friend to the poor," and of another bandit, "He robbed from the rich and he gave to the poor.") [2]

Fisk fired the first gun at the meeting. It was an injunction by Judge Barnard restraining the voting of "illegal" and "bogus" shares—the shares issued to J. P. Morgan and others by Ramsey—in fact, restraining the voting of any but those shares of which the Erie-Fisk-Gould party knew they had a majority. Under these circumstances the Ramsey-Morgan party decided their only hope was to prevent an election and secured an injunction restraining the inspectors from receiving the votes. Fisk was prepared for the move, and prior to the serv-

ing of the injunction his meeting removed the inspectors and
elected new ones to whom the injunction did not apply. Ramsey thereupon served another injunction restraining the voting
of certain shares, but these shares were voted by a receiver appointed by Fisk.[3]

The upshot of these maneuvers emphasized Fisk's control
of the stockholders' meeting, and the Ramsey-Morgan party
withdrew to organize a rival meeting. Fisk, prepared as usual,
served an injunction on the meeting restraining the Ramsey
inspectors from receiving votes on certain shares, and an order
of arrest, issued the day before by Judge Barnard, on Ramsey
and three other Albany & Susquehanna officers. From another
judge Ramsey immediately secured an order of release on bail.
Each party now elected its own board of directors (the Ramsey board including J. P. Morgan), and adopted resolutions
accusing each other of "fraud, violence, criminal and morally
reprehensible practices."[4]

Nothing being decided by the stockholders' meeting the war
flared up again in litigation—seven more lawsuits, more injunctions, contempt-of-court proceedings and many arrests.
Complete demoralization prevailed on the Albany & Susquehanna Railroad—built to serve the people. Indignation flamed
forth at the outrage, whereupon the Attorney General of the
State of New York, in the name of the People, brought suit
against Morgan, Gould, Ramsey, Fisk and forty-two others to
determine who were legal directors of Albany & Susquehanna,[5]
throwing the case into the up-State courts—precisely what
Morgan had maneuvered for.

Although Gould and Fisk retained control of Erie's board
of directors in the October elections, their position was shaken
by Black Friday and other developments. Appreciating the
situation, and while preparing for the Albany & Susquehanna
legal battle in the State Supreme Court, Morgan executed a
flank movement against Gould and Fisk. In November, Ramsey, as an Erie stockholder, secured a Supreme Court order

suspending Gould, Fisk and their confederates from serving
as officers and directors of Erie, "by reason of gross misconduct
and abuse of their respective trusts and offices." Ramsey's suit
was brought under a New York statute authorizing the Supreme Court "to suspend any director of a corporation when-
ever it shall appear that he has abused his trust." In the petition Ramsey charged that Gould, Fisk and their confederates
were "unscrupulous usurpers who, by a sort of legerdemain,
usurped control of the stockholders' property," stole millions of
Erie's money, impaired its credit and good repute, used the
company's money for their gold speculations and corrupt political purposes, paid not a single dividend, and so demoralized
service on the Erie as to bring "calamities of unusual horror,
damage and death." In addition to suspending Gould, Fisk
and their confederates as officers and directors, the Court enjoined them "from exercising any right, privilege or authority,
in respect of the company, or its franchises, rights of property,
in any capacity whatever, until further order of the court."
The Erie directors not suspended, moreover, were ordered not
to elect new directors or have anything to do with the suspended directors and officers.[6]   ·

Apparently the buccaneers' defeat was final and crushing.
"The Erie Ring Crushed," jubilated the New York *Times:*
"Messrs. Gould, Fisk and their fellow conspirators are stript
of the authority they have abused and the power they have
prostituted. Justice, though tardy, is on the right track at
last." [7]

Jubilation was premature, however, and Morgan's flank
movement not as successful as appeared. The suspension order
was issued on November 23 and served the next day. Gould
and Fisk barricaded themselves in the Erie offices, protected
by armed guards, and defied the Court's order. Again illegality
resorted to the Law. An up-State judge temporarily in New
York City and outside his own jurisdiction was induced to issue an injunction staying all proceedings on the order sus-

pending Gould and Fisk and forbidding its service. Then reliable Judge Barnard issued an injunction forbidding Ramsey to proceed with the suit, reinstating Gould and Fisk and forbidding them "from neglecting to carry out any order of the board of directors" of Erie.[8] Contempt proceedings. More injunctions. Arrests. Large lawyers' fees. Newspaper indignation at the proceedings. In the midst of this melodramatic litigation Gould slipped off to Albany, and in his own peculiar fashion secured from the Legislature an act prescribing that no suit could be brought in a State court to remove corporation directors by any private party aggrieved, but only by the State's Attorney General.[9] And the Attorney General, at the moment, was Gould's man.

While repulsed in his flank movement, Morgan conquered in the main offensive against the Erie conspirators. In December, 1869, the Supreme Court of the State of New York rendered its decision in the Albany & Susquehanna case. The election of the board of directors "headed by J. Pierpont Morgan" was declared "unquestionably valid," that of the Gould-Fisk party procured through conspiracy and fraud. Gould, Fisk and their associates were "perpetually restrained" from bringing any new suits and proceedings in the case, and the Morgan-Ramsey party authorized to recover all costs.[10] Immediately Morgan leased the Albany & Susquehanna Railroad to the Delaware & Hudson Canal Co., and the price of the stock rose to 100, yielding excellent profits.[11]

The decision was too favorable to the Morgan-Ramsey party, and on appeal the Court sustained the legality of the Morgan directors' election but reversed the decision on costs and new suits and proceedings.[12] But new proceedings did not interest Jay Gould any more. In 1872 he was ousted from Erie by a group of English stockholders using Gould methods against Gould.

For years these English stockholders had been trying by legal means to oust Gould from control of Erie in order to

JAY GOULD

Brown Bros.

WILLIAM H. VANDERBILT

stop the plundering and resume dividends. Becoming impatient of the law's impotence, they determined to use other than legal means. Gould provided the opportunity by deciding to make Erie "respectable" with a new board of directors of responsible businessmen (among them Junius Morgan, whose firm represented Erie in London). Learning of this plan the old directors offered themselves for sale to a party representing the English stockholders, the sale put through by payment of $300,000 and Gould ousted. General Daniel Sickles, American minister to Spain on leave of absence to direct the campaign against Gould, received $150,000 for his services in bribing the Erie directors. The whole coup cost $750,000.[13] Bischoffsheim & Goldschmidt, the London bankers who organized the conspiracy against Gould, secured the English representation of Erie.

But old Junius Morgan had his revenge, compelling the payment of $70,000 as the price of giving up a contract for the sale of Erie bonds. Bischoffsheim & Goldschmidt recouped themselves for this and the costs of ousting Gould from the proceeds of Erie bond sales.[14] The new management sued Jay Gould for restitution of money stolen from Erie ($9,000,000) and Gould settled for $5,000,000, the settlement including an agreement that he should be consulted in the working of the road and allowed to buy 200,000 shares of Erie stock at the market price. Gould did this knowing that the news of his settlement would push up the price of Erie stock, upon which he sold his shares, the profit, said Gould, "reimbursing me for the money I have paid to Erie."[15] On top of which the securities Gould turned over for the settlement were found to be worth only $200,000.[16] Out of defeat, as in the Black Friday conspiracy, Jay Gould snatched more millions. The transaction impressed British journals as indicating "a very unhealthy state of commercial morals"—with which the new York *Times* agreed.[17]

J. P. Morgan's victory over Jay Gould and Jim Fisk im-

pressed contemporary opinion, which decided that "this contest, waged not only by litigation but by force of arms, made
Mr. Morgan universally respected as an able financier." [18]
This was a new conception of the financier, indicating the
trend of the times. Defeating the men who had imposed their
will upon Cornelius Vanderbilt and terrorized the business
community was an achievement marking the emergence of a
dominating personality. The older bankers were either afraid
of Jay Gould and Jim Fisk, mixed up in their schemes or pursuing similar schemes of their own; moreover, they were often
too dignified to adopt the rough-and-tumble tactics required
under the circumstances. But Morgan was not. He met force
with force, guile with guile, methods which Morgan subsequently combined with the technique of using the concentrated power of massed money to conquer his objectives. The
combination was irresistible.

CHAPTER XIII

GOVERNMENT FINANCING: 1871-79

> *"Collar that Dormouse," the Queen*
> *shrieked out. "Behead that Dormouse!*
> *Turn that Dormouse out! Suppress him!*
> *Pinch him! Off with his whiskers."*
> ALICE IN WONDERLAND

J. PIERPONT MORGAN's struggle against Jay Gould and Jim Fisk, revealing the age and Morgan's characteristics, and indicating more important events to come in railroad affairs, was an interlude. The House of Morgan emerged as a definite American financial power by means of international finance, in a struggle against Jay Cooke and in the midst of the government financing of 1871-79 which refunded $750,000,000 of national bonds, the larger part through the House of Morgan.

Jay Cooke in 1871 was the dominant American financier, a peculiar combination of fox and parson, constructive builder and reckless speculator, patriot and unscrupulous money-maker, plus some of Barnum's ballyhoo talents. Cooke was a tower of strength to the government in financing the Civil War, his sale of bonds (yielding him commissions of $7,187,-000)[1] being facilitated by wily political intrigues, corruption of the press and securing the confidence of small investors. Other bankers were more of a liability than an asset to the government, often speculating in gold and government credit, while Jay Cooke cannily combined profit and loyal service. His almost monopolistic supremacy in the sale of War bonds (which anticipated many modern ideas of popular bond sales, in spite of his misleading slogan, "A national debt is a national blessing") aroused enmity in the financial community,

competitors being mercilessly trod underfoot by Cooke in his
march to power. This enmity was sharpened after the War by
the establishment in New York City of a branch house of Jay
Cooke & Co., even former friends now becoming rivals. The
new company was immediately successful.[2]

In 1869 Jay Cooke acquired control of the Northern Pacific
Railroad, chartered during the Civil War by speculators without money of their own and granted 47,360,000 acres of public
lands by Congress.[3] The terms on which the company was
reorganized offered prospects of fabulous profits. Cooke & Co.
agreed to advance Northern Pacific $500,000 and in return re-
ceived $20,000,000 stock as a bonus, one-half of the remaining
$60,000,000 stock for introducing and selling $100,000,000 of 7.3
per cent Northern Pacific bonds, and one-half of the stock in
the Lake Superior & Puget Sound Land Co. organized to exploit the railroad's enormous land grants. As construction
proceeded, the balance of $40,000,000 Northern Pacific stock
was to be distributed to a pool upon subscribing $5,600,000 cash
in stock and bonds.[4] It was a stupendous speculation. Affable
and benign, as if on the Lord's business, Jay Cooke "sweetened" members of Congress and other prominent men with
Northern Pacific stock and bonds in order to secure their influence with government and public: the company's Congressional lobby was stigmatized "as a gang of plunderers and
beasts of prey."

New York and Philadelphia capitalists, excluded from the
gigantic speculative enterprise, inspired venomous attacks upon
Cooke and the Northern Pacific. One of the most bitter and
persistent antagonists was Anthony J. Drexel, soon to become
J. P. Morgan's partner. This enmity originated in the Civil
War when Drexel & Co., the largest banking house in Philadelphia, were thrust aside in the scramble for government
financing business by the new house of Cooke & Co. The Congressional demand for an investigation of Jay Cooke's Civil
War financing was inspired by Drexel, while his Philadelphia

Ledger maintained an unremitting criticism of Cooke and the Northern Pacific.[5]

In order to strengthen his international financial affiliations and dispose of Northern Pacific bonds in Europe Jay Cooke organized the firm of Cooke, McCulloch & Co. in London, the former Secretary of the Treasury being chosen as a partner partly because his name "suggested an alliance with the government which was likely to impress Europe very much."[6] The new firm could not secure a site near the Bank of England, but were comforted by the "consoling thought" that they were "not farther away from the 'Old Lady' than Morgans' or Barings'." Nearly all the London bankers with American affiliations felicitated McCulloch, old Junius Morgan being "particularly attentive." But rivalry was sharpened, all the more as the Cookes in London tried to get the profitable American naval agency away from the Barings.[7]

The antagonism between Cooke and the other bankers broke out in open conflict in 1871, when the Treasury decided to refund $200,000,000 of Civil War bonds. Expecting to get the business, the Cookes met immediate opposition. Drexel secretly maneuvered against Cooke. Levi P. Morton, of Morton, Bliss & Co. and his English partner, Sir John Rose, appeared in Washington, tried to get the new loan and almost succeeded.[8] Congressional agitation assailed the Cookes' power over the government and insisted that the bonds be sold directly by the Treasury, which Secretary Boutwell decided to do.

Banking houses in this country and Europe were appointed agents for the loan, among them Dabney, Morgan & Co. and J. S. Morgan & Co. The books were opened March 6, 1871, and were to close in twenty days. But most of the bankers in New York City, including Dabney, Morgan & Co., were indifferent to the loan's success, disapproving of direct government sales, and did not act on their appointment as agents. By March 22 only $20,000,000 had been subscribed, one-third being through Cooke & Co. Nor were the European bankers sympathetic and their attitude decided the loan's failure, a total of only $60,000,000 being subscribed.[9] The indifference of the financial community killed the loan.

Failure definitely assured, Morton, Bliss & Co. formed a syndicate in opposition to Cooke to get the balance of the loan. The struggle flared up again. But Secretary Boutwell decided on the Cookes, Congresssional agitation being quiescent. Cooke organized two syndicates, one American and the other European. Participation in the European syndicate was offered to the Morgans, Barings and Morton, Rose & Co., but they declined to accept. The syndicate operations were immediately and strikingly successful, $130,000,000 of bonds being disposed of on which the Cookes cleared $3,000,000 profit. Levi Morton afterward praised the operation, expressing regret that he had rejected the offer to participate because of the belief that a new house (Cooke, McCulloch & Co.) could not successfully head a foreign syndicate.[10]

Capitalizing the advantages of success, Cooke, McCulloch & Co. secured the American naval agency in London.[11] The opposition was temporarily smashed and Jay Cooke supreme in the American financial world.

In June, 1871, the Morgans and Drexels combined forces, Charles H. Dabney retiring from Dabney, Morgan & Co., which now became Drexel, Morgan & Co. It was an important alliance. The Drexels were powerful bankers with excellent foreign connections which the alliance strengthened, while the Morgans strengthened their American connections. Drexel & Co. had dominated the banking field in Philadelphia before the coming of Jay Cooke (against whom they now prepared more vigorous offensives). The origins of the Drexels were curious. The father, Joseph Drexel, was an immigrant portrait painter who wandered all over Mexico and South America before settling in Philadelphia. There, abandoning art, he made money buying and selling "wild-cat" currency issued by State banks, became a broker dealing in gold from California, and gradually built up a successful banking business which was inherited by the sons.[12] Drexel, Morgan & Co. purchased for $945,000 property in Wall Street on which a chastely dignified building was erected, significant of power and prestige.[13] Contemporary opinion spoke of the "great house of the Drexels," [14] but in fact Morgan was the active moving force, although still comparatively unknown beyond the inner circles. The House of Morgan now consisted of Drexel, Morgan & Co., New York, Drexel & Co., Philadelphia, J. S. Morgan & Co., London, and Drexel, Harjes & Co., Paris (afterward Morgan, Harjes & Co.).[15] It was a formidable combination, marking the definite emergence of J. Pierpont Morgan, prepared to dispute with Jay Cooke for American financial supremacy.

Morgan himself directed the new struggle against Cooke which broke out in 1873, again over national financing. As usual Morgan was in the shadows while other men appeared publicly: but his were the strategy and driving force.

Although indisputably the most important contemporary financier, Cooke's power was never the financial dictatorship created by Morgan in later years, personal and institutional characteristics determining the differences. Astute and of extraordinary ability, Cooke only partly had the capacity to impose himself on other men and compel their obedience. Under the prevailing conditions of savage competition in finance, where every one was on the make, the fox might go far but the quality of the wolf was indispensable to maintain (if not secure) supremacy. Cooke never had Morgan's terrifying capacity to bludgeon antagonists into submission. The House of Cooke, moreover, concentrated on itself and not on the creation of a system as the basis of its supremacy. Morgan conquered and maintained supremacy not only by his capacity to compel obedience, but by institutionalizing his supremacy in a system of which the House of Morgan was the concentration point, and in which other financiers participated *under Morgan's overlordship*. When in after years Morgan spoke, he spoke for the system, an order almost automatically obeyed by financiers and their institutions; when Cooke spoke, he spoke simply for his House, arousing competitors to hostile combination and action. That happened now, not only competition for new business but another struggle against Jay Cooke's supremacy, in which the Cookes recognized "young Morgan and Morton" as their most active and important rivals[16]—Morgan, thirty-six years of age, and Morton, much older but accepting Morgan's leadership.

With power Morgan was beginning to be himself, to manifest the talents of organizing and ruling which were fundamental in his character. His silence, originally considered "dull," appeared as the concomitant of power, of temperamental peculiarity, now that Morgan could decide in terms of orders and not discussion, ruling Drexel, Morgan & Co. He dominated associates or they ceased being his associates. Formerly dependent upon the prestige of J. S. Morgan & Co., which buoyed him up while accumulating power (the breath of his being), J. Pierpont Morgan was becoming master in his father's House—and his own. Aggressively energetic, absorbed in business, no longer the speculative fledgling of the Civil War, Morgan prepared the campaign against Jay Cooke, whose downfall was indispensable to his own financial supremacy.

Already in 1871, while still flushed with the success of the syndicate operations, the Cookes were afraid of competition in government business. They suspected the Rothschilds might form a syndicate of their own to get further refunding loans. "Jealousy toward our house," wrote a Cooke partner, "would make such a combination remarkably easy." This development was forestalled by the House of Cooke and the Rothschilds combining forces in an offer to Secretary Boutwell for new refunding business, an offer temporarily declined.[17]

Meanwhile agitation against Jay Cooke increased, instigated by his rivals, public resentment at the Northern Pacific "robbery," and the discontent of small businessmen, farmers and labor. Their contribution of large sums to the Republican party in the 1872 campaign,[18] Grant's re-election, and the fact of "sweetened" politicians in Washington being under financial obligations to them, convinced the Cookes that they would secure the new government business. It was a mistake, this dependence upon "sweetened" politicians, who are as unreliable as their principles. Morgan never made the mistake, contemptuous of politics and politicians. (In spite of this contempt, however, Morgan maintained a general interest in politics, of the most reactionary sort, never respondng to any progressive principle, and contributing generously to the Republican party. In 1872 Drexel, Morgan & Co. signed a manifesto of bankers and businessmen urging Grant's re-election, in spite of his administration's abysmal incompetence and corruption, for "the general welfare of the country, the interests of its trade and commerce, and the consequent stability of its public securities.")[19]

When the Treasury decided on a new loan in 1873 Jay Cooke was disturbed by the opposition which immediately appeared and infuriated by Secretary Boutwell's hesitancy in giving his House the business. Morgan organized a syndicate composed of Drexel, Morgan & Co., J. S. Morgan & Co., Baring Bros. and Morton, Rose & Co., and this syndicate waged war on the Cookes and the Rothschilds—J. P. Morgan in the shadows and Levi Morton in the open.

The Ways and Means Committee of the House of Representatives held meetings on the new loan, there being considerable sentiment in Congress for the direct sale of bonds by the Treasury. William B. Duncan, of Duncan, Sherman & Co., appeared before the committee to urge direct government sales, claiming that syndicate operations took "United States bonds out of the hands of small investors and put them in the hands of bankers, brokers and large investors, where they were liable to be affected by the frequent fluctuations in the money market."[20] Levi Morton, appearing for the Morgan syndicate, ridiculed Duncan's argument and insisted, "I do not know of any other method of negotiating a government loan except by bankers."

CHAIRMAN: You propose to become a member of the next syndicate?

MORTON: We do.[21]

This bland insistence of the Morgan-Morton party for a place in the sun infuriated the Cookes, who were outraged by Secretary Boutwell's procedure of apparently encouraging the opposition. But the opposition campaign was clever. While Cooke asked for the whole business, Morgan and Morton simply insisted on equal participation. Moreover, the opposition developed an annoying political campaign—Morton lobbied publicly and secretly, President Grant was influenced [22] and a species of political blackmail levied on the government concerning its dependence upon Cooke & Co. There was a collapse of the house of cards Jay Cooke had built with "sweetened" politicians. While the Ways and Means Committee declined to recommend any action on the loan, Secretary Boutwell decided to compromise, dividing the $300,000,000 of bonds equally between the Morgan-Morton syndicate (including J. S. Morgan & Co. and the Barings) and the Cooke syndicate (including the Rothschilds).[23]

The compromise was a Morgan victory as his syndicate had simply insisted on equal participation, which was granted, a victory achieved by exploiting the general distrust and fear of Jay Cooke and by mobilizing the Morgans' international financial power. Most of the loan was to be placed in Europe, and the formidable combination of J. S. Morgan & Co., the Barings and Drexel, Harjes & Co. offset the Rothschilds' support of Cooke. But the victory was equally important in the struggle for American financial supremacy.

Operations to dispose of the loan in the United States were directed by Morgan, Morton and Fahnestock (a Cooke partner). In advertisements to the American public signed Jay

Cooke & Co., Drexel, Morgan & Co. and Morton, Bliss & Co. the syndicate emphasized its "connections in Europe and America which insure the placing of the entire remainder of 5 per cent bonds." Prospective buyers were urged to act immediately as "it is expected that the affiliations in Europe will be very large, and perhaps more than sufficient to absorb the whole loan." [24] Books were opened on February 4 and the next day Junius Morgan sent a cable of "confident tenor." [25]

But something went wrong. Perhaps the antagonists could not work smoothly together. More important, business was unsound, money tight, underlying conditions preparing the panic that was to break loose within a few months. Subscriptions were meager. By February 16 only $13,500,000 had been subscribed in the United States and a few millions in Europe. [26] Fright assailed the syndicate members, and they implored Secretary Boutwell not to issue the call for $100,000,000 on February 9, but to postpone action. [27] Upon definite news of the loan's failure in London speculators forced up the price of gold. [28] The Cooke party spoke sarcastically of their "distinguished associates" and Jay Cooke hoped they would "back out," considering them a hindrance rather than a help. [29] But Morgan and Morton did not back out, and the bond operations limped on their way. Then the syndicate called upon Secretary Boutwell to scale down the call to $50,000,000, which was done. [30]

In spite of the loan's failure, Morgan had conquered a measure of financial equality with Cooke, whose prestige was severely lowered and whose House was to disappear in the great panic of 1873.*

* In 1873 J. Pierpont Morgan received the accolade of membership in the Union League Club. Organized to sustain Abraham Lincoln in the prosecution of the War, the Union League Club from the start proposed to organize the "élite of the élite" in the new money aristocracy coming to power, an inner circle of the powerful to influence legislation and social life generally. The Club sought its members among three classes: (1) "Men of substance and established high position socially," (2) "Clever men, especially of letters, wits and artists who have made their mark," and (3) "Promising young men who

General uneasiness preceded the panic—tight money, developing industrial recession, and a dangerously top-heavy financial superstructure reared upon unrestrained speculation (particularly in railroads and land). The collapse of railroad speculation precipitated the panic. In September two brokerage houses failed in New York City, with one of which Daniel Drew was identified.[31] Then the New York branch of Cooke & Co. suspended, without consulting Jay Cooke, compelling suspension of the parent branch in Philadelphia. The panic spread like wildfire, there being forty important suspensions in two days in New York City alone.[32] Cooke & Co. crashed owing largely to their enormous burden of practically useless Northern Pacific collateral acquired in the course of unsound speculative manipulations. Sales of Northern Pacific bonds, calculated upon to sustain the whole speculation, had slackened and almost ceased because of public distrust produced by revelations of how the Crédit Mobilier had plundered the Union Pacific and smeared corruption over the national government.[33] But Jay Cooke was determined to proceed with the Northern Pacific, being in too deep to retire, and made still larger advances to the company, while the immense speculation in land by the Lake Superior & Puget Sound Land Co. still further sapped Northern Pacific's resources and hastened its insolvency.[34]

Jay Cooke specialized successfully in securing the confidence of small investors, and these were now victims of the crash. One was "a poor old woman who holds a $500 Northern Pacific bond, all her earthly wealth." Another wrote the financier: "I worked twenty years to get that little sum of $360

should be drawn in and nourished with care, but especially those rich young men who don't understand what their place can be in American society." In 1864 the Union League Club adopted resolutions in favor of immigrant contract labor, "the establishment of agencies through which the various classes of employers may obtain the particular operatives they require." (Henry W. Bellows, *Historical Sketch of the Union League Club of New York, 1863-79*, pp. 13, 65.)

together. You told me and my little girl when we went to the bank to get our money that all was safe." These letters, according to Jay Cooke's biographer, "of the most pitiful kind, were calculated to increase Mr. Cooke's mortification." [35] The crash was complete and final.*

Five years of business depression followed the 1873 panic, accompanied by agrarian distress, severe unemployment, wage reductions and an upflare of social discontent. Mercantile failures involved immense losses. [36] The Granger movement assumed new vigor in its expression of agrarian discontent, while the Greenback Party proposed "cheap money" legislation and in 1878 secured substantial representation in Congress. Labor burst forth in the great strikes of 1877, which were stigmatized as "revolutionary." Discontent, as usual, developed attacks upon the banks, and bankers in convention assembled expressed "grave apprehensions as to the future of the banking system in the United States... popular hostility toward the banks has probably never been so widespread." [37] The combined farmer-labor revolt frightened industrialists, financiers and politicians. Mild reform proposals were savagely rejected, strikes ruthlessly crushed and unemployed demonstrations dispersed by force. Its liberal principles cracking under the strain, the *Nation* insinuated that farmers were "thieves and swindlers" in demanding lower freight rates which meant carrying their grain "for a trifle." [38] Henry Ward Beecher, himself the recipient of $20,000 a year and whose church had been organized as a profit-making enterprise by real-estate speculators, sermonized against labor amid the applause of Plymouth's congregation: "Is the great working class oppressed? Yes, undoubtedly it is. God has intended the great to be great and the little to be little.... The trade union, originated under the

---

* After his discharge from bankruptcy Jay Cooke invested $3,000 in a silver mine, against the advice of his friends. The mine proved fabulously rich, and in 1879 Cooke sold his share for $1,000,000, assuring a comfortable old age. (E. P. Oberholtzer, *Jay Cooke*, Vol. II, pp. 522-26.)

European system, destroys liberty....I do not say that a dollar a day is enough to support a workingman. But it is enough to support a man! Not enough to support a man and five children if a man insist on smoking and drinking beer....But the man who cannot live on bread and water is not fit to live." [39] Christ's teachings were consumed in the flames of social war.

Capitalist enterprise, in the midst of social war, consolidated its financial supremacy by proceeding with refunding the national debt and resuming specie payments. This involved a series of national loans by means of which J. P. Morgan emerged definitely to financial power.

Early in 1876 Drexel, Morgan & Co. organized a syndicate which secured a government issue of $5,883,000 5% bonds against the competition of August Belmont representing the Rothschilds.[40]

In 1877 the House of Morgan participated in a refunding syndicate composed of August Belmont & Co. (the Rothschilds), Drexel, Morgan & Co. (J. S. Morgan & Co.), J. & W. Seligman & Co. (Seligman Bros.) and Morton, Bliss & Co. (Morton, Rose & Co.).[41] Morgan dominated the American combination. After the new Secretary of the Treasury, John Sherman, had secured a revision of the contract and more favorable terms,[42] the syndicate proceeded with its operations. The loan combined refunding and resumption purposes, the syndicate selling $235,000,000 bonds (at 4½ and 4 per cent) for redemption of 6 per cent bonds and $40,000,000 to secure gold for the resumption of specie payments. Most of the bonds were sold at an advance of one to four points.[43] In this financial operation, it was reported, the syndicate made a profit of $25,000,000, of which $5,000,000 accrued to Drexel, Morgan & Co.[44]

The operation ceased owing to the syndicate's belief that popular agitation for repeal of the resumption act (which set January 1, 1879, for resuming specie payments) and agitation for unlimited coinage of silver would prevent further sales of bonds.[45] Depression and discontent strengthened the movement for cheap money. The Greenback Party, with fourteen members in Congress, was making alarming progress in its agitation for payment of the national debt in greenbacks and repeal of the resumption act, a program accepted by a newly organized labor party, the National Party. Social as well as financial issues were involved. Redemption of Civil War bonds in gold meant increasing the principal's value by 35 per cent.[46] As after the Revolution redemption of the worthless paper currency enriched a clique of speculators (including Robert Morris and Governor George Clinton), so the resumption of specie payments enriched a small group of bondholders—while depression oppressed the people.

Labor and the farmers, moreover, felt that cheap money would end depression, while the farmers' mortgage burdens would be eased and agricultural prices increased. As against this, bankers wanted a gold currency to insure financial stability and the bondholders to increase the value of their bonds. It was a triangular class struggle in which economic facts overwhelmed labor and the agrarians, scoring another inevitable conquest for business enterprise.

Secretary Sherman, however, in 1878 again proceeded with his resumption plans, in spite of Congressional and popular opposition. The Morgan-Rothschild syndicate secured an issue of $50,000,000 4½ per cent bonds payable in gold coin or bullion for resumption purposes.[47] Attacks on the loan and resumption flared up again, particularly in the West, but on January 1, 1879, specie payment was resumed.[48]

Resumption had been preceded by a steady rise in the value of greenback currency and prepared for by the Treasury's accumulation of gold, but its success was still doubtful. In March foreign bankers unanimously predicted that gold would again move to Europe and threaten resumption.[49] Secretary Sherman met this by an issue of $25,000,000 4 per cent

bonds sold in London by the Rothschild-Morgan syndicate in
order to prevent the shipment of gold from this country to
Europe.[50] But the situation remained unfavorable, and the
Commercial and Financial Chronicle asked, "Where is the
prosperity promised with resumption?"[51] At this juncture an
immense grain shortage in Europe created an increased demand and higher prices for American wheat, stimulating the
largest grain exports in our history. Agricultural prosperity
accelerated industrial revival and general business prosperity.
The situation, moreover, favored resumption owing to Europe
being compelled to pay for its grain imports in gold. During
three months in 1879 Europe sent large shipments of gold to
the United States, averting the danger of Europe draining away
American gold. Resumption was assured by the grain crop of
1879 and the large exports of the next two years.[52] Agitation
for cheap money declined owing to farmers receiving higher
prices for their products, the object aimed at by the inflation-
ary Greenback proposals.

In the refunding operations the financial community was not
enthusiastic in its offers and pressed the treasury for concessions. Secretary Sherman was compelled to revise one contract, and in the resumption loan of 1878 the terms offered
by the national banks were unacceptable, the Morgan-Rothschild syndicate offering more favorable terms.[53] The struggle
for power among the bankers, however, resulted in better
terms than might otherwise have been secured. "I knew of the
sensitive jealousy between the banks and bankers," said Secretary Sherman, "and between the old syndicate and prominent
and wealthy firms who wished to participate in any new syndicate, and were jealous and suspicious of each other."[54] The
Rothschild-Morgan syndicate's great profits were made in the
1877 operation, but later Secretary Sherman secured the advantage by manipulating the financiers' distrust and jealousy
of each other.

Financial competition still prevailed. Fifteen years later it was another story, J. Pierpont Morgan dominating the financial system and largely imposing *his* terms upon the government. But in 1877 Morgan's supreme power was still to come, and journals described the refunding syndicate as the "Belmont Syndicate," after August Belmont, the American representative of the House of Rothschild.[55] The Morgans, however, participated in the syndicate as equals of the Rothschilds, then the most powerful banking house in the world, and the alliance emphasized the fact that Drexel, Morgan & Co. now occupied the place of the House of Cooke, formerly the Rothschilds' American ally.

By 1879 the House of Morgan had definitely emerged as a dominant power in American finance, largely through its international financial affiliations and operations.

PART FOUR

MORGANIZING RAILROADS

CHAPTER XIV

FINANCIERS: OLD AND NEW

*"When you have to turn into a chrysalis—
you will some day, you know—and then
after that into a butterfly, I should think
you'll feel it a little queer, won't you?"
"Not a bit," said the Caterpillar.*
ALICE IN WONDERLAND

IN THE decade 1879-89 the House of Morgan consolidated its financial power and developed the institutionalized mechanism for the control of investment resources and of industry which distinguished its subsequent development.

The Morgans' financial power manifested itself in the 1884 panic when their intervention was asked to restore confidence. Preceded and accompanied by depression in trade and industry, severe unemployment and tight money, the panic produced many bank failures and a stock-market crash. In the midst of the panic Cyrus W. Field (the first transatlantic cable's projector and promoter) sent a cable to Junius Morgan urging action by his House to restore stock-market confidence:

"Many of our businessmen seem to have lost their heads. What we want is some cool-headed strong man to lead. If you should form a syndicate in London to buy through Drexel, Morgan & Co. good securities in this market, I believe you would make a great deal of money and at the same time entirely change the feeling here." [1]

Canny old Junius Morgan had made large purchases to great advantage which he considered beneficial to the stock market, but did not think a syndicate "desirable" or "necessary." [2] The circumstances were unfavorable and the stock market shifted for itself. Field's proposal, however, indicated the contemporary feeling of the financial community and its recognition of the Morgans' leadership—a leadership expressed by the House of Morgan in other stock-market crashes, particularly in 1907 and 1929.

In 1889 the Morgans' financial power manifested itself in another and more characteristic way. J. P. Morgan had secured control of many important railroads, combining financial power and direct railroad power in a fashion new to American finance. Control of Northern Pacific by Jay Cooke & Co. was an isolated, speculative enterprise, not much different from similar enterprises except that Cooke was a banker, while the Goulds and Vanderbilts were essentially entrepreneurs manipulating railroads. Morgan's railroad empire, on the contrary, was the direct product of developing finance assuming new forms and functions. In 1889 the House of Morgan convened a conference of railroad presidents, at which Morgan presided and issued ultimatums—"bankers triumph" and "presidents surrender," declared the New York *Times*.[3] "Morganization," the control of finance over industry, and, consequently, the centralization of industry and finance, made its definite appearance.

In 1879 the House of Morgan was essentially an old-style financial institution—dealing in foreign exchange, placing American securities in Europe, gathering together the scattered capital of innumerable investors by selling stocks and bonds, and participating in government financing. By 1889 the House of Morgan still did all these things, but in addition it participated directly in corporate affairs, combining, consolidating, centralizing, imposing the mastery of finance over industry by the institutionalized control of investment resources and of corporate industry itself.

The empire J. Pierpont Morgan carved out of American industry is often interpreted in terms of the man's personality. Clearly his truculent and domineering character, animated by an overwhelming urge to power, could not satisfy itself with the traditional function of the investment banker as an intermediary between corporate enterprise and the investor, where it might control corporate enterprise. But the form of expression of Morgan's will to power, the technique of that power, was determined by forces more decisive than personality—by the complex of new industrial and financial relations, of class forces and class power, of the revolutionary transformation of American economic life.

Morgan was by inclination and circumstances a banker, and a *conservative* banker, his conservatism projecting itself financially, politically and socially. Jay Cooke might pioneer railroads through the wilderness and others create an industry out of a dream, but either was repugnant to Morgan. This sound, conservative banker consolidated enterprises—never pioneered them. Yet Morgan was to personify the revolution which transformed the financier from an agent of industry into its master.

Sound, conservative banking means an adjustment to facts —the practical facts of prevailing business procedure. As business changes banking must change, otherwise it becomes unsound. A change here, an adjustment there, never beyond the limits of immediate needs and profit—in this accretive fashion Morganization shaped its technique. The immediate task, seldom the far-flung objective, absorbed Morgan, at once the strength and weakness of the man. Concentrating upon immediate tasks determined by the dynamic problems and changes of American business enterprise, Morgan moved unimaginatively, massively but irresistibly, with the irresistibility of economic compulsion, to the Morganization of industry by means of new financial procedure and institutions, imposing the control of the financier over industry and integrating industry and finance.

Before the Civil War industry operated overwhelmingly in small units under control of individuals or partnerships.

People directly interested in an enterprise subscribed the capital, seldom large, and usually participated both in ownership and management. The banks' functions were almost exclusively commercial, financing the mercantile movement of the products of industry. The merchant capitalist was the dominant entrepreneurial factor. As industry developed the industrial capitalist superseded the merchant capitalist in importance. But although originally organized by industrial capitalists, the corporation assumed such large dimensions and required such large amounts of capital that it thrust the industrial capitalist into the background, or made him dependent upon stockholders and financiers. As corporate industry consolidated and combined, becoming still larger, the financial capitalist became the most important factor in business enterprise.

These changes produced a system of complex financial relations and institutions, multiplying and modifying the banks, developing other financial institutions, and creating a new type of financier—changes which, while appearing before the Civil War, acquired maturity during the period 1870-1900.

Where commercial banks (as their name implies) originally simply provided the money to finance the movement of goods from producer to consumer, they now financed industrial corporations to produce goods by making loans for working capital and by purchasing corporate bonds. These banks, moreover, participated in the business of investment houses by means of loans on new corporate issues pending their absorption by the investing public, and often directly engaged in promotions. The banks combined their old commercial functions with general investment operations.

The financial changes produced by corporate enterprise developed the trust company. Combining commercial and direct investment banking of all sorts, trust companies acted as fiscal agents of corporations, registrars and custodians of securities, depositaries under reorganization agreements, and in other

ways served corporate enterprise and paralleled its development, both growing rapidly and simultaneously after 1880.

As insurance companies grew in size and resources they also
became important factors in financing corporate business enterprise, being immense reservoirs of investment capital.

These developments enlarged the scope and power of investment bankers. Before the Civil War investment houses
engaged primarily in securing foreign capital, as in the case
of Peabody & Co., and in financing canals, railroads and other
large-scale enterprises. As corporate enterprise began to dominate business investment banking assumed larger importance.
Industry concentrated, requiring more capital which was gath-
ered up by banks and investment houses and placed at the
disposal of large-scale enterprise.

The multiplication of stockholders separated corporate ownership and management. Corporations grew larger, stockholders were deprived of all functional participation in industry beyond the initial act of investment, simply receiving the
income on their securities. The trust company, acting as trustee
for individuals and estates and serving as investment expert for
investors, assuming all investment responsibility, emphasized
the separation of corporate ownership and management, since
the investor now did not even choose his investments. This increasingly large class of non-managing investors provided most
of the capital required by corporate enterprise (where this
capital was not accumulated by reinvestment of profits).

One of the first consequences of the separation of ownership
and management was usurpation of control by the buccaneers,
who manipulated and plundered the property of scattered
stockholders. Competitive skullduggery aggravated the situation. Corporate enterprises began to combine to strengthen
their competitive position, simultaneously strengthening the
buccaneers' opportunity for plunder. Buccaneering and ruthless competition created business disturbances, lowered the

general level of profits, and upset the complex relations of corporate business.* Stabilization was necessary.

Industrial concentration and combination produced measurable stabilization, but then arose the problem of stabilization among the combinations whose unrestrained competition was more disastrous than among petty enterprises. The separation of ownership and management, which gave the buccaneers the opportunity to plunder, now gave the bankers the opportunity to intervene and usurp control. While financiers often engaged in buccaneering practices, finance itself was a stabilizing force, compelled to emphasize the constructive aspects of the new economic order. Banks, and particularly investment bankers, who originally acted almost exclusively as intermediaries between corporations and investors by the sale of securities, now participated actively in corporate management, determined the personnel and larger policy of boards of directors, created community of interest and co-operation among combinations, and imposed financial control over corporate business.

Financial concentration accompanied industrial concentration. Larger industrial units required larger banking units. Banks amassed larger resources, consolidated and combined. Investment bankers acquired control of banks and other financial institutions and their investment resources, combining control of the sources of money and of the corporate users of money, centralizing industry and finance. Out of this amalgamation of functions and institutions arose the power of the new-style financiers, particularly of the House of Morgan.

This interlocking of industry and finance constituted the fundamental aspect of Morganization, of the financial pene-

---

* Buccaneering practices were, in general, also determined by unprincipled competition, by the predatory aspects of capitalism. There was no separation of ownership and management in Standard Oil, owned at the time by a small clique of stockholders, yet Rockefeller's enterprise was extremely piratical. There was this important difference: Rockefeller plundered competitors and the public, not his own enterprise, while the buccaneers plundered as well enterprises under their control.

tration and control of industry. There was another important aspect. The complexity of modern industry demands centralization, a measure of unified regulation and control over economic life. Ruthless, unrestrained competition disorganizes and demoralizes. Corporate combinations introduced measurable unity in their particular industry, but often clashed with each other. Morganization emphasized community of interest among corporations and the masters of corporations, appearing as a force acting against the worst buccaneer practices and the business disturbances provoked by economic civil war. This was a phase of the larger problem of regulation and control which society in the shape of its government declined to act upon, and which was usurped by the investment bankers, by Morganization.

Of all investment bankers J. Pierpont Morgan most clearly recognized the importance of the new developments and most thoroughly acted in accordance with that recognition. Still, other bankers (particularly James Stillman and George F. Baker) participated in the development of an institutionalized mechanism for the control of investment resources and of corporate industry—an inevitable financial development of concentrated capitalism. Morgan secured supreme power owing to peculiar temperamental characteristics.

The centralization of industry and finance during 1870-1900 constituted a transition period, and transitions offer an opportunity for dictatorships. Relationships which subsequently become completely institutionalized function, during their development in the transition period, largely through personal expression and compulsion. The system of financial centralization and control institutionally expressed itself in the dominance of the House of Morgan, but equally through the personal ascendancy and dictatorship of Morgan himself. His overwhelming impulse to dominate other men, to rule, and the capacity to get his rulership accepted, was a decisive factor in his own ascendancy and the supremacy of the House of

Morgan. It was not enough to develop the new financial technique: Morgan had to engage in a tooth-and-claw struggle with antagonists, with men in his own camp, to browbeat, impose and dominate. The arrogant self-confidence, the aggressive personality, the streak of ferocity which terrorized lesser men—all were important in Morgan's emergence to power out of savage economic civil war.

To Morgan power meant dictatorship—he knew no other way to rule. He disposed of men, money and property in the same brusk fashion, compelling obedience, savagely breaking down resistance. While developing his dictatorship over railroads, the president of one road approached Morgan to protest against an ultimatum:

PRESIDENT: You can't ask us to turn over our whole road to you!

MORGAN: Your roads! Your roads belong to my clients.[4]

Which meant: "Your roads belong to me, I shall do what I consider necessary, issue the orders and you must obey."

Morgan inspired fear, overwhelming fear and unquestioning obedience, but he also inspired confidence and loyalty. Self-confident, massively solid, one knew where he stood, a quality particularly important in transitions when changes are frequent and bewildering. "A man always has two reasons," said Morgan, "for the things he does—a good one, and the real one." [5] Morgan seldom gave the "good" reason for what he did, either to himself or to others, but frankly gave the real one—a quality of cynical arrogance, perhaps, but also of honest realism. Such a man never indulges in daydreams, or envisages far-flung objectives, or permits imagination to pioneer the originality which may be dangerous. Morgan was not original nor of pioneer temperament, but the practical organizer and ruler, moving irresistibly to supreme financial power.

CHAPTER XV

RAILROAD DEMORALIZATION

*The players all played at once, quarreling
all the while, and fighting for the hedge-
hogs; and in a very short time the Queen
was in a furious passion, and went stamp-
ing about, and shouting "Off with his
head!"*

ALICE IN WONDERLAND

THE buccaneer practices of Jay Gould and Jim Frisk provided
J. P. Morgan's first opportunity to participate directly in railroad affairs; but outside of the struggle for control of the
Albany & Susquehanna, Morgan (up to 1879) had scarcely
departed from the old-style investment bankers' limited function of selling stocks and bonds. In 1879 the House of Morgan
emerged as a railroad power by means of a transaction involving William H. Vanderbilt and the sale of New York Central
stock in England—a transaction determined by Morgan's
international affiliations and linked up with important aspects of the movement centralizing industry and finance.

Upon the old Commodore's death William H. Vanderbilt
inherited the New York Central system, a railroad empire in
itself. Cornelius Vanderbilt had done an important constructive job of railroad consolidation, New York Central becoming
one of the most efficient systems in the country; but in his
onward sweep to empire the old Commodore had corrupted
legislatures, ruthlessly crushed competition and provoked
enormous public antagonisms. Enmity against the New York
Central was all the sharper because of the large dividends paid
on stock 40 per cent of which was water.[1] William H. Vanderbilt inherited the antagonisms provoked by his father and him-

self provoked new antagonisms. Morose, unimaginative, parsimonious, contemptuously disliked by his own father, the younger Vanderbilt had neither the force nor the engaging piratical flair which made people like Cornelius Vanderbilt while infuriated by his actions. Public hostility broke loose unrestrainedly, in the press, legislature and municipal councils, Vanderbilt being denounced as a "dangerous monopolist" (and often threatened with blackmail by corrupt politicians).[2] This hostility was intensified by Vanderbilt's stupidly arrogant attitude of "The public be damned!" The New York Legislature threatened to impose heavy taxation upon the Central system, in which Vanderbilt owned 87 per cent of the stock, while the State's investigation of the railroads revealed many damaging facts, particularly New York Central's connection with John D. Rockefeller's use of secret discriminatory rates, rebates and drawbacks to crush competitors.[3] Commodore Vanderbilt would have fought tigerishly back but the son scurried to cover.

Vanderbilt discussed the situation with Morgan, to whom capitalists now went with large propositions. Two issues were involved: Vanderbilt wanted to scatter some of his stock to avoid the cry of "monopolist," and to prevent a threatened competitive war between New York Central and the Wabash, St. Louis & Pacific Railroad (in which Morgan was interested). The decision was to sell $25,000,000 of Vanderbilt's stock in England and conclude a Central-Wabash alliance, accomplishing four purposes:

Prevent the threatened rupture between Wabash and the Central.

The new stockholders, being English, secured an important influence hampering possible hostile legislative action.

Increasing the number of stockholders, in general, helped break down the monopolist one-man ownership argument. "Concentration of ownership has hitherto exposed the New York Central to many attacks," said the *Railway World*, "and the diffusion of its stock will lessen the number of its enemies and increase the number of its influential friends." [4] As diffusion of stock ownership increased it created a class of small stockholders which, while still a small minority of the American people, was sufficiently influential to blunt public hostility to corporate enterprise.

Finally, as the New York Central developed from a railroad of 700 miles into an infinitely larger system, one-man ownership was impossible. Corporate concentration transformed the managing industrial capitalist into the absentee financial capitalist. The sale scattered some of Vanderbilt's holdings, securing diversity of investment and safety; the important final development being that diversification, emphasizing the separation of ownership and management, facilitated the introduction of financial control over industry.

Morgan insisted, as a condition of the stock sale, that his House receive representation on Central's board of directors —which would have infuriated the Commodore. But Vanderbilt yielded, reluctantly. Morgan's demand expressed the drift toward more direct banking participation in corporate industry.

The utmost secrecy prevailed in the discussions between Morgan and Vanderbilt. Reports of the contemplated sale were acrimoniously discussed in Wall Street as "dishonorable stock-jobbing rumors," no one believing that Vanderbilt would sell. [5] Confirmation of the sale, which astonished the market, was characterized as "one of the most remarkable railroad transactions." [6] Drexel, Morgan & Co. organized a syndicate including J. S. Morgan & Co., August Belmont & Co., Morton, Bliss & Co. and Jay Gould, Morgan being head of syndicate (and always, from now on). Vanderbilt's stock was easily sold in England, a tribute to the international financial dominance of the House of Morgan. The Morgan syndicate bought the stock at 120 and sold at 130, realizing a profit of $3,000,000. [7] J. S. Morgan & Co. became general agents of New York Central in London, Morgan himself was elected to the board of direc-

tors representing the new English stockholders, and Drexel,
Morgan & Co. secured the fiscal agency of the Vanderbilt
railroad system. Concluding an alliance, Wabash secured two
directors on the New York Central board and an outlet to
the Atlantic, while Central secured southwestern traffic under
Wabash control. In 1883 Wabash was leased to the Missouri
& Pacific Railroad, of the Jay Gould system.[8] In addition,
Drexel, Morgan & Co. were fiscal agents of the Pennsylvania
Railroad. The House of Morgan emerged as a railroad power,
interlocking railroad systems by means of financial penetration.

The larger aspects of the New York Central transaction were
recognized by the *Commercial and Financial Chronicle,* which
said: "This new combination clearly has for its ultimate aim
a union under one head of the system of roads from New York
to the great Northwest, and then on to San Francisco."[9] The
importance of the stock sale as a phase of the combination
movement determined Morgan to participate aggressively in
railroad affairs. Out of this participation developed the Morganization of the railroads as an expression of the new technique
of financial centralization and control.

In the background of Morgan's decision, as an immediate,
practical problem, was the demoralization prevailing among
the railroads, depressing investment values and producing
widespread discontent. The demoralization was particularly
acute during the years 1879-89, the situation being aptly characterized by Charles Francis Adams, then president of the
Union Pacific Railroad:

"Stockholders are complaining; directors are bewildered;
bankers are frightened.... The railroad system, especially in
regions west of Chicago, is to-day managed on principles
which must inevitably lead to financial disaster.... The dishonest methods of rate-cutting, the secret system of rebates,
the indirect and hidden payments made to influence the course
of traffic resorted to or devised in the last two years are un-

precedented in the whole bad record of the past.... There is an utter disregard of fundamental ideals of truth, fair play and fair dealing." [10]

Demoralization among the railroads was a direct consequence of their whole history, a fascinating mixture of magnificent enterprise and downright thievery, of the absence of unified national transportation plans, and of the contemporary insistence that competition should prevail in an industry where competition was particularly bad.

American railroads up to 1880 were largely built with public money. Federal, State and municipal governments contributed $700,000,000 for railroad construction and grants of 155,000,000 acres of public lands—an empire of 242,000 square miles, larger than France and four times the size of New England. About 40 per cent of the legitimate construction costs were paid by public money. [11] If profits on the sales of land received from the government are added, the whole cost was borne by the people in the shape of government aid. This undoubtedly facilitated railroad construction, but it also encouraged speculation and plunder. For government aid was accompanied by complete independence of the railroads from government control, on the theory of private competitive business enterprise. That benevolent old uncle, the government, should "come across" financially but must not interfere. Under the prevailing conditions of lack of government control, very loose corporation laws, unrestricted competition and speculation, political corruption and low business morals, thievery and demoralization inevitably developed among the railroads.

Plundering usually started with securing government aid by bribery, railroad promoters smearing a dirty trail of corruption over legislatures. Where bribes were not forthcoming, legislators often blackmailed "bribes" by threats of preventing favorable or initiating hostile action—business plundered the government and politics plundered business. Most of the railroad promoters were flagrant speculators with little money of their own, money being raised by selling bonds to the public, often at heavy discounts, disastrously piling up fixed charges. Promoters appropriated most of the stock as bonus, cash subscriptions from stock seldom exceeding 30 per cent of the railroad's construction costs and frequently almost nothing.[12] Land grants were another source of speculative profit for promoters and directors. Still another means of making illegitimate profit was construction of the railroad, usually undertaken by promoters and directors organized in a separate construction company charging enormously high prices. The most scandalous construction frauds were those of the Crédit Mobilier, which charged the Union Pacific $93,546,000 for construction against the legitimate cost of $50,000,000—the Crédit Mobilier organizers being the promoters of Union Pacific (which received money and public lands from the Federal government).[13] Every mile of Western railroads cost 35 per cent to 50 per cent more than legitimate construction costs.[14] The railroads were marvels equally of engineering enterprise and speculative plunder.

But that was not all. After their construction the railroads often came under control of buccaneers—the plunder of Erie by Daniel Drew, Jay Gould and Jim Fisk was characteristic, as was the struggle for control of the Albany & Susquehanna Railroad, in which J. P. Morgan beat back the buccaneer offensive. The buccaneers disregarded business and the public. People indignantly asked: "Who can measure the iniquity of the railway wreckers who have used their power for nefarious purposes—stolen franchises, cheated their stockholders, and perverted the most powerful and beneficent instrumentality ever placed at the disposal of man?"[15]

Plundered by buccaneers, the railroads were further tormented by unrestrained competition (which encouraged buccaneering). Railroads waged war on each other for new business, producing ruinous rate wars, demoralizing the railroads financially and throwing many of them into bankruptcy. Nor did rate wars materially help the public, since lower rates in one case were offset by higher rates in others, while discriminatory rates flourished. Railroads tried to regulate rates by pooling agreements, but these were illegal and there were always railroad managements precipitating rate wars by breaking agreements. The threat of a rupture of peaceful relations between New York Central and the Wabash was one cause of the Morgan-Vanderbilt transaction in Central stock. Consolidation measurably regulated competition and rates, but it was opposed by public opinion, and railroads waged rate wars in spite of consolidation.

Demoralization made investment in railroads unsafe and unprofitable. The buccaneers plundered investors as much as they plundered business and the public. In spite of most railroad bonds offering 7 per cent, the average interest in 1886 was 4.7 per cent, while the average yield on stock was only 2 per cent (including "watered" stock).[16] In 1876 railroad bonds in default represented 39 per cent of the total, and in 1879 sixty-five roads capitalized at $234,000,000 were sold under foreclosure.[17] One year later bankrupt railroads represented 20 per cent of total mileage and capitalization.[18] The business depression of 1873-79 was only in part responsible for the financial demoralization: in the ensuing period of prosperity the situation grew worse instead of better.

Disgruntled railroad investors demoralized the general investment market, a development directly concerning the House of Morgan in its investment-banking operations. Railroad demoralization, moreover, inflicted heavy losses on foreign investors, many of whom had purchased their securities through the Morgans. Foreign investors owned $251,000,000 of railroad bonds in default.[19] The *Bankers' Magazine* estimated that between 1873 and 1879 European investors in American enterprises had lost $600,000,000 by bankruptcy or fraud, and declared that "this despoiling of European investors has been going on for more than a generation."[20] In Germany, one financier declared, an American railroad bond could not be sold "even if signed by an angel." [21] In England the *Statist* said: "The consequences of rate wars on American railways are proving so disastrous to the holders of securities, and the prospects are so gloomy, that some heroic remedy must be resorted to, else the whole investment will be lost." [22]

This situation directly threatened the House of Morgan, the power of which still depended upon its international financial affiliations and the import of capital by the United States. Moved largely by the immediate, practical problem of restoring foreign confidence in American securities, J. Pierpont Morgan decided to intervene more actively in railroads. The intervention was to have other and more important consequences than the original purpose.

CHAPTER XVI

REORGANIZING RAILROADS

*She noticed a curious appearance in the
air: it puzzled her very much at first, but,
after watching it a minute or two, she
made it out to be a grin, and she said to
herself, "It's the Cheshire Cat."*

ALICE IN WONDERLAND

THE House of Morgan's penetration of the railroads developed
by reorganization of bankrupt roads, out of which arose the
Morganized system of financial centralization and control. In
developing the new system J. Pierpont Morgan moved from
the particular to the general, the general policy being shaped
slowly out of the particular problems and tasks imposed upon
the financier by railroad demoralization, bankruptcy and reorganization in terms of stabilized finances, profits and investment-banking operations.

These railroad reorganizations revealed the essential Morgan
quality—constructive force, an acute sense of financial values,
ruthless determination in pursuing objectives, never abandoning the practical, and the spirit of dictatorship in imposing
his will upon other men. When Morgan reorganized a railroad he told the managers bluntly, almost brutally: "The road
now belongs to *me!*" Some growled, others admired, all obeyed
and admitted he got things done.

An increase in demoralization and bankruptcy, particularly
by the promotion of "blackmail" railroads, facilitated the Morgan penetration.

In 1880-82 there was an addition of 34 per cent to the country's railroad mileage, of which not more than one-third was
justified by existing business.[1] Some of the new railroads

anticipated future needs, others were built to strengthen the power of large consolidated roads, and still others simply to make money for the promoters. Competition sharpened, rate wars multiplied, earnings declined and bankruptcy flourished.

The prevailing demoralization was made still worse by the fact that many of the new railroads were "blackmail" enterprises, deliberately predatory in character. These blackmail enterprises secured profits from three sources: on the sale of bonds to the public, by the construction-company device promoters used to plunder the treasury by charging exorbitant building prices, and by sale of the new railroad to the competitor whose lines it usually paralleled.

One of these blackmail enterprises was the Nickel Plate, paralleling the New York Central from Buffalo to Chicago, built at a nominal price to sell on extortionate terms. A disastrous rate war ensued (complicated by another rate war with Erie), in which Vanderbilt broke a pool agreement in order to meet the menace of the Nickel Plate and bankrupt it. A campaign was organized to compel Vanderbilt to buy, unscrupulous means being used such as circulating rumors that Jay Gould contemplated purchase to wage war against Central. In the end Vanderbilt had to buy out the competitor.[2] Then a new blackmail threat appeared in the form of the New York, West Shore & Buffalo Railroad, built to parallel New York Central and dragoon it into an extortionate purchase.

Claims of low capitalization in comparison with that of other railroads and particularly the watered stock of New York Central induced the public to buy West Shore bonds in large amounts. The promoters, including General Edward F. Winslow, John Jacob Astor, George M. Pullman and General Horace Porter, organized a construction company to build the road, its anticipated outlay being $29,000,000 against which it was to receive $75,900,000 in West Shore stock and bonds.[3] This plundering contributed directly to West Shore's insolvency, together with more than ordinary mismanagement. Receivership made matters worse—rates were cut in order to secure business and compel New York Central to buy the West Shore, in 1884 working expenditures were more than gross earnings, and next year the road defaulted on its interest. Vanderbilt was pressed to buy West Shore but refused, favoring a war of extermination. Meanwhile the rate war went on, West Shore did not earn enough for operating expenses and New York Central's net earnings declined alarmingly.[4]

Three different plans of reorganizing the West Shore were abandoned owing to Vanderbilt interposing obstacles in his decision to wage a war of extermination. In 1886 * Drexel, Morgan & Co. undertook the reorganization as part of a larger policy to produce more harmonious relations among the railroads.

The success of Morgan's West Shore reorganization, according to contemporary opinion, "was much greater than anticipated." [5] It was drastic, the bondholders being offered $25,000,000 of 4 per cent bonds for their $50,000,000 of 5 per cent bonds. The bondholders' committee tried to secure better terms but reported that their efforts had been in vain, Drexel, Morgan & Co. rejecting all modifications. Two shares of old West Shore stock were exchanged for one in the new company and assessed $5. Morgan compelled Vanderbilt to accept the agreement, West Shore being leased to New York Central on its guarantee of principal and interest on the bonds of the new company, J. S. Morgan & Co. becoming its London agents.[6]

This reorganization of West Shore depended upon W. H. Vanderbilt, whose acquiescence Morgan secured by using the pressure of another reorganization—the South Pennsylvania Railroad, a parallel railroad Vanderbilt himself was construct-

* In 1886 Drexel, Morgan & Co. joined with a group of other bankers in petitioning the governing committee of the New York Stock Exchange not to list an issue of $3,500,000 Georgia State bonds on the ground that Georgia had repudiated $8,000,000 of bonds issued by the "carpet-bag" government in 1868-72. (Henry Clews, *Fifty Years in Wall Street,* p. 287.)

ing to compete against the Pennsylvania Railroad. Allied with Vanderbilt in this enterprise were the Philadelphia & Reading and Lake Shore Railroads and a group of capitalists including John D. Rockefeller, Andrew Carnegie, Stephen B. Elkins and Henry C. Frick.[7] It was a formidable combination, Rockefeller participating as part of a campaign to force secret rates, rebates and "drawbacks" from the Pennsylvania, which resisted his demands. President George D. Roberts of the Pennsylvania branded the proposed railroad "blackmail" and prepared to fight vigorously.* The situation threatened disastrous rate wars among three powerful railroads, increasing the prevailing demoralization.

But Vanderbilt, never very courageous, became frightened and decided to withdraw, against the wishes of most of the other capitalists interested in the South Pennsylvania project. Andrew Carnegie asked Roberts to buy the new road, but Roberts declined. Then A. J. Drexel, upon Vanderbilt's suggestion, approached Roberts, who replied, "I am not anxious to buy a hole in the ground." [8]

This was in 1885. Morgan had just returned from Europe, and criticism there of American railroad demoralization still rang unpleasantly in his ears. Most American railroad securities listed on the London Stock Exchange were paying nothing to their owners. This directly affected Morgan as an international banker. Moreover, he was actively interested in both the Pennsylvania and New York Central, and a war between the two was not in accord with the conception of community of interest which was now Morgan's policy. In his own words, Morgan decided that "something should be done to bring more harmony among the trunk lines." [9]

Morgan's decision involved reorganization of West Shore

* The Pennsylvania Railroad in 1869 had itself begun construction of a parallel railroad, against the Baltimore & Ohio, which answered by invading the Pennsylvania's territory, producing rate wars, litigation and lobbying for legislative favors. (Edward Hungerford, *The Story of the Baltimore & Ohio,* pp. 103-6.)

and South Pennsylvania. This meant fighting Vanderbilt, who while anxious for a compromise on the South Pennsylvania was determined to wage a war of extermination against West Shore; the group of capitalists associated with Vanderbilt, including John D. Rockefeller maneuvering his Standard Oil monopoly; the Philadelphia & Reading management, out after competitive advantages over the Pennsylvania Railroad, and the Pennsylvania itself whose president was determined not to compromise.

Opposition seldom frightened Morgan, however, simply nerving him for the struggle—merciless, domineering, bigger than the men who disputed his power. Although his proposals were usually peaceful compromises in the interest of all concerned, emphasized by his insisting on community of interest instead of destructive competition, they often met the opposition of men accustomed to other manners, men who resented the Morgan overlordship accompanying the community-of-interest proposal and whose opposition had to be forcibly overcome. At an investigation by Pennsylvania's Attorney General Morgan described his procedure to compel harmony:

"I made a trip to Philadelphia and suggested to President Roberts that if the Pennsylvania Railroad was prepared to take the South Pennsylvania for bonds or any other security that bore 3 per cent, I thought the thing could be carried through. Roberts doubted the policy or the ability of the Pennsylvania Railroad Co., as such, to buy off or in any other way interfere with what might be considered rival roads. Later I arranged a meeting on my yacht between Roberts, Thompson, Chauncey Depew [president of New York Central and Vanderbilt's Man Friday] and myself. At the meeting there was practically an agreement reached on the plan ultimately carried out." [10]

That meeting on the *Corsair,* Morgan's yacht, was curious and not precisely peaceful. Morgan had approached the problem in terms of personal power: "I decided," he said, "that something should be done." The developing dictator proposed an agreement to Roberts, which the Pennsylvania's president angrily rejected. The *Corsair* steamed idly to and fro. Roberts and Depew did the talking; the massive Morgan, six feet and two hundred pounds of him, sprawled in a chair, truculently silent, smoking his eternal big black cigar, intervening in the discussion now and then in his sharp, brusk fashion. The *Corsair* steamed idly on, until nightfall. Roberts maintained his objections, insisting on war and punishment of the South Pennsylvania promoters. But to insist on war meant not only fighting the powerful Vanderbilt interests but probably also Drexel, Morgan & Co., the Pennsylvania's own fiscal agents. In addition to Morgan's financial power and personality there was his argument, in Roberts' words, "that some understanding should be had among the larger railroads of the country with the view to securing remunerative rates of traffic and to securing harmony among the lines." [11] By Morgan's plan New York Central was to acquire West Shore and the Pennsylvania the South Pennsylvania. Roberts finally yielded.

"We then went to work with Vanderbilt," Morgan's testimony proceeded, "it being believed that sufficient influence could be brought to bear to induce him to supply a majority or more of the South Pennsylvania subscriptions." [12]

Vanderbilt did. Of the "influence" used Morgan said nothing. The problem was not to induce Vanderbilt to sell South Pennsylvania but to buy West Shore, Morgan making one dependent upon the other. Vanderbilt accepted, acceptance being a "peace offering" to the Pennsylvania [13]—and to the House of Morgan.

A provision of the Pennsylvania State constitution prevented the Pennsylvania Railroad from purchasing a competing line. "In order to evade this provision," said the *Railroad Gazette,*

"J. Pierpont Morgan will be the nominal purchaser." [14] Morgan blandly explained this transaction on the witness-stand:

"Roberts said it was necessary for some one to be the purchaser of the South Pennsylvania other than the Pennsylvania Railroad. As a firm we [Drexel, Morgan & Co.] could not do this, but as an individual feeling the importance of what was at stake, I was prepared to do what I could and to give the use of my name and signature to act as purchaser of one for the other." [15]

It was not as simple as all that, being an evasion of the law— but of a law, however, which permitted a blackmail enterprise such as the South Pennsylvania. Things had to be done in spite of the law. Ten years later, in another railroad case, Morgan asked Elbert H. Gary's opinion on the law involved:

GARY: I don't think you can legally do that.

MORGAN (*stormily*): Well, I don't know as I want a lawyer to tell me what I cannot do. I hire him to tell me how to do what I want to do. [16] . . .

In answer to Roberts' objection that buying South Pennsylvania and consolidating it with the Pennsylvania meant helping the promoters out of a bad mess, Morgan had said: "Oh, no, they'll not get out whole." They didn't. Capitalization and debts were drastically scaled down, after which 3 per cent bonds were issued to the South Pennsylvania promoters—a considerable financial sacrifice for Vanderbilt, Rockefeller and the others. [17]

Violent protests met the settlement, particularly from the Philadelphia & Reading and Pittsburgh interests seeking a competitor to the Pennsylvania Railroad. Morgan ignored the protests. The Philadelphia & Reading accused Vanderbilt (himself a large stockholder in the road) of treachery as after an agreement with him Reading had purchased stock in South Pennsylvania and spent considerable money constructing terminals to make connections with the new railroad. [18] Under pressure from disgruntled interests Pennsylvania's Attorney General investigated the whole transaction, but to no avail.

During these struggles Philadelphia & Reading was in receivership, the direct consequence of financiering considered scandalous by contemporary opinion, aggravated by factional disputes among stockholders and considerable litigation. An important railroad, Philadelphia & Reading owned immense coal and iron mines in the acquisition of which it had piled up oppressive fixed charges, increased still more by attempts to secure a coal monopoly and crush competitors. High dividends were paid on watered stock while bonded indebtedness increased disastrously. Bankruptcy came in 1880, reorganization, and bankruptcy again in 1884.[19]

For two years Philadelphia & Reading interests had unsuccessfully tried to agree on a reorganization plan. After discussing the situation with President Roberts of the Pennsylvania and other railroad and coal interests, Morgan offered to reorganize Reading. The first requirement in Morgan's plan, developing his system of community of interest, was maintenance of "harmonious relations," particularly in the coal business, "in order that suitable prices may be obtained for coal produced and shipped." Morgan pledged himself "to bring about satisfactory arrangements with all the anthracite roads, and also the trunk lines, which shall secure to the Philadelphia & Reading Railroad Co., when reorganized, its just share of the business at remunerative rates."[20] Reading's fixed charges were to be scaled down severely and the floating debt wiped out by assessments upon the stockholders. The Morgan syndicate was to advance $15,000,000, 5 per cent of which was to be its compensation plus 6 per cent on all advances, control of the reorganized company to be vested in a voting trust[21]— that is, a group of trustees exercising all the voting power of the stockholders.

A considerable minority considered Morgan's reorganization

plan oppressive, and a sharp struggle developed. This compelled comparatively unimportant modifications of the original plan, including minority representation on the reconstruction committee and enlarging the syndicate by $4,000,000 additional subscriptions, the agreement providing that the "names and amounts of subscriptions be approved by J. Pierpont Morgan." [22] Control of the reorganized Philadelphia & Reading was vested for five years in a voting trust composed of Morgan and four others [23]—assuring control by the House of Morgan.

In the midst of these reorganizations Morgan had his first clash with Edward H. Harriman. The victory was Harriman's.

This clash was reminiscent of the struggle with Jay Gould and Jim Fisk for control of the Albany & Susquehanna Railroad, except in the resort to physical force. Entering the railroad field by buying a financially demoralized railroad, reorganizing and selling it at a large profit by playing the Pennsylvania against New York Central, Harriman was now a director and power in the Illinois Central Railroad. Illinois Central had a lease on the Dubuque & Sioux City Railroad which expired in 1887, and Harriman was authorized to get control of the road by negotiation or stock purchase. Learning of this, a group of Dubuque stockholders decided to "squeeze" Illinois Central by extorting more for their stock than the market price. Their stock, a majority, was placed in the hands of Drexel, Morgan & Co. for sale, Harriman buying up the balance. [24]

Apparently Morgan controlled the situation, having the majority stock and able to dictate terms. But Harriman was aware of some things Morgan overlooked. At the Dubuque stockholders' meeting Harriman controlled a majority of the stock present, and he rejected all proxies as illegal in Iowa. This struck a blow at the Morgan party and created an uproar, but was not catastrophic. Then, amid sheer amazement and indignation, Harriman calmly rejected the stock held by Drexel,

Morgan & Co. on the ground that it was signed by Drexel, Morgan & Co. personally and not as trustees. Imperturbably Harriman silenced all protests, the only stock voted being his own and that of his associates.[25] Sharp work, but effective.

The result, as in the case of Albany & Susquehanna, was the election of two boards of directors (one including J. P. Morgan) and throwing the case into the courts. But Morgan was compelled to accept Harriman's terms for the Dubuque stock.[26] Harriman's victory surprised Wall Street, it being Morgan's first defeat and by an antagonist comparatively unknown. Morgan developed a violent dislike of Harriman, whom he could never intimidate (sufficient cause for dislike!), which became hatred as the two men clashed again in later years. Most of Morgan's few defeats were inflicted by Harriman.

Morgan met another setback in his plans for control of the Baltimore & Ohio Railroad, an aggressive competitor which rejected harmony with other lines, cut rates and clashed repeatedly with the Pennsylvania. Drexel, Morgan & Co. offered to raise money for Baltimore & Ohio on two conditions: the management to be put in competent hands satisfactory to Morgan, and an arrangement be made with the Pennsylvania on the basis of general community of interest. The offer was accepted, Samuel Spencer becoming president. Spencer's management met opposition; and the opposition, maintaining that Drexel, Morgan & Co. were trying to get control of the Baltimore & Ohio, ousted Spencer after one year in the presidency.[27]

In 1888 Drexel, Morgan & Co. were completely successful in reorganizing C. P. Huntington's Chesapeake & Ohio Railroad. The reorganization followed the general Morgan pattern—including five-year control by a voting trust composed of Morgan and two others.[28] A Morgan representative was elected president of the reorganized company,[29] close business relations and community of interest being established with other railroads under control or influence of the House of Morgan.*

Morgan's railroad reorganizations were constructive but drastic, opposition being ruthlessly suppressed, finance imposing its will equally upon managements and stockholders. The profits were very large, reorganization commissions ranging from $1,000,000 to $3,000,000—"for knowing how to do it and doing it." [30] Morgan's railroad reorganizations developed three decisive aspects:

Financial reorganization. The insolvent railroad was financially rehabilitated and put on a paying basis—the pressing immediate problem.

Consolidation and community of interest. Morgan's reorganizations always lessened competition among the railroads either by direct consolidation or establishing harmonious relations on the basis of community of interest. In the case of the South Pennsylvania and West Shore—consolidation; in the others— community of interest. This community of interest was established by Morgan (or his representatives) participating in the directorates of reorganized railroads and compelling harmony with other railroads with which the House of Morgan was affiliated.

Control. By a variety of means—the voting trust, stock purchase and interlocking directors—the House of Morgan retained control of reorganized railroads, originally to insure fulfilment of reorganization agreements and later as an expression of deliberate Morganization.

In these railroad reorganizations Morgan was a financier directly participating in the control of industry, imparting new functions to investment banking, and gradually mastering the

---

* While reorganizing railroads J. P. Morgan was penetrating other corporate enterprises, becoming, for example, a director in the Western Union Telegraph Co., under Jay Gould's control. By organizing to build parallel telegraph lines, cutting rates and the older company's profits, manipulating the stock and other characteristic means, Gould acquired control of Western Union. (Henry Clews, *Forty Years in Wall Street*, p. 629.)

most powerful men of his age. Out of the conditions and problems of railroad reorganization emerged the larger aspects and final character of Morganization—the consolidation, combination and centralization of industry and finance by institutionalizing the control of finance over industry. Industrial and financial developments imposed a definite pattern upon the railroad reorganizations of the House of Morgan.

CHAPTER XVII

DEVELOPING FINANCIAL DICTATORSHIP

She was a little startled by seeing the
Cheshire Cat sitting on a bough of a tree a
few yards off. It had very *long claws and*
a great many teeth, so Alice felt it ought
to be treated with respect.

ALICE IN WONDERLAND

THE House of Morgan's reorganizations imposed consolidation
and community of interest upon particular railroads. In terms
of profit Morgan might have stopped there, but there were
other considerations. Unrestrained competition and demoralization still prevailed, and they affected Morgan's reorganizations. Immediate problems merged in the general. Unity and
order were indispensable among the railroads as a whole. Consolidations, pools and gentlemen's agreements had tried to
produce unity and order, and failed miserably: some force
outside the railroad managements was necessary. J. Pierpont
Morgan decided on larger intervention, expressing his own
impulse to impose order and rule, and the new functions being
assumed by finance as the balance-wheel in the complex relationships of large-scale business enterprise.

In 1889 Morgan mobilized the financial power of his own
and other investment-banking houses to compel community
of interest among the Western railroads, where buccaneering
and demoralization flourished most disastrously. Upon invitation of the House of Morgan and its affiliates the Western
railroad presidents, powerful men usually brooking neither
interference nor control, met in conference under Morgan's
chairmanship to consider establishing harmonious relations
among themselves in place of unrestrained competition and

rate wars. Most of the presidents came under duress, compelled by necessity and the threatening character of Morgan's financial mobilization. The New York *Times* interpreted the conference's decisions in terms of "bankers triumph, railway presidents surrender," marking the definite emergence of Morgan's financial dictatorship.

While the conference met to consider the problems of railroad demoralization in terms of unrestrained competition, rate wars and community of interest (including industrial and financial centralization), there was a larger political problem: public antagonism and government intervention.

Morganization was not simply a financial technique. New economic functions and institutions are not developed by economic changes alone, but are modified and shaped by political forces expressing the clash of different class interests in the community. Morganization assumed the institutionalized importance of a technique imposing the control of finance over industry in the midst of the onward sweep of concentrated capitalism, of the violent antagonisms aroused and the consequent struggle of class against class. Morgan's reorganizations and consolidations solved the immediate problems of competition, insolvency and profits, but they did not solve the larger problem of the antagonisms aroused by the railroads' oppressive power and their share in the development of industrial combination.

Themselves large aggregations of corporate capital, railroads were mighty factors in the crushing of small-scale industry and free competition by industrial combinations. While economically inevitable, combinations were accompanied by the oppression of small businessmen, farmers and workers, who revolted and asked plaintively: "What can be done to insure the enterprises of men of moderate means against the overwhelming competition of aggregated wealth?"[1]

The crushing of small-scale industry and competition by corporate enterprise, which produced Morganization, arose out

MORGAN AT FORTY-FIVE

JAMES J. HILL

of the urge for more efficient production, making larger industrial units mandatory. Inefficient, wasteful, ruthless, competition itself compelled combination. But combinations waged
the battle of competition by other means than economic efficiency. Receiving secret railroad rates and rebates effectively
helped corporate enterprise crush competitors. Profit margins
were not large and even a small difference in shipping rates
might mean the difference between business success or failure.
This meant that competition, theoretically waged by improving
technological efficiency and cheapening the price of goods,
might favor a comparatively inefficient but unscrupulous corporation receiving lower railroad rates as against a more efficient competitor. Manufacturers and railroad magnates made
secret agreements discriminating against other manufacturers,
the purpose being competitive gains and not efficiency.

John D. Rockefeller characterized the age in his systematic,
unscrupulous use of discriminatory railroad rates in building
up the Standard Oil monopoly. In 1872 Rockefeller's South
Improvement Co. made an agreement with the Erie, New
York Central, Lake Shore and Pennsylvania by which these
railroads agreed "to maintain the business" of the South Improvement Co. "against loss or injury by competition, and to
that end shall lower or raise the gross rates of transportation
... as may be necessary to overcome such competition"! The
Rockefeller oil interests not only received lower rates but a
"drawback"—that is, the railroads agreed to pay the Standard
Oil interests the excess in rates charged their competitors.[2]
Curiously, Vanderbilt, Roberts and other hard-boiled railroad
magnates accepted an agreement exclusively in Rockefeller's
interest.

Sanctimonious John D. not only made it difficult for competitors to ship oil, but every barrel they did ship yielded him
a profit. A storm of indignation compelled revocation of the
agreement when its terms became public. In later years Rockefeller ascribed Standard Oil's success to its cheapening the

gathering and distribution of oils, using the most efficient methods and encouraging exports. True, but improvements were neither exclusive with Standard Oil nor decisive in winning the battle of competition, which was waged by means of intrigues, discriminatory railroad rates, business blackmail and expropriating competitors' property. Standard's competitors used the same methods where they could—a savage struggle for survival, all means being justified in terms of prevailing business skullduggery. In spite of public condemnation, Standard Oil persisted in extorting discriminatory rates from railroads, afterward secured by John D. Rockefeller becoming a power himself in the railroads, particularly New York Central, Erie and Pennsylvania. Rate discrimination was general * and infuriated small businessmen to revolt.

The farmers also were in revolt. Developing capitalism subordinated agriculture to industry, crushed the old agrarian democracy. A fringe of prosperous farmers was enriched by rising land values and investments in stocks and bonds, but the majority did not prosper much. While agricultural productivity increased immensely, output per man rising more than threefold in twenty years, the farmers' relative share of the national income declined considerably. Tenancy and mortgages increased steadily, while declining prices made it difficult for the farmers to get out of debt. Railroads in particular and monopoly in general aroused agrarian wrath. Where farmers were not oppressed by excessive rates they were outraged by scandalous discriminations favoring one agricultural community against another. Frequently pioneers settled in the wilderness upon promise of a railroad which never materialized and were stranded, speculative promoters profiting from sales of land received in grants from the government. The farmers' prosperity depended upon cheap transportation, to

* The Anthracite Coal Combination, maintained by railroads as mine operators in control of 75 per cent of the anthracite coal fields, later coming under Morgan's control, crushed its competitors by denying them transportation facilities. (Arthur T. Hadley, *Railroad Transportation*, pp. 68, 95.)

secure which they often invested in railroads which then charged high rates, paid no dividends or went into bankruptcy, the farmers' stock being wiped out in reorganizations. Railroad magnates insisted lower rates would be ruinous, as dividends were already small—but these dividends were paid on "watered" stock. The Granger movement, organizing the agrarian revolt and condemning railroads as guilty of "arbitrary extortion and opposed to free institutions,"[3] captured control of several State legislatures and imposed severe regulations upon the profits, operation and political relations of the railroads. Much of this legislation was nullified by court decisions, the railroads high-handedly insisting that neither nation, State nor public could interfere with their operations, but the movement persisted until a measure of government control emerged.

Labor revolt assumed the form of strikes and union organization. Crushed during the Civil War, unions now multiplied and developed real power. Industrial productivity increased almost 100 per cent, and while real wages rose considerably this was partly offset by recurring business depressions and severe unemployment. The concentration of wealth sharpened discontent, the industrial and financial aristocracy amassing enormous riches: in 1888, 100 persons owned more than $3,000,000,000, including John Jacob Astor, $150,000,000; John D. Rockefeller, W. K. Vanderbilt and Jay Gould, each $100,000,000; and J. P. Morgan, Junius Morgan and A. J. Drexel, $25,000,000 each.[4] These fortunes, even if cut in half as they should be, were then startlingly large, although they were to become larger. If the magnates of money were contemptuous of the public, they were brutal toward labor.

Again the railroads characterized the general situation. Conditions of labor were almost unbearable, low wages accompanied by denial of elementary rights. When in 1877 railroad managements announced a 10 per cent reduction in wages discontent flared up in a great strike movement. The Pittsburgh

Chamber of Commerce, while condemning the strikes as "insurrection, widespread anarchy, and an organized war of rebellion against all constituted authority," admitted that the "wages received were insufficient to support life, and it was everywhere apparent that strikes would assuredly result from the repeated and swift recurring reductions of the wages of the men."[5] Another series of strikes broke out on Jay Gould's Western railroads in 1884-86, in which the unions, at first successful, were finally crushed as Gould had crushed the Telegraphers' Union. Unionism was given short shrift by Morgan's reorganized railroads and wages often cut on pleas of "economy."

General opinion insisted that the railroads were "striving to stem the tide of gross mismanagement and personal, local and corporate rivalry, which has been destructive of the property they were pledged to protect, by striking a blow at the wages of overworked men: they give another turn to the screw upon wages, but make no efforts to reform themselves."[6]

Ideals of petty industry, of free competition, animated the war of small businessmen, farmers and labor against the railroads and other corporate combinations. Competitive individualism, the product of petty capitalist enterprise and pioneer traditions, rejected equally laws for the protection of labor and protection of the public against corporate abuses—and these laws, consequently, were behind the standards of most other nations. Necessity partly modified this individualist ideology, which hampered the introduction of government regulation and control. Legislatures under control of agrarian Grangers passed laws imposing regulation on the railroads, in spite of violent opposition, the constitutionality of which was sustained after preliminary reverses. But State regulation was insufficient, considering the interstate character of railroads and the Supreme Court decision that States could not regulate interstate traffic. In 1884-86 the struggle converged in an overwhelming campaign for legislation by the national government, and in 1887 Congress passed the Interstate Commerce

Act, a compromise measure neglecting the decisive issue of rate-making but prohibiting rebates and discriminations of all sorts, pooling and traffic agreements, and other abuses, the Interstate Commerce Commission being established to enforce the law.[7]

Railroads opposed the Interstate Commerce Act publicly and secretly while judicial decisions emasculated the Commission's powers.[8] In spite of the Act and the Commission, rebates and discriminations persisted (Standard Oil being still the most scandalous beneficiary). There developed agitation for still more regulation and a growing threat of possible government ownership of railroads.

The immediate effect of the Interstate Commerce Act was to increase demoralization among the railroads. In spite of public antagonism consolidation had proceeded steadily: where in 1870 the New York Central with 700 miles was considered one of the world's great railroads, by 1889 twenty-eight railroad systems ranging from 2,000 to 5,000 miles controlled 44 per cent of all mileage.[9] The lessening of competition by consolidation was supplemented by partly successful agreements on rates (as in price pools among industrial combinations) but these agreements were now illegal. Competition broke forth disastrously, aggravated by the construction of unnecessary and parallel railroads.

Government regulation and control could function effectively only on the basis of definite, unified railroad systems; but the Interstate Commerce Commission and public opinion, animated by the theory of free competition, condemned consolidation and combination. Nor did the Commission act to prevent construction of unnecessary and parallel railroads, since the theory was that competition meant lower rates and better service, although in fact it meant demoralization.

Railroad men considered new construction the most serious danger. After condemning Congress for not "creating governmental checks upon unnecessary construction," the *Railway World* called upon the bankers for action:

"The extent to which the impending danger [of a new era of feverish construction] may run must depend very largely upon the custodians of credit.... The peril may be arrested if banks and bankers will do their part toward discouraging all questionable railway loans.... The railroad speculators must be told that there is no money for them."[10]

This, then, was the situation: Public clamor against the railroads compelled government action. But government action was largely nullified by its insistence on competition and the railroad managements' opposition. Competition and mismanagement wrecked profits: in 1888, although gross earnings increased 3.5 per cent, net earnings decreased 6 per cent.[11] Aggravating the situation (for the railroads) loomed the threat of more thorough regulation if not government ownership.

J. P. Morgan decided to intervene on a larger scale. A "Private and Confidential Circular" was issued by Drexel, Morgan & Co., Brown Brothers & Co. and Kidder, Peabody & Co., all of them railroad powers, particularly the House of Morgan. The circular called the Western railroad presidents to a conference at Morgan's home to form an association to enforce provisions of the Interstate Commerce Act and "maintain public, reasonable, uniform and stable rates."[12] Financial power moved definitely to impose its control.

The first conference in December, 1889, adopted a preliminary agreement to maintain rates for sixty days after January 1. Jay Gould was a hold-out, preferring buccaneering independence. "The railroad officers who were present," said Morgan optimistically, "were earnest in their wish to secure a lasting peace. I consider the Western rate wars as practically at an end." Meanwhile more comprehensive plans were to be worked out and another conference scheduled for January, 1889.[13]

Most of the Western railroad presidents came unwillingly to the conferences—but they came. Some declined. One president declared publicly that "no combination of bankers can set up to whip the country's railway managers into line like so many senseless cattle." The Chicago & Alton Railroad refused to participate in the conference, arguing that it was not in harmony with the Interstate Commerce Act, but giving the real reason in the words: "We don't need any conservators over our property just yet. We are responsible to our security-holders, not to Wall Street." [14] Morgan's conferences and proposals meant imposing the control of financiers over independent railroad managements, an emerging financial dictatorship, and managements resisted.

Morgan presided at the conference on January 8. The bankers' representation included Brown Bros. and Kidder, Peabody & Co., powerful investment institutions which accepted Morgan's directives, and also important foreign affiliations—J. S. Morgan & Co., the Barings and others. It was an overwhelming amalgamation of financial power, mobilized by Morgan, aggressive and threatening, prepared to compel obedience. Most of the Western railroad presidents were there, including Jay Gould of Missouri Pacific and Charles Francis Adams of Union Pacific. The conference was considered so vital that Eastern railroad presidents participated, including George D. Roberts of the Pennsylvania and Chauncey M. Depew of New York Central (of which roads the Morgans were fiscal agents). The conferees represented perhaps two-thirds of the nation's railroad mileage, upon which Morgan proposed to fasten financial mastery.

At this conference finance, under overlordship of the House of Morgan, represented some of the more constructive aspects of business, moving to impose unity and control upon corporate enterprise. The situation offered an opportunity for the expression of Morgan's characteristics—his dislike of disorder and competition, his insistence upon order and business efficiency, his impulse to rule and dominate other men.

The conference met in Morgan's library, amid books, manu-

scripts and art which had probably seen the kings of old imposing their royal will. Now another royalty emerged—the
royalty of financial power. For this was not a conference of
equals, but a conference met to accept an ultimatum. Massive,
threatening, accepting the responsibility of power, Chairman
Morgan delivered the ultimatum in his usual direct fashion:

"The purpose of this meeting is to cause the members of this
association to no longer take the law into their own hands
when they suspect they have been wronged, as has been too
much the practice heretofore. This is not elsewhere customary
in civilized communities, and no good reason exists why such
a practice should continue among railroads." [15]

This was more than direct—it threatened. Behind the threat
loomed an immense financial power which, not sufficiently
institutionalized to compel customary obedience, spoke in
terms of J. Pierpont Morgan's personal power. It was something new to the railroad presidents, accustomed to doing as
they pleased, making forays on each other from their baronial
domains, and defying the government. They disliked it intensely, as much as feudal barons disliked the development of
kingly power. Roberts expressed the feeling clearly—the same
Roberts upon whom Morgan had imposed his will in the
South Pennsylvania case. Said Roberts:

"Speaking on behalf of the railroad people of this country,
I object to this very strong language, which indicates that we,
the railroad people, are a set of anarchists, and this is an attempt to substitute law and arbitration for anarchy and
might." [16]

This plain speaking did not soften tempers and antagonisms.
Then A. B. Stickney, of the Chicago, St. Louis & Kansas City
Railroad, objected to the conference's secrecy: "The public are
sure to think we are conspiring to do something that we ought
not to do." [17]

Morgan, in his direct, massive fashion insisted on the objective—creation of a permanent organization of some sort in

which could be concentrated the power to maintain rates. Tempers and antagonisms flared forth again, and Charles Francis Adams, who had rehabilitated the demoralized and discredited Union Pacific and within a year was to be thrown out by Jay Gould, did some plain speaking of his own:

"The difficulty in railway management does not lie in an act of legislature, State or national, but does lie in the covetousness, want of good faith, and low moral tone of railway managers, in the complete absence of any high standard of commercial honor. Now the question we are to decide here to-day is whether any gentleman representing a railroad company is prepared to stand up and say before the public and before us that he is opposed to obeying the law, and, further, that in matters of controversy he prefers to take the law into his own hands rather than submit to arbitration." [18]

An unanswerable challenge. The railroad presidents insisted that legislative interference was responsible for the prevailing demoralization where in fact their own behavior was the primary cause. No one accepted Adams' challenge. The Interstate Commerce Act must be enforced, he insisted, "both among yourselves and all others—it is a law, and as such it should bear with equal weight upon all." [19] The conference elected a committee of three to draw up a plan of organization based upon the original agreement incorporated in Morgan's circular and discuss it with members of the Interstate Commerce Commission who, while not present, had come to New York because of the conference's importance.

The conference reconvened on January 10. Charles Francis Adams reported for the organization committee, proposing the formation of an Interstate Commerce Railway Commission composed of presidents who were to be held "strictly and personally" accountable for enforcing the Interstate Commerce Act and maintaining rates. Other provisions included a Board of Managers to meet monthly or on special call; special committees to regulate changes in rates, disagreements to be decided by the Board or by arbitration; a fine of $250 for violations of decisions, and a fund out of which these fines would be paid to which each railroad was to contribute from $1,000 to $5,000.[20]

Acrimonious discussion again, the railroad presidents' competitive individualism being shocked by the regulatory proposals. Roberts complained of Morgan's "harsh language" ("but I can stand it if the others can") and slashed out at bankers "who, with all their horror of railroad wars and cut rates, are usually ready to help along disturbing factors by selling the securities of any parallel railroad originated." [21] Morgan replied, aware of financial power and accepting its responsibility:

"In regard to the bankers and the construction of parallel lines, I am authorized to say, I think, on behalf of the banking houses represented here that if an organization can be formed practically upon the basis submitted by the committee, and with an executive committee able to enforce its provisions, upon which the bankers shall be represented, they are prepared to say that they will not negotiate, and will do everything in their power to prevent the negotiation of, any securities for the construction of parallel lines, or the extension of lines not approved by that executive committee. I wish that distinctly understood." [22]

This declaration reveals Morgan's purpose—a compact organization including financial representation with power to regulate rates, enforce decisions, and control railroad construction. But the proposal did not meet with approval and a looser form of organization was adopted by the Western presidents, who pledged their personal word of honor that rates would be maintained. Chauncey Depew read a resolution on behalf of the Eastern presidents accepting the conference decisions.

After the conferees adjourned and left Morgan's home the Western presidents must have had a slight change of heart. They immediately held another meeting of their own (apparently upon Jay Gould's initiative) "in order to separate the discussion from the banking interests," said a spokesman, who added: "We did not swallow whole the arrangement evidently prepared for us." [23] This was simply a gesture, however, the new meeting making unimportant modifications in the organization plan.

Opinion on the conference agreement varied. There was much indifference and skepticism, "officers of railroads under considerable pressure from the banking interests were outspoken in their approval of the plan," and some insistence that it was the greatest financial movement since Morgan's West Shore settlement. [24] The *Commercial and Financial Chronicle* was "disappointed" in its expectations of "more radical action," [25] while the *Railway World* criticized the bankers and threatened: "The railwaymen of the country are a very independent set of gentlemen when they are aroused, and stockholders will very generally support them." [26]

Railroads accepting the plan were not enthusiastic. The Chicago, St. Louis & Kansas City, through its president, A. B. Stickney, wrote to Drexel, Morgan & Co. that although the plan was "undoubtedly a step forward, the effect will be inconsequential." [27] Events justified the opinion. Some of the railroads refused to accept the agreement, others withdrew, new rate wars broke out and the old conditions crept back in spite of the Interstate Railway Association and the presidents' "word of honor" to maintain harmonious relations.

Demoralization expressed itself in a continuous decline in the prices of railroad stocks. [28] The situation was so bad that T. B. Blackstone, president and chief stockholder of the Chicago & Alton, urged ownership by the Federal government of all interstate railroads: "If things go on as now," he said, "in ten years all the roads will be hopelessly bankrupt." [29] Neither bankers nor railroad men wanted government ownership, but the danger, from their standpoint, was serious, since Blackstone's proposal measured the desperation of prevailing conditions. Government ownership, moreover, was being urged by agrarian and labor radicals, who were becoming strong politically (particularly in State legislatures) and whose program included government ownership of trusts as well as railroads.

Meanwhile Morgan, undismayed by the failure of his efforts, proceeded to develop community of interest where his power was larger than in the Western railroads. He put through an agreement between the Pennsylvania Railroad and the Vanderbilt lines for co-operation by means of an Advisory Council "with power to decide all questions of common interest, to avoid wasteful rivalry and to establish uniformity of rates between competitive points." [30] By implication the agreement included the reorganized railroads under control of the House of Morgan.

His financial dictatorship still only developing, Morgan had to await an appropriate opportunity for again intervening in the Western railroad situation. He could act decisively only within limits, by the force of favoring events, and still more by convincing, cajoling or threatening men upon whom he could not impose forcibly. Morgan let the Western railroads fight each other for two years, and acted at the moment when demoralization was again acute, expressed in declining security prices and complaints by stockholders. Then, mobilizing his financial affiliates, Morgan issued another invitation for a conference, which met in the library of his home on December 15, 1890.

This time the railroad presidents came more willingly, realizing the danger and prepared to discuss Morgan's proposal for a revision of the "Gentlemen's Agreement" of 1889. Sixteen Western railroads sent their presidents or other officers, among them Jay Gould, A. B. Stickney, C. P. Huntington, Thomas F. Oakes, James J. Hill and Russell Sage. Morgan again was chairman and Samuel Spencer (now a partner in Drexel, Morgan & Co) was secretary.[31]

More peaceful than its predecessor, there was one acrimonious flare-up in the conference, provoked by Stickney, formerly president, now chairman of Chicago, St. Louis & Kansas City, who said he had no confidence in agreements:

STICKNEY: I have the utmost respect for you, gentlemen, individually, but as railroad presidents I wouldn't trust you with my watch out of sight.

OAKES: Have you reached that opinion recently, Mr. Stickney, or did you entertain it when you were a president? [32]

Jay Gould relieved the tension by telling a story about Daniel Drew. At one time Drew went into a Methodist Church while a revival was in progress, and listened to a convert telling how sinful he had been, lying, cheating and robbing men of their money in Wall Street. Greatly interested, Drew nudged a neighbor and asked:

"Who is he, anyhow?"

"That's Daniel Drew," was the reply. [33]

Now interested in stabilizing railroad values, Gould proposed an agreement for centralized control of rates to run five years. The conference considered his plan too strong and calculated to arouse public hostility, particularly among the agrarian Grangers.

Dominating the conference, Morgan proposed the more moderate Vanderbilt-Pennsylvania agreement, saying:

"After much consideration, I suggest this simple, comprehensive and effective plan." [34]

Morgan's proposal was adopted, all being in favor except the Chicago, St. Louis & Kansas City Railroad. The new agreement provided for an Advisory Board, composed of the president and one director of each of the railroads, with authority to appoint arbitrators, commissions and other representatives to carry out decisions. By a four-fifths vote the Advisory Board was empowered to establish uniform rates between competitive points, and decide all questions of common interest between members of the Association. The agreement was to be in force at least six months after January 1, 1891, withdrawals being permitted after ninety days' notice. There were no penalties provided for breaking faith.[35]

Wall Street, which had awaited the conference "expectant, but critical, inclined to wait for results," [36] was disappointed and railroad stocks declined, while railroad men did not believe the presidents would stick to the agreement. Stickney, the die-hard, declined to participate in the new arrangement, insisting the "Advisory Board is not impartial and disinterested," and that "I do not propose to have competing railroads run the business of my railroad." [37] Morgan, however, expressed confidence in a public statement:

"I am thoroughly satisfied with the results accomplished. The public has not yet appreciated the magnitude of the work. Think of it—all the competitive traffic of the roads west of Chicago and St. Louis in the control of about thirty men. It is the most important agreement made by the railroads in a long time, and it is as strong as could be desired." [38]

The conferences did not accomplish Morgan's objective. They produced, however, measurable results in partial community of interest, becoming complete some years later by means of consolidations, combinations and financial centralization and control. Of Morgan's financial intervention in railroad affairs the *Commercial and Financial Chronicle* said:

"When the party that furnishes all new money needed, and the party that owns the old money invested, and the party managing the corporation, meet, the result means revolution. The word 'revolution' is a strong word. But what else can the result be? An arrangement, if it is worth anything, covers a total change in the animus of management.... There is a certain state of society when the freebooter is tolerated; there is a state of railroad development when the system of each man for himself, without respect to word or method, is endured. But a situation is revealed which demands that the ambitions of each road must be subordinated to a union and comity in action which community of interests requires." [39]

There was the crux of new developments—"change in the animus of management." Originally combined with ownership, management was directly responsible to ownership. Now there was separation, management being responsible to a mass of stockholders, helpless, concerned simply with dividends, deprived of all functional participation in the corporations they "owned." This meant a measure of irresponsibility among managements, and control of corporate combinations by men who did not own them (or who had just sufficient ownership to insure control). Competing managements had to be disciplined, unified, made to work together. Stockholders, scattered, helpless, owning without managing, could not do it: investment bankers assumed the task, managements becoming responsible to them.

At the conferences Morgan, representing finance in its newer functions, waged a threefold struggle—against independent railroad managements, bankers financing parallel lines, and the government.

While the final expression of concentrated capitalism, centralizing industry and finance in an overwhelming amalgam, Morganization had to meet the opposition of forces within capitalism itself. Railroad managements resisted the imposition of financial control (as managements of industrial corporations resisted later). Morganization meant crushing competitive independence, yielding under financial pressure, control of the industrial capitalist by the financier, arousing almost as much opposition among corporate interests as in the general public.

Morganization, moreover, meant struggle against the government, implicit in Morgan's proposals at the conferences. There was an Interstate Commerce Commission to regulate the railroads—a problem of public policy—yet Morgan proposed another organization of larger scope and power to im-

pose regulation under financial control. There was a measure
of illegality in all this, imposed, however, by economic facts
in conflict with outworn theories of free competition, by the
need of suppressing inefficient, wasteful competition by consolidation and combination. It was not the illegality of Jay
Gould's thievery and corruption but the illegality of economic
compulsion, shaping economic functions and institutions in
accord with new conditions.

Society in the shape of its government permitted Morganization to develop. Government imposed scarcely any control
on rate wars, construction of parallel lines, issuance of securities for that purpose, and other abuses of competitive railroad
enterprise. The problem was one of consolidation and combination, of unified social control of transportation, but government
was satisfied to impose negative prohibitions. Inevitably others
accomplished the necessary task.

Starting as a financial problem of reorganizing bankrupt
railroads, Morgan's activity soon became an expression of the
drift toward consolidation and combination. Community of
interest was another form of combination, measurably contributing to unification of the railroads under definite financial
control. Within ten years six great railroad systems emerged,
four of them under control or influence of the House of
Morgan.

Financial centralization and control appeared first on the
railroads, since they constituted the largest aggregations of
corporate capital with ownership and management most separated owing to the multiplication of stockholders. But the
technique of financial centralization and control was destined
to appear among industrial corporations, in answer to the
same problems of competition, combination and the separation
of ownership and management—finance assuming the task
shirked by society in the shape of its government of imposing
regulation and control upon industry. Finance subordinated
industry to itself instead of both being subordinated to larger

social controls. The economist might still speak of free competition, of "an invisible hand" shaping and directing economic activity. The immense industrial forces generated by concentrated capitalism could not be shaped and directed by an "invisible hand," involving the wastes and convulsions of economic civil war. Combination, centralization and control were indispensable.

But Morganization was animated by no social purpose or policy, moving within the limits of profit, control and power, imposing tribute in the performance of a socially necessary task. Corporate combination and centralization solved problems of competition and profit, but not the social problem of their oppressive power and the antagonisms aroused. Financial centralization and control, moreover, strengthened the power of concentrated capitalism, making it easier to crush the resistance of small businessmen, farmers and labor. Inevitably class hatreds and conflicts were aroused, expressing the clash of the old and the new economic systems. Industrial combination and financial centralization (including Morgan's personal dictatorship) developed in the midst of an implacable social war.

PART FIVE

TRANSITION

CHAPTER XVIII

MORGAN, CLEVELAND, BRYAN

> *"Not like cats!" cried the Mouse, in a
> shrill, passionate voice. "Would you like
> cats if you were me?"*
> *"Well, perhaps not," said Alice, in a
> soothing voice; "don't be angry about it."*
> *"Our family* always *hated cats," cried
> the Mouse, who was trembling to the end
> of his tail. "Nasty, low, vulgar things!"*
> ALICE IN WONDERLAND

THE violent class antagonisms aroused by concentrated industry and its financial expression, Morganization, flamed forth
in the bitter campaign of 1896 in which the agrarian radicals,
led by William Jennings Bryan and supported by labor and
middle-class radicals, seized upon the silver issue in an aggressive struggle for political power. Plutocracy mobilized all
its resources to beat down the menace, stigmatizing Bryanism
(an expression of legitimate if inchoate discontent) as anarch-
ism, communism and revolution, a revolt against government,
God and the Ten Commandments.

On the Saturday before Election Day the bankers, brokers,
manufacturers and merchants of New York City staged an
immense demonstration against Bryan—a parade of 80,000
men (including, parenthetically, two women!) marching from
morning until night. And as they marched they sang:

> *We'll hang Bill Bryan on a sour apple tree,*
> *As we go marching on!* [1]

The city was decked in flags, particularly Wall Street, where,
it appears, J. Pierpont Morgan's banking house "made the
finest and most ornate display," using one hundred eight-foot

flags.[2] In line were the city's richest men (and their employees who had been given the day off with pay and the "suggestion" to parade). This parade of plutocracy the Rev. Dr. Emory Haynes acclaimed in the spirit of the lowly Nazarene: "The success in life's struggle presented there has never before in the history of this world been brought into one such mass, the largest flower ever yet blooming on the human stock.... It was Plymouth Rock all under Broadway for miles, and the feet that trod it were as firm in resolve as those of the Pilgrims who founded this Republic."[3] The parade's Grand Marshal was General Horace Porter, ten years earlier engaged in the "blackmail" West Shore enterprise and its plundering construction company, now an employee of the Vanderbilt interests. One section consisted of 5,000 bankers and brokers, and as they passed the reviewing stand there was a yell:

"Where's Pierpont Morgan?"

All the spectators craned their necks, but were doomed to disappointment.

Morgan was not on parade.[4]

But Morgan was an important issue in the campaign, marking his emergence out of the financial shadows to become the symbol of the "money power" and "plutocracy" against which Bryanism and its successors thundered. Violent denunciation assailed Morgan, whom Homer Davenport pictured in his cartoons as a financial plug-ugly in company with $$$-spangled Mark Hanna and sanctimonious Andrew Carnegie dripping the blood of the Homestead strikers. The government bond issue of 1895, underwritten by a Morgan syndicate and intended to safeguard the gold standard, constituted the particular charge against Morgan, but this was identified with the larger issue of trustified capitalism. "The people," said W. J. Bryan, "will vote against the bond syndicates and the trusts."[5]

The essential features of the 1895 bond issue were the financial helplessness of the government and the hard terms extorted by the bankers. That was enough in itself for criticism and

agitation. But this issue merged in larger economic and political issues, an apparently ordinary financial transaction becoming an explosive in the clash of class against class. J. Pierpont Morgan was not the savior of his country nor Grover
Cleveland its betrayer, the bond issue being determined by the
prevailing economic and class relationships.

Resumption of specie payments was insured by the substantial prosperity prevailing after 1879, agitation for "cheap
money" becoming quiescent. Then business depression appeared again, culminating in the disastrous panic of 1893
with its agrarian and industrial distress, severe unemployment
and business failures. The Greenback agitation for "cheap
money" revived in the form of proposals for the free and
unlimited coinage of silver money on an equal basis with gold.
This meant currency inflation, since the price of silver had
declined about one-half in terms of gold. Farmers favored
inflation (as they had periodically since the beginning of the
republic) in order to secure higher prices for their products
and ease their mortgage-debt burdens which had almost tripled
in twenty years; silver-mine owners financed the free-coinage
agitation, as placing silver on a parity with gold meant securing
higher prices for the product of their mines; and small businessmen and labor generally believed that "cheap money"
might produce business revival. The silver agitation in Congress resulted in the compromise of the Silver Purchase Act,
by which the Treasury was to buy a definite amount of silver
monthly and issue notes against it redeemable either in gold
or silver at the Secretary's discretion. This was unsatisfactory
to the agrarian radicals, and in 1892 they organized the People's Party on a platform stigmatizing the gold standard as
"a vast conspiracy against mankind." [6] The immense distress
prevailing in 1893 and after increased discontent and made free
silver a dominant issue.

Unlimited coinage of silver, considering its price decline,
threatened the Treasury's gold reserve accumulated to insure

specie payments, and it meant complications in foreign trade
and finance, gold being the international monetary standard.
The possibility of a suspension of specie payments brought its
inevitable results. Foreign exchange rates began to rise and
European investors to sell American securities, compelling
gold exports—gold secured from the Treasury by redemption
of legal-tender notes which the Treasury was legally compelled
to re-issue. The deficiency in government revenues produced
by the 1893 panic aggravated the situation, ordinary bills being
paid out of the gold reserve. President Cleveland forced repeal
of the Silver Purchase Act, but the outflow of gold went on,
banks and individuals hoarded the metal, and the Treasury's
reserve fell below the statutory limit of $100,000,000 considered
necessary to insure gold payments.[7]

In secret discussions with a Treasury representative the
bankers (including J. P. Morgan) insisted that the gold standard was in danger, proposing the sale of bonds abroad as the
only means to secure gold and check its outflow. But the
Treasury wished to avoid bond issues, and instead Secretary
John G. Carlisle appealed to banks all over the country for
gold, but the gold supplied was again withdrawn. By January, 1894, the Treasury's reserve fell seriously, compelling immediate action.[8]

The Treasury decided to secure gold by a public issue of
$50,000,000 5 per cent bonds to sell at 117. Bankers did not
like this public issue and its terms (they had previously rejected
a proposal for a bond issue to secure gold from abroad because
its terms were not acceptable). The bids were so slow that
failure appeared probable, compelling Secretary Carlisle to
hurry to New York and make a personal appeal to the bankers
in spite of his repugnance for such procedure.[9] Nothing was
decided at the conference, the bankers insisting they could not
do anything; but realizing the danger, a group of banks, led
by the United States Trust Co., took up the bonds. The reserve
declining again, the Treasury appealed to the banks to supply

gold, and, the response being slight, decided in November upon another bond issue of $50,000,000 at public subscription. Public bids were slow and low, and a Morgan syndicate obtained the issue on an "all or none" basis, its terms being better than the others. But the bond issues did not help much, as almost half the gold came out of the Treasury itself by redemption of legal-tender notes to secure gold with which to buy bonds: the gold pumped into the Treasury was pumped out again. The adverse movement of foreign exchange, moreover, compelled large gold exports.[10]

In these bond issues Morgan did not appear as the "savior of his country"—at least not to his financial associates. James Stillman, president of the National City Bank, an affiliate of Standard Oil and almost as powerful as Morgan, made an interesting revelation years later in discussing with a friend the events of 1894:

STILLMAN: The Treasury begged Morgan for $50,000,000, which he refused, thundering "Impossible!" Then they came to see me and I went round to see what I could do. Morgan was greatly upset and overcharged, nearly wept, put his head in his hands and cried: "They expect the impossible!" So I calmed him down and told him to give me an hour and by that time I cabled for $10,000,000 from Europe for Standard Oil and ten more from other sources and came back. I told Morgan: "I have $20,000,000." "Where did you get them?" And when he heard—*il bondit de l'abîme de désespoir au pinacle de bonheur,* and became perfectly bombastic and triumphant as the savior of his country.

FRIEND: And he took all the credit?

STILLMAN: Of course. But then you see, he is a poet; Morgan is a poet.[11] ...

Congress condemned the bond issues and they provided only temporary relief. Europe drained out gold, business depression persisted and the banks hoarded gold. By January, 1895, the Treasury's gold reserve again fell considerably below the statutory limit and still more gold was shipped to Europe. In a special message to Congress President Cleveland urged the importance of maintaining gold payments and asked for authority to issue gold bonds. Of this message Morgan said:

"Everybody knows what I think of it. The president is absolutely right. The only remedy is the one he recommends—the issuance of a gold bond, a bond the principal and interest of which is payable specifically in gold." [12]

While Congress violently discussed Cleveland's plea (clearly foreshadowing rejection) the Treasury's gold reserve on February 2 fell to $42,000,000,[13] threatening suspension of specie payments. The President was urged by friends to confer with the bankers but refused, owing to his bitter feelings against them for their behavior in the government crisis.[14]

Meanwhile secret negotiations (the secrecy inflaming public opinion) went on between bankers and Treasury representatives. It was now clear that gold could not be secured by sale of bonds to American banks, the gold being immediately withdrawn by the endless chain of note redemption and re-issue, and by gold exports, but only by means of an international syndicate that would draw gold from Europe. This gave control of the situation to the international financiers, the Morgans and the Rothschilds. August Belmont was the Rothschild representative but Morgan dominated the proceedings. Belmont went to Washington to confer with Secretary Carlisle.[15] Then a Treasury representative asked to see Morgan and they met in secret conference in New York. To this representative Morgan said:

"I will undertake to get the gold necessary abroad, provided it is left in my hands to undertake, and, if I succeed, that you will make a private contract for the gold." [16]

This the Treasury was loath to do, insisting on a popular loan which Morgan categorically rejected. But gold was flowing to Europe, the gold reserve sinking, and breakdown threatened. Helpless in the emergency, at the mercy of the bankers and the situation, the Treasury agreed to a private negotiation and concluded an agreement. Then Secretary Carlisle sent the Morgan syndicate a letter abandoning the negotiation [17] and the fat was in the fire.

Morgan acted immediately. He sent Belmont to Washington and by telephone urged Carlisle not to make public acknowledgment of abandonment of the private negotiation: "I ask you at least to delay until Mr. Belmont and myself shall have an interview with the President." Carlisle agreed and Morgan set out at once for Washington. [18]

Cleveland at first refused to see Morgan but agreed on February 7, the same day Congress rejected his plea for authority to issue gold bonds and while new gold withdrawals threatened to wipe out the Treasury's reserve. At the conference were Cleveland, Morgan, Secretary Carlisle and the Attorney General. Morgan complained of the treatment received from the Treasury in rejecting the original bond agreement:

CLEVELAND: Mr. Morgan, whatever may be in all that, another offer of bonds for public subscription, open to all bidders, has been determined upon. [19]

MORGAN: My decided view is that an immediate supply of gold from Europe is the only means of averting a panic and widespread disaster. [20]

Cleveland was determined on a popular loan, while Morgan insisted on a syndicate operation. A tense discussion went on. The situation imposed its will on Cleveland: the Treasury's gold reserve continued to sink ominously, he was determined to maintain the gold standard, and apparently only the international bankers could get the gold. Finally Morgan suggested that the government secure gold under a Civil War act authorizing the Treasury to buy gold bonds or notes of the United States, the Morgan syndicate to supply the gold and receive government bonds in payment. Cleveland accepted the suggestion. [21]

Under the new agreement the Morgan syndicate was to deliver to the Treasury $65,000,000 of gold for which they received $62,000,000 4 per cent bonds at 104. The agreement included two features not in previous bond issues: the syndicate agreed to secure half the gold abroad and "to exert all financial influence and make all legitimate efforts in their power to protect the Treasury against withdrawals of gold, pending the complete performance of this contract." [22] This meant that the syndicate agreed not only to secure gold elsewhere than the Treasury but to prevent gold exports by control of the foreign-exchange market.

In this agreement the Morgan-Belmont syndicate imposed its own terms which "were extremely harsh," declared a dispassionate financial historian fifteen years later; "they measured with little mercy the emergency of the government." [23] Contemporary opinion in the financial community agreed that the terms were "excellent from the bankers' point of view," the syndicate driving "a hard bargain with the Administration." [24] The new bonds yielded 3.75 per cent interest as against 3 per cent for those of 1894. The syndicate offered a concession, a proposal for 3 per cent bonds payable specifically in gold (as against "coin" which meant either gold or silver). [25] But there was no danger of this offer being accepted, as it implied an attempt to force legislation on Congress which would surely be rejected—as Congress did when Cleveland asked for the necessary authorization.

This syndicate operation meant unusually large profits. The bonds were secured from the government at 104, offered by the syndicate at 112, the price rising to 118 and as high as 123. [26] Morgan was always touchy on this subject, and refused to reveal the profits to Senator Vest at a Congressional investigation of the bond issue:

VEST: What profit did your House make upon this transaction?

MORGAN: That I decline to answer. I am perfectly ready to state every detail of the negotiation up to the time that the bonds became my property and were paid for. What I did with my own property subsequent to that purchase I decline to state.

VEST: You decline to reveal the profits made by your firm?

MORGAN: I do, sir.[27]

The syndicate profits ranged from seven to twelve million dollars, which the *Bankers' Magazine* justified as "making a profit out of market prices that were actually created and sustained by their own actions." [28] ...

Morgan directed the syndicate's operations. A friend who asked for details of their plans before subscribing was told: "Can't give you any particulars. If you want to make some money and have got the gold, subscribe. If not, *au revoir.*" [29] There was a tremendous scramble for the bonds. Morgan personally received subscriptions, and in front of his office men cursed and struggled for a place in the long line, many still lingering after the sale was over.[30] The bonds were oversubscribed six times in New York; and in London, where half the issue was placed by J. S. Morgan & Co. and the Rothschilds, subscriptions were more than ten times the amount of the bonds.[31]

While the Morgan-Belmont syndicate's operations were successful, the relief was again only temporary. The syndicate carried out its agreement to get gold elsewhere than the Treasury, and J. P. Morgan & Co.* spent considerable amounts of money to prevent gold exports by control of the foreign-exchange market. They succeeded for a time, aided by industrial revival and renewed European purchases of American securities. Then rising prices increased imports and checked exports, Europe again sold American securities (owing to speculation forcing up their prices), and the consequent adverse balance

---

* In 1895 Drexel, Morgan & Co. became J. P. Morgan & Co. owing to the death of A. J. Drexel. Although a part of the Morgan firm, Drexel & Co. of Philadelphia retained its old name for local purposes. The Paris firm became Morgan, Harjes & Co. J. S. Morgan & Co. of London retained the name. (*Bankers' Magazine*, December, 1894, p. 87.) In 1894 J. Pierpont Morgan, Jr., became a member of his father's firm.

of international payments again forced gold exports, much of the gold being secured from the Treasury by means of note redemption.[32]

By January, 1896, the Treasury's gold reserve was down to $61,000,000. Morgan organized ancther syndicate for a private negotiation, but wrote President Cleveland that he would co-operate should the government decide on a new bond issue at public subscription.[33] Morgan's organization of a syndicate unleashed opposition in Congress and the press. Cleveland, however, had independently decided upon a public issue, securing much better terms than granted the previous year by the Morgan syndicate. The new bonds, $100,000,000, were offered to the highest bidders, bids ranging from 110.6 to 120, J. P. Morgan & Co. securing $38,000,000 at the former price.[34]

The Morgan-Cleveland bond issue of 1895 let loose a storm of widespread criticism. The secrecy inflamed public opinion and the extortionate terms were everywhere condemned. W. J. Bryan in Congress criticized the issue unsparingly, particularly the bankers' offer to accept 3 per cent if the bonds were made specifically payable in gold: "It is a contract with men who are desirous of changing the financial policy of this country, and they come to us with the insolent proposition, 'We will give you $16,000,000 in thirty years * if the government of the United States will change its financial policy.' Never before has such a bribe been offered to the people of a free country." Bryan ended characteristically: "Bondage is ephemeral, liberty is eternal. The West and South will unite successfully to resist and overcome the cruel demands of the East." [35] Flamboyant, but expressing the mood of millions of people. The Populists in Congress declared the bond issue was a move to demonetize silver and meant "fastening the burden of perpetual debt upon the people." [36] Nor was criticism limited to the silver agitators. "Sound money" men also con-

* The saving in interest accruing to the Treasury on 3 per cent bonds instead of the 4 per cents.

demned the Morgan-Cleveland agreement and its extortionate
terms, incensed by the secrecy of the proceedings and the humiliating dependence of the government upon the bankers.

Criticism concentrated upon Cleveland. Silver Democrats
were bitter while gold Republicans sniped at him for partisan
purposes. Scapegoats are always being created. Determined to
maintain the gold standard, Cleveland had to get gold from
those who could get it: the bankers. Cleveland's ideal, the ideal
of competitive capitalism, was the absolute separation of government and banking, with the consequence that banks imposed their control upon government. In an emergency, European governments turned to banks under state control, but in
the 1895 emergency the American government had to accept
the bankers' terms. A measure of control had been imposed
upon railroads and trusts, but scarcely any upon financial institutions, in spite of the national-bank system.

The Morgan syndicate of 1895 was not simply a syndicate
but the expression of a centralized financial mechanism. By
means of stock ownership, interlocking directors and affiliations J. P. Morgan & Co. had under their control or influence
powerful commercial banks and other financial institutions,
centralizing investment and banking resources. Nor was the
House of Morgan the only centralizing force. There were
wheels within wheels, and competing financial groups, some
of which were almost as powerful as Morgan, particularly the
National City Bank under the aggressive management of James
Stillman (who co-operated with the Standard Oil interests).
While community of interest largely prevailed among the
groups (in 1896 one of the Morgan partners became a director
in National City) there was also considerable rivalry. Stillman
by and large accepted Morgan's supremacy but smiled cynically
at his arrogance and delight in the display of power.

The financial centralization being accomplished by Morgan,
Stillman and others represented an interlocking of banking institutions independent of government action and control.

There being no central banking institution (such as the Bank of England), the government was helpless in an emergency and dependent upon the House of Morgan, which imposed its own terms—and this Morgan interpreted as an ordinary business transaction, apparent in his testimony at the Congressional investigation: What I did with the government bonds after they became my property is my own business.

This clash between government and the centralized banking power (which flared up in the Money Trust investigation of 1912, the grilling of Morgan on the witness-stand, and the struggle over the Federal Reserve System) constituted another expression of the transformation of the old economic order by the new. Grover Cleveland was caught in the cleft stick of the old and the new, characterizing the transition by clinging to the old (as in his ideal of separating government and banking, which meant yielding power to the financial oligarchs) yet compelled to accept the new by the compulsion of economic necessity itself. The small businessman was excellently represented by Cleveland—independent, belligerent, stubborn, yet cannily accepting the inevitable.

The magnitude of the storm aroused by the Morgan-Cleveland bond issue was determined by the general revolt against concentrated industry and finance. Bryanism expressed the accumulated class resentments of a generation. The radicals had compelled adoption of the Interstate Commerce Act to regulate railroads, with scarcely any immediate tangible results. They had compelled adoption of the Anti-Trust Law in 1890 forbidding "combinations in restraint of trade," couched in terms, however, which were easily evadable legally and which did not prevent new trusts organizing. Popular discontent insisted upon necessary reforms, but these were either rejected or emasculated after becoming laws.

To increase government revenues and "equalize" tax burdens, Congress in 1894 imposed a tax of 2 per cent on incomes of $4,000 and over—arousing the fury of the well-to-do who damned it as confiscatory and the harbinger of communist revolution. Ward McAllister, the social mentor of the new money aristocracy, who boasted of being allowed in Windsor Castle's kitchen "to inspect the preparations for the royal lady's dinner," and who said, "If you see a man with a shabby coat, cross the street to avoid him"—McAllister expressed the mood of the plutocracy when he threatened the rich would go abroad if the income tax was levied.[37] The following year the Supreme Court, by one of its clear-cut five-to-four decisions which are such unanswerable proof of the Court's wisdom, declared the income-tax law unconstitutional—after one of the judges, originally in favor of the law, changed his opinion, and in spite of the Court twenty-five years earlier having upheld the Civil War income tax.[38] This decision, in the midst of industrial depression, severe unemployment and declining government revenues, was a contemptuous slap in the face of popular discontent, particularly as heavy indirect taxation oppressed recipients of small incomes.

Government, apparently an impartial arbitrator in class disputes, was flagrantly manipulated to favor the dominant industrial and financial interests. These interests supplemented their economic power by control of legislation through corruption and other means, business and politics becoming indistinguishable, and unscrupulously pursued their predatory purposes. Under these conditions progressive legislation was almost impossible, and if adopted was usually declared unconstitutional by the courts. This sinister control of government operated against small businessmen, farmers and labor, inflaming the discontent arising out of other grievances.

Since 1890 agricultural prices had declined steadily, but there was no decline in the interest farmers, who waged perpetual war against insolvency, had to pay on their mortgages or in their disproportionately large tax burdens. In 1895 twice as many bushels of wheat were necessary as seven years before to pay the interest on a mortgage. The farmers, naturally, favored an unlimited coinage of silver to increase agricultural prices and decrease their mortgage payments—which was just as naturally opposed by capitalists and bankers. Agriculture, moreover, contributed much of the costs of industrialization, particularly in the high prices of manufactured goods and the low prices of farm products. These grievances were colored by the pioneer characteristics of independence and individualism —the frontier, in its resistance to business enterprise, producing a legion of radical ideas and movements, clinging to the ideals of free competition.

Discontent among small businessmen, who found it increasingly hard to compete against trustified industry, was increased by the 1893 panic in which they suffered disastrously, there being three times as many failures as in 1873 and the liabilities 50 per cent larger.[39] Small business was still antagonistic to trustified enterprise instead of accepting it, making the necessary adjustments and operating within its limits, as is being done to-day.

Labor discontent was intense and widespread. Real wages had increased but were partly offset by recurring depressions and unemployment, while the 1893 panic created immense suffering among the workers, unprecedented unemployment being accompanied by wage cuts and bread lines. Labor as much as the farmers participated unequally in economic progress— probably the most potent source of permanent discontent. Social legislation developed slowly, heart-breakingly, legislatures often rejecting the most elementary protective proposals. Strikes were frequent and usually crushed. The anthracite miners, almost brutalized by their underground labors, affirmed their humanity in an impressive strike, and met the savage opposition of government, judiciary and the public. Andrew Carnegie's use of armed guards in the bloody suppression of the Homestead strikers (mostly foreigners working at very low wages) became an issue in the 1896 presidential campaign, as did Grover Cleveland's intervention in the great railroad strike of 1894. This strike was clearly victorious when President Cleveland set the precedent of using Federal troops in labor disputes and broke the strike, acting under "authority" of the Interstate Commerce Act which had never been intended for such use. Even the *Bankers' Magazine* declared Cleveland "perverted" the Act "to protect those whom the government notoriously has never compelled to obey it, nor punished for breaking it." [40]

The discontent of small businessmen, the farmers and labor converged on Bryanism, a sort of drag-net of social revolt. If the issue had been simply unlimited coinage of silver, Bryanism would never have aroused the unrestrained fury and apprehensions of dominant plutocracy. Free silver meant disorganizing the currency and disturbing business, but no more and no more fatal than in the Civil War (and later the World War). But the radicals pressed other proposals—government ownership of railroads and banks, dissolution of the trusts, modification of the Supreme Court's power, popular election of United States Senators, prohibition of injunctions in labor disputes and approval of the boycott, an income-tax law and other measures. Some of these measures were impossible of realization, being against the facts of economic development, others have since been realized without producing a communist revolution—but at the time the victory of Bryanism meant a new balance of class power in government, temporarily at least, and the prospect frightened industry and finance. ("You make me think of a lot of scared hens," said Mark Hanna to a group of capitalists. James J. Hill wrote to J. P. Morgan that the McKinley managers "should get to work *at once*.... There is an epidemic craze among the farmers and to some extent among those who receive wages or salaries." [41])

Abusive and savage, the 1896 campaign appeared to threaten another civil war in the fury of the class and sectional passions aroused. The Bryanites unmercifully assailed the plutocracy of organized wealth as plunderers and despoilers of the people.

John D. Rockefeller, Andrew Carnegie, J. Pierpont Morgan and other magnates of capital were lampooned for crimes real and unreal—indicating that silver was simply an expression of more fundamental issues. Finance crowned the developing new economic order, typified by the House of Morgan, and this fact, not only the 1895 bond issue, provoked violent castigations of Morgan—which he ignored in his usual silent, arrogant fashion. The industrial and financial aristocracy retorted by declaring that the struggle against Bryanism was a struggle of civilization and barbarism, their characterization of the radicals as a revolutionary mob suggesting the same fear and hatred of democracy and the masses that animated the Wits of Junius Morgan's Hartford. Directed by the Mark Hanna whose creed was that "no man in public life owes the public anything," the plutocracy mobilized all its resources against Bryanism. William McKinley's victory was assured by an enormous campaign fund secured by levies upon corporations—Standard Oil alone giving $250,000—the threat of manufacturers to shut down if Bryan was elected, and the desertion of many farmers owing to rising wheat prices caused by crop failures in Europe and South America.[42]

Bryan's defeat consolidated the power of dominant capitalism. It was the last appearance of the frontier as a force in American politics, the final upsurge of Jacksonian democracy and its homespun equalitarianism. Business enterprise conquered, and thereafter revolts proceeded largely within its limits. The frontier, perpetually renewed, fluid in its class relations, aggressive and independent, flamed in action in the Revolution, the Civil War and the post-war radical movements. It produced the radical ideas and the causes which discontented labor and small businessmen usually accepted. Now the frontier was no more, limited by the Pacific Ocean and beaten by the development of business enterprise. The ideals of business (fed by the frontier's spirit of competitive individualism) were to conquer the rebels—and Bryan himself, a development implicit in many of his utterances during the 1896 campaign:

"The man who is employed for wages is as much a businessman as his employer, the attorney in a country town is as much a businessman as the corporation counsel in a great metropolis, the merchant at the crossroads is as much a businessman as the merchant in New York, the farmer who goes forth in the morning and toils all day is as much a businessman as the man who goes upon the board of trade and bets upon the price of grain, the miners who bring forth the precious metals are as much businessmen as the few financial magnates who corner the money of the world." [43]

"Clad in the armor of a righteous cause" the Bryanites insisted on getting *their* place in the sun of business prosperity along with the plutocracy. The struggle was to flare up again, subside, assume new forms and purposes, but definitely accepting and merging in the dominant system of business enterprise. Bryan himself was to end as an enterprising realtor. And on a day not far off William Jennings Bryan, as Secretary of State, was to order the conveyance of J. Pierpont Morgan's body from Italy to the United States for honorable burial.

CHAPTER XIX

MORGAN'S RAILROAD EMPIRE

*She went on growing and growing, and
very soon had to kneel on the floor; in
another minute there was not even room
for this, and she tried the effect of lying
down with one elbow against the door,
and the other arm curled round her head.
Still she went on growing, and, as a last
resource, she put one arm out the win-
dow and one foot up the chimney.*

ALICE IN WONDERLAND

IN June, 1895, J. P. Morgan returned from an European trip on
business of the bond syndicate. A statement being expected
from him the stock market practically halted its operations,
and continued to mark time in spite of an hour's delay in issuance of the statement. Morgan said, "The feeling abroad is very
strongly in favor of American securities, the issues recently sold
selling at large premiums and other negotiations pending,"
after which the market got to work again.[1] Morgan's "commanding position" was commented on by the New York
Tribune:

"There are only a few Wall Street interests of moment which
J. P. Morgan & Co. have not some connections with. Reorganization of the United States Cordage Co., of which J. Pierpont
Morgan is one of the largest securityholders ... Northern Pacific and Erie reorganization plans ... developments in the
New York and New England railroad situation ... expected
settlement of difficulties in the anthracite coal trade ... operations of the government bond syndicate in its control of the
exchange market to prevent gold exports ... large blocks of
American railroad securities sold abroad by Morgan & Co."[2]

Active in government financing, already represented on the directorates of many industrial corporations (finance penetrating industry), the House of Morgan engaged most intensely in Morganizing railroads. In July, one month after his return from Europe, Morgan called a conference of Eastern railroad presidents to restore rates between Chicago and New York. A pool had been dissolved by refusal of one of the roads to stay in, rates secretly cut by all the roads, and another rate war flourished merrily. The conference decided promptly to restore rates on the basis of the pool agreement, Morgan's success creating "surprise" among railroad men.[3] But this surprise was unjustified, Morgan being now the most powerful single force in American railroads.

At the conferences of railroad presidents in 1889 and 1890 Morgan had not sufficient power to compel acceptance of all his proposals. The "gentlemen's agreements" to maintain rates were compromises, almost immediately broken. Unrestrained competition and rate wars flared up again, demoralization increased, and within one year railroads began to reap the whirlwind of mismanagement and plunder. Between 1890 and 1895 one-third of railroad mileage went into bankruptcy—15,630 miles in 1890-92 and 40,550 in 1893-95,[4] the panic accelerating the process of disintegration. By reorganization of these bankrupt corporations the House of Morgan built up its railroad empire, *imposing* community of interest.

Reorganization and concentration of railroads under direct financial control was for a time almost a monopoly of the House of Morgan. Still satisfied with the simple function of floating securities, the other bankers were not direct railroad powers (except Speyer & Co., on a small scale). In its reorganizations the House of Morgan was helped by its international financial affiliations (particularly the Rothschilds, now a Morgan ally), since considerable blocks of American railroad securities were owned in Europe. Out of Morgan's activity developed the later general direct participation of banking houses in railroad affairs.

Up to 1889 retaining control by the House of Morgan of reorganized railroads was largely for reorganization purposes; now control was definitely for purposes of Morganization, to create a railroad empire under direct financial mastery.

This appeared clearly in the reorganization out of which emerged the Southern Railway, a consolidation of thirty-five corporations into the South's largest railroad system and the basis of Morgan's empire.

The Southern Railway's predecessor was the Richmond & West Point Terminal Co., itself a series of combinations loosely united by stock ownership and leases. By 1891 the Richmond system, although consisting of three north and south lines as far northwest as Cincinnati and dominant in its territory, was financially demoralized owing to fraudulent capitalization, mismanagement, speculative manipulation of its stock by directors and their plundering of the treasury.[5] Moreover, according to a report by Drexel, Morgan & Co., the system's physical condition was poor, much of the mileage unprofitable, and management inefficient.[6] The directors asked a committee, including representatives of Speyer & Co. and Kuhn, Loeb & Co., to suggest plans for financial reorganization, but the plans were rejected. After another unsuccessful attempt at amicable reorganization, a number of prominent banks, independently of the Richmond's directors, asked Drexel, Morgan & Co. to reorganize the company, in which request the directors were compelled to join. Accepting the offer, the House of Morgan subsequently declined to go on with the reorganization owing to insufficient assurance of support from all interests.[7]

By 1893 most of the Richmond Terminal roads were in receivership and another appeal for reorganization to Drexel, Morgan & Co. was accepted.[8] The Morgan reorganization provided for physical improvement of the roads, reduction of fixed charges, large new stock issues and cash assessments. Sweeping away the loose combination of many separate corporations, reorganization and consolidation produced a unified system of almost 7,000 miles which later strengthened itself by purchase of Mobile & Ohio (notoriously indiscriminate rate cutter)[9] and control of other lines, becoming the South's dominant railroad system. In spite of scaling down bonds, capitalization increased 27 per cent (the Morgan reorganization commission being $750,000 in common stock plus $100,000 cash),[10] no dividends being paid on the stock for twenty years.[11] Control was vested in a voting trust including J. P. Morgan and George F. Baker,[12] president of the First National Bank affiliated with the House of Morgan.

The next road to become Morganized was the unfortunate Erie, a property still sick from the manipulations of Jacob Little, Daniel Drew, Jay Gould and their successors, which staggered into receivership in the panic year 1893. Erie's reorganization provoked another clash between J. P. Morgan and E. H. Harriman.

Morgan's reorganization plan met considerable opposition. The opposition of an English committee was overcome by J. S. Morgan & Co.,[13] but American opposition persisted. A combination of August Belmont & Co., Kuhn, Loeb & Co., the United States Trust Co. and Harriman insisted Morgan's reorganization plan was "unjust" and "financialy unsound," but Morgan ignored the protest and at the Erie stockholders' meeting dominated the proceedings completely.[14] Belmont, Kuhn-Loeb and the United States Trust withdrew their opposition, "leaving it to you," they said to Morgan, "to do what in our opinion is dangerous." [15] But Harriman still carried on the fight, forming a protective committee.

Being only a small owner of bonds, Harriman was not much interested financially in Erie's reorganization, apparently intervening as part of his struggle for a place in the sun of railroad power. Harriman carried the case to the courts where he met defeat, the only result being to increase Morgan's dislike of the man.[16] But criticisms of the reorganization were justified, as within a year Erie defaulted on its interest, compelling modifications to lower fixed charges instead of raising them.[17] The Erie system was unified by consolidations and control passed to the House of Morgan, which in addition received compensation of $500,000 (and expenses) for its services.[18]

More interesting and important was reorganization of the Philadelphia & Reading Railroad. The Reading, reorganized by Morgan in 1887, came under control of a group of Philadelphia capitalists (including George M. Pullman) and Arthur McLeod who, as president of the road, initiated a vigorous campaign of expansion and consolidation.[19] The House of Morgan, still fiscal agents of the Reading, frowned upon this campaign, but McLeod said, "I would rather run a peanut-stand than be dictated to by J. P. Morgan," [20] and went ahead with his plans. The consequent clash was disastrous, producing Morgan reorganization and control.

Pursuing the old Reading policy, McLeod tried to build up a coal monopoly on the basis of the road's immense coal holdings, acquiring control of other coal-producing roads by stock purchase and interlocking directorates. Coal prices suddenly rose, arousing public hostility.[21] Building up a system of 5,000 miles the Reading connected with manufacturing regions where it could sell its surplus coal, and invaded New England by acquiring partial control of the Boston & Maine.[22] It appeared as if a new railroad power was in the making.

But Reading's campaign of expansion aroused the animosity of powerful interests represented by the House of Morgan. The Pennsylvania Railroad felt itself threatened, while the Vanderbilts, who had substantial stakes in the coal industry, disliked McLeod's monopolistic purposes. As if this was not enough, Reading invaded New England where railroad control was an appanage of the Vanderbilts and the House of Morgan. This was the final straw, and a combination of Morgan, Van-

derbilt and Pennsylvania interests determined to crush the interloper.

Active war raged in New England between Reading and
the Vanderbilts, with Morgan directing the Vanderbilt interests. Reading scored some coups, but was beaten in the struggle
for control of the Old Colony line, which merged instead with
New York, New Haven & Hartford (in which J. P. Morgan,
Chauncey Depew and William Rockefeller were directors).[23]
The New Haven victory made the Pennsylvania Railroad officials "jubilant" as Old Colony carried their freight to New
England and its control by Reading would have shut the
Pennsylvania from that territory except under terms amounting
to tribute.[24]

The McLeod-Reading program of expansion meant borrowing very large amounts of money, at 9 per cent interest, owing
to the financial antagonisms aroused,[25] and in 1893 they tried to
sell bonds. Although Reading's fiscal agents, Drexel, Morgan
& Co. refused to take the issue and Speyer & Co. did instead,
becoming Reading's bankers.[26]

Drexel, Morgan & Co. now waged open war upon McLeod,
sold Reading stock and depressed its price.[27] A large block of
stock owned by the Philadelphia capitalists, used as collateral
for Reading loans, was sold out and still further depressed
prices, the Morgans now buying stock for control.[28] The financial pressure being too great, Reading went into bankruptcy
with McLeod appointed receiver. Adequate banking support
lacking, isolated by a financial *cordon sanitaire,* McLeod was
compelled to resume banking relations with the Morgans and
finally retired, beaten, a Morgan representative becoming receiver.[29] Under Morgan's reorganization the Reading retired
from New England and gave up its program of expansion, in
spite of which the new company's capitalization increased considerably. By means of a voting trust (including Morgan)[30]
Philadelphia & Reading became a part of Morgan's railroad
empire. The House of Morgan had ruthlessly crushed a rebel

and interloper in the developing system of community of interest.

Among the railroads thrown into bankruptcy in 1893 was the Union Pacific which, after being plundered by the Crédit Mobilier and Jay Gould, was partly restored financially and in the confidence of the people in the territory it served. It came again under control of Gould and his predatory manipulations. The result was an old story. A reorganization committee, including Morgan, struggled unsuccessfully with the problem of reconciling conflicting interests and refunding Union Pacific's debt to the government instead of making cash payment.[31] His reorganization plan meant sacrificing much of the Federal government's financial interest in Union Pacific and was opposed in Congress (complicated by political attempts at blackmail). Discouraged, the committee abandoned its task, particularly as Morgan did not consider Union Pacific a profitable property. Things drifted in confusion for a while, when Jacob H. Schiff of Kuhn, Loeb & Co. was asked to form a reorganization committee and go ahead. Schiff answered:

"But that is J. P. Morgan's affair; I don't want to interfere with anything that he is trying to do." [32]

Informed that Morgan had abandoned the task as hopeless and impressed by the opportunity of a reorganization of such magnitude, Schiff went to Morgan and asked him about it.

"I am through with the Union Pacific and want nothing to do with it," said Morgan. "You are at liberty to go ahead and do what you like with it, and I will give you what help I can. But I am disgusted with the political wire-pulling which defeated our committee's plans in Congress." [33]

Kuhn, Loeb & Co. now proceeded with the Union Pacific reorganization, but by 1896 they felt powerful influences secretly working against them and thwarting their plans. It being suggested that Morgan, disgruntled, was the cause, Schiff went to see him and received the answer, "Not I" and the promise to find the culprit. Some time later Morgan sent for Schiff and told him:

"It's that little fellow Harriman, and you want to look out for him." [34]

Harriman, then simply a power in Illinois Central, had intervened in the situation and actively intrigued to get himself in the reorganization. Sentiment was being inflamed against the Schiff committee in Congress, the press and among stockholders. Schiff sent for Harriman, who proposed to join forces providing he was made chairman of the executive committee of the reorganized road, a proposition Schiff rejected. But Harriman persisted and was finally taken in.[35] The reorganization was successful, the road recapitalized and the government debt paid in cash, Union Pacific emerging as a most profitable system of 5,400 miles and the reorganization syndicate securing $6,000,000 compensation.[36]

Morgan's mistake in yielding up Union Pacific was serious. He not only thought it less valuable than Erie,[37] but his action permitted the rise of a formidable combination with which he was destined to clash. Kuhn, Loeb & Co. and Harriman decided to finance the reorganization through the National City Bank, known since 1891 as a Standard Oil bank.[38] Originally forced to depend upon its own financial resources, as bankers who wanted "sure things" considered oil too speculative, Standard Oil proceeded to build up large cash reserves and act as their own bankers independently of Wall Street. Accumulating an immense reservoir of money capital Standard Oil penetrated Wall Street, acquiring interests in railroads and banks, among them National City. In the reorganized Union Pacific, Standard Oil received two memberships on the board of directors.[39] A challenge to the supremacy of the House of Morgan was to come from this combination of the Rockefellers, Harriman, Kuhn-Loeb and the National City Bank.

The Union Pacific was the only important reorganization in which the House of Morgan did not participate. Among the other reorganizations that of the Northern Pacific Railroad stands out as vitally affecting the balance of railroad power, making the House of Morgan a factor in the Northwest. After the failure of Jay Cooke & Co. financially demoralized Northern Pacific, it was reorganized in 1875 and, under control of Henry Villard, made steady progress. In 1883 Drexel, Morgan & Co. organized a syndicate which floated $18,000,000 Northern Pacific bonds, Morgan becoming a director.[40] Bankruptcy in 1893 interrupted a policy of expansion which piled up excessive fixed charges and aroused much criticism. Kuhn, Loeb & Co., John D. Rockefeller and other large interests failed in their efforts to save the road from bankruptcy.[41] A struggle developed for control of Northern Pacific which ended in reorganization by J. P. Morgan & Co. in conjunction with the Deutsche Bank (large amounts of Northern Pacific bonds having been marketed in Germany) and the Great Northern Railroad interests under control of James J. Hill.

A railroad man of extraordinary ability, Hill emerged as an important magnate by acquiring control of the St. Paul & Pacific Railroad under circumstances which clearly suggested conspiracy, betrayal of trust and fraud practised upon foreign bondholders.[42] Out of this road developed Great Northern. In 1884 Hill and Great Northern, under an old and forgotten land grant, claimed 65,000 acres in the Dakotas. In the intervening twenty years the wilderness had been settled by men and women who knew nothing of the land grant. Sustained by the courts, Great Northern began to evict the farmers, who appealed to Congress which compromised by permitting Great Northern to select an equal area of land elsewhere. In this exchange Great Northern received valuable mineral lands (although the original grant was non-mineral).[43] Hill and his associates had long coveted Northern Pacific, as it operated in much of the Great Northern's territory, and in 1889 they formed a combination to wrest control from Henry Villard, but failed. The Northern Pacific's bankruptcy * offered another opportunity, but Hill secured the road only after a struggle and Morgan's intervention.

The reorganization of Northern Pacific, as usual, reduced fixed charges but increased total capitalization considerably. Control was vested in a voting trust including J. P. Morgan, August Belmont and a representative of the Deutsche Bank.[44] James J. Hill and his associates in Great Northern acquired $26,000,000 of reorganized Northern Pacific stock, in order, wrote Hill to Morgan, to bring the two roads "together as nearly as possible in general policy" by "the holding of a large and practically a controlling interest in both companies by the same parties." [45] It was a merger of interests essentially uniting Northern Pacific and Great Northern, although not open consolidation, Hill writing an associate that they must "bear in mind the opposition to the consolidaton of the two companies." [46] The Hill system now moved definitely in the Morgan orbit, J. P. Morgan & Co. becoming Great Northern's bankers in place of Kuhn, Loeb & Co.[47] This combination offset that of Harriman, Kuhn-Loeb and the Rockefellers in control of Union Pacific (and later of Southern Pacific), the combinations balancing each other temporarily.

All these reorganizations (in general charge of Charles H. Coster, a Morgan partner specializing in railroads) were a consequence of the piratical financiering which, according to Henry Clews, "constituted the chief source of the phenomenal fortunes piled up by our railroad millionaires and direct frauds upon the public." [48] Reorganization required lessening financial burdens on the railroads and meant scaling down the

* While Northern Pacific was in bankruptcy the receivers twice and severely cut wages and the workers went on strike. An injunction was issued by a judge of the United States Circuit Court prohibiting the workers to leave their employment or get others to leave. The Judiciary Committee of the House of Representatives, after an investigation, characterized the injunction as "an abuse of judicial power without authority of law" and "an invasion of the rights of American citizens." But the strike was broken. (Gustavus Myers, *History of the Great American Fortunes,* Vol. III, pp. 384-85.)

equity of bondholders who had provided most of the money for construction. "Cruel things" were done to small investors in reorganizations [49]—cruel still, although forced by previous plundering. But while bonds suffered stock was pampered. In recapitalizing reorganized railroads Morgan generously issued new stock, capitalizing prospective earnings to the limit, the company emerging with smaller fixed charges but larger total capitalization. Out of the new stock issues the Morgan syndicates (and others) secured most of their profits. Financially necessary, reorganization expropriated small investors.

Reorganization of railroads strengthened consolidation and the creation of systems which facilitated the imposition of financial control since they still further separated stockholders from "their" property. Independent entrepreneurs were either discredited by bankruptcy or, owing to the increasingly large size of consolidated systems, could no longer carry on without the financial resources of the great banks. Stockholders were numerous and scattered (thousands of them in Europe), and this multiplication of stockholders,* originally favoring the independent entrepreneur, now favored control by financiers. Strategic stock ownership, interlocking directorates and financial community of interest insured control of immense systems. By 1900 the overwhelming bulk of railroad mileage was concentrated in six dominant systems:

Harriman—20,245 miles; Vanderbilt—19,517; Morgan—19,073; Pennsylvania—18,220; Gould—16,074; Hill—10,373. [50]

But the power of the House of Morgan was much larger than appears. J. P. Morgan & Co. were fiscal agents of the Pennsylvania, Vanderbilt and Hill systems in which they owned large amounts of stock, while Morgan was a director and member of the executive and finance committees of New York Central (heart of the Vanderbilt system), director in

---

* The multiplication of stockholders was used to resist regulatory legislation. "Legislating against corporations!" said one magnate. "You are legislating against yourselves. To-day every large corporation has thousands of stockholders." (*Report of the Industrial Commission*, Vol. I, p. 1165.)

twenty other railroads, and a power in Great Northern. More-over, the House of Morgan centralized an interlocking finan-cial community of interest among the railroads. Morgan was instrumental in harmonizing the relations of the Pennsylvania and New York Central by means of a compromise lease of the Chesapeake & Ohio.[51] George F. Baker, of the First National Bank, was a director in many railroads, and First National was a Morgan affiliate. Morgan centralized control of his own rail-road system by means of interlocking directorships held by himself, his partners and representatives, but many of these held directorships in roads outside the Morgan system. Thus Charles H. Coster, a Morgan partner, was voting trustee in the reorganized Baltimore & Ohio, and Samuel Spencer, president of Morgan's Southern Railway, a director in Chesapeake & Ohio, Milwaukee & St. Paul and Northern Pacific.[52] Only two systems were outside the orbit of Morgan's influence—the Harriman and the Gould. J. Pierpont Morgan was the dominant railroad power.

The working of Morgan's power is illustrated in the way he secured control of the Central Railroad of New Jersey. George F. Baer, president of Philadelphia & Reading, a Morgan road, learned that Baltimore & Ohio proposed buying Jersey Central.* What happened was described by Baer at a govern-ment hearing:

"I at once went to Mr. Morgan and told him the situation was most alarming; that it would be the ruin of the Reading property if an antagonistic company got control of the Jersey Central.... He told me to keep my own counsel and look up the whole subject and see what could be done.... I made a report in a week's time.... When I got home one night in Reading there was a call on the telephone and Mr. Morgan

---

* In 1896 Baltimore & Ohio was in financial straits and on the verge of bankruptcy. J. P. Morgan & Co. offered to raise money, but the terms in-volved control of the road and were rejected. (Edward Hungerford, *The Story of the Baltimore & Ohio*, Vol. II, p. 206.) The B. & O. later came under Morgan's influence.

was there, telling me to come to New York immediately. I went to New York the next morning. Mr. Morgan said to me: 'What do you think is the fair price [of Jersey Central stock]?' I said: 'I have named what I think is a fair price in my report.' He called for George F. Baker [chairman of the Jersey Central board]. We sat down and dickered for about five minutes until Mr. Baker said they would take 160, and I said I would advise that, and I went to the phone and called up Mr. Welsh and Mr. Harris, who were with myself a majority of the executive committee, and they said yes, and the deal was closed. That is the whole story." [53]

Reorganization, consolidation and Morganization of the railroads solved problems of finances and profits but not the social problem of their control. Oppressive conditions persisted. The Morganized railroads flouted regulations of the Interstate Commerce Commission. In spite of the law secret rates and rebates flourished in favor of industrial combinations against their competitors. "Discriminating favors are granted chiefly to large shippers," reported the Industrial Commission to the government. "The effect of the penalties of the Interstate Commerce Act has been still further to limit the preferences to a few shippers, since this makes it more possible to secure secrecy.... Railway discriminations foster trusts and combinations." [54] Consolidation improved efficiency and economy in operation but strengthened the railroads' oppressive powers. "At no time in the history of American railroads," concluded the Industrial Commission, "has the need of efficient, wise and firm supervision by public authority of the terms and conditions of transportation been more imperatively demanded than at the present time." [55] But the Morganized railroads resisted public control and engaged in aggressive struggles against the government, a decisive aspect of the centralization of industry and finance.

The railroad empire of the House of Morgan included an empire in coal. Five railroads through subsidiaries dominated anthracite coal ownership and produced two-thirds of the output,[56] four of the roads being in the Morgan system and one in the Vanderbilt (the Vanderbilts also owning considerable stock in the Morgan roads). The railroads crushed independent operators by charging excessive transportation rates, or compelling them to agree forever not to ship over other roads.[57] Independent operators retaliated by securing a provision in the Pennsylvania State constitution prohibiting railroads from owning and operating coal mines,[58] but this provision was easily evaded and legally, by means of subsidiary companies which received lower rates than the independents.[59] Agreements and pools among the coal roads were prohibited by the Interstate Commerce Act, but there was no change except for a series of investigations and legislation. Slowly but relentlessly the independent operators were crushed.

By 1898 there were only a few independent operators. Among the independents were Simpson & Watkins, influential supporters of a proposed new railroad to compete against the coal roads and secure lower rates.[60] This was a two-fold menace to the Morgan system and New York Central—as railroads and as coal producers. Action being necessary, J. P. Morgan & Co. bought up Simpson & Watkins for $5,000,000, the stock being put in control of the Guaranty Trust Co.[61]

The sale of Simpson & Watkins meant temporary abandonment of the proposed new railroad. The project was revived by the Pennsylvania Coal Co., another independent operator. Erie, which had been carrying the Pennsylvania's coal, appealed to Morgan who began to buy Pennsylvania Coal stock for control. After considerable difficulty and paying high prices (the average price was $552),[62] Morgan succeeded and turned the stock over to Erie.[63] This purchase was considered a "bold stroke" which "completely upset plans" of the independents to compete against "large vested interests."[64] By this stroke most of the independent coal producers were eliminated as competitive factors. J. P. Morgan & Co. received the large commission of $5,000,000 from Erie.[65] The price Erie paid was considered "excessive," the "highest ever paid for such properties." [66] But not in terms of control of coal.

J. Pierpont Morgan's complete and almost dictatorial power in the anthracite industry revealed itself clearly in the great miners' strikes of 1900 and 1902.

Ruthless in oppression of independent operators and the public, the anthracite railroads were still more ruthless toward the miners. Working under extremely dangerous conditions, the miners averaged monthly earnings of $12.95 and up, depending on employment.[67] They were often paid in scrip, compelled to trade at company stores and live in company houses from which they were mercilessly evicted in case of strikes. Unions were distasteful to the coal barons, and crushed. Industrial feudalism flourished. A series of wage reductions which "brought the miners and their families to the verge of starvation" provoked general strikes in 1894 and 1897. "The employers," said the New York *Tribune,* "deliberately adopted a course of action which has established conditions of peculiar hardship at the mines." [68] The strikes were brutally repressed— the miners being stigmatized as "dangerous swarms of foreigners," [69] that is, immigrants who constituted the human raw material of industry, ruthlessly driven and oppressed. Another strike broke out in 1900, alarming Mark Hanna and the Republican party in the midst of a presidential campaign against W. J. Bryan. Hanna interviewed Morgan, "the railroad presidents received their orders," and the miners' compromise terms were accepted.[70]

But in 1902 there was another strike, forced upon the miners by the coal barons, and no presidential election. Recognition of the union was an important issue. Mark Hanna, who considered that unionism should be tamed rather than antagonized, again intervened and appealed to Morgan over the heads of the presidents of the anthracite railroads to accept arbitration. No action. Evictions, starvation and troops appeared in the strike regions. After an interview with Morgan, John W. Gates was willing to wager 100 to 1 against the strike. George F. Baer, president of the Philadelphia & Reading (a Morgan road and the largest coal operator) declared:

"The rights and interests of the laboring man will be protected and cared for by the Christian men to whom God has given control of the property rights of the country. Pray earnestly that right may triumph, always remembering that the Lord God Omnipotent still reigns." [71]

The industrial and financial aristocracy, as is the custom of aristocracy, identified itself with the Almighty. Dependent upon the barons' money, the Church in the coal regions accepted and magnified the feudal credo. God, it appeared, was on the side of the larger profits. Meanwhile the miners grimly persisted in their strike, although starving and manhandled (in Pennsylvania) by the Coal and Iron Police, mercenaries commissioned by the State but hired and paid by the railroad and coal companies.

Financial opinion was that "J. P. Morgan dominates the coal situation and can dictate to the coal operators." [72] But Morgan declined to intervene, although aware of his own power, being apparently satisfied with affairs. This appeared in an interview:

REPORTER: What action, if any, will you take?

MORGAN: What action can I take? Why is it necessary for me to take any?

REPORTER: Will you take any action?

MORGAN: Why should I? I am not president of the coal companies.

REPORTER: Is there any chance of arbitrating the strike?

MORGAN: I know nothing about the matter. Why don't the papers leave matters alone? Why should you stir things in this way instead of leaving them to settle matters among themselves?

REPORTER: The operators have already said you will not interfere.

MORGAN (*quickly*): I have not said that I will not interfere, or that I will interfere.[73]

A few days later, after a conference in the offices of J. P. Morgan & Co., George F. Baer *did* say: "Morgan does not mean to interfere." [74]

Public opinion was against the coal barons, inflamed by their arrogance and a threatened coal famine. Morgan, the master of anthracite, publicly disavowed responsibility while his satraps fulminated against the strikers and "the tyranny of monopolistic combinations of labor," defying public opinion. The "Christian men" who had built up monopolistic combinations of capital by economic force and financial control objected to labor combining in unions for self-protection. The union offered arbitration, public opinion approved the offer, but the coal barons refused to arbitrate. Pressure on Morgan to intervene in favor of arbitration produced no results. Infuriated by the refusal to arbitrate an organization of businessmen in the coal regions appealed to President Theodore Roosevelt to compel arbitration:

"Is J. Pierpont Morgan greater than the people? Is he mightier than the government? ... Morgan has placed a ban upon us which means universal ruin, destitution, riot and bloodshed.... We appeal from the king of the trusts to the President of the people." [75]

The strike was six months old, there was a coal shortage and suffering among the poor in cities, and still the coal barons rejected arbitration. In answer to an appeal from the Governor and Attorney General of Pennsylvania, Morgan said in substance: "Tell the miners to go back to work. Then, and not till then, will we agree to talk about concessions." [76]

Sensing public opinion and developing his campaign to impose a measure of civilized procedure upon the magnates of industry and finance, President Roosevelt intervened, urging arbitration. The strikers accepted, the magnates, according to Roosevelt, "insolently" declined, refusing "to consider the public had any rights in the matter." [77] Aroused, Roosevelt made plans for military seizure of the mines. [78] There were secret conferences between Secretary of State Elihu Root and Morgan at the Union League Club in New York City, and later in the night on Morgan's yacht the *Corsair*, [79] at which Root emphasized Roosevelt's decision to compel arbitration under threat of government operation of the mines. Morgan's hand was forced and, master of anthracite, appeared at the White House to inform the President that the coal operators accepted arbitration. [80]

There was a bit of comedy in the drama. At a White House conference Robert Bacon and other Morgan coal representatives were "nearly wild" when Roosevelt proposed to include a union-labor man among the arbitrators. They became "more and more hysterical" in their opposition as Roosevelt insisted, although admitting that failure to agree might mean social war. Then Roosevelt accepted a compromise—"I have not the slightest objection to doing an absurd thing," he said, "when it is necessary to meet the objections of an absurd mind, and I will cheerfully appoint my labor man as an 'eminent sociologist.'" There was "instant and tremendous relief," and when informed on the telephone Morgan "eagerly" ratified the compromise. [81] J. Pierpont Morgan bent to the storm, but his was still the power.

CHAPTER XX

INTERNATIONAL FINANCE AND IMPERIALISM

> *"How am I to get in?"* asked Alice again
> *in a louder tone.*
> *"Are you to get in at all?"* said the
> *Footman. "That's the first question, you*
> *know."*
> *It was, no doubt; but Alice did not like*
> *to be told so.*
>
> ALICE IN WONDERLAND

THE bond issues, the Bryan revolt, the Morganization of railroads and the struggles of class against class were all aspects
of the same movement—the transformation of economic and
political life by concentration of industry and centralization
of financial control. This produced an immense accumulation
of investment capital which in the United States was absorbed
in the development of a continent, but which in the industrialized nations of Europe broke through national limits after
new markets to conquer.

Originally satisfied to sell manufactured goods to other peoples not yet in the orbit of capitalism, the industrialized nations now compelled them to build railroads, factories and
develop their natural resources, enterprises requiring large
amounts of capital and machinery. Monopolistic aggregations
of industry and finance, usually operating through the great
banks, feverishly seized upon new markets and undeveloped
lands in which to dispose of goods and capital, accompanied by
political pressure and military force. Assuming the "white
man's burden" (on an exceptionally profitable basis) was the
rationalization of an imperialism ruthlessly and cynically oppressive; but, in fact, the "white man's burden" was simply the

necessity of maintaining "law and order" in undeveloped lands in order to insure profits.

Imperialism operates by means of the export of capital, facilitated by diplomatic and military force. Up to 1875 the export of capital was overwhelmingly British, invested in every country of the world. By 1885, however, other European nations (particularly Germany, issuing its challenge to Britain) began to export capital and an imperialistic scramble developed for colonies, protectorates and spheres of influence, parceling out the "backward" portions of the world among their financial and industrial interests. Capital acquired an irresistible international mobility, and wherever it penetrated the consequences were revolutionary. It broke up old civilizations and modes of living, and compelled savages to become "civilized" overnight. The export of capital meant an increase in European industrial prosperity and brought new comforts to certain groups of people in the lands being "penetrated," but simultaneously produced misery and horrors—colonial wars and massacres, barbarous servitude, imperialistic conquest and oppression of "backward" peoples. While the world was progressively drawn together in a larger unity by the development of international industrial and financial relations, the imperialistic nations' rivalry in the export of capital drove inexorably to armed conflict. Europe complacently accepted the "little colonial wars" against "backward" peoples—dreamed, even, of universal peace—while the "little wars" prepared the great catastrophe of 1914....

J. S. Morgan & Co. was actively identified with the British export of capital. When the Barings crashed in 1890, owing to speculative investments in Argentine securities, J. S. Morgan & Co. were as active as the Bank of England in preventing the crash becoming a panic. In fact, British opinion considered J. S. Morgan & Co. instrumental in "working out the salvation of the financial world after the Argentine collapse." [1] British capital had flowed into Argentina recklessly and in large amounts, and fraud tainted many of the securities. In 1889 the Argentine wheat crop failed, there was a revolution and financial panic. The government imposed taxes on the profits and deposits of private banks, and on the profits of all foreign enterprises in Argentina. The American minister protested, some American enterprises being affected.[2] Most of the invested foreign capital was British, and Britain used financial pressure to make the Argentine government come to terms, which withdrew the obnoxious taxes and instead taxed more heavily the necessities of life of the poor. The government, moreover, had suspended payments on the Argentine national debt, mostly foreign, and withdrawn guarantees to the railroads owned by British investors. After considerable discussion and pressure, J. S. Morgan & Co. settled the issues, the settlement being approved by the Argentine Committee of which Lord Rothschild was chairman. The railroad guarantees were confirmed and Argentine's national debt refunded by means of a $75,000,000 loan underwritten by J. S. Morgan & Co. with interest at 6 per cent, although most of the bonds refunded carried much lower interest, some as low as 3½ per cent.[3]

(In the midst of these transactions Junius Spencer Morgan died in Monte Carlo, in 1890, from an accident while out driving. There were no changes in the House of Morgan, J. Pierpont Morgan having been master of the House for many years.) ...

Imperialism is not only smeared with the blood of "backward" peoples but with financial frauds and thievery. Among the scandals of imperialism was the Panama Canal Co. promoted by French financiers after the Suez Canal, which the French had built, became British property through Disraeli's manipulations. Blackmail, corruption and thievery from the start tainted the Panama Canal Co. Fraudulent means were used to induce people to invest, shares illegally disposed of, and everybody bribed who could influence the enterprise favorably or unfavorably—ministers, legislators and ordinary

politicians, journalists, bankers and diplomats. Persons who
were not bribed, blackmailed bribes. The construction frauds
were enormous, while the financiers who promoted the enterprise amassed fabulous profits. Although originally estimated
to cost $114,000,000, expenditures were shot up to $400,000,000
and the canal still only one-third completed.[4]

Bankruptcy intervened and the scandal was aired publicly
in 1893, wrecking many political and financial reputations
(and almost driving Georges Clémenceau from public life).

American opinion was against construction of the canal by
foreign capitalists and under foreign governmental control,
particularly the French, considering their Mexican adventure
during the Civil War. President Rutherford B. Hayes insisted
that any Isthmian canal should be under American control,
and Congress agreed with him. There were some proposals
and one attempt to construct an American canal across
Nicaragua, but they were abandoned. The government did
nothing, although its opposition was plain. Considering the
state of American opinion, the French Panama Canal Co.
organized, through Seligman Frères of Paris, an American
Committee to "protect the interests" of the project in the
United States, composed of J. Pierpont Morgan, Jesse Seligman and Charles Lanier (of Winslow, Lanier & Co., an investment house closely co-operating with J. P. Morgan & Co.).
J. & W. Seligman & Co. were American agents of the Canal
company, carrying on all purchases and other transactions, the
purpose of the Committee being simply to influence public
and government opinion, for which service each member of
the Committee received $400,000.[5] The bankers, after former
President Grant declined the offer, induced R. W. Thompson
to resign as Secretary of the Navy and accept the chairmanship
of the American Committee at $24,000 a year, lobbying in
Congress and at sessions of the House Committee on Foreign
Affairs.[6] The affair was investigated by a Congressional com-

mission, the chairman of which tried to find out why Thompson was chosen:

PATTERSON: Why was Mr. Thompson selected as chairman? He was not a great financier, was he?

SELIGMAN: No, but he was a great statesman and lawyer.

PATTERSON: But you offered the place to General Grant. Now, he was a great soldier, a popular idol; but he was not a great lawyer, or financier, or great statesman, was he?

SELIGMAN (*smilingly*): Well—

GEARY: There may be some difference of opinion on that point.

SELIGMAN: General Grant was a bosom friend of mine, and I always look out for my friends.[7]

Admitting he knew American sentiment was against the Panama Canal Co., Seligman said: "A committee of representative men here, identified with the Canal company, would have the effect of creating a more favorable sentiment among the American people."[8]

That was the sole purpose of the American Committee—to influence public opinion. J. Hood Wright, one of the most active partners in the House of Morgan, testified that Drexel, Morgan & Co. had nothing to do with the Canal company's purchases, expenditures or other banking business, although they had helped the Seligmans buy the (American built and owned) Panama Railroad for the French company.[9]

PATTERSON: Was not the moral and business influence of these three great banking houses given to the enterprise?

WRIGHT: In what respect?

PATTERSON: So far as affecting public opinion in the United States was concerned.

WRIGHT: I presume so.

PATTERSON: Was that not sufficient, in a large degree, to mold public opinion in favor of the Panama Canal Co.?

WRIGHT: That I am not prepared to answer.[10]

The protests aroused by affiliation of Morgan and other

American bankers with the French project to build a canal across the Isthmus of Panama was provoked by the belief that it violated the Monroe Doctrine. This Doctrine, originally proposed to prevent European territorial expansion in the Americas, was developing another purpose: the economic domination of Latin America. By tariff manipulations the United States tried to control Latin-American trade, and at the first Pan-American Congress in 1889 proposed a customs union of the Americas (directed against European trade) which the Latin-Americans rejected. In the dispute with Great Britain over Venezuela President Grover Cleveland did much to impart an imperialistic character to the Monroe Doctrine when he insisted it meant that the United States is sovereign on the American continents and its fiat law.

In the Venezuelan dispute, while business and the press generally supported Cleveland, the financial community was extremely lukewarm. The threat of war was not taken seriously. Recalling recent races in which British yachts had been beaten, London bankers cabled the New York Stock Exchange:

"When our warships enter New York Harbor we hope your excursion boats will not interfere with them."

To which the New York Exchange replied:

"For your sake it is to be hoped that your warships are better than your yachts." [11]

But when the war threat loomed up more dangerously and stocks declined, financiers protested vigorously. Morgan was "appalled" by Cleveland's ultimatum to Britain. The work of a lifetime, he said, was in danger of destruction: "I have labored to build up such relations of confidence between the United States and the money markets of Europe that capital from there could be secured in large sums for our needs, and here is a threatened disaster that will put an end to our borrowing." [12] In 1895 J. Pierpont Morgan was apparently unaware of American "imperial destiny," considering international relations in exclusively financial terms. The United States being still dependent upon foreign capital, nothing should be done, according to Morgan, to disturb the import of capital.

There was no war, and in spite of Cleveland's imperialistic interpretation, the Monroe Doctrine economically remained largely a claim on the future.

Still, problems of world power dimly interested Morgan. He became identified in 1896 with J. A. Scrymser in the project for a Pacific cable. Scrymser had organized the Mexican Telegraph Co. and spread a network of telegraphs and cables over South America, competing aggressively with the British. President Grant had urged a Pacific cable, but Cyrus W. Field and others abandoned the project. Expressing the government's interest, Vice Admiral David D. Porter wrote to Field that the route via the Sandwich Islands was preferable "as I have no doubt they will ultimately become a part of the United States," adding: "It can easily be seen what an advantage this freedom of communication would be to our people in the great race for supremacy in China ... wealth and power to the successful nation." In 1891 the Senate passed a bill for a subsidy of $200,000 yearly for a cable from San Francisco to Hawaii and thence to Japan and New Zealand, but the House rejected the bill. In 1896 Scrymser and Morgan organized the Pacific Cable Co., capitalized at $10,000,000. The Scrymser-Morgan company maintained a large lobby with considerable influence in Congress. Asked why the government should grant a subsidy, Scrymser replied: "We have got to go into a field already occupied by English companies." The Pacific Cable Co. received a franchise from the Hawaiian government, which provided for approval by the State Department, but Secretary Hay disapproved and the scheme was abandoned.[13]

Although still importing capital the United States was developing an export of capital, the extension of which produced the seedlings of imperialism. By 1898 American investments in Mexico, Cuba and the Caribbeans amounted to $350,000,-000.[14] American business enterprise began to penetrate other nations. In 1877-82 "enthusiasm" prevailed for investments in Mexican railroads, American promoters securing concessions for 5,000 miles, some of the roads built being extensions of our Southwestern systems.* The Mexican Central, largest of the railroads, was an American-British property, while Collis P. Huntington had promoted the Mexican International. There were isolated American investments in mines, railroads and plantations scattered all over Latin America, producing considerable manipulation of governments, politics and soldiers. W. R. Grace & Co. secured mining and railroad concessions in South America; the American Fruit Co. staked out its empire in Central America, building plantations, railroads, stores and ships, and an American concern, the San Domingo Improvement Co., bought the debt of $850,000 a Dutch company held from the Dominican government—the first economic hold on San Domingo which later produced American occupation.[15] And Standard Oil, of course, was spreading petroleum and investments all over the world.

This American export of capital was scattered, the expression of independent and isolated entrepreneurs, not a definitely organized financial movement. There was consequently no scramble for colonial territory (and also because American capitalism was still absorbed in the industrialization of its own continental areas).

Before the Civil War the Southern States favored territorial expansion in the Caribbeans in order to strengthen slavocracy and provoked the war with Mexico. They suggested purchasing Cuba, a proposal rejected by Spain and frowned upon by the North. After the Civil War territorial expansion was considered slavocratic, and neither W. H. Seward's declamations

---

*British, French and American promoters plundered the Mexican government, which generously subsidized railroads. Thus the Vera Cruz (British) Railroad, capitalized at $40,000,000, could have been built for $10,000,000, yet paid 5 to 12 per cent. Corruption and construction frauds flourished, one source of profit being unnecessary mileage to get the government subsidy. (Matias Romero, *Railways in Mexico*, p. 8.)

on "Manifest Destiny" nor President Grant's imperialistic schemes overcame the prejudice. Moreover, conquest of the West absorbed the nation's imperial energy. But the progress of manufacturing developed larger exports and foreign markets assumed new importance. Particular corporate enterprises, such as Standard Oil and the American Fruit Co., had large international interests. American foreign investments, although small, were concentrated in the Caribbeans and influential beyond their amount. And the European scramble for new markets, immediate and potential ("pegging out claims on posterity") inevitably influenced American policy, particularly as the country approached industrial maturity. Assuming the "white man's burden," the United States plunged into the war with Spain.

The Spanish-American War did two things: it consolidated the power of the plutocracy and it developed an American colonial empire. Spain was easily crushed, much as a man might crush a fly on a summer's day.* The war unloosed imperialistic ambitions. Cuba was occupied and converted into an American protectorate and Porto Rico annexed—assuring American hegemony in the Caribbeans. The islands were invaded by American banks. There was a controversy over disposal of the Philippines—and war between Filipinos and Americans who had previously jointly fought against the Spaniards, the Filipinos claiming independence, which President McKinley insisted he solved in this fashion: "I went down on my knees, and prayed Almighty God for light and guidance, and one night it came to me, to take them all, to educate the Filipinos and uplift and civilize and Christianize them." But McKinley also said: "What we want is new markets, and

* To finance the war the government issued $200,000,000 of 3 per cent bonds for direct sale to the people. J. P. Morgan & Co. organized a syndicate which bid for the whole amount of the loan. This was a gesture, the syndicate declaring: "We know the loan will be subscribed for independently of this action" and "we have no wish to interfere with the popular loan." The loan was a big success, being subscribed five times over. One-half of the subscriptions were for $500 or less. (*Bankers' Magazine*, July, 1898, pp. 121, 131.)

as trade follows the flag, it looks very much as if we were going to have new markets."[16] The Philippines were annexed, and Hawaii, Porto Rico, the Samoan Islands. Within a year the United States acquired a colonial empire of 170,000 square miles and 12,000,000 population (including Cuba). Only five years previously Cleveland had refused to sanction annexation of Hawaii!

Trade and investments beckoned in the Orient. Financial interests favored territorial annexation. "It is as a base for commercial operations," declared Frank A. Vanderlip, later president of the National City Bank, "that the Philippines seem to possess the greatest importance, pickets of the Pacific standing guard at the entrance to trade."[17] The *Bankers' Magazine* said: "The extension of American territory will give new scope for banking and other business enterprises."[18] Asia loomed as the coming great mart of trade and investments. The threatened break-up of China and its partition by the European powers and Japan led the United States to proclaim the "Open Door" there (while bolting the door in the Philippines and the Caribbeans). The "Open Door" policy originally meant freedom of trade but was later broadened to include freedom of investment. Our "splendid isolation" was finally broken by American troops co-operating with the troops of other powers in suppressing the Boxer revolt.

These events paralleled an extraordinary development of business prosperity. After four years of intense depression prosperity revived in 1897, initiated by large American harvests and crop failures abroad. Commodity and stock prices began to rise. The Spanish War accelerated prosperity by its demands for munitions and supplies, its brevity preventing a business reaction. Particularly prosperous was the iron industry, production increasing in two years by 40 per cent.[19] Exports multiplied, and Europe considered protecting its markets against the invasion of American manufactures. Business failures declined. Industrial combination proceeded feverishly. Rising prices stimulated business. Bank reserves and profits flourished like the green bay tree. Speculation broke loose, concentrating prosperity.* Easy money. There was an immense accumulation of investment capital and of American credits on Europe's money markets. Then, for the first time, the United States loaned considerable money to other nations.

Dominant in American finance and its international affiliations, the House of Morgan naturally led in the new development of lending American money abroad. In 1899 J. P. Morgan & Co. negotiated conversion of the entire Mexican debt of $110,000,000 at 96 and 97 less 1 per cent commission.[20] While considerable amounts of American money were invested in Mexican oil, mines and railroads, the foreign debt was held exclusively in Europe and much of it represented extortion practiced upon the Mexican government. Included in the Morgan syndicate were J. S. Morgan & Co. and the Deutsche Bank (which was becoming the financial driving force of German imperialism, actively struggling for promotions, concessions, spheres of influence, and financing the Berlin-Bagdad railroad). "The striking feature of this conversion," according to contemporary financial opinion, "is that it has been undertaken by an American banking house, J. P. Morgan & Co., and that these bankers have co-operating the most substantial American and European financial interests."[21] There was another striking feature: the decision of Porfirio Diaz, Mexico's perpetual president, to conclude an alliance with American finance, whose support was important in maintaining his oppressive régime.

The profits in foreign bonds being superior to United States bonds, investors were eager to subscribe. Sweden secured a loan of $10,000,000 through the National Park Bank, Germany

* In 1899 there was a minor panic in Wall Street produced by a break in the market. Several Stock Exchange and other firms suspended. J. P. Morgan & Co. loaned $1,000,000 at 6 per cent, although rates were much higher in the open money market, and organized a syndicate of banks to lend another $9,000,000. (*Commercial and Financial Chronicle,* December 23, 1899, p. 1277.)

$20,000,000 through Kuhn, Loeb & Co., and there were minor Latin-American loans as well as loans of $10,000,000 to European cities.[22] In 1900 a syndicate organized by the National City Bank placed an issue of $25,000,000 for the Russian government, secured by mortgage on a railroad being built in the oil regions to facilitate distribution of petroleum products [23]— an expression of Standard Oil's far-flung international interests, the National City Bank acting as Standard's agent.

Britain's imperialistic war against the Boers produced the "novel" situation of British borrowings in the American money market. In 1900 J. P. Morgan & Co. floated a loan of $15,-000,000 for the British government, another of $28,000,000 a few months later (American investors securing $4,000,000 more direct in London), another of $100,000,000 in 1901, and still another of $80,000,000.[24] These loans were all oversubscribed. The unexpectedly stubborn resistance of the Boers to benevolent assimilation in the interest of mine-owners and Cecil Rhodes' dream of empire (on a financially profitable basis) placed a severe burden on the British exchequer, and one-fifth of the war costs were financed by American loans underwritten by the House of Morgan.

All these foreign loans, particularly the Morgan loans to Great Britain, were greeted as "a significant index of the progress of New York toward a commanding position among the world's money markets," while at the American Bankers Association meeting in 1900 (among those present being the president of the National Bank of Commerce, a Morgan institution) one of the speakers said amid general approval: "These developments have contributed to bring New York into the circle of international money markets and have raised the question whether the star of financial supremacy is not to move westward from the precincts of Lombard Street to our own chief city." [25]

The American loans to Britain coincided with other events which made J. Pierpont Morgan an object of popular curiosity and imagination. He loomed as a sort of financial wizard, simultaneously making loans to other nations, organizing the Steel Trust, buying British ships to organize still another trust, acquiring Europe's art treasures and mingling with its kings. The man's appetite was apparently insatiable—Gargantuan! In European eyes Morgan personified the "American menace" to Old World industry and art, while in England they asked plaintively, "Where will he stop?" All of which created chuckles of delight. "Great man, J. P. Morgan," said Senator Mark Hanna. "No telling where he'll stop. I wouldn't be surprised to hear he was getting up a syndicate to buy the British Empire. It isn't safe as long as he's over there." [26]

But there were aspects to financial expansion other than delight in the "Morganization" of Europe. There was the unpleasant aspect of colonial war waged by American troops in the Philippines, which the financial community accepted as the price of carrying "the white man's burden," the *Bankers' Magazine* complacently declaring:

"Nations whose citizens have large interests abroad must necessarily encounter many difficulties, which may sometimes be settled by diplomacy, but which frequently can only be overcome by force of arms. The employment of armies naturally drifts into what is called conquest.... The United States, having become a lender of its surplus resources, must follow the methods which such development requires, and it has the advantage of the experience of other nations." [27]

But this imperialistic complacence was not shared by all the American people. There were many who remembered the traditional American policy (when the United States was neither a creditor nation nor a colonial power) of encouraging international freedom and the struggles of oppressed peoples against their oppressors. Shamed by a brutal colonial war these Americans, clinging to older ideals, declined to accept the fact that an imperialistic nation on the make could not afford to be squeamish—any more than the magnates of industry and finance. War against the Filipinos meant fulfilling "manifest imperial destiny"—don't be soreheads!

Imperialism and the Philippines shared honors with the trusts as issues in the 1900 presidential campaign. William Jennings Bryan emphasized anti-imperialism, although he prevented probable rejection of the Philippine annexation treaty by inducing several Democratic senators to vote in its favor. In answer to the claim that colonial expansion was unconstitutional a general retorted: "We have outgrown the Constitution... and it is not worth while to discuss it."[28] (The Supreme Court settled the issue by declaring expansion constitutional.) Bryan's opposition to imperialism was hampered by the fact that Democratic as well as Republican businessmen desired new markets, among them cotton merchants in the South. The Democrats' opposition to imperialism was parochial, characteristic of the ideology of small businessmen who cannot see beyond their noses—objecting to imperialism in Asia but favoring it nearer home in the Caribbeans. Anti-imperialism fell flat. Nor was the campaign as vituperative in its expression of class antagonisms as in 1896. The Spanish-American War blunted the clash of class against class, "reconciled" East and West, and, according to financial opinion, produced "an era of national good feeling."[29] Business was prosperous, the farmers favored by higher prices and not in a radical mood, Mark Hanna satisfied labor with declamations on the "full dinner pail," and in general people preferred not to be disturbed. Bryan was overwhelmingly beaten.

The years 1890-1900 constituted a transition period during which concentrated capitalism and finance conquered power, emphasized by colonial expansion and overwhelming Republican victory in the presidential election.

But financial supremacy did not come to New York. Foreign loans almost ceased being floated in the United States, the export of capital becoming dominantly the direct investments of American business in Canada, Latin America and Asia, in the form of enterprises owned by American corporations, particularly oil, mines and other natural resources. Active imperialism limited itself to the Caribbeans and the Philippines, although issuing a challenge to Europe in China and preparing for the future. Instead of making New York the world's money market, American finance, under leadership of the House of Morgan, proceeded to consolidate, combine and recapitalize industry, establishing more firmly the foundations of industrial concentration and financial control.

CHAPTER XXI

OVERTONES: 1901

> *"What was that?" inquired Alice.*
> *"Reeling and Writhing, of course, to be-*
> *gin with," the Mock Turtle replied; "and*
> *then the different branches of Arithmetic—*
> *Ambition, Distraction, Uglification and De-*
> *rision."*
>
> ALICE IN WONDERLAND

THE new century! ...

After glorifying the old century's "achievements in science and in civilization" a speaker at New York City's celebration said: "I express the earnest wish that the crowning glory of the coming century shall be the lifting up of the burdens of the poor, and peace and good will."[1] ... The New York *Tribune* greeted the new century with a cartoon picturing the old as a hag flying away accompanied by the bats of superstition, religious intolerance, ignorance, slavery and war.[2] ... In China and the Philippines colonial war was being waged upon an outraged people. ... Prof. Simon Patten lamented that economic changes had "not advanced wages nor relieved misery" as much as anticipated.[3] ... In New York City's sweatshops men and women toiled ten to twenty hours a day for starvation wages.[4] ... The anthracite coal miners were recovering from the recent strike, in the course of which 2,000 child strikers demonstrated, one-third of them boys of eight to ten years forced into the mines by their fathers' low wages.[5] ... J. Pierpont Morgan was asked to consolidate some enterprises in Boston, bought the Mannheim collection of 241 antique objects, and the relics of Marie Antoinette, including her fan and a lock of her hair set in crystal.[6] ... At the Paris Exposition models of American warships attracted attention—"since the

Spanish-American War Europe has a great respect for the
U. S. Navy." [7] ... Asked what he thought he could do with an
education, one student replied: "The degree of Harvard College is worth money to me in Chicago." [8] ... New York City
was in the midst of one of its perpetual campaigns against
corruption and vice, against the alliance of crime, politics and
business—the same conditions flourishing in most large cities. [9]
... Within two weeks of the new century's birth they lynched
a Negro out in Kansas after dragging him from jail:

MOB: Don't hurt him! We'll burn him! (*To Negro*)—
Confess!

NEGRO (*steadily*): I am innocent!

MOB: You lie! (*One huge fellow strikes the Negro three
times in the forehead.*) Confess!

NEGRO: My God, men, I have told you that I am innocent.
I can't tell you any more!

MOB: He lies! Burn him! (*After the Negro is burned, the
crowd scrambles for relics—bits of charred flesh, pieces of
chain, scraps of wood, anything.*) [10]

Mrs. William Astor greeted the new century with a magnificent ball patronized by 600 of the élite, receiving "alone in
the drawing-room, which was decorated with mauve orchids
in golden vases. Mrs. Astor has continued to wield the only
scepter possible in a democratic country—that of womanly
kindliness, refinement, discretion and tact." [11] ... William Wal-
dorf Astor had just been compelled to retire as director in
American banks owing to renunciation of his citizenship and
acceptance of a British title. [12] ... J. Pierpont Morgan's daughter
Louisa received a marriage settlement of $1,000,000 (plus gifts
of a tiara and collar of diamonds)—a squad of police had to
keep the crowd in order at the wedding. [13] ... John D. Rockefeller greeted the new century by distributing gold pieces (not
silver dimes) among "the railwaymen, expressmen and others
who help him during the year; to the help on his place, the
minister and the sexton of the Baptist Church" (which also re-

ceived $2,000 for improvements).[14] ... At the Woman's College
of Baltimore they burlesqued Consuelo Vanderbilt's marriage
to the Duke of Marlborough amid decorations of cabbage heads
draped in ribbons and "choir boys" in kimonos:

BISHOP: Dukey, wilt thou have this woman to be thy beloved wife? Wilt thou love her, honor her, board her, lodge
her, so long as ye both shall live?

DUKE: You bet!

BISHOP: Consy, wilt thou take this man to be thy dearly
beloved? Wilt thou serve him, disobey, scold and rule him
until he dies?

CONSUELO: Yum, yum.[15]

Feeble stuff! There is suspicion that the girls thrilled to the
aristocratic aura in spite of the mockery—they mocked, but
they loved. American aristocratic marriages provided their own
burlesque. Consider an aftermath of Jay Gould's illegitimate
millions. In November, 1900, George J. Gould secured a court
order appointing him trustee for his sister, Anna Gould, who
four years previously married Count Boni de Castellane. She
received a dowry of at least $3,000,000 and an income of
$600,000 yearly, all of which the Franco-American aristocrats
spent in four years plus debts of $4,485,000—Count Boni's
theory being that acceptance by Parisian society depended upon
"amazing" the aristocracy with lavish expenditures.[16]

The economic changes producing the House of Morgan also
produced changes in the American aristocracy. Henry Clews
wrote:

"In the United States Nature's nobility is at the front, as
against the parchment nobility of England and the Continent.
The English nobility makes a sorry showing beside our
wealthy Americans. The modern nobility springs from success
in business." [17]

The glory of self-flattery! But the older aristocracy of money
went high-hat and bolted its doors against the newly rich.
That dynamic phantom, Henry Adams, bitingly observed:

"Setting aside the few, like Pierpont Morgan, whose social position had little to do with greater or less wealth ... scarcely any of the very rich men held any position in society by virtue of his wealth, or could have been elected to any office, or even into a good club." [18] The parvenus of yesterday contemptuously declined the company of the newer parvenus. After all, money was so common, so plentiful, growing like manna in the desert.

Industrial revolution transformed the nation, an immense constructive accomplishment on the basis of which clever and predatory men accumulated large fortunes. These fortunes represented tribute upon economic progress; few fortunes were acquired by ordinary producers, or by scientists, inventors, engineers and technicians whose work was at the basis of the industrial revolution. In Wall Street they said: "It's the third or fourth man who cleans up on inventions"—not the inventors, few of whom acquired fortunes (or even received decent payment).

Separate the constructive and the predatory aspects of large fortunes, and the predatory dominates overwhelmingly. They expropriated the public domain—government records are full of cases of fraud and theft. They plundered the nation's natural resources, recklessly and wastefully. They sold tainted food to the people, and to soldiers in the Spanish-American War. They captured the places where wealth produced by others could be intercepted and accumulated. Circumstance often meant fortune. Vegetating on their ancestral acres, farmers became suddenly rich (the work of Providence, in Sunday School mythology) by the growth of population and cities or the discovery of oil and minerals. Speculators plundered corporations, manipulated the stock market, engineered "corners" in the grain and produce exchanges. They crushed competitors, oppressed labor, juggled law. Businessmen extorted millions out of government and politicians blackmailed businessmen. In the larger cities the "community of interest" between vice, crime and politics produced many respectable fortunes (at least one of which became "aristocratic" by buying a castle in Britain). The money was there to get: they got it. And how they loved it! Cornelius Vanderbilt left most of his money to William and the other children threatened suit. William H. Vanderbilt compromised by personally delivering $500,000 to each of his sisters. One of the husbands said to Vanderbilt:

"William, these bonds fall $150 short of the $500,000, according to the closing prices of this day's market."

Laughing sardonically, Vanderbilt gave a check for the balance. The husband of another sister said:

"By the way, if you conclude to give the other sisters any more, you'll see that we fare as well as any of them, won't you?"

"Well, what do you think o' that!" said Vanderbilt.[19]

Most of the rich men were "big" because of the mighty economic forces represented by their fortunes. "I am more than a little puzzled to account for the instances I have seen of business success—money-getting," said Charles Francis Adams. "I have known, and known tolerably well, a good many 'successful' men—'big' financially—men famous during the last half century; and a less interesting crowd I do not care to encounter. Not one that I have ever known would I care to meet again, either in this world or the next; nor is one of them associated in my mind with the idea of humor, thought or refinement. A set of mere money-getters and traders, they were essentially unattractive and uninteresting."[20] Unattractive, yes, although some of the buccaneers were very engaging persons; but uninteresting, not wholly, since they contributed to organizing a new economic system, represented a cycle of civilization. The Adams criticism, moreover, was couched in the spirit of the old agrarian-mercantile aristocracy which industrialism overwhelmed—but were the progenitors of Adams' aristocracy "men of humor, thought and refinement"? The origins of any aristocracy are uncouth and unlovely, predatory: out of feudal banditry arose the European aristocracy.

Money was aristocracy now. But money was *so* plentiful, and there were so many new millionaires, of whom the old millionaires did not approve socially. An aristocracy likes to feel itself exclusive, although it never is, the newer aristocrats always conquering or absorbing the older. The feeling developed that money's not enough, and it began to make an important social difference whether money was acquired ancestrally or contemporaneously. They gilded the lily of money, acquiring distinctions other than money (money buying the distinctions).

Some acquired ancestors, which is an easy thing to acquire.

Others bought titles for their daughters (a few choosing expatriation and complete identification with the European aristocracy). Aristocratic marriages became a football in the game of social prestige.

Mrs. William Astor erected social spike-fences, ruling the élite of the "Four Hundred" under the tutelage of Ward Mc-Allister who started by fawning upon the aristocracy of money and then bullied its women socially.

All competed in aristocratic splurges—buying mansions, equipages, livery and art.

The trappings of culture are indispensable to aristocracy. Millions were acquired overnight: why not culture? The aristocracy of money transformed its mansions into art galleries, plundering Europe of its paintings and sculptures, its furniture and tapestries, occasionally transporting castles stone by stone and re-erecting them in the American scene. They sat in the chairs of royalty, these pretenders to aristocracy, admired royal decorations, slept in beds formerly slept in by kings and their concubines. Characteristic was Henry C. Frick "in his palace, seated on a Renaissance throne under a baldacchino and holding in his little hand a copy of the *Saturday Evening Post.*" [21]

Majesty overwhelming! Below, in the depths, was the stupefy-ing bric-à-brac art of stuffy middle-class homes.

Collecting art signified aristocratic distinction. Old Junius Morgan was an art patron, and J. Pierpont Morgan started collecting in his youth. William H. Vanderbilt, while miserly, spent large sums on his private art gallery, in which, how-ever, no nudes were permitted by the impeccably moral mil-lionaire. Vanderbilt's artistic ideals are revealed by the fact that "he did not continue to make a collection of Ameri-can pictures after he had come into possession of his fortune, since he was able to buy the *best and most costly* in the world." [22]

The craze for art afflicted all the millionaires. They com-bined in 1893 to finance the meretricious magnificence of the Chicago World's Fair, where Morgan, striding through the Palace of Fine Arts, unfeelingly said that the French exhibits must have been selected by chambermaids,[23] and the directors talked as though art "was a stage decoration, a diamond shirt-stud, a paper collar." [24] (Yet there were in the Fair flashes of artistic promise most of which never flowered, but the Fair started ragtime on its conquest of the world!)

Most of the millionaires displayed deplorable taste, buying art as they bought stocks, bonds, politicians and business enter-prises. Morgan's taste was much finer—unimpeachable within its museum limits. His agents ransacked Europe systematically, organizing the search for art as he organized trusts. By 1900 Morgan's collections were extraordinary, and kept on growing: paintings, sculptures, books, manuscripts, autographs, antiqui-ties, miniatures, watches, tankards, spoons, church ornaments, porcelains, tapestries—all the raw material of splendid mu-seums, an accumulation of art "worth" $50,000,000.[25] It was useful to build up American museums, to make available for study the cultural heritage of Europe. But museums are simply the curators of culture, not the creators of culture.

The sentimental, almost romantic streak in Morgan, which

he otherwise repressed, manifested itself wantonly in the splendor and magnificence of his art collections. The magnificence of these ornaments of an older aristocracy! The splendor of having them for the buying! It yielded Morgan immeasurable delights; and while he appraised with the cold eye of the businessman, he bought in the spirit of the playboy at liberty to express himself. In one of the imposing rooms of an old castle was a gorgeous tapestry, which James Stillman hesitated to buy because of the price:

STILLMAN (*slowly*): I suppose I oughtn't to, but it's a great temptation.

MORGAN (*gaily*): Always resist everything, Stillman, except temptation.[26]

Nor did Morgan resist feminine temptation. The man who, in youth, defied death for the sake of love, now plucked women as the spoils of power. The masters of money (with exceptions, among them moral John D.) sported women as they sported money and art. "Self-made" men acquired women of the "great world," discarding the wives of their years of struggle, as in the case of one of the Steel Trust presidents whose actress-wife despoiled him of millions and then used the money in efforts to make a European noble marriage. Those born to the purple acquired seraglios in the style of Renaissance merchant princes, imitated by the "self-made" millionaires. There were many women in Morgan's life, beauty and youth becoming jewels in the crown of power. The affairs were in the grand style, grandly scornful of what people might say. There was never any scandal—Morgan awed his women, and he was generous. He pensioned them, married them off, found them husbands (who were delighted, apparently, to marry a discarded Morgan mistress)—in the manner of the kings of old.

The mastery of money, art, women—*there* was power, splendor, magnificence, the love of which led a witty English archbishop to nickname Morgan "Pierpontifex Maximus." He did things in the grand style, bought grandly, lived grandly, driven

by a nostalgia for the grandeur of the older aristocracy of
blood and iron: of all European cities Morgan felt most at
home in the grandeur that is Rome,[27] and he died there. ...

There were many aspects to the plunder of European art by
American millionaires. It responded to temperament. It as-
suaged an emptiness of life. It expressed contemporary civilization in glorifying things (except that art things possessed an
aura of aristocracy). Curiously mingling the magnificent, pathetic and clownish, the acquisition of art treasures meant, essentially, the new aristocracy identifying itself with the older
aristocratic traditions and trappings, separating itself from the
multitude, acquiring the glory of exclusive cultural gilt.

But however ornamental gilt is, it is not culture. Culture is
dynamic, not ornamental, the vital urge to live and create. Art
collections adorned the masters of money, but beneath was
an emptiness of creative cultural life, the scars inflicted on
nature by ruthless exploitation, the squalid factory towns, New
York City's vile slums, Pittsburgh's steel hells, Chicago's
smelly braggadocio, Boston's cobwebby culture. Before the
Civil War there had been the beginnings of an American
culture; it was crushed by feverish, unregulated industrialism.
Where John Pierpont urged finer ideals of life, J. Pierpont
Morgan collected museum pieces. The aristocracy did not encourage American artists, preferring the thrill of contact with
the dead artists patronized by an older aristocracy. Meanwhile
American culture drooped, but the aristocracy sported mu-
seums in its mansions.

If acquiring art treasures constituted its culture, the aristocracy of money's *noblesse oblige* was philanthropy. They all
gave to the church, naturally, since the dominant religion of
the Old Testament sanctified the predatory and acquisitive
impulses. By 1900 philanthropy was an indispensable item in
the aristocracy's budget. Men who plucked with the right hand
distributed philanthropic largesse with the left. It was not the
generous giving of George Peabody, much more calculating

and businesslike. "The rich are blind," said **Abram S. Hewitt**, millionaire philanthropist. "There is not one among them who is giving what he would give if his conscience were properly aroused. The rich in contributing are but building for *their own protection*. If they neglect so to build, barbarism, anarchy and plunder will be the inevitable result." [28] The Rockefellers calculatingly used philanthropy to influence public opinion, transforming John D. from the hyena of yesterday into the "grand old man" of to-day.

The philanthropic impulse was apparently alien to Morgan, and he scorned the hypocrisy of cultivating public opinion by means of philanthropy. He made generous religious gifts— $4,500,000 to the Cathedral of St. John the Divine, $300,000 to St. George's Church (of which Morgan was a warden) and $100,000 to the Y. M. C. A., in addition to many secular contributions and art gifts.[29] But Morgan was an inconsiderable philanthropist in comparison with Rockefeller and Carnegie, not having their peculiar desire for "good works."

While having no peculiar desire for "good works," Morgan loved the Church, its ceremonial majesty and medieval grandeur. The incense of the Church, wafted up to the mighty of heaven, is also incense for the mighty of earth. Morgan lavishly entertained Church dignitaries (in spite of their gibes at "Pierpontifex Maximus"), and he repeatedly greeted European prelates coming to the United States. The Church represented neither piety nor morality to Morgan—simply an appanage of aristocracy.

Culture and philanthropy constituted the ornamental façade of substantial power—the control of a mighty nation's immense economic resources. Capitalism had conquered the old order after forty years of industrial progress, ruthless exploitation and social war, out of which emerged the world's most efficient and powerful economic system. The multiplication of goods and comforts improved standards of living in all levels of society, although very unevenly. Yet, by and large, human values were suppressed in favor of money values, acquisition and accumulation being the dominant ideals sanctified by religion, morality and custom. In greeting the new century a clergyman insisted: "Wealth concentrated in the hands of the very rich is not such a public calamity as a great many seem to think. They must use their money for the public good." [30] Exactly what the Rev. Joseph Morgan said in 1732 ("A rich Man is a great friend to the Publick, while he aims at nothing but serving himself") and Samuel J. Tilden in 1877 ("Men of colossal fortunes are in effect, if not in fact, trustees for the public"). In this civilization progress only incidentally meant social improvement, the liberation of life: it meant ownership, money and power, ideals oppressing the prospector in the wilderness, the farmer on his farm, the worker in the factory, the storekeeper in village and town, and the master of the House of Morgan. In terms of power American capitalism now aspired after an imperial destiny.

On the issue of imperial destiny William McKinley was overwhelmingly re-elected to the presidency. He said: "I observe that majorities rise with prosperity and that the American people never fail to support the flag." [31] ... The day after McKinley's victory enthusiasm raged on the New York Stock Exchange, speculators celebrated by forcing up prices, and men, women and children came "to see the fun." [32] ... Venezuela threatened to disposses American asphalt concessionaires, and the Secretary of State acted to protect American rights. [33] ... In China the Powers indulged an orgy of "massacre, rapine, loot and destruction of villages—in the name of Christian civilization," said the New York *Times*. [34] The United States, associated with the Powers, protested against the barbarism, acted as a moderating force and prevented the dismemberment of China by insistence on the "Open Door" (which favored American interests)....In the Philippines American troops waged colonial war in the usual fashion against the rebels insisting on independence. "Damn, damn, damn the Fili-

pinos!" sang the civilizing troops. First Lieutenant Griffith
wrote home: "We had one killed and two wounded, while the
enemy fared much worse. We took no prisoners. We have absolutely no respect for the Filipinos in any way; they will lie,
steal, stab you in the back, but will not stand up and fight.
One good solution of the trouble would be to turn loose about
3,000 American Indians here." Soldiers sang:

> *"Underneath the starry flag,*
> *Civilize 'em with a Krag!"* [35]

PART SIX

STEEL—MORGANIZING INDUSTRY

CHAPTER XXII

INDUSTRIAL AND FINANCIAL COMBINATION

*"Don't talk nonsense," said Alice; "you
know you're growing too."
"Yes, but I grow at a reasonable pace,"
said the Dormouse, "not in that ridiculous
fashion."*

ALICE IN WONDERLAND

COMPLEX developments are simple in origin. The Morganization of industry and finance arose out of improvements in
technology, in the methods of producing and distributing
goods. Inventions and engineering constituted a spiraling force
continuously disturbing the economic equilibrium, destroying
old industries and creating new ones, multiplying the production of goods and broadening national and international markets, increasing the size of industrial enterprises, compelling
the introduction of new industrial and financial institutions
and relationships. The inventor's gadgets and the engineer's
technique prepared the complex economic changes which
transformed modes of living, instigated social and colonial
wars, and forged the supremacy of industrial and financial
combinations. J. Pierpont Morgan, in the institutionalized operations of his banking house, was the multiplied, concentrated
expression of all these forces.

The distinguishing feature of modern industry is the machine. Machinery crushed the handicrafts (arousing the artisans' protest) and then machinery began to war upon machinery. Inventions and improvements made old machines
obsolete, and the new machines, being more expensive, required more capital and larger plants. Manufacturers combined
their plants and capital in corporations, which aroused the

protest of independent petty producers. Corporate industry and continuously improving technology increased the output of goods faster than the increase in the purchasing power of markets. Increasing competition for sales was waged by productive efficiency cheapening the price of goods, but this often meant lowering profit margins disastrously. Some enterprises failed, others enlarged their size, and still others combined. Small producers declaimed furiously against combinations (although themselves always on the alert to increase the size of their own enterprises). But the profits of combinations, which lessened but did not destroy competition, invited the investment of capital in new competitive enterprises or more efficient machinery, again increasing the output of goods. Competition flared up disastrously, profits declined, and combinations of combinations (trusts) developed to restrict competition more completely and insure profits. All business enterprises grew in size, but unevenly, some more than others, embittering competition and developing war against combinations.

Restricting competition, not improving efficiency, was the primary purpose in organizing trusts, accomplished by either buying out competitors or crushing them by merciless competition and unscrupulous predatory tactics. Standard Oil, the first trust organized in 1882, was particularly notorious for restricting competition and crushing competitors. Another purpose was to secure the large profits accruing to promoters of trusts. In organizing the Standard Distilling & Distributing Co., for example, the underwriters, for each $100,000 cash advanced to buy plants, received $250,000 in stock and the promoters another $150,000.[1] All the trusts (except Standard Oil) were heavily overcapitalized, six-fold in some cases, owing chiefly to the immense profits of promotion and the excessive prices paid to acquire plants. Overcapitalization was usually made good by monopoly prices. The predatory aspects of the trust aroused antagonisms, but they were not decisive, the

movement of combination being determined by the technological and financial facts of an inescapable concentration of
industry.

The House of Morgan did not engage actively in the early
trust and combination movement. It was, however, among the
organizers of the General Electric Co. in 1892, J. P. Morgan
and Charles H. Coster (a Morgan partner) being directors
and three other members of Drexel, Morgan & Co. trustees of
the new corporation. General Electric, co-operating harmoniously with the Westinghouse Electric Co., dominated the electric industry.[2] When the National Cordage Co (Cordage
Trust, in control of 90 per cent of the industry) crashed in 1893
owing largely to its speculative, marauding management which
paid a heavy cash dividend in the very month of insolvency,
Morgan, a substantial stockholder, participated in the company's reorganization.[3] There were important financial interests and directorships in other industrial corporations (including Western Union Telegraph). But railroads were still the
most inviting object of financial control, owing to their demoralization and the almost complete separation of ownership
and management, and the House of Morgan concentrated on
carving out its railroad empire, penetration and control of
industry being only in the preparatory stages. Others pioneered industrial combination.

In spite of the immense antagonisms and struggles they
aroused, there were by 1897 only eighty-two industrial combinations with an aggregate capitalization slightly in excess of
$1,000,000,000.[4] Declared illegal in their original form of com-
binations of separate corporations the stock of which was vested
in and voted by a board of trustees, the trusts evaded the law
by reorganizing as single corporations owning the plants or
stock of affiliated enterprises. But public and legislative antagonism persisted, trusts being stigmatized as extortionate, concentrating opportunity and wealth, and a menace to republican
institutions. The organization of new trusts was discouraged

by this antagonistic mood and by the depression following the 1893 panic, when many trusts shivered or crashed owing to their overcapitalization and plundering managements.

But the discouragement was temporary. William McKinley's election to the presidency strengthened the dominant industrial and financial interests, prosperity revived in 1897, accumulation of capital and speculation developed feverishly, and corporate combination assumed overwhelming proportions. In the one year 1898 combinations were formed with an aggregate capitalization of $916,000,000 [5]—almost equal to the capitalization of all previously organized combinations. By 1900 a Congressional Industrial Commission reported that "industrial combinations have become fixtures in our business life" and urged that "their power for evil should be destroyed and their power for good preserved"—regulation instead of extermination.[6]

Railroads being now largely reorganized, stabilized and under definite financial control, Morgan prepared for new conquests. The House of Morgan was the most active agency in the combination movement which swept American industry after 1898 and assured the supremacy of concentrated capitalism.

The basic industry of steel flourished after the revival of prosperity, while the Spanish-American War and the Boer War created large demands for iron and steel. Prices increased two-fold and output three-fold. The dominant factor in the steel industry was Andrew Carnegie, whose company was the largest, most integrated, and completely independent of financial control. Carnegie was a merciless competitor and the smaller concerns consolidated in order to compete. In the three years 1898-1900 there were eleven consolidations in iron and steel, representing an aggregate capitalization of $1,140,000,000 and setting the pace for other industrial combinations.[7]

At this time the House of Morgan's only direct participation in the steel industry was through two directorships in the Illinois Steel Co. and the Minnesota Iron Co.[8] In 1897 John W. Gates approached J. P. Morgan & Co. with a proposal to combine wire and nail manufacturers, which was accepted and then rejected owing to the outbreak of the Spanish-American War and the poor financial showing of the companies to be consolidated.[9] Then in 1898 Morgan organized the Federal Steel Co., making the House of Morgan a dominant (but not dominating) factor in the iron and steel industry.

The Illinois Steel Co. felt itself menaced by the competition of Andrew Carnegie, who believed neither in "community of interest" nor in pooling agreements but in competitive war to the limit—and competition in the iron and steel industry *was* war, unscrupulous, ferocious and devastating. Carnegie's company had not only the advantage of size but of integration (in control of all stages of manufacture from raw materials to finished products), particularly in iron-ore resources. Illinois Steel depended completely upon others for ores and fuel and was also weak in transportation. The proposal was made to J. P. Morgan & Co. to consolidate the Illinois Steel Co., the Minnesota Iron Co., and the Lorain Steel Co., in order to produce an integrated combination capable of competing with Andrew Carnegie.[10] Morgan accepted the proposal.

Robert Bacon, director in two of the companies to be consolidated, and Elbert H. Gary directed the organization of the new combination. J. P. Morgan & Co. acquired the stock of the constituent companies and sold it to the newly organized Federal Steel Co., capitalized at $200,000,000 (half issued).[11] Gary was elected president and among the directors were J. P. Morgan and Robert Bacon.[12] There were also representatives of Standard Oil interests on the board (they had been in control of the Minnesota Iron Co.),[13] but Federal Steel was a Morgan company. The new combination, an integrated enterprise, owned its sources of ore and fuel, plants, ships and railroads.[14] As in the case of all industrial combinations, Federal Steel engaged in an aggressive campaign for export markets.

The House of Morgan strengthened its power in the steel industry by promoting two other consolidations—the monopolistic National Tube Co. and the American Bridge Co., capitalized at $80,000,000 and $70,000,000 respectively.[15] Itself a formidable combination and financially affiliated by means of J. P. Morgan & Co. with National Tube and American Bridge, the Federal Steel Co. was able to bludgeon the Carnegie Steel Co. into a pooling agreement as equals[16]—an illegal agreement.

Large profits accrued to the House of Morgan from these consolidations. Testifying before the Industrial Commission, President Gary declared that Federal Steel paid only the "comparatively small sum" of $200,000 commission to J. P. Morgan & Co.[17] That was the cash payment. But there were two other sources of profit. The House of Morgan owned the majority stock of the corporations to be consolidated, and there was a profit on the sale of this stock to the Federal Steel Co.[18] In return for supplying $4,800,000 cash and their services the Morgan syndicate, moreover, received a block of Federal Steel stock on which the probable profit was $4,450,000.[19] In the National Tube and American Bridge promotions the Morgan syndicate received $27,500,000 in stock of the new corporations in payment of services.[20]

These profits were not unusual. Fifteen combinations organized in 1899 paid up to 20 per cent of their capitalization to promoters.[21] Immense overcapitalization (up to 65 per cent)[22] was produced by capitalizing bonuses to interests being consolidated, promoters' profits and prospective earnings. Yet such was the speculative enthusiasm of investors, the accumulation of investment capital produced by increasing profits and concentration of income, and the earning power of combinations that the "watered" stock sold usually at very good prices.

Although president of Illinois Steel (for the quaint reason that "it was safer to have him in the concern than out")[23] John W. Gates was not included in the Federal Steel combina-

JOHN W. GATES

JAMES STILLMAN

tion. Several directors refused to serve with him while Morgan felt that "property is not safe in his hands." [24] Flamboyant, stooping to all means in the pursuit of money, an unscrupulous manipulator of corporate property, Gates resembled the man with whom Morgan had clashed in the old days —Jim Fisk. This inveterate gambler (his favorite expression was "bet you a million") was extraordinarily resourceful, as is shown by the first step he took up the ladder of business success. While salesman for a barbed-wire concern Gates secured so many orders that he decided to start a plant of his own to fill them. He did—in violation of the duty to his employers and of patent rights. An injunction being issued against him, Gates moved the plant beyond its jurisdiction. Unable to outwit the resourceful Gates, his employers decided to license him as a legitimate manufacturer [25] ... and within a few years John W. Gates dominated the barbed-wire industry. Contemptuously shoved out of Federal Steel by his former associates, "Bet-you-a-million" Gates organized another consolidation, the American Steel & Wire Co., which yielded him an unusually large promoter's profit. But apparently the resourceful Gates manipulated another promoter out of his share of the profits, being sued on the claim of violation of agreement. It transpired at the trial that part of the new combination's stock was missing, and A. G. Fox, plaintiff's counsel, asked John W. Gates about it:

Fox: The testimony shows that $26,000,000 of the $90,000,000 of the Steel Wire Company's stock is missing. What became of it?

GATES: I don't know.

Fox: Have you got any of it?

GATES: No, I never got a cent's worth of it. [26]

This was characteristic. The corporate situation invited the manipulations of men such as John W. Gates—and they were legion. Corporation clashed against corporation, stockholders were scattered, helpless and functionally unnecessary, owner-

ship, management and control separated. The task of combination was assumed by cliques which manipulated things to their
own profit. This aroused even businessmen who believed in
the "let alone" policy to admit that measures were necessary
to protect stockholders.[27] Most of the promoters flitted from
enterprise to enterprise, speculating, plundering, building up
nothing permanent—except their own swollen fortunes.

But neither stockholders nor promoters' profits were decisive
factors in the combination movement. In his railroad reorganizations and industrial combinations Morgan extorted all
the profit there was, naturally. The movement itself, however,
was determined by more fundamental economic forces. Competition, efficiency and integration compelled concentration
and concentration compelled combination. Large-scale combinations could not be organized without the banks and investment houses mobilizing the necessary financial resources. Industry depended upon finance. Starting in the local banks,
the influence of finance over industry converged upward and
concentrated in the great financial houses—accumulating investment resources, supplying capital and credit to industry,
reconciling antagonistic interests, imposing a measure of centralized direction and control.

J. Pierpont Morgan was not a financial wizard but chief
of a financial general staff. The man was neither brilliant nor
speculative in temper, in spite of that little gold corner during
the Civil War, his characteristics being overwhelming self-
confidence, the passion for order, an almost mastiff-like clinging to objectives, and the merciless driving energy of supreme
organizing talent—the broadsword and not the rapier. Morgan
operated in military terms—carefully worked-out campaigns,
massed movements, an irresistible concentration of money at
the decisive point and moment. (His massive, unimaginative
character, however, made him a better tactician than strategist,
explaining his Union Pacific and other mistakes.) Mathe-
matically inclined, Morgan was uncannily adept in the statistics

of finance, swiftly mastering the essential figures in any proposition. He hated disorder, competition, division of authority,
and manipulated the financial resources of others as if they
were his own. Morgan was a supreme organizer and ruler,
precisely the man to institutionalize the developing financial
mechanism of concentrated capitalism.

At the basis of Morgan's towering structure of financial
control was the investment house of J. P. Morgan & Co., private
bankers and as such independent of government supervision.
While the firm could not issue banknotes or receive government deposits, it was under none of the restrictions imposed
on commercial banks and other financial institutions. J. P.
Morgan & Co. were a partnership usually composed of twelve
partners and the master (the ribald in Wall Street spoke of
"Jesus Christ and the Twelve Apostles") unified in the majority interest and dynamic personality of J. Pierpont Morgan.

Sagacious in his judgments of men, using men whom
he despised, Morgan was usually hard-boiled in the choice of
partners—except for the soft, almost sentimental streak which
insisted on cropping out in spite of stern repression by the burly
master of money. It expressed itself in the interview with James
Stillman when the strong, silent man, with his eternal big
black cigar, almost wept. It expressed itself in the curious liking
for good-looking young men, many an incompetent crashing
the gates of the House of Morgan on his looks. "When the
angels of God took unto themselves wives among the daughters of men," they said in Wall Street, "the result was the
Morgan partners." [28] This preference for Greek gods as partners was often unfortunate, particularly in the case of Robert
Bacon, whose masculine beauty conquered women but was
helpless against financial wolves. In spite of this weakness
(or idiosyncrasy) Morgan was uncannily lucky in his choice
of partners—from Charles H. Dabney and the Drexels to
Charles H. Coster, Egisto P. Fabbri (an Italian financial
genius), George S. Bowdoin, J. Hood Wright and others.

Wright came with Drexel & Co. in 1871. Coster became a partner in 1884, devoting himself to railroad reorganization; he was a director in fifty-nine corporations, and completely absorbed in business.[29] Morgan secured their unfaltering loyalty and co-operation, energizing and mercilessly driving them (and himself). The life of the Morgan partners was short, if not precisely merry: by 1900 they were all dead, the men who had helped build up the House of Morgan by their organizing talent and capacity for team-work under their chief, most of them worn out by the terrific strain.[30]

The work of J. P. Morgan & Co. was completely departmentalized. One partner devoted himself to finance, another to railroads, each according to his particular talent. All of the partners held numerous directorships in enterprises under the control or influence of the House of Morgan, as did the master himself. From the offices in Wall Street radiated a thick network of relationships representing financial control of the most important aspects of American economic life. Policy was always determined by Morgan himself, and his overwhelming impulse for domination made him supervise even petty details. At least once a year Morgan went to Europe, and his partners were under orders to cable him on all transactions involving over $5,000,000 and on all matters of policy.[31] By cable came Morgan's decisions. The master insisted on retaining his mastery.

In addition to their major investment operations J. P. Morgan & Co. dealt extensively in foreign exchange, received deposits from corporations in which they were interested, and did a general banking business. As investment operations assumed larger and larger dimensions the House of Morgan multiplied its resources by securing control of commercial banks and other financial institutions. At the time of the bond issue in 1895 it was observed that J. P. Morgan mobilized "the powerful coterie of banks, life insurance and trust companies."[32] These institutions, gathering together the money capital of scattered investors, accumulated immense resources and began to engage in investment operations of their own.

By 1900 all financial institutions were competing for investment business. Commercial banks, although limited by law to commercial transactions, dealt actively in stocks and bonds, and participated in promotions. Trust companies, almost free of any restrictions, participated in investment operations of all sorts, and competed with the investment bankers. Life-insurance companies went into banking, buying control of trust companies and commercial banks, making life-insurance money directly available for the investment business of banking institutions under their control or influence (and often for the speculative promotions of their officers and directors). The rigid separation of functions of financial institutions broke down. In the case of the National City Bank, its aggressive investment operations made it a formidable competitor of investment bankers—underwriting promotions of its own, financing speculative promoters directly, and even engaging in stock-market manipulations. This was considered "banking heresy," departing from the commercial functions imposed upon banks,[33] but it expressed the drift toward concentration of industry, centralization of financial control, and the development of new financial relationships and institutions.

The banks, trust companies and insurance companies constituted the heart of concentrated capitalism, pumping the blood of money and credit into the channels of business. Centralization of functions was completed by centralization of control imposed by dominant investment bankers, who levied upon the resources of all financial institutions, originally by simple co-operation and then more directly by combination and control. The House of Morgan, by stock ownership, affiliation, interlocking directorships and community of interest, concentrated banking and life-insurance resources into an overwhelming money power.

J. P. Morgan & Co. acquired direct control of the National

Bank of Commerce in New York City, of which Morgan himself was vice-president and director. This bank was interlocked with the First National Bank, which always worked harmoniously with the House of Morgan and had representatives and affiliates of the House on its board of directors, including James J. Hill and John A. McCall, president of the New York Life Insurance Co., Morgan being the largest stockholder next to the president, George F. Baker.* [34] With large resources of their own, these Morgan banks penetrated other banks and financial institutions. By means of stock ownership and interlocking directorships the House of Morgan, First National and the Bank of Commerce secured control of the Liberty, Chase, Hanover and Astor National Banks.[35] The influence of this combination radiated to banks outside of New York City: thus J. P. Morgan was a large stockholder in the First National Bank of Chicago, while James J. Hill (an affiliate of the House of Morgan and substantial stockholder in the Baker-Morgan First National Bank of New York) was a stockholder and director in many out-of-town banks.[36]

From control of national banks the House of Morgan proceeded to control of trust companies, which were growing phenomenally, owing to their paralleling the development of corporate industry and being free of the rigid legal restrictions imposed upon State and national banks. Trust companies were soon strong enough to reorganize and finance corporations directly, and by 1900 their resources were as large as those of ordinary banks. The House of Morgan organized its own trust company (the Bankers Trust) some years later, and at this time it was in measurable control of at least five trust companies. First National dominated the Manhattan Trust while J. P. Morgan & Co. were represented by directors in the

* Although comparatively unknown to the general public, George F. Baker was almost as powerful and active an agency in the centralization of industry and finance as J. P. Morgan of whom he was an independent but always cooperating ally, Baker's interests being interlocked with all the more important interests of the House of Morgan.

Morton (which Morgan later merged in his own trust company), Union, Commercial and Fidelity Trusts.[37]

Life-insurance companies constituted another reservoir of financial resources, and two of the most important were dominated by J. P. Morgan & Co. For years the president of the New York Life Insurance Co. had been under Morgan's control, while George W. Perkins, vice-president of the New York Life, retained the posts of trustee and chairman of the finance committee (and a $25,000 salary) after he became a partner in the House of Morgan in 1901.[38] James J. Hill was a director in the Equitable Life,[39] and J. P. Morgan chairman of the finance committee of the Mutual Life, three of whose trustees were directors in Morgan's National Bank of Commerce.[40] This was the period when officers and directors of life insurance companies did pretty much as they pleased, the laws being lax, and prepared the scandals which shocked public opinion a few years later.

The centralization of financial institutions by stock control, interlocking directorates and community of interest was accompanied by an increase in their size and resources. Smaller bankers resented and resisted this development, and their own interests being now endangered they began to speak in Populist strain of the "money power." [41] But banks had to increase their size and resources in order to serve concentrated corporate business. Combination begets combination, and industrial and financial consolidations paralleled each other. Within two years Morgan's National Bank of Commerce consolidated twice and almost tripled its resources.[42]

One aspect of financial centralization was institutionalizing the control of investment resources. The banks and other financial institutions under control of the House of Morgan represented immense resources. This simplified investment operations: in organizing a syndicate Morgan simply allotted subscriptions to institutions under his control and they took them. The mobilization of this massed power of money assured the success of Morgan's promotions.

Another aspect of centralization was institutionalizing the financial control of industry. The House of Morgan held inter-locking directorships in banks, life-insurance and trust com-panies, and these in turn held directorships in each other and in the railroad and industrial combinations under control of the House of Morgan and in which the House held its own directorships. Morgan himself was a director in twenty-one railroads and three insurance companies, in Federal Steel, Gen-eral Electric, Western Union, Pullman Car Co. and other cor-porations.[48] His partners also held scores of directorships (fifty-nine in the case of Charles H. Coster) [44] and still other scores were held by directors in the affiliated enterprises of the House of Morgan.* Interlocking directorates interlocked industry and finance. In this centralization of industry and finance the equilibrium was maintained by the House of Mor-gan in the final authority of J. Pierpont Morgan.

The centralization of industry and finance expressed the increasingly complex network of relationships developed by business enterprise. Roughly, experimentally, predatorily, busi-ness developed the institutional arrangements of centralized direction and control. Financial integration paralleled indus-trial integration. Unrestricted competition threatened to upset the economic equilibrium and compelled combination. Indus-trial and financial enterprises were scattered, their functions separated: centralization combined and unified them. This necessary unification of economic life was a task for conscious social engineering, but it was left to business enterprise, usurped by the investment bankers who acquired an immense power

* An illustration: J. P. Morgan & Co. were directly represented on the board of directors of the Liberty National Bank. In addition four of the directors represented the First National Bank, two the United States Steel Corporation and one the Central Railroad of New Jersey—all of them enterprises under control or influence of the House of Morgan. (*Bankers' Magazine*, September, 1901, p. 435.)

which was used primarily for the production of profits. The plundering aspects of centralization were determined by its unregulated development and the predatory character of business enterprise, not by centralization itself.

The institutional arrangements centralizing industry and finance were being simultaneously developed by all the important investment bankers, but by none on the gigantic scale of the House of Morgan. Standard Oil and its affiliated interests constituted the only rival power.

While the House of Morgan represented finance penetrating industry, Standard Oil represented the transformation of industrial capitalists into financial capitalists. The profits of John D. Rockefeller's monopolistic combination were unbelievably large—in twenty-four years, up to 1906, it paid $548,-436,000 in dividends, for ten years at the rate of 39 per cent.[45] While paying these huge dividends and creating a score of millionaires, Standard Oil built up immense cash resources by retaining a goodly part of the earnings in the business. The Standard and its masters (the Rockefellers, Henry H. Rogers, Oliver H. Payne, William C. Whitney and others) were all speculatively inclined, and of their operations one financier said:

"With them manipulation has ceased to be speculation. Their resources are so vast that they need only to concentrate on any given property to do with it what they please. . . . There is an utter absence of chance that is terrible to contemplate." [46]

Standard Oil was independent of the banks, being itself a great bank with immense cash resources which were used, together with the resources of its masters, to acquire control of other industrial corporations, railroads and financial institutions. The banking interests of the Standard combination converged on the National City Bank of New York. Itself the largest bank in the country, Morgan's Bank of Commerce being second, National City dominated five other banks and a number of life-insurance and trust companies, its aggressive policy of consolidation and expansion setting the pace for other banks.[47] National City combined with the Rockefeller interests, Edward H. Harriman and Kuhn, Loeb & Co. in the Union Pacific reorganization (retaining one-third of the stock), wrested control of their railroads from the decadent progeny of Jay Gould, organized industrial combinations, acquired important foreign affiliations, and developed their own interlocking directorates imposing financial control over industry. Among the directors of the National City Bank were William Rockefeller, Harriman and Jacob Schiff (of Kuhn, Loeb & Co.), co-operating in the struggle for power.[48]

The National City Bank led the movement by which commercial banks assumed the functions of investment institutions. It was accused of "banking heresy" in "departing widely from the pursuits of commerce and lending itself to the uses of the promoter, the financier and even the stock gambler." [49] All of which was true, but couched in terms of the separation of commercial and investment functions prevailing in the older competitive capitalism. The centralization of industry and finance unified functions and operations. James Stillman, the National City president, was as much of an investment banker as commercial, and his system of financial control was comparable to Morgan's. Always grave (he was known as "Sunny Jim" among the bright young men in Morgan's office), Stillman was harsh, saturnine and sardonic,[50] with the touch of cynical indifference which distinguishes the over-civilized man from the more primitive men who become dictators. Stillman might have towered over Morgan under more stabilized conditions, but in an age of transition and rough-and-tumble struggles, out of which dictatorships emerge, Morgan's inbred self-confidence, burly autocratic force and simple lust after power constituted an overwhelming advantage.

By 1900 the Stillman-Rockefeller-Harriman-Schiff combination was almost as powerful as the House of Morgan (and its affiliates, George F. Baker and James J. Hill), Stillman alone being a director in forty-one railroads, industrial corporations, and banks and other financial institutions.[51] There was measurable community of interest between the two groups—Robert Bacon, of J. P. Morgan & Co., was a director in the National City Bank and they met in other enterprises.[52] But there was also definite competition, antagonism and animosity. The Rockefellers were jealous of Morgan's arrogant power and ruffled by his contemptuous dislike (weren't they also, by God, kings of industry and finance?). A man of intense dislikes, Morgan exceedingly disliked the spidery, sanctimonious, moneymaniacal John D. (the sentiment never being disguised), and the dislike was aggravated by the fact that Rockefeller was one of the men Morgan could not bludgeon but must treat as an equal. Prejudices sharpened the struggle for mastery.

The House of Morgan, for a time, was threatened by the Rockefeller-Stillman group, which in 1899 organized the Amalgamated Copper Co. Its financing aroused considerable criticism, the promoters receiving $30,000,000 of the $75,000,000 capital stock, the public buying "in shoals." [53] Amalgamated Copper was one of the larger combinations, an effort at its organization by J. P. Morgan & Co. producing deadlock, after which it was underwritten by the National City Bank, Robert Bacon becoming a director (a concession to community of interest).[54] The Rockefeller-Stillman combination organized other trusts, penetrated public utilities and substantially increased the resources of the National City Bank,[55] all of which appeared to threaten the House of Morgan's dominance. Then Morgan organized the United States Steel Corporation and decided the mastery.

CHAPTER XXIII

STEEL TRUST

"Curiouser and curiouser!" cried Alice.
"Now I'm opening out like the largest tele-
scope that ever was! Good-bye, feet!" (for
when she looked down at her feet, they
seemed to be almost out of sight, they
were getting so far off).

ALICE IN WONDERLAND

ORGANIZATION of the United States Steel Corporation consolidated the supremacy of the House of Morgan in industry and
finance. Decided upon in December, 1900, it was an accomplished fact within four months. The giant corporation logi-
cally emerged out of the iron and steel industry, where output
and concentration were both steadily increasing.[1] Wall Street
financiers had doubted its practicability, the proposed combination, they said, being "so vast as to make it impossible for even
Morgan to finance the operation," and doubts persisted after
the preliminary announcement of plans, although the general
agreement was that only Morgan *could* "swing the deal."[2]
Investors and speculators joyously acclaimed the Steel Trust
while opponents of Morganized capitalism bitterly assailed it
as another monopoly in restraint of trade. British steel magnates were depressed—the United States had not only become
the world's largest producer of iron and steel, it now threatened
Britain's foreign markets, increasing export sales being an
important objective of the United States Steel Corporation.

The idea of this giant combination was not original with
Morgan; urged by others, it grew upon him as changing
conditions compelled action, almost forced upon him, but
when he acted it was swiftly and overwhelmingly.

Instead of peace, consolidation in the steel industry produced the threat of more dangerous competition, as the competitors disposed of larger resources. There were four dominant groups. The Carnegie company was the most powerful, an industrial barony making war on all the others. Morgan trailed Carnegie with Federal Steel, National Tube and American Bridge. The third group was composed of the Tin Plate and three other combinations, heavily overcapitalized enterprises dominated by two brothers, William H. and James H. Moore, notorious and predatory promoters. Finally, the Rockefeller interests were the most important factors in producing and transporting iron ores, owning Lake Superior Consolidated Iron Mines in the Mesabi range, railroads and ships.[3] On the fringe, distrusted by all, was John W. Gates and his American Steel & Wire Co., eager to snatch any stray millions the others might let go. Most of the steel companies were dependent upon Carnegie for crude steel, and none were as integrated and self-sufficient. In trying to become more integrated and independent they threatened each other's interests and particularly the interests of the Carnegie Steel Co. The prevailing equilibrium was unsatisfactory, but to disturb it meant unloosing ferocious and disastrous competitive war.

Under these conditions combination naturally suggested itself. Any combination depended upon acquiring control of Andrew Carnegie's company—it was the most important steel enterprise, and its exclusion, moreover, meant savage competitive reprisals. The Moore brothers and Henry C. Frick (formerly Carnegie's partner, the two now waging an acrimonious personal and legal war against each other) prepared plans for . a combination and offered Carnegie $147,000,000 for his property, posting a large cash option. Disturbances in the money market and other factors compelled abandonment of the plans and Carnegie pocketed the option of $1,170,000—arousing Frick's violent curses.[4] Merging Federal Steel and the Carnegie Co. was discussed by the two presidents, Elbert H. Gary and

Charles M. Schwab, but they could not reach an agreement.[5] The Rockefeller interests then considered the proposed combination and approached Carnegie, the immense potential profits arousing their appetites. Dominating the situation and knowing it, the canny Andrew raised his price to $250,000,000, which the Rockefellers considered too high and abandoned the proposition.[6] There was another reason for the abandonment, however, revealing an advantage of the House of Morgan in the struggle for supremacy. The Rockefeller interests were not in a position to finance such a huge enterprise as the proposed steel combination. Still essentially industrial capitalists, their first consideration was Standard Oil and their resources consequently not so mobile as a financial capitalist's; nor did they possess adequate machinery to draw upon the investment resources of the public (in spite of the affiliated National City Bank). The proposed combination required generous public participation. While not as large as Standard Oil's, the resources of the House of Morgan had the complete mobility of financial capital, and, moreover, J. P. Morgan & Co. as an investment house was able to secure the necessary public participation by means of its institutionalized control of investment resources.

Only Morgan could organize the steel combination, but he rejected the proposal when it was urged upon him by John W. Gates and others. Of an interview with Morgan on the proposed combination, E. H. Gary said: "I did not receive any encouragement."[7]

Then the latent competitive danger began to emerge. Morgan's National Tube Co., to secure larger integration in its operations, adopted plans to provide its own crude steel which it had been buying from the Carnegie Co. Carnegie swiftly retaliated with a proposal to build an immense tube plant to compete with Morgan's company.[8] Fedral Steel replied with threats to build a competitive structural steel plant.[9] That was all Carnegie needed. The apostle of international peace was in business a confirmed militarist, unscrupulously waging war against his competitors and his workmen (as much a factor in his success as adoption of the most progressive technical ideas in production). Urging his managers that "after peace is gone the worst policy in the world is 'gentle war,'" Carnegie in quick succession issued threats to construct a sheet steel plant, wire-rod and hoop mills, ore-carrying ships on the Great Lakes and a railroad from Pittsburgh to the Atlantic Ocean paralleling the Pennsylvania Railroad (a Morgan affiliate).[10] These plans threatened all the steel interests—Morgan, the Rockefellers, the Moores and Gates. Since none of the prospective belligerents believed in "gentle war" (the Rockefellers had tried to sandbag Carnegie on ore prices and transportation rates, but were compelled to yield) the situation meant, according to contemporary business opinion, "plunging the steel industry into a war which would prove disastrous to some of the weaker combatants and costly and wearing to the strongest."[11]

Carnegie was not bluffing in threatening the most powerful combinations in industry and finance—Morgan and the Rockefellers. He was the only important industrial capitalist left, in complete control of his own enterprise and independent of Wall Street financiers—the Henry Ford of his day. Carnegie's threats meant danger. He would undoubtedly have emerged victor out of any sustained competitive struggle, while the others might have met disaster owing to overcapitalization.

Nor was Carnegie mad. He did not want a war of extermination but to compel his competitors to buy him out. Carnegie was old and eager to retire—at his own price. The canny Andrew realized that the buyer must be J. P. Morgan, and his campaign of threats was craftily directed at the Morgan interests in particular. "Buy or fight!" was the ultimatum.[12] In a sense Andrew Carnegie created the United States Steel Corporation by his campaign to compel Morgan to act on the proposed combination.

Morgan's interests and power were now directly threatened, and competition was repugnant to him. Moreover, the steel magnates were frightened by Carnegie's threats. The Rockefellers rejecting an appeal to intervene, the magnates concentrated their efforts on Morgan, who now felt that action was necessary. The final convincing argument, it appears, was made by Charles M. Schwab.[13] Convinced at last, Morgan's imagination caught fire at the prospect of organizing the gigantic combination and he mobilized all his massive energy and immense resources for the task.

Organizing the United States Steel Corporation was largely a problem of prices to be paid the enterprises it combined. Morgan's three steel companies would enter any combination proposed by their master. The other companies (except possibly the Rockefellers) were eager to sell and come in—at a price. This problem of price was crucial, and the final decision was Morgan's, which he confirmed twelve years later while testifying in the Congressional investigation of the Money Trust:

UNTERMYER: Did you fix the prices?

MORGAN: I approved the prices; yes.

UNTERMYER: It was left to you, was it not, to determine the prices at which they should go in?

MORGAN: Yes; but I was not always able to get it at the price at which I thought it should go in.[14]

No, Morgan did not always get the right price. But he did not permit price to interfere with his plans, simply increasing the final capitalization. In large measure high prices were forced upon Morgan. The proposed combination aroused the cupidity of all the interests involved.

Federal Steel, National Tube and American Bridge offered no problem—they would go in at Morgan's price. But the price Andrew Carnegie asked astonished even Morgan. Carnegie had previously offered to sell for $157,000,000 and then $250,000,000, and in an answer to a lawsuit by Henry C.

ANDREW CARNEGIE

JOHN D. ROCKEFELLER

Frick he had sworn that the Carnegie Steel Co. was worth much less than $250,000,000.[15] The price Carnegie now asked of Morgan was equivalent to $447,000,000 in cash and in bonds and stock of the United States Steel Corporation.[16] Morgan accepted—the Carnegie property was indispensable, and the old fox knew it. Carnegie received four times as much as the Federal Steel Co., much of the difference representing the "price of peace." [17]

Some months later Carnegie and Morgan met on an Atlantic liner.

"Do you know, Pierpont," said Carnegie (the royal Morgan always winced at Carnegie's use of "Pierpont"), "I have been thinking it over, and I find I made a mistake. I should have asked you another $100,000,000."

Morgan answered frankly and unfeelingly, "If you had I should have paid it." It seems he added: "If only to be rid of you!" Carnegie, so they said in Wall Street, was so soured that he could take no more toast and marmalade.[18]

The original plan was to buy the Carnegie company and combine it with Federal Steel and its two affiliates. But that meant a combination incomplete in itself, in terms of raw materials, transportation and products manufactured, and incapable of dominating the steel industry. It meant, moreover, the probability of a competing combination as formidable as Morgan's being organized by the Rockefeller, Moore and Gates interests. United States Steel was consequently broadened to include twelve corporations, securing complete integration from ores and fuel to finished products, dominating the steel industry.[19]

As plans broadened prices went up. All the corporations included in the combination were heavily overcapitalized, their common stock representing simply water and prospective earnings, yet they received enormously inflated prices—the Moore companies $145 of new stock for $100 of the old.[20] Scores of new millionaires were created. The dickering for still higher prices was staggering, many little hold-up games being put over. But there were limits and the limit was reached in the case of John W. Gates, who asked a price for American Wire & Steel higher than the already high prices being paid. Morgan refused. At a conference at Morgan's office Gates' bluff was called in a framed-up scene arranged by Gary:

MORGAN: Gentlemen, I am going to leave this building in ten minutes. If by that time you have not accepted our offer, the matter will be closed. We will build our own plant. (*Morgan leaves the room.*)

GATES: Well, I don't know whether the old man means that or not.

GARY: You can depend upon it he does.

GATES: Then I guess we will have to give up.

GARY (*to Morgan, who has been sent for*): The gentlemen have accepted your proposition.

MORGAN: Is that right?

GATES: Yes.

MORGAN: Now let's go home.[21]

Still, "Bet-you-a-million" Gates was paid a good price, even if he did not get the "little extra" he was trying to force out of Morgan. In exchange for its stock, the market value of which was only $60,000,000, American Steel & Wire received $110,000,000 in United States Steel stock.[22] Although excluded from the new corporation's management (Morgan told Gates: "It will be impossible for you to enter the directory. You have made your own reputation. Good day, sir.") [23] the feelings of Gates were salved by the major share in promoters' profits of at least $11,600,000.[24]

The proposed combination now assumed definite shape. (In the midst of these momentous transactions the House of Morgan casually organized another combination, the Hartford Carpet Co.) [25] Arrangements completed with the most important iron and steel enterprises, prices and profits agreed upon, United States Steel appeared an accomplished fact. But while the new combination was wholly integrated in manufactures, in undisputed control of the most important iron and steel products, it was still weak in its sources of raw materials. The Carnegie Co. held extensive leases on iron mines, but they were leases, supremacy in raw materials being retained by the Lake Superior Consolidated Iron Mines owned by the Rockefeller interests. Its objective being complete integration and self-sufficiency, United States Steel had to control an ample ore supply of its own, otherwise it would be at the mercy of the Rockefellers. Moreover, Consolidated Iron Mines might become the basis of another steel combination. The Rockefeller company had to be acquired.

When urged to see John D. Rockefeller about the purchase, Morgan refused—"I don't like him," he said. But more than dislike animated Morgan. He could not bludgeon Rockefeller, as he bludgeoned others, and his arrogance resented negotiating with an equal. But John D. held the whiphand, and Morgan sent him a message to call at his office to discuss the purchase. Enjoying the situation and probably smiling his spidery smile, Rockefeller replied that he never went downtown and invited Morgan to make a social call. Morgan did, fuming at what he considered an affront.

Morgan started to talk business, but Rockefeller said: "I am not in business. You must see my son."

The comedy proceeded, Rockefeller chuckling, Morgan fuming. He sent for John D. Rockefeller, Jr. "I understand your father wants to sell and has authorized you to act," said Morgan bruskly. "How much do you want?" But the son was worthy of the father:—

"I have no information that my father wants to sell," young Rockefeller replied, and Morgan staring silently, added: "If that is all, Mr. Morgan, I bid you good afternoon." [26]

Angry, his dignity ruffled by the cat-and-mouse play, Morgan refused to reopen the subject. But the iron mines were indispensable to United States Steel. Still riding the high-horse

Dignity, Morgan asked Henry C. Frick to negotiate with Rockefeller. The price finally agreed upon was larger than the "outside" figure estimated by Gary, and in answer to his protest Morgan said: "Would you let a matter of $5,000,000 stand in the way of success?" [27] Rockefeller extorted exceptionally favorable terms, more favorable than others received, pressing his advantage to the limit.

There was an unsavory taint about the Rockefeller ownership of the Consolidated Iron Mines which Morgan bought for the United States Steel Corporation. The mines, located in the Mesabi Range of Minnesota, had almost fabulous reserves of easily worked iron ore. They were discovered by the Merritt family, seven men of the old breed of pioneers who, in spite of jeers, suffering and discouragement, persisted in their search for the iron they felt sure was in the Mesabi. They were not businessmen, these hardy pioneers who conquered nature, and they lost what they found: enmeshed in the almost imperceptible iron meshes of finance, the Merritts saw their mines become the property of John D. Rockefeller. In 1911, during the investigation of the Steel Trust by a committee of the House of Representatives, Leonidas Merritt told the story—an old man still bewildered by the magic manipulation of John D. It appears that the Rev. F. T. Gates, the Oil King's almoner ("serving the Lord and John D. Rockefeller") [28] particularly aroused the resentment of Leonidas Merritt for his share in the magic business:

MERRITT: Rev. Dr. Gates explained to me how he was a preacher and how honest he was, and how pious John D. Rockefeller was.

CHAIRMAN: Did he congratulate you on your piety and on your being a Christian?

MERRITT: He seemed glad that we were Christian people. [29]

The Rev. Dr. Gates, who introduced the Merritts to John D. Rockefeller, was, for a Man of God, curiously active in the financial transactions between John D. and the unsuspecting pioneer. Leonidas Merritt told this story:

"It was in 1893 and times were panicky.... I knew our boys were suffering for money up there. Well, I, of course, appeared to be worried, and this man Gates—I saw him almost daily—I was led to believe that if we would make a consolidation of all these interests Mr. Rockefeller would help—and through Gates I began to take small loans of Mr. Rockefeller, for which I put up good collateral of these mines and stocks.... There came a time when they suggested that I put up a whole bundle of securities, and get what money I wanted—that is, from time to time. My brother gave me power of attorney to put up securities for him, which I did.... I began to be unable to borrow. Mr. Gates told me that Mr. Rockefeller was hard up, and, by golly, I believed it at the time. Anyway, I began to get uneasy." [30]

The Rev. Dr. Gates urged the consolidation upon Leonidas Merritt and arranged for him to see John D. Rockefeller. ("Come into my parlor," said the spider to the fly.)

"Well," proceeded Merritt, "I went up there and met Mr. Rockefeller. I went into Mr. Gates' office. Mr. Rockefeller came in and shook hands with me, and he was as gentlemanly a sort of man as you have met. He had a kindly face and a brotherly sort of manner.... He said, 'Go ahead and make this consolidation. I do not want to have your stock. I am past speculating, but I have money that I would gladly invest in these bonds and I will buy your bonds.' He then said, 'I will make things easy.' Such talk as that captured me. I told him that I would do it, and he got up then and we shook hands. I expressed my approval of my good fortune in meeting a gentleman like him." [31]

But it was not such good fortune. The series of loans finally amounted to $420,000, made on a "call" basis which the Merritts did not clearly understand. Then came proposals, intrigues, complications, and finally the demand to pay up in twenty-

four hours, an utter impossibility. John D. Rockefeller took
over the Merritts' collateral—"and I have never seen it since,"
said Leonidas Merritt. There was a lawsuit in which the Merritts charged Rockefeller with fraud and secured judgment for
$940,000, but the case on appeal was sent back for retrial.
Destitute and overwhelmed by Rockefeller's financial and legal
resources, the Merritts settled for $520,000 and a retraction of
their charges of fraud.[32]

In this tortuous fashion and for less than $1,000,000 John D.
Rockefeller secured possession of the Lake Superior Consolidated Iron Mines, for which J. P. Morgan paid $79,417,000 in
United States Steel stock.[33] The immense reserves of iron in
these mines assured the Steel Trust supremacy in raw materials
and competitive impregnability.

This transaction decided, the United States Steel Corporation
in April, 1901, was launched upon a world astonished by the
super-trust's enormous size and capitalization of $1,400,000,000.
There were immediate demands for government investigation
and action, but Attorney General Knox answered, I know
nothing and can do nothing.[34]

Organization of the United States Steel Corporation reveals
clearly the House of Morgan's system of institutionalized financial control as the apex of the developing centralization of
industry and finance, and the interlocking relations of the
system's different phases.

The starting point was direct corporate control. In Federal
Steel, American Bridge and National Tube the House of
Morgan had a definite basis for any proposed combination.
The stockholders offered no problem. Control of three steel
corporations (plus general financial considerations) developed
a community of interest with the Rockefellers, J. W. Gates and
others in companies available for combination. The problem
was simplified immensely by financial control of industry operating through interlocking directorships and community of
interest.

After securing the agreement of companies merging in the combination, the problem was to dispose of an enormous amount of new securities. This was accomplished by means of the institutionalized control of investment resources. Morgan decided upon participations and allotted their shares to the banks, life-insurance and trust companies under the immediate control of his House, and to the financial institutions under control of allies in the community-of-interest system (such as the Rockefeller-Stillman National City Bank). These institutions were seldom consulted as to their shares: they were simply told what the share was, and took it, retaining some of the securities and passing others on to their affiliates.

The formidable concentration of financial interests and investment resources converged on United States Steel's board of directors, among the twenty-four directors being representatives of the House of Morgan (J. P. Morgan and Robert Bacon), the Rockefellers, National City, First National and other banks and financial institutions as well as representatives of the merged corporations.[35] This final interlocking of the interlocked masters of industry and finance mobilized almost irresistible forces in the promotion of the United States Steel Corporation.

One of the vital problems of this concentration of financial forces was to dispose of enormous masses of securities issued by the steel combination, which was heavily overcapitalized. According to the Bureau of Corporation, after investigating the United States Steel Corporation, the tangible assets of its constituent enterprises were worth $682,000,000 and the market value of their securities when acquired was $793,000,000, against which the new corporation issued $303,000,000 bonds, $510,000,000 preferred stock and $508,000,000 common.[36] All of the common stock and two-thirds of the preferred represented nothing but speculation, promoters' profits and capitalization of prospective earnings. United States Steel insisted, in 1902, that its tangible assets were worth $1,457,000,000.[37] A simple calculation proves the absurdity of the claim. In 1929 United States Steel had assets of $2,286,000,000 [38] which, allowing for the decline in the purchasing power of money, would represent a trifle less than the 1901 "assets"—after twenty-seven years of expansion, the reinvestment of billions in earnings, and an increase in surplus from $25,000,000 to $700,000,000! Obviously, the United States Steel Corporation was not worth more in 1901 than in 1928.

Most of the enormous overcapitalization represented promoters' profits. As syndicate managers, J. P. Morgan & Co. received $12,500,000 in addition to profits secured as participating subscribers in the syndicate, which distributed profits of $50,000,000 among its members.[39] Including previous underwriting commissions of the constituent companies (but excluding large amounts of common stock issued as bonus with preferred for property or cash), more than $150,000,000 of United States Steel stock was issued to promoters for their enterprising services.[40]

Since the Morgan Steel syndicate's commission was in the form of stock in the new corporation, the profits were realized by sale of the stock. Speculation was rampant, all sorts of watered stocks eagerly bought by the public, whose appetite seemed insatiable, and every one dreamed of fabulous profits. Multiplying stockholders meant increasing promoters' profits —there was nothing in watered stocks unless the public bought them. The whole mechanism of Morgan's institutionalized control of investment resources was mobilized to sell United States Steel stock. In addition, sales were manipulated on the Stock Exchange to create the semblance of investment activity and shoot up the price of the new issues, the celebrated manipulator, James R. Keene, being employed for the purpose: "Half a million of the shares were dealt in during the first two days of their appearance on the Stock Exchange; the next week's record was a million. The greater part of this was doubtless merely 'matching of orders' by the syndicate's agent,

through the medium of other brokers; but the public did not
know this. It caught the speculative fever; even in thrifty Western towns and New England country villages, the gossip of
an evening was apt to concern itself with 'Steel.' " [41] The operation was unqualifiedly successful.

In the welter of clashing interests, plots to sandbag higher
prices from the new corporation and complicated financial
problems, J. P. Morgan maintained his undisputed control.
Compelled to yield here and make concessions there, his was
the final decision on prices and particularly on officers and
directors of United States Steel. In the Money Trust investigation Morgan testified:

UNTERMYER: Did you name the entire board of directors?

MORGAN: No. I think I passed on it.

UNTERMYER: Did you not, as a matter of fact, name the
board and pass out a slip of paper containing the names?

MORGAN: I cannot say that no one else helped me in it.

UNTERMYER: Did you not only pass on it and approve it, but
did you not further select the board and determine who should
go on and who should stay off?

MORGAN: No, I probably did the latter.

UNTERMYER: Yes, and having determined who should stay
off, you necessarily determined who should go on?

MORGAN: I am quite willing to assume the whole responsibility.

UNTERMYER: I want the fact.

MORGAN: Whoever went on that board went with my approval.

UNTERMYER: And from time to time whoever has gone on
the board has gone on with your approval, has he not?

MORGAN: Not always.

UNTERMYER: Has he gone on against your protest?

MORGAN: No, sir. [42]

In testifying, Morgan blandly tried to push away the
honor of having determined the Steel directors; but, in fact,

he did, dominating the Steel Trust. Under the system of community of interest Morgan granted directorships to John D. Rockefeller and others of the Standard Oil group (and some minor groups), but the majority of the directors represented the House of Morgan and its affiliated enterprises. J. P. Morgan and two of his partners were among the directors. Robert Bacon, one of Morgan's partners, was chairman of the finance committee. Elbert H. Gary, another Morgan representative, was chairman of the executive committee—and this committee, which met daily and whose powers when not in session were vested in its chairman, governed the United States Steel Corporation.[43] Control was definitely maintained by the House of Morgan and its master.

United States Steel's board of directors represented an overwhelming concentration of financial power, the Corporation itself an overwhelming concentration of industrial power. Upward of 60 per cent of the nation's iron and steel output was produced by the Steel Trust, and it owned over 1,000 miles of railroads, 112 ore vessels and immense reserves of iron ore (at least 700,000,000 tons), coal, limestone and natural gas.[44] Completely integrated and mechanized, pioneers in the introduction of automatic machinery, the Corporation's plants were marvels of productive efficiency. Iron and steel is the basic industry, on which all industry depends, continuously enlarging its output to satisfy the insatiable demands of an iron and steel age. The United States Steel Corporation dominated this mighty industry and the House of Morgan dominated the Corporation . . . and other industrial enterprises, and railroads, and banks, life-insurance and trust companies, centralizing industry and finance, acquiring power overwhelming.

CHAPTER XXIV

THE ATTITUDE TO LABOR

*I passed by his garden, and marked, with
one eye,
How the Owl and the Panther were sharing
a pie:
The Panther took pie-crust, and gravy,
and meat,
While the Owl had the dish as its share of
the treat.*

ALICE IN WONDERLAND

THE United States Steel Corporation was challenged by labor
within three months of its organization. A series of strikes
broke out to unionize all the Corporation's plants and compel
acceptance of collective bargaining. J. Pierpont Morgan met
the challenge: "There can be no compromise," he said.[1] Unionism was crushed.

While themselves actively combining corporate enterprises,
the industrial and financial magnates denied labor the right
of combination. Business organized in chambers of commerce,
trade associations, corporations and trustified combinations of
corporations. But business, by and large, mobilized against
unionism: labor was to be disorganized, unprotected by the
might of combination. Unions developed only by means of a
tooth-and-claw struggle against the employers. Although the
Industrial Commission reported in 1900 that combinations
manifested no hostility to unions but were inclined to favor
them,[2] this was untrue testimony: combinations violently resisted unionism. Dictatorship characterized combination—the
dictatorship of financiers over stockholders and management,
and the dictatorship of management over labor. Unionism de-

veloped in none of the corporate combinations (except rail-roads).

The House of Morgan was definitely against unionism, al-though occasionally making concessions to public opinion. In the coal strike of 1900 Morgan rejected arbitration (which implied recognition of the miners' union) and accepted arbitra-tion in the coal strike of 1902 only under pressure of President Theodore Roosevelt. In 1903, in reference to a union-shop agreement in one of his affiliated enterprises, Morgan said: "If I have any authority to cause that agreement to be broken, it will be broken." The temper of the House's affiliates was expressed by George F. Baer, president of Morgan's Philadel-phia & Reading Railroad, during the shopmen's strike of 1901: "The union is not to be recognized. We will employ any one we please." [3]

This temper dominated the United States Steel Corpora-tion. Most of the constituent companies were non-union. Mor-gan's National Tube Co. had been "pretty steadily non-union from the beginning" and Federal Steel had only a small union in one plant, while John W. Gates' American Steel & Wire Co. was completely non-union.[4] The former Carnegie men in the Steel Corporation (Charles M. Schwab, Henry C. Frick and others), who had deliberately provoked the bloody Home-stead strike in order to crush unionism, were particularly hos-tile to labor; one of them said: "If a workman sticks up his head, hit it." [5]

When the workers stuck up their heads in the strike of 1901 the United States Steel Corporation hit them, and hit them hard.

In some of the plants of three of the Corporation's con-stituent companies the Amalgamated Association of Iron, Steel and Tin Workers was fairly strong, wage scales being agreed upon by union and management. In 1901 the Amalgamated Association asked that the new wage scale include all the plants of the three companies [6]—which meant extending the union to plants where it was not recognized. The managements declined, and United States Steel's board of directors, insisting the issue was unionism and not wages, declared: "We are unalterably opposed to the extension of union labor." [7]

The Amalgamated Association declared a general strike in all the plants of the Steel Trust—essentially a strike for collective bargaining and recognition of the union—and offered to arbitrate the issues. Considerable dependence was placed by the Amalgamated Workers upon the support of public opinion, which was inflamed against the monopolistic steel combination, but the public did not respond to their struggle. The United States Steel Corporation declined to arbitrate, its justification being: "It will be better for the business interests, now the fight is on, to let it go to a finish, which means the defeat of the workers." [8] J. Pierpont Morgan backed up the Corporation. He said:

"There has been no settlement and there can be no compromise. The position of the operating companies is perfectly simple and well understood, and, so far as I am concerned, has my unqualified approval." [9]

The strike was doomed to fail. There was little response to the call for a general strike. The Amalgamated Association had only 13,800 members, United States Steel 168,000 employees.[10] Moreover, the Amalgamated was an exclusive union, composed of cliques of skilled workers who declined to organize all the workers in a plant, interested only in securing better conditions for their own particular group. In fact, although mechanization decreased the number and importance of skilled workers, the Amalgamated fought efforts to organize all the steel workers, skilled and unskilled, in one union— integrated unionism to parallel integrated industry. The workers previously scorned were now called upon to strike to help the Amalgamated, and most of them declined.

At a conference between Steel Corporation and union officials in J. P. Morgan's office terms were offered the strikers, although Charles M. Schwab and other die-hards were against offering any terms. But the terms meant the union's defeat— the Amalgamated to withdraw the demand for unionizing non-union plants and accept the "open shop," its minimum scale of wages being accepted. The strikers rejected the terms, insisting that "Morgan's offer will in time kill the Amalgamated." [11] Declaring his determination to break the strike if the terms were not accepted within one week, Morgan at another conference angrily refused to make concessions.[12] The strike lingered on, but it was hopeless. Finally a settlement was signed by the Steel Corporation and the union in J. P. Morgan's office, by which the Amalgamated agreed not to endeavor to organize non-union mills and workers in return for recognition in the few union mills where it had been previously recognized—except, however, in the union mills which had become non-union during the strike.[13] Unionism in the iron and steel industry was annihilated.

Against unionism the United States Steel Corporation offered paternalism determined by self-interest. In 1902 it introduced a system of employee stock ownership, which was rationalized by one of the directors, Abram S. Hewitt: "The harmony of capital and labor will be brought about by joint ownership in the instruments of production, and what are called 'trusts' merely afford the machinery by which such ownership can be distributed among the workmen."[14] (In the 1902 coal strike Hewitt opposed arbitration and urged "stern repression.")[15] Most of the employee stockholders, however, were limited to the better-paid managerial and supervisory employees; moreover, by 1908 employee stockholders had declined from 26,399 to 5,409, out of almost 200,000 employees, and their shares from 47,551 to 12,339.[16] The corporation also introduced a bonus system and profit-sharing for those who expressed "a proper interest in the welfare of the Corporation."[17] Only four or five per cent of all the employees participated in profit-sharing, reported Elbert H. Gary: "Sometimes the percentage is less.... The majority of them are in excutive positions."[18]

All of these paternalistic measures were designed to attach employees to the corporation, particularly the men in managerial, supervisory and other "key" positions. The mass of workers did not profit materially, nor was it necessary, since their unity was broken by the "loyalty" of the favored groups. Elbert H. Gary developed the system. As much opposed to unionism as the Carnegie men, Gary preferred to circumvent unionism by guile—strikes might discredit the United States Steel Corporation, the position of which was none too secure owing to public antagonism.

But Gary's velvet glove covered a hand of steel. Where the workers did stick up their heads, they were hit and hit hard. Gary's system, however, was to prevent the sticking up of heads. Paternalism was one means, organized espionage another, making workers in the Steel Corporation's plants "suspicious of one another, of their neighbors and of their friends."[19] This espionage was directed against strikes and unionism—members of unions or union agitators were reported to management by the spies and immediately thrown out. It worked. Benevolent feudalism flourished.

The benevolence of United States Steel's feudalism was more apparent than real, being chiefly malevolent. Elbert H. Gary frequently complimented himself and his associates on their "enlightened policy" of voluntarily increasing wages.[20] They did—in a sense, and as all employers did during this period. Rising prices compelled wage increases, but by 1915 the average of real wages for all workers was no higher than in 1895, and stationary during the twenty years.[21] Wages and prices were rising together (and profits more than either wages or prices), but wages did not increase in terms of purchasing power, of the goods wages could buy. The average yearly money earnings of iron and steel workers were $553 in 1901, $588 in 1905, and $665 in 1912, but in terms of purchasing power earnings were 1 per cent lower in 1912 than in 1901 and 5 per cent lower than in 1895.[22] Combination increased profits but not wages.

Other conditions among the iron and steel workers were worse than their wages. Immigrants were given the preference as more easily managed, and their racial prejudices exploited to prevent organization—the human raw material of industry and profits. A survey by the Russell Sage Foundation revealed frightful misery among the workers of the United States Steel Corporation—unsanitary Corporation houses, large industrial hazards, the twelve-hour day (often twenty-four-hour stretch) and the seven-day week—78 per cent of the workers toiled twelve hours a day.[23] Most contemptible was the Corporation's justification of the twelve-hour day—the workers wanted it because they could make more money! [24] Of course—wages were so low that lower hours accompanied by lower wages meant sheer starvation: men do not work twelve hours a day because they like it. Almost inhuman conditions prevailed under benevolent feudalism. But the Steel Corporation belligerently rejected all proposals for improvements. "Men owning property," declared J. P. Morgan, "should do what they like with it." [25] Characteristically feudal, this was the spirit of Morganized industry and finance. John Pierpont had insisted: You can't be let alone in your business if it doesn't serve humanity. The grandfather's passion for human rights had become in the grandson a passion for the rights of property.

CHAPTER XXV

ASPECTS OF MORGANIZATION

> *"I'll be judge, I'll be jury," said cunning*
> *old Fury; "I'll try the whole cause, and*
> *condemn you to death."*
> ALICE IN WONDERLAND

THE Morganization of industry meant financial dictatorship over labor, managements and stockholders. Stockholders, of course, received more consideration than labor, but it was consideration tempered by the "unbridled arrogance"[1] of financial magnates. Labor was to receive its wages and keep quiet, stockholders receive their dividends (if any) and keep quiet: the magnates ruled.

Being scattered and deprived of all active participation in the corporations they owned, stockholders might resent but could not resist unbridled and arrogant control by financial magnates. P. A. B. Widener, a director in the United States Steel Corporation and other affiliated enterprises of the House of Morgan, met considerable stockholder opposition in manipulating a lease of the Metropolitan Street Railway of New York to another corporation in 1902. The stockholders' meeting, of which Widener was chairman, proceeded in this fashion:

WIDENER: The tellers will now take the vote.

STOCKHOLDER: We wish a discussion of this matter. Let us discuss it before we vote for it.

WIDENER: Well, you can vote for it and discuss it afterward.

STOCKHOLDER (*amazed, incredulously*): Do you mean to say that we must vote and then discuss?

ANOTHER STOCKHOLDER: You wish us to be executed first, then tried, is that it? We object to voting before discussion.

WIDENER (*bored, smilingly*): Well, sir, you may withhold

your vote until after the discussion. The Chair orders that the vote shall be taken.[2]

The vote was taken (without discussion) and Widener's lease jammed through, the whole thing being prearranged by the clique in control. Nor did the opposition represent the stockholders, simply another financial clique trying to secure control.

Many factors determined the Morganization of industry— technological developments, industrial concentration, the increasingly complex character of business enterprise and the dependence of industry upon finance. But Morganization acquired undisputed control only because the multiplication of stockholders separated ownership from management. The House of Morgan and other financial masters of industry did not own the corporations under their control. Nor was ownership necessary. Stockholders being scattered and numerous (43,000 in the case of United States Steel) control was easily usurped by minority interests, particularly when these interests were institutionalized in the formidable combination of the House of Morgan. The Morganization of industry was accomplished by a complex system of stock ownership, voting trusts, financial pressure, interlocking of financial institutions and industrial corporations by means of interlocking directorates, the community of control of minority interests—all dependent upon stockholders who did not participate in management, who could not easily combine to assert their ownership, and whose concern was limited to dividends. Morganization trampled upon stockholders and the stockholders liked it— providing Morganization "delivered the goods" in the form of increased stock values and frequent (and large) dividends.

J. P. Morgan frankly admitted his belief in making corporations so large that their managements would be independent of the stockholders, which meant dependent upon the financial masters of industry. At the trial of a lawsuit against one of his corporations Morgan testified:

"We do not want financial convulsions and have one thing one day and another thing another day. The policy on which the future of the company depended should be continued. I wanted the people who should have it should be independent. I wanted the stock put so nothing could interfere with ... the policy we had inaugurated. J. P. Morgan & Co. might be dissolved, I might die, and we wanted the road to go on prospering just the same on the old lines. It was our idea to organize a holding company with a capital so large that no rival corporation could purchase a controlling interest in it and so wrest away the control." [3]

Arranging things so competing financiers could not wrest control from the House of Morgan also meant wresting control from stockholders. There is no suggestion in Morgan's words of anything but control by financial magnates, and centralizing control was immediately the most important aspect of Morganization. Corporate combination, of which Morganization was the final expression, included:

Restricting competition to control prices and insure profits.

Industrial integration to insure larger productive efficiency.

Overcapitalization and enormous promoters' profits.

Insuring control by financial interests.

The argument of larger efficiency was most frequently used to justify industrial combinations, but it was the least important consideration of promoters and financiers—usually an *after* consideration. "The only serious objection to trusts," said James J. Hill in 1902, "has been the method of creating them—not for the purpose of manufacturing any particular commodity in the first place, but for the purpose of selling sheaves of printed securities which represent nothing more than good will and prospective profits to promoters." [4] These profits, supplemented by considerations of competition and control, determined whether or not to organize any particular combination. The economic justification of combination was simply exploited or ignored.

But productive efficiency, the least consideration of promoters and financiers, was the decisive factor in the success or failure of combinations. By 1903 there were 440 trustified combinations capitalized at $20,379,000,000, dominating the nation's business.[5] Much of the capitalization was water, 50 per cent in the case of the United States Steel Corporation. Many combinations so completely neglected the factor of productive efficiency that they crashed. In others, labor, engineers and management combined to increase efficiency, output and earnings, and so squeezed the water out of capitalization. United States Steel, it was prophesied, would crash owing to its over-capitalization. But the Corporation was an integrated enterprise, dominating the iron and steel industry (and prices). Labor, engineers and management accomplished marvels of productive efficiency, making good the speculation of the financiers. By 1907 United States Steel had reinvested $208,000,000 of its earnings on improvements and additions;[6] and by its policy of reinvesting part of its large earnings the Corporation acquired tangible assets for every penny of its capitalization.* But while usually facilitating productive efficiency, combination was not its primary cause. Combinations often repressed efficiency; and, in general, while productive efficiency increased 25 per cent between 1899 and 1914,[7] the increase was much larger in the preceding twenty-five years when competitive conditions still prevailed. Efficiency was comparatively unimportant since combination, control of markets and rising prices insured substantial profits.

United States Steel did not neglect the factor of productive efficiency, nor did it neglect the factor of public opinion. Although the McKinley Administration decided it was not illegal, the Steel Trust *did* dominate the iron and steel industry; and the advent of Theodore Roosevelt to the presidency

* The period after 1900 was one of continuously rising prices, including the price of securities, which automatically helped to squeeze water out of over-capitalized combinations.

initiated action against trusts (including, in 1905, government investigation of United States Steel). Appreciating its vulnerability to attack, the Steel Trust magnates decided to make it a "good corporation." While adopting some of Standard Oil's organization forms (particularly executive-committee management), the Steel Trust did not adopt the Standard policy of crushing competitors. Its financial reports were much more complete than customary, the Steel Trust insisting it "has nothing to conceal." [8] And apparently it abolished the practice of permitting directors to receive advance information for purposes of stock-market manipulation. [9]

Most of the "good corporation" business, however, consisted in the personality and utterances of Elbert H. Gary, whom Nature apparently cast for the job. Gary was as formidably respectable as widow's weeds, as priggishly moral as an old-maid Sunday-school teacher.* Frequently he delivered moral discourses to his associates. Steel's directors received a $20 gold piece for attendance, the directors present claiming the fees of absentees and dividing them. Then, all the directors being inveterate gamblers, they decided to match for the gold pieces. Gary squirmed uncomfortably for a time and then spoke up nobly: "I told them that I was brought up not to believe in gambling and I thought the board of directors of the United States Steel Corporation should set a good example." [10] The old sinners to whom gambling was the breath of life smiled cynically and continued to match gold pieces. But Gary loved

---

* Elbert H. Gary found the perfect biographer in Ida M. Tarbell, who from the extreme of making John D. Rockefeller a devil of melodrama swung to the other extreme of making Gary a plaster saint, incidentally picturing J. Pierpont Morgan as a sort of sentimental grandpa. Gary tells the story of a disagreement between himself and Morgan on United States Steel policy. Gary went to Morgan determined to resign: " 'I am going to leave you. You must decide the question. I think I can bring the board of directors to ratify whatever you decide.' He got up and, putting his arm around my shoulder, said: 'My dear boy, I would not do that for anything in the world, you shall have your way.' " (Ida M. Tarbell, *The Life of Elbert H. Gary*, p. 171.) All of which Ida accepts adoringly, and more of the same. But it wasn't exactly the way Morgan managed.

to deliver moral discourses, much as a toothache loves to ache. He kept discoursing on the immorality of matching gold pieces, and the custom was finally abandoned—Gary's priggery was of the annoyingly irresistible sort.

In spite of the ecstasy it aroused in his feminine biographer, Gary's morality had a rhinoceros streak somewhere. For eight years this St. George of business associated with John W. Gates, the saint and the sinner each profiting from the association. Nor did Gary crack under the moral strain. Morgan never adopted the manner of moral righteousness, his cynical nature scorning subterfuges, but Morgan could not stomach Gates as Gary did and threw him out of his system. The cynic in practice shamed the moralist.

Gary's priggery was probably offensive to Morgan, yet the shrewd master of money (and of men) knew whom he could use. Compact of all the copy-book virtues, calculatingly moral and morally calculating, Gary was just the person to set up the respectable "front" of the United States Steel Corporation. This "front" was determined by more important considerations than Gary's morality. While not a monopoly, the Steel Trust "regulated" competition by the weight of its immense resources. Standard Oil developed out of competition by crushing or absorbing competitors: it had to *become* dominant. Dominant upon its organization, in control of 65 per cent of the iron and steel industry, United States Steel did not have to resort to the competitive skullduggery of Standard Oil, and worked harmoniously with competitors, regulating competition and prices. Its dominance and the new campaign against trusts compelled United States Steel to tread softly; in spite of which, and its abolition of some of the worst corporate abuses, United States Steel clashed with the government: it was, after all, in a system the other parts of which had no peculiar reasons for being "good."

Morganization, the system of financial centralization and control, ignored larger social and political interests, which

ELBERT H. GARY

EDWARD H. HARRIMAN

Morgan considered only as they affected his operations. An enthusiast likened Morgan to a "force of nature" [11]—and he was, in the crude sense of being contemptuous of larger consequences. The centralization of industry and finance meant efficiency, profits, power—the social and political consequences were unimportant. But society could not afford to be contemptuous of consequences, of an unregulated industrial and financial power dominating business and government. In 1901 the *Bankers' Magazine* admitted frankly:

"The growth of corporations and of combinations tends to strengthen the forces which seek to control the machinery of the government and the laws in behalf of special interests. ... The productive forces are the purse-bearers. The businessman, whether alone or in combination with other businessmen, seeks to shape politics and government in a way conducive to his own prosperity. As the business of the country has learned the secret of combination, it is gradually subverting the power of the politician and rendering him subservient to its purposes. That government is not entirely controlled by these interests is due to the fact that business organization has not reached full perfection." [12]

Morgan despised politics but politics could not afford to despise Morgan. Morganization was inextricably identified with politics in the sense that politics expresses class forces, issues and struggles. The centralization of industry and finance aroused antagonisms. Labor was oppressed, stockholders and small business trampled upon. "Men owning property should do what they like with it," insisted J. Pierpont Morgan. That was too much—even business enterprise imposes limitations upon the rights of property, if only to protect the property of others (which Morganization manipulated in its operations). The antagonisms aroused compelled intervention by society in the shape of its government. Government and the House of Morgan were to clash.

PART SEVEN

DOMINANCE

CHAPTER XXVI

THE MORGAN-HARRIMAN CLASH

"Is that the way you manage?" Alice asked.
The Hatter shook his head mournfully. "Not I!" he replied. "We quarreled last March—just before he went mad, you know—" (pointing with his teaspoon to the March Hare).

ALICE IN WONDERLAND

THE Steel Trust consolidated J. Pierpont Morgan's towering structure of financial control over industry. It appeared as if the power of the House of Morgan was unchallengeable. But there developed a challenge from a magnate Morgan had clashed with before—Edward H. Harriman, mobilizing the resources of the Standard Oil oligarchy and its affiliates.

This clash arose out of the struggle for control of Northern Pacific, a Morgan-Hill road which Harriman tried to wrest away from its masters. The clash revived the conditions when community of interest was still undeveloped and railroad magnates made baronial forays upon each other, contemptuous of the public welfare.

Coming to power in the midst of industrial and financial civil war, of struggles for mastery producing severe business disturbances, Morgan waged war upon the disturbers of business peace, emphasizing and imposing community of interest. The system of community of interest was not only the logical development of increasingly complex economic relations, it was also the form of expression of the House of Morgan's power. In its final aspects, consequently, community of interest operated under the overlordship of the House of Morgan, which insisted on stabilization, peace and the *status quo*. But as the system assumed Morgan's supremacy, the *status quo* was itself an aggression, since it barred the way to others yearning after larger power. Community of interest represented a dynamic equilibrium which might at any moment be upset by the emergence to power of men who felt their development repressed by the House of Morgan's dominance.

The other magnates recognized Morgan's supremacy, but many of them resented it and intensely disliked the man. Much of it was dislike of jackals for the tiger, and much of it was produced by Morgan's arrogance and contempt of the lesser men about him. Morgan had few friends and scarcely any intimates, and never asked advice even of his partners. He simply issued his ultimatums: "I'll do this" or "I won't do that," and whichever it was settled the matter. The syndicate participations of associates were decided by Morgan himself and they accepted unquestioningly. Once one of them suggested that he did not like going into a particular syndicate, to which Morgan icily replied: "You can stay out, but do not think you will share with us again." [1] This to his associates—consider, then, Morgan to his antagonists! There was something terrifying in his appearance—an aggressive jaw, monstrous nose (of which he was acutely sensitive), shaggy, lowering eyebrows, fiercely penetrating eyes—massive, truculent and overbearing, merciless as the economic forces he represented. Intense in his hatreds, Morgan never forgot or forgave an affront, and he was easily affronted. Of iron resolution, Morgan implacably and ruthlessly pursued his objectives: if it meant trampling upon men, trample! He was a man to make many enemies, who winced particularly under his contempt of bombast, bluff and cant (of which there is so much in captains of industry). They dared not challenge J. Pierpont Morgan, these enemies, but they lay in wait—and hoped.

Only the Standard Oil oligarchy was powerful enough to challenge the House of Morgan. While resenting Morgan's power and disliking the man, it accepted community of interest, however, there being too much at stake to risk a clash. But Standard Oil was not averse to an indirect challenge, gloating and helping when Harriman threw down the gauntlet to Morgan, the consequent struggle combining financial and personal motives.

While the Standard Oil oligarchy was busily piling up its millions, drawn from industry, finance and unscrupulous stock-market manipulations, E. H. Harriman was still largely a man on the make; and where the oligarchy was uninterested in adventures unless they were safe and yielded fat profits, Harriman was adventurous, a dreamer of dreams who as much as Morgan yearned after supreme power. Harriman acquired control of Union Pacific in 1898, proved it a gold mine, and then in quick succession reorganized Chicago & Alton, became chairman of the executive committee of Kansas City Southern and a member of its voting trust, director in Baltimore & Ohio, and early in 1901 bought control of Southern Pacific (in spite of the opposition of its fiscal agents, Speyer & Co.).[2] In all of these moves, and in acquiring interests in other railroads, banks and insurance companies, Harriman worked with the Standard Oil oligarchy, the National City Bank, Kuhn, Loeb & Co. and the Goulds. Now one of the two or three most important railroad magnates, Harriman dreamed of an ocean-to-ocean transportation system, and of other roads and ships circling the world. Fulfilment of these plans, however, meant disturbing the community-of-interest equilibrium and challenging the House of Morgan, which directly or indirectly controlled most of the railroads necessary to create Harriman's transcontinental system.

Meanwhile James J. Hill (an affiliate of the House of Morgan) was in control of Northern Pacific and practically merged it with his other road, the Great Northern. Desiring an outlet to Chicago for the two northwestern railroads, Hill in 1897 considered buying the Chicago, Burlington & Quincy, but temporarily abandoned the plan.[3] Harriman, who also desired an outlet to Chicago, was aroused: acquisition by the Morgan-Hill interests of Burlington (which between the Missouri River and Denver closely paralleled Union Pacific) not only deprived his roads of an outlet to Chicago but threatened future expansion. In 1899 Harriman approached the Burlington management with an offer to buy; and when the offer was rejected he held a conference with James Stillman, of the National City Bank, Jacob H. Schiff, of Kuhn, Loeb & Co., and George J. Gould, at which it was decided to secure control of Burlington by buying the stock in the open market. But the market supply of stock was scarce, much of it being held by scattered small investors, the price rose, and the syndicate sold most of its stock at a profit, suspending operations.[4]

The Morgan-Hill forces now got into action, of which procedure Morgan subsequently said:

"I think it was in 1898 or 1899 that I made up my mind that it was essential that the Northern Pacific should have its eastern terminus in Chicago, in the same way as the New York Central, of which I am a director, has its western terminus there. ... From a study of the question I came to the conclusion that there were three lines available—the St. Paul, the Chicago, Burlington & Quincy and the Wisconsin Central. I wanted to take the St. Paul. Soon after that I met Mr. Hill—he wanted the Burlington. He didn't agree with me, but acquiesced.... The St. Paul directors said we could not have the road. Being unwilling to buy the stock, we decided to abandon the transaction. I told Mr. Hill to see what he could do with the Burlington. He took up the negotiations and carried them through."[5]

In this question Morgan was parochial, being simply interested in the Chicago terminus (which any one of the three roads would give) while Hill dreamed of competition with Harriman, control of the Western railroad empire and the markets of the Orient, all of which the Burlington's acquisition facilitated. The deal went through quickly and secretly, organized as a stroke against the Harriman interests. Hill approached the Burlington directors, who agreed to sell the stock at 200 (although the market price was below 180). The offer being accepted by Hill, Northern Pacific and Great Northern jointly bought the Burlington's stock, issuing bonds in payment—and adding 8,000 miles to the Morgan-Hill railroad empire in the Northwest.[6]

Then J. P. Morgan went to Europe, where he was accorded "royal honors" as the "Steel King." [7] ...

The Burlington's sale shocked the Harriman interests, which tried to secure control but failed. Harriman then had a conference with Hill at the home of George F. Baker and asked that Union Pacific be given a one-third interest in Burlington. It was a legitimate proposal under the community-of-interest system. But Hill declined even to consider the request—supremacy in the West and the Orient beckoned. "Very well," said Harriman, "it is a hostile act, and you must take the consequences." [8] Hill did not take the threat seriously: was he not in control of Burlington's stock?

But to Harriman the issue was now larger than Burlington. The *status quo* was an aggression, the Morgan-Hill system repressed his plans. Considering Hill the aggressor, Harriman retaliated by a slashing offensive: to snatch control of Northern Pacific by buying up the majority of its stock, acquiring its half-interest in Burlington and Northern Pacific itself. It meant transcontinental rail supremacy for Harriman and, through his affiliations with Standard Oil, more power in the larger spheres of industry and finance. It meant, moreover, humiliating J. P. Morgan, the man who sneeringly spoke of him as "that little fellow."

Purchasing control of Northern Pacific was a stupendous enterprise, requiring $78,000,000 (and secrecy). But Harriman levied upon Union Pacific's cash and credit, upon the National City Bank and Kuhn, Loeb & Co., while in the shadows skulked the Standard Oil interests indirectly helping Harriman and prepared to pounce upon Morgan should the offensive conquer.

Secretly the Harriman and Union Pacific forces, under direction of Kuhn, Loeb & Co., proceeded to buy up more than half of Northern Pacific's capital stock. They met no opposition, the House of Morgan being completely unaware of danger, while Hill afterward said that he had not believed it "at all likely that anybody would undertake to buy in the market control of $155,000,000 of stock." [9] So unsuspicious were the Morgan-Hill people, so conspiratorial the purchases, that J. P. Morgan & Co. sold 10,000 shares of stock and Northern Pacific itself 13,000 shares, tempted by the high prices.[10] In one week the stock went from 101 to 117 and kept rising, Wall Street considering the rise an "enigma." [11] But they sold just the same, at a good profit, and the Harriman forces accumulated more and more stock.

Out in Seattle Hill finally became suspicious, owing to the enormous transactions in Northern Pacific and the rising prices. Rushing to New York he went to see Jacob Schiff, who informed him that Kuhn, Loeb & Co. were buying for Harriman—and control.

HILL: But you can't get control. The Great Northern, Morgan and my friends were recently holding $35,000,000 to $40,000,000 of Northern Pacific stock, and so far as I know none of it has been sold.

SCHIFF: That may be, but we've got a lot of it. You secretly bought the Burlington and refused to give us a fair share; now we're going to see if we can't get a share by purchasing a controlling interest in the Northern Pacific.

HILL: It can't be done.[12]

But after surveying the situation Hill was convinced that it could be done, and urged immediate action upon Robert Bacon of the House of Morgan. The threat being urgent, they cabled to Morgan, who was then in Aix-les-Bains.

"When the news came to me," Morgan afterward testified,

"I hadn't any doubt about the facts of the matter. Something must have happened. Somebody must have sold. I knew where certain stocks were, and I figured it up. I feel bound in all honor when I reorganize a property and am morally responsible for its management to protect it; so I made up my mind that it would be desirable to buy 150,000 shares of stock, which we proceeded to do, and with that I knew we had a majority of the common stock, and I knew that actually gave us control." [13]

But much more was involved than simply protecting a property Morgan had reorganized: his whole towering structure of financial control was threatened by Harriman's offensive, the success of which meant upsetting the dynamic equilibrium of community of interest upon which largely depended the House of Morgan's dominance.

Mobilizing all its forces (the order to buy Northern Pacific stock meant war to the limit), the House of Morgan sent its agents into the market under direction of an experienced manipulator. The price of Northern Pacific stock went up, but price was utterly unimportant in the struggle for control. Harriman also bought, and still the price went up. Europe sold and garnered fat profits.[14] Expecting to buy later at lower prices, speculators sold for the decline, accumulating a large "short" interest. But Northern Pacific stock was being bought for control, the speculators miscalculated, and then developed, according to contemporary financial opinion, "one of the most serious and yet unnecessary panics New York has ever experienced." [15]

When it appeared, on May 9, 1901, that Northern Pacific stock was "cornered" in the sense of scarcely any being available, the panic broke. Speculators who had sold "short" made frantic efforts to secure stock to "cover" and hysterically bid up the price. Some stock appeared—in one case a special train was chartered to deliver a few hundred shares, and in another an invalid was carried in an ambulance to the bank to get some shares out of his strong-box.[16] These shares were snatched up quickly, but they could not still the storm. The price went up, up—200, 300, 1,000, all in one hour, and no stock available.[17] Brokers went crazy. The market broke, and all other stocks declined. Money rates shot skyward. In an effort to undo the harm the struggle for control of Northern Pacific had created, J. P. Morgan & Co. organized a syndicate of banks (in which the National City Bank did not participate) to loan $20,000,000 in the market, at 40 per cent to 60 per cent.[18] Then the House of Morgan and Kuhn, Loeb & Co. agreed not to insist on immediate delivery of Northern Pacific stock, and later decided on a price of 150 (although Robert Bacon at first resisted the proposal, fearing J. P. Morgan & Co. might lose some of their stock).[19]

As Northern Pacific rose in price other stocks declined from 15 per cent to 40 per cent—United States Steel from 46 to 24.[20] While the Morgan-Harriman clash was the immediate cause of the panic, the circumstances were more than favorable for a break in the stock market. An unparalleled speculative mania had prevailed since early in the year. The crop of millionaires created by the Steel Trust tossed their millions into the market. New combinations (enormously overcapitalized) encouraged speculation. The Standard Oil oligarchy massed its immense resources in the market, making $50,000,000 out of Amalgamated Copper manipulations alone (the manipulators forcing up the price, selling "short," then forcing the price down).[21] Speculators insisted a "new order of things" had come (as they did in 1929), the market was a mass of maddened bulls, and the *Commercial and Financial Chronicle* deplored this unbridled speculation's effect "on the morals of the community." [22] But while stock prices rose to dizzy heights corporate earnings did not, making collapse inevitable.

Meanwhile Morgan, in Europe, kept closely in touch with developments and upon news of the panic rushed immediately from Aix-les-Bains to Paris. He was excited, worried and in a towering rage: all over the office of Morgan, Harjes & Co. they could hear him swearing at the "idiots" and "rascals." Securing permission that his cablegrams to and fro be given precedence, Morgan studied the situation and issued orders. A reporter seeking an interview was threatened with "murder," but he persisted:

REPORTER: Don't you think, that since you are being blamed for a panic that has ruined thousands of people and disturbed a whole nation, some statement is due the public?

MORGAN: I owe the public nothing.[23]

After the smoke of battle cleared away, the Morgan and Harriman cohorts both claimed victory, Hill being particularly insistent that "J. Pierpont Morgan controls Northern Pacific." [24] The situation was this: the House of Morgan had bought 150,000 shares of Northern Pacific common stock, controlling a majority of this stock, while the Harriman forces had a majority of the preferred. Apparently Morgan was in control. But the preferred stock had equal voting rights with the common, and the Harriman holdings constituted a clear majority of both stocks. The Northern Pacific board of directors, however, had power to retire the preferred, and the Morgan-Hill forces threatened to do this, insuring their control. Harriman secured opinions that retiring the preferred stock was illegal and prepared to fight.[25]

But while Harriman was prepared to fight, his allies were not. Morgan had clearly manifested his determination to retain control of Northern Pacific, mobilizing all his resources, if necessary: resistance meant another and more disastrous clash. The Standard Oil jackals, still skulking in the shadows, decided not to pounce upon an aroused Morgan. Kuhn, Loeb & Co., frightened, worked for settlement and peace: they might make a foray against the House of Morgan, but war might mean their annihilation. The suave, unctuous Jacob Schiff, never very courageous, almost fawningly urged peace and friendship. Alone, Harriman was helpless. The embattled forces held a conference at which it was decided to "leave the composition of the Northern Pacific board in the hands of J. P. Morgan personally," agreeing upon a truce until Morgan's arrival in July.[26]

Morgan's final settlement was in accord with the system of community of interest—under his own overlordship. Five vacancies were created in Northern Pacific's board of directors, for which Morgan named J. J. Hill, E. H. Harriman, William Rockefeller, H. McK. Twombley and Samuel Rea.[27] Two of these new directors were out-and-out Morgan men and two others identified with the community-of-interest system (the older directors being Morgan-Hill representatives). Moreover, while Harriman became a member of the executive committee, the other five members were definitely affiliated with the House of Morgan.[28] The settlement, in a sense, was a partial Harriman victory, since he secured representation in Northern Pacific (which included Burlington), but Morgan retained the final control, although making concessions to community of interest.

Still, the Morgan-Hill forces were not satisfied with the situation. What had happened once might happen again. They decided to consolidate their control of Northern Pacific and Great Northern in a fashion making impossible their capture by rival interests. The means adopted was incorporation of a holding company, the Northern Securities Co., capitalized at $400,000,000, which acquired substantially all the stock of Northern Pacific and Great Northern.[29] Another corporation was organized to lease the Burlington, the stock being divided equally between the Hill-Morgan and Harriman interests. In Northern Securities itself the House of Morgan was dominant: it owned 120,000 shares, Hill was president, and twelve of the fifteen directors were Morgan-Hill representatives, the Harriman interests being granted three.[30]

The Northern Pacific settlement on the basis of community of interest was discussed by Morgan while testifying in a suit against the Northern Securities Co.:

COUNSEL: You knew that the Union Pacific was a competing line with the Burlington and that they had attempted to wrest your property away from you. What was the object in putting their representatives on the board?

MORGAN: Simply to show everybody concerned that J. P. Morgan & Co. were acting under what was known as the community-of-interest plan and that we were not going to have a battle in Wall Street.

COUNSEL: What is the community-of-interest theory?

MORGAN: That a certain number of men owning property should do what they like with it...and act toward mutual harmony.

COUNSEL: There has never been a representative of the Union Pacific on the board of the Northern Pacific before?

MORGAN: No; and I think those people were most surprised themselves. It was a most unusual thing to do with a competing interest, but showed we had nothing to fear from them.[31]

The clash revealed that railroads were still the playthings of competing, self-aggrandizing groups. Disposition of Burlington, of Northern Pacific itself, was decided by financial and manipulative power, not by the requirements of the railroads and public welfare. Morgan's settlement affirmed community of interest, under the overlordship of the House of Morgan, and it affirmed that community of interest operated in terms of the profits and power of the men in control. "Men owning property," said Morgan, "should do what they like with it and act toward mutual harmony." Harmony among the men in control and independent of any other control. J. P. Morgan rejected the right of government and public opinion to interfere with vested interests or to regulate their power and actions.

CHAPTER XXVII

REVERSES: MORGAN IN DANGER

> *She heard a little shriek and a fall, and a crash of broken glass.*
> *"Sure I don't like it, yer honor, at all, at all!" "Do as I tell you!" This time there were two little shrieks, and more sound of broken glass.*
> ALICE IN WONDERLAND

WHILE organizing the United States Steel Corporation and in the midst of the clash with Harriman, the House of Morgan prepared another giant combination—the International Mercantile Marine. This new combination was to become in transatlantic shipping what the Steel Trust was in the iron and steel industry—the dominating factor, capable of regulating (if not stifling) competition.

Intense competition prevailed in transatlantic shipping, rate wars being frequent and disastrous to profits. International conferences tried to apportion business and prevent competition.[1] J. P. Morgan's proposal was to combine the American, British and German lines—an international trust dominating the shipping business. It was a grandiose project, but failed lamentably, initiating a series of reverses which shook the House of Morgan's towering structure of financial control.

Acquiring two American lines, Morgan in April, 1901, bought the British Leyland Line,[2] and then proceeded to discuss an international combination. But the proposed combination was to be under American control and met unrelenting opposition in Britain and Germany, where it was interpreted in terms of American seizure of maritime supremacy.

The German lines at first negotiated with Morgan and then

withdrew. Although insisting that "I do not anticipate much harm from the appearance of the Morgan group in the ship-owning business," Albert Ballin, of the Hamburg-American Line, proposed measures to retain German lines under German control, a proposal emphasized by the *Berliner Tageblatt:* "Steps must be taken at once to protect our lines from Ameri-can action." [3] Germany's imperialistic projects were involved, and in the conferences to organize action against the American menace Kaiser Wilhelm himself participated.

Insisting that "Morganizing the Atlantic" threatened Brit-ain's maritime supremacy, British opinion protested against the proposed combination, the *Daily Mail,* in particular, bitterly and persistently assailing Morgan.[4] The House of Commons appointed a committee "to devise means for heading off some of the ruinous effects" of Morgan's combination.[5] One result was withdrawal of the Cunard Line, which received a large subsidy from the government "for the express purpose of meet-ing the conditions created by the Morgan combination." [6] But Morgan's prices meant such large profits that British ship-owners (in spite of arguments on "national interest") found them irresistible: the Leyland management bluntly declared Morgan's terms were so extravagant they could not do other-wise than accept in the interest of the shareholders, while a very high British shipping authority said, "The vendors made an exceptionally good bargain, which it is probable the pur-chasers will soon find out." [7]

The negotiations (in which J. Pierpont Morgan, Jr., actively participated) were drawn out, Morgan was compelled to modify his plans, but by the end of 1902 the combination was organized and the International Mercantile Marine Co. in-corporated, capitalized at $170,000,000. It included the Atlantic Transport, American, Leyland, White Star, Dominion and Red Star lines.[8] International Mercantile Marine was heavily overcapitalized. As in the case of the Steel Trust, extravagant prices were paid for the companies to be combined. Atlantic

Transport secured $12,000,000 in International Marine stock for its $3,000,000 stock outstanding, while shareholders in the merged British lines received $22,500,000 in cash plus generous amounts of stock in the new combination.[9] J. P. Morgan & Co. were paid $652,000 for organization expenses; and the Morgan syndicate, which provided $50,000,000 in cash, received all of International Marine's $50,000,000 bonds and $27,500,000 in stock.[10] Control was completely American, only five of the thirteen directors being English. American control was vested in the House of Morgan. J. P. Morgan, Charles Steele and P. A. B. Widener were three of the five voting trustees, and among the directors were Steele, Widener, Charles W. Perkins (who were also members of the finance committee), George F. Baker and Charles H. Hyde.[11]

But International Marine was one of Morgan's major mistakes, based on miscalculations. The market for new issues was congested, owing to the multiplication of combinations, and the public refused to buy International Marine stock. This refusal was sharpened by the 1903 panic, and the Morgan syndicate had to carry the new stock.[12] Another miscalculation was the impression that the new Republican Congress might grant a ship subsidy, but it did not. Immediately after International Marine's organization, depression developed in the ocean-carrying trade, and the company's first annual report showed earnings had been considerably higher *before* the combination.[13] British and German competition became more intense, the governments granting larger ship subsidies.

Clearly Morgan was developing faith in the magic potency of combination *in itself*. But the justification of combination was either in the monopolistic control of prices (or rates) or in improved productive efficiency. International Mercantile Marine offered neither—there was not much improved efficiency; and its share of transatlantic business being under 40 per cent, International Marine could not stifle competition or control rates. The unwieldy combination was a flat failure, the general impression being that Morgan had committed a major blunder—and this was emphasized in 1914 when International Mercantile Marine suspended interest payments, receivership coming the following year. The reorganization drastically reduced capitalization, aroused considerable litigation, and lessened control by the House of Morgan.[14]

International Mercantile Marine typified the reckless organization of combinations which flourished during 1901-3, stimulated by the immense profits yielded by the Steel Trust. Among them was the United States Shipbuilding Co., styled the "Shipbuilding Trust," which cast largely unmerited discredit upon the House of Morgan.

Originated by John W. Young, son of the Mormon prophet, United States Shipbuilding was characterized by misrepresentation and fraud from the beginning. Edward H. Harriman and James Stillman allowed their names to be used as "consenting" to serve on the board of directors, but then withdrew.[15] Underwriting was undertaken by the newly organized Trust Company of the Republic, in which Standard Oil interests were represented. Extravagant prices were paid for properties: the owner of one small plant, who would have sold gladly the previous year for $100,000, received twenty times that amount.[16] Charles M. Schwab, then president of United States Steel, approached the Shipbuilding promoters and suggested they buy the Bethlehem Steel Co., being "carried" for him by the United States Steel Syndicate. The offer was delightedly accepted, Bethlehem being a substantial property. People insisted that Schwab was crazy, but it was the craziness of the fox. He received $10,000,000 in Shipbuilding stock and $10,000,000 in bonds for Bethlehem (for which he had paid $7,246,000 in cash).[17] The bonds, strangely, carried voting rights, giving Schwab control of the combination, the promoters appearing exceptionally gullible. The underwriting failed disastrously. Ill from an overabundance of "indigestible securities," the public refused to buy Shipbuilding stock, in spite of John W. Gates

being engaged to "make a market." [18] The promoters had lied
unblushingly to the Trust Company of the Republic, reporting
that a French syndicate had agreed to take a large block of the
stock, but this turned out as simply the "lending of names"
for a commission by discredited financiers (one of whom had
been in prison). [19] Bethlehem was the only subsidiary which
met expectations, and the Shipbuilding board, under Schwab's
control, favored Bethlehem in the disposal of available capital.
Earnings being poor and the public refusing to buy the company's securities, money was borrowed from the Trust Company. But to no avail. The Shipbuilding Trust crashed into
bankruptcy, dragging down the Trust Company of the Republic. Reorganization plans favored Schwab, who drove "as hard
a bargain as his fortified position allowed." Bondholders began
legal action, charging "fraud and mismanagement" in Schwab's
interest, the proceedings revealing misrepresentation, manipulation and fraud. After the merry war of litigation, Bethlehem
Steel in 1904 took over the Shipbuilding assets, and Charles
M. Schwab emerged as an independent steel producer. [20]

This ingenious transaction, considered by contemporary
opinion a major financial scandal, produced much ill-will
against Morgan, in spite of the statement: "Neither the firm of
J. P. Morgan & Co. nor any of the partners ever had any connection with the inception, organization or financing of the
United States Shipbuilding Co., nor have they ever received
or owned any of its securities." [21] The Morgans were involved
as managers of the United States Steel Syndicate, which owned
Bethlehem Steel and acted in its sale to Schwab and transfer
to the Shipbuilding combination. J. P. Morgan & Co. received
as bonus $5,000,000 of Shipbuilding stock (which was after-
ward sold to Schwab for $75,000). [22] John W. Gates insisted
there was an agreement with Schwab and Morgan for the
priority sale of their stock, but Morgan did not sign the agreement, Schwab apparently signing for both. [23] J. P. Morgan &
Co., however, were not wholly passive in the promotion, send-

ing the following cablegram to Morgan, Harjes & Co. in Paris: "Charles M. Schwab and his friends are interested in the new shipbuilding company, and would be glad to have you take as cordial view as is consistent." [24] But although the Shipbuilding Trust was not a Morgan promotion, it intensified the public ill-will against the House of Morgan created by the International Mercantile Marine fiasco.

At this time "Bet-you-a-million" Gates specialized in stock-market manipulations, organization of the United States Steel Corporation signalizing his retirement from the iron and steel business. Among other manipulations Gates and his associates would buy small railroads not included in the large systems, plunder them and then use them for predatory manipulations. In this fashion they secured control of the Louisville & Nashville Railroad, the blackmail purpose being to compel J. P. Morgan & Co. to buy (against the head of which, moreover, Gates had many grudges). Success marked the conspiracy. The road might be used to demoralize Morgan's Southern Railway, and one night G. W. Perkins routed Gates out of bed, asked his price and received the reply: "As you want the stock so badly, I will let you have it if you will pay me $10,000,000 more than it cost." [25] The offer was promptly accepted, the Louisville & Nashville being merged with the Atlantic Coast Line, a road within the Morgan orbit.

Testifying in an investigation of complaints of mergers and combinations violating the Interstate Commerce Act, J. P. Morgan was asked about the Louisville & Nashville transaction by B. M. Young, counsel of the Railroad Commission of Kentucky:

YOUNG: Did you fear Gates would disturb the Southern railroad situation?

MORGAN: I did. I don't think him a proper man to be in control of that railroad.

YOUNG: How did you think Gates would injure Southern railroads?

MORGAN: I don't know exactly. I knew his men had no experience in handling railroads, and I didn't think his people the proper men.[26]

Meanwhile "Bet-you-a-million" Gates boasted gleefully of having "put one over on the old man," and Wall Street merrily agreed with him, the *Commercial and Financial Chronicle* commenting ironically:

"The Gates venture seems to have been a most wonderful affair. [After buying control of Louisville & Nashville] they knew where to go. They had been a party to dealings with J. P. Morgan & Co. before. Besides, they had no doubt heard of Mr. Morgan's skill as a rescuer. Passing all other lesser occasions, that page of history never can be blotted out when the country was on the ragged edge of the silver precipice, when confidence was gone, when foreign exchange was way up, when gold was flowing out in a flood, and all the gold left in the Treasury was being prepared to leave the country in twenty-four hours—no one can forget how when this climax was reached the President called upon Mr. Morgan for help and within an hour after he had received authority the marvel was worked of a complete restoration of confidence, a change in the foreign exchange market and a reversal of the gold current. We hardly need add that Mr. Gates and his friends were rescued." [27]

This was in 1902. A few years later Morgan met another reverse, to which his old enemy Harriman contributed. For some years Harriman had desired to become a member of Erie's board of directors and proposed it in 1903. The Erie board had no objections—but what would Morgan say? His antipathy to Harriman was notorious. When the directors approached Morgan he said that "the matter rests entirely with the board and the president," whereupon Harriman was elected a director.[28]

Some time later Morgan urged Erie to buy the Cincinnati, Hamilton & Dayton Railroad and "to move quickly,

for there are other purchasers after it." [29] The vendors submitted a statement to Morgan indicating that the road was
solvent, when in fact it was not earning its fixed charges and
practically bankrupt. Manipulated and plundered by speculative syndicates, the road was palmed on Morgan, who bought
and sold it to Erie for $12,000,000, Erie's president authorizing
the purchase without any investigation. It appears there was
some opposition to the deal,[30] but Morgan's authority prevailed. The road proved a heavy drain on Erie, and its insolvency was soon manifest. Harriman urged the Erie's president to see Morgan and have the sale rescinded, which the
president did—palpitatingly. Then Morgan appeared before
the board of directors and offered to buy back the Dayton
at the price Erie had paid, the offer being accepted. The
generosity of Erie's master warmed the bosoms of its directors
and they adopted a resolution, "suitably engraved, under Erie's
corporate seal, and signed by every director," thanking J. Pierpont Morgan "for his extraordinary service and assistance to
the company," first for buying the railroad and then for
"his magnificent, unparalleled, and absolutely voluntary offer
himself to assume the entire purchase." [31] There is in all this
more than a suggestion of the servility considered Asiatic. Two
days after the agreement the Cincinnati, Hamilton & Dayton
Railroad was thrown into bankruptcy.

A much more serious reverse for the House of Morgan was
the decline in United States Steel stock. After a short lull produced by the 1901 stock-market panic speculation revived and
again flourished rampantly. Recklessly overcapitalized combinations, such as International Mercantile Marine and the
Shipbuilding Trust, issued floods of new stock which they
could not dispose of. Morgan spoke of "undigested securities," but insisted that most of them were sound and their issue
justified.[32] Europe withdrew from the New York money market, sensing coming catastrophe. In the Autumn of 1902 money
became tight and banks began to compel syndicates to settle,

and as the syndicates could not sell their new issues they were forced to sell seasoned stocks and bonds. The market broke in 1903 and a panic developed. There were many bankruptcies among overcapitalized combinations. United States Steel suspended dividends and did not resume until two years later, while its common stock declined from 50 to 8 and the preferred from 95 to 49.[33] Other combinations suspended dividends and their stocks declined seriously.

United States Steel was the most important industrial affiliate of the House of Morgan and the particular pet of Morgan himself. It now appeared as if the corporate giant might crash. Ten years later, in the Money Trust investigation, Morgan testified:

MORGAN: I began to have doubts when the stock went to $8 a share.

UNTERMYER: Your doubts did not interfere with your buying heavily?

MORGAN: No, I bought all I could.

UNTERMYER: You were getting the advantage of other people's doubts at that time?

MORGAN: Nobody ever sold it at my suggestion, sir.

UNTERMYER: No, I did not mean to assume that.

MORGAN: I know.[34]

J. P. Morgan & Co. urged clients and others to buy Steel, insisting it was a good investment. Morgan's organization of the world's largest trust had captured popular imagination, and small investors all over the country invested their savings in United States Steel, fascinated by the prospect of large profits and their association with the financial Titan: "You see, J. P. Morgan says—" Most of the small investors now sold, their courage and imagination not being equal to the strain of the stock's downward plunge, and many of them were ruined. Nor was their action wholly unjustified, seasoned investors prophesying disaster for the Steel Trust, of which Carnegie said that its common stock was water and the preferred air. Confidence in United States Steel was also impaired by a proposed conversion of $200,000,000 7 per cent preferred stock into 5 per cent bonds, in the belief bonds might appeal more to investors than the preferred, considered distinctively speculative. The syndicate was to receive 4 per cent commission of which 25 per cent went to J. P. Morgan & Co. as syndicate managers. Minority stockholders and the press vigorously condemned the proposed conversion, declaring the Morgan commission "excessive" and a deliberate attempt to "milk" the Corporation. Owing to the opposition and unpleasant notoriety the plan was abandoned in 1903.[35]

This financial miscarriage, the disastrous drop in the price of United States Steel stock, the ill-fated International Mercantile promotion and the Shipbuilding Trust scandal created popular clamor against the House of Morgan. Cheated of the magic profits which did not materialize, investors who had almost worshiped Morgan as a financial Titan now pictured him as a financial pirate, the plunderer of widows and orphans (how they were overworked, these tear-wringing widows and orphans, both by the magnates and their antagonists!). More annoying to Morgan, probably, were the gibes at his mistakes: the demi-god of 1901 became the charlatan of 1903.

Expressing the popular mood, *Judge* pictured Morgan as a discredited magician and gibed at him in almost rhythmical prose:

As a floater of schemes
Pierpont Morgan seems to be losing his grip.
His appealing gaze at the investors that will not invest is a most
*   pathetic one*
Considering that a brief handful of moons agone
The speculator was quite as helpless in his gaze as is the song-
*   bird in the eye of the rattlesnake.*
Mr. Morgan used to float better than he knew,
And now he sinks better than he ever floated.

The day of his greatness is gone, never to return.
The soul of the old money magician
Experiences a thrill of keen, reminiscent pain.
With his divining-rod he can still cause the water of inflation
    to spout forth,
But no man seems to hanker after this rainbow-tinted water for
    fear he may, through imbibing it, become financially
    typhoided.
The undoing of the erstwhile king of financiers
Is largely due to his confidence in the inability of the public to
    see through his kaleidoscopic methods.
In the eyes of the financial world
He is not so conspicuous a figure of all-round grandeur
As he recently was.
The intelligent financier, in looking him over casually and
    critically,
Is reminded of a certain man in the Scriptures
Whose woebegone countenance but served to illustrate the fact
    that his glumness was due to a bellyful of east wind.[36]

The threat in the combined reverses was real. Some bankers said that J. Pierpont Morgan would never regain his financial prestige. Carnegie laughed, Harriman smiled, the Standard Oil oligarchy gloated. There might yet be a Morgan butchery to make a Roman holiday.

At the basis of the threat to the House of Morgan was the stampede (produced by the "silent panic" of 1903) to realize on huge masses of undigested and indigestible securities manufactured by trust promoters, and of which Morgan had issued more than his share. J. P. Morgan & Co. had to depend upon their own resources and the resources of their affiliates to meet the price declines in securities issued by the House, which was not over-strong in its liquid reserves. The Rockefeller-Harriman interests, on the contrary, had very large cash resources, were never in danger, and gleefully used the oppor-

tunity to "knife" Morgan. But silently, still arrogantly, Morgan
met the crisis in the manner of aggressive dictatorships. They
were trying to "knife" him?   Very well—Morgan issued an
ultimatum: Any one who had ever been assisted by the House
of Morgan and now declined, upon request, to assist the Morgans and their affiliates, would never again receive business
recognition by the House of Morgan.[37] This was not revenge,
but dictatorship threatening its antagonists, an offensive calculated to disorganize the enemy's forces. It worked—an aroused
Morgan was dangerous, and, after all, power still inhered in
the House of Morgan in spite of reverses. Nor was business
recognition ever again granted men who, upon request, denied
the assistance asked.

The reverses assailing the House of Morgan were accompanied by a new revolt against corporate combinations which
produced and was strengthened by the Supreme Court's decision, in March, 1904, ordering dissolution of the Northern
Securities Co. This decision constituted a serious reverse piled
upon other reverses.

Many Western governors greeted the formation of Northern
Securities with hostility, the Governor of Minnesota declaring
no stone would be left unturned to prevent the contemplated
consolidation. Minnesota initiated legal action, and then President Theodore Roosevelt intervened, Attorney-General Philander C. Knox starting dissolution proceedings on the ground
that Northern Securities violated the anti-trust laws. These
proceedings constituted the second clash between Morgan and
Roosevelt, the President recently having compelled the master
of money to come to terms during the anthracite strike. The
suit against Northern Securities was decided upon in secret,
and Morgan knew nothing about it until the report appeared
in the newspapers. Wall Street furiously condemned the action.
Morgan broke out in one of his violent fits of rage, and rushed
to Washington to interview Roosevelt and Knox:

MORGAN: Why didn't you let me know of the suit?

ROOSEVELT: That is just what we did not want to do.

MORGAN: If we have done anything wrong, send your man [meaning Attorney-General Knox] to see my man [meaning one of the Morgan lawyers] and they can fix it up.

ROOSEVELT: That can't be done.

KNOX: We don't want to fix it up, we want to stop it.

MORGAN: Are you going to attack my other interests, the Steel Trust and the others?

ROOSEVELT: Certainly not, unless we find out that in any case they have done something that we regard as wrong.

After the interview Roosevelt said to Knox: "That is a most illuminating illustration of the Wall Street point of view. Mr. Morgan could not help regarding me as a big rival operator, who either intended to ruin all his interests or else could be induced to come to an agreement to ruin none." [38]

If the government suit enraged Morgan, the interview with Roosevelt humiliated him, compelled him to eat humble pie— he who, until recently, had gone his royal way undisturbed. Roosevelt's behavior was something new—since McKinley's election the magnates of industry and finance had come to look upon the government as their "big brother." The President infuriated the magnates still more by his denunciations of Morgan, Hill and Harriman as "malefactors of great, wealth." Morgan acquired a dislike of Roosevelt during the coal strike, which became violent, unreasoning hatred, mounting in fury as the President attacked others of Morgan's combinations. ...

The government secured a victory in the lower courts, which enjoined the Great Northern and Northern Pacific Railroads from allowing Northern Securities to vote their stock or pay it any dividends. On appeal, this ruling was affirmed by the Supreme Court in a characteristic five-to-four decision.

In its majority opinion the Court insisted that Northern Securities was an "illegal combination or conspiracy in restraint of trade," that its purpose to destroy competition "was

concealed under very general words that gave no clue whatever to the real purpose," and that "if the Anti-Trust Act is
held not to embrace a case such as is now before us, the plain
intention of the legislative branch of the government will be
defeated." [39] The minority opinion insisted just as positively
that Northern Securities was *not* in restraint of trade, and
indicated the weakness of all anti-trust decisions by pointing
out that "the decree, whilst forbidding the use of the stock by
the Northern Securities Co., authorizes its return to the alleged
conspirators, and does not restrain them from exercising the
control resulting from ownership." [40] The men in control
would simply exercise their control in some other form. "I do
not expect to hear it maintained," said Justice Holmes in his
dissenting opinion, "that Mr. Morgan could be sent to prison
for buying as many shares as he liked of the Great Northern
and Northern Pacific, even if he bought at the same time and
got more than half the stock of each road." [41] In emphasizing
the issue of competition, the Supreme Court majority forgot
that there was no competition between Northern Pacific and
Great Northern before the organization of Northern Securities.

The order of dissolution against Northern Securities disturbed and unsettled the stock market, but financial opinion
quickly concluded that the decision was "inconsequential,"
since "Congress cannot prevent, if it would, any individual
from purchasing more than a majority of the stock of competing roads; that being true, the community-of-interest idea
is invulnerable and a way will be devised for making it feas-
ible." [42]

All of which was true, but did not touch the real issue.
Supreme Court decisions, of course, could not restore competition or annihilate the system of community of interest: the centralization of control over industry and finance was inescapable. The importance of the Northern Securities decision lay
in affirming the power of the Federal government to regulate
corporate combinations, constituting an important stage in

President Roosevelt's campaign for regulation of the trusts and railroads. This campaign developed into a war between government and the magnates, in the course of which government imposed some limitations upon J. P. Morgan's theory that "men owning property should do what they like with it." In one of its aspects, Morganization was a struggle against government regulation and control: Morgan was against the "leave alone" policy of competition, but favored the "leave alone" policy of letting the magnates of industry and finance do as they liked. Among the railroads, the final outcome was regulation of rates, accounting, valuation and financing, and machinery for the control of wages and labor conditions.

Another clash between Morgan and Harriman developed out of the dissolution of Northern Securities. The Morgan-Hill directors decided to distribute the stock pro rata. Harriman objected, insisting that each party receive the stock it had originally put in Northern Securities, which meant Harriman receiving the majority stock in Northern Pacific instead of minority holdings in the two roads.[43] At a conference in the offices of J. P. Morgan & Co. Harriman's proposal was rejected, the decision being to let the courts settle the dispute. Reports of a "friendly suit" were vigorously denied by Harriman's attorney, and it was reported that "Rockefeller wants the Northern Pacific." [44] After a series of injunctions and lawsuits, the United States Supreme Court decided against Harriman, who subsequently sold Union Pacific's holdings in Northern Pacific and Great Northern at a profit of $58,000,000.[45] Harriman persisted in being a thorn in the flesh of Morgan, snatching from him control of Erie some years later. . . .

The series of reverses in 1902-4 shook the House of Morgan's towering structure of financial centralization and control —but shook it only, being too solidly organized to be seriously affected by anything short of a major catastrophe. Aggressively, ruthlessly, Morgan beat down enemy attacks and compelled wavering affiliates not to desert his dictatorship. He was comparatively inactive for three years, undertaking no new enterprises of magnitude, placing his house in order. Events, moreover, favored Morgan in his simple faith: You can't be a bear on America, prosperity will revive: wait! By 1905 unprecedented prosperity prevailed. Dividends being resumed, United States Steel stock rose above its original prices.[46] Tottering combinations assumed new vigor, earnings piled up, more combinations were organized, the securities of which the public again bought eagerly, and speculation flourished—until business crashed again in 1907. Morgan used the intervening period of prosperity to accumulate large liquid reserves; never again the 1902-4 experience! When the 1907 panic came the House of Morgan was in shipshape condition to resist the storm, while others were not: out of the panic came unchallenged acceptance of J. Pierpont Morgan's supremacy....

In the midst of reverses, moreover, the House of Morgan broadened, deepened and consolidated its system of financial centralization and control. It organized in 1902 one of the most successful combinations, the International Harvester Co. Capitalized at $120,000,000, organized to control the market and develop exports, and combining the McCormick Harvester Co. and four other large manufacturers of agricultural machinery, International Harvester easily dominated its industry.[47] The profit of J. P. Morgan & Co. in this promotion was $2,957,000, and the new enterprise was substantially Morganized: George W. Perkins and Henry P. Davison (one already a Morgan partner, the other prospective) were two of the three voting trustees of International Harvester, Perkins was vice-president and chairman of the finance committee, and the directors included Perkins, Elbert H. Gary and Charles Steele (another Morgan partner).[48]

The broadening and deepening of the House of Morgan's power was facilitated by developments among its industrial affiliates. Thus the General Electric Co., which since its organization had moved within the Morgan orbit, was by now more than a manufacturing concern. General Electric had abandoned the practice of its predecessors in promoting local traction and lighting companies, but resumed the practice in another form. The enormous expansion in electrical manufactures and profits piled up large resources, and through a holding company General Electric began to develop and acquire control of public-utility corporations in the more important sections of the country.[49] Its affiliates strengthened the House of Morgan's financial control of industry.

Financial control of industry, in the final analysis, was determined by control of financial resources upon which the House of Morgan's dominance depended. In the midst of reverses J. P. Morgan & Co. consolidated their financial power. The National Bank of Commerce, directly under Morgan's control, absorbed the Western National Bank, its board of directors becoming a concentration of the most important industrial and financial interests, including George F. Baker, James B. Duke, Chauncey M. Depew, Daniel Guggenheim, Otto H. Kahn, A. W. Mellon, Elihu Root, George J. Gould, Thomas F. Ryan and Levi P. Morton. Owing to pressure of other business, Morgan resigned as vice-president but retained his posts in the board of directors and the executive committee.[50] J. P. Morgan & Co. acquired a large interest in the Liberty National Bank (with which the First National Bank had long been associated) and secured two directors.[51] The House of Morgan now organized its own trust company, the Bankers Trust Co., no stock being offered to the public, its officers and directors being all Morgan affiliates.[52] Another concentration of industrial and financial forces, under Morgan's system of community of interest, was the Trust Company of America, which absorbed two other trust companies, its directors including George W. Perkins, P. A. B. Widener, Samuel Spencer (president of Morgan's Southern Railway), W. K. Vanderbilt and Charles W. Morse.[53] Through these banks and other affiliations the House of Morgan penetrated more completely the life-insurance companies, while its associates in other cities adopted the same procedure (as in the case of Charles S. Mellen, president of Morgan's New York, New Haven & Hartford Railroad, becoming a director in the First National Bank of Boston).[54]

Out of the House of Morgan's control of financial resources developed its control of industry which was used to secure still larger control of financial resources—an overwhelming centralization of industry and finance capable of resisting the most serious reverses.

CHAPTER XXVIII

DEVELOPING IMPERIALISM

See how eagerly the lobsters and the turtles all advance!
They are waiting on the shingle—will you come and join the dance?
Will you, won't you, will you, won't you, will you join the dance?

ALICE IN WONDERLAND

THE House of Morgan expressed the major developments of American industry and finance as they approached maturity, seldom in their initial stages. One reason was that J. Pierpont Morgan dreamed no dreams, never tried to pierce the future and anticipate coming events. The other reason was impersonal and more important—as the most active agency stabilizing and centralizing industry and finance, integrating capitalism, the House of Morgan necessarily expressed developments in their larger aspects and as they assumed definite shape. As in the case of industrial combination, which it did not pioneer but dominated at the decisive moment, the House of Morgan was identified with the larger aspects of American financial imperialism, seldom with the pioneering.

In 1902 J. P. Morgan & Co., Belmont & Co. and the National City Bank applied to the New York Stock Exchange to list Russian rentes, preliminary to more listings of foreign securities.[1] This was the backwash of the movement to make New York City the money center of the world, of which Wall Street had dreamed in 1900. But the threat to London did not materialize. By 1903 most of the British and German bonds bought by Americans the previous two years had been repurchased by Europe.[2] Instead of lending money abroad American financiers began to borrow there to finance new corporate combinations and to sustain speculation.[3] American financiers temporarily lost their interest in foreign loans.

But foreign loans are simply one aspect of the export of capital and imperialism, which is an international struggle for supremacy in the monopolization of the world's markets, natural resources and investment opportunities by loans or direct investments (including political and military force).

Almost all the industrial combinations under control or influence of the House of Morgan engaged actively in the struggle for international supremacy, directly investing large amounts of capital in other countries. United States Steel acquired iron mines in Cuba and competed aggressively for foreign markets and raw materials, ultimately compelling the European steel magnates to come to terms by means of an agreement; International Harvester built plants in Canada, Russia, Germany and France, and General Electric in Japan and China.[4] To secure more business for Northern Pacific and Great Northern, James J. Hill organized an aggressive campaign for markets in Oriental countries: "preparing to challenge England," said Hill, "for our share of the business," adding, "the Orient belongs to us and we should control it."[5] In 1904 J. P. Morgan & Co. bought $5,000,000 of Canadian Northern Railroad bonds.[6] The Vanderbilt interests acquired Canadian railroads connecting with New York Central, while Morgan-Hill efforts to extend the power of their Northwestern railroad system to Canada provoked charges in parliament that they were trying to get control of the country's railroads and mines.[7]

In 1901 J. S. Morgan & Co. secured control of London's underground railway system preparatory to another of Morgan's combinations; but the following year control was snatched away by the Speyers and Charles T. Yerkes, the Chicago traction magnate.[8] The British press considered the affair "J. Pierpont Morgan's second defeat in this country" (the first being the failure to buy the Cunard Line for International Mercantile Marine).[9] To finance Yerkes' traction projects in London, Speyer & Co. issued an American loan of $17,000,000, which was oversubscribed.[10]

At this period, however, American capital was most active in Latin America, although still subordinate to Britain, France and Germany (except in the Caribbeans).

Immediately upon their liberation from Spain, Cuba and Porto Rico were invaded by American banks and business enterprises, which soon acquired control of banks, railroads, sugar plantations and ports. The American Fruit Co. owned plantations and docks in Cuba, and the Bethlehem Steel Co. through a subsidiary operated mines and mills.[11] In 1904 the Speyers floated a Cuban loan of $35,000,000, partly subscribed by American investors.[12] Economic subjection implies political subjection, and Cuba was transformed into an American protectorate by means of the Platt Amendment which limited the new republic's treaty-making and financial powers and gave the United States the right of military intervention—the first exercise of this right in 1906 presaging a series of interventions.

American capital flowed turbulently into Mexico after the discovery of oil in 1901. Edward L. Doheny and his associates acquired large oil fields and when the British appeared an aggressive struggle for supremacy developed, strengthening the tyrant Porfirio Diaz, spreading corruption and instigating political disturbances.[13] In 1902 Edward H. Harriman secured from Dictator Diaz a concession to build a railroad as an extension of his Southern Pacific, running through fabulously rich mineral regions, and in 1903 the Speyers floated a loan of $12,500,000 for the Mexican government.[14]

While concentrating on the Caribbeans and its colonial empire, American capital did not altogether neglect South America. J. P. Morgan & Co. bought the Transandine Railroad, Anglo-American financiers secured an immense rubber concession in Bolivia, copper mines were acquired in Chile, W. R.

Grace & Co. expanded their mercantile and banking business, and other American corporations directly acquired large interests.[15]

All this activity was climaxed by the Panama Canal, which confirmed American supremacy in the Caribbeans, brought closer together the Philippine and Caribbean colonial empire, provided a shorter ocean route to the Orient's markets, and insured American sea power.

Considerable mystery still shrouds the events leading up to the American government's purchase, in 1902, of the "rights" of the old Panama Canal Co. of France, which expired in 1904, although the political and financial motives are clear. The project of a Nicaraguan canal was making headway when Philippe Bunau-Varilla, representing the old French company, got in touch with William Nelson Cromwell, an expert in reorganization of bankrupt corporations. Cromwell incorporated (with dummy directors) the New Panama Canal Co. which took over the old company's assets, and still another company, the American Panama Canal Co., to "Americanize" the canal. A $5,000,000 syndicate was formed to finance the new corporations.[16] "Exclusively empowered" to act for the New Panama Canal Co., Cromwell made the sale to the United States government for $40,000,000. The Roosevelt Administration then asked Colombia, in return for $10,000,000, to cede by perpetual lease a strip of territory through the Isthmus. Considering the terms unfair, in view of the larger payment received by the French company for its worthless "rights" and "assets," the Colombian Congress refused to ratify the treaty. Cromwell, Bunau-Varilla and their associates were not to be balked, and they were desperate as the French company's concession expired in 1904, after which they would have nothing to sell. Confident of American support, the conspirators determined on forcible action.

In 1903 an insurrectionary movement broke out in the City of Panama in favor of an independent republic, in which the employees of the Panama Railroad (under Cromwell's control) were particularly active. The insurrection broke out the day after the United States cruiser *Nashville* arrived at Colon. Colombia rushed troops to the disaffected area, but they were blocked by the *Nashville* and its marines, who prevented an attack upon the insurgents. Three days after the revolution President Roosevelt recognized the Republic of Panama, and twelve days later the Canal treaty was signed.[17] To criticisms of his procedure Roosevelt some years later cynically retorted: "I took the Canal Zone and let the Congress debate, and while the debate goes on the canal does also." [18]

The Republic of Panama appointed J. P. Morgan & Co. its fiscal agents, in co-operation with Cromwell. Of the $10,000,000 received by the new republic from the American government, Morgan and Cromwell paid it $4,000,000 outright, the balance being "invested permanently, for the benefit of the nation," in New York real-estate mortgages.[19] The Morgans were also fiscal agents of the Panama Canal Co. of France, to whom the United States paid $40,000,000 for its "assets" and "rights." Morgan and his son, J. P. Morgan, Jr., were active in the transfer of the money, which the Treasury deposited in ten banks, all of them Morgan institutions or moving within the Morgan orbit.[20] J. S. Morgan & Co. in London made the final transfer to the Bank of France.

Not only was there criticism of President Roosevelt's intervention in the Panaman revolution, but considerable speculation on "who got the money" paid by the government to the French company. In 1906 the Senate Committee on Interoceanic Canals investigated the transaction. Asked about the payments, Cromwell said that $25,000,000 had been paid to the liquidator of the old French company and $15,000,000 to the New Panama Canal Co., of which $3,000,000 was still in the treasury.[21] But Cromwell refused to reveal the final distribution of the money: he knew who got the money, but would not tell, although his refusal shrouded the affair in mystery and suspicion.[22] Cromwell was the chief actor in the whole transaction, and he and his associates undoubtedly cleared large profits.

The New York *World* and Indianapolis *News* persisting in asking "Who got the money?" and making damaging accusations, President Roosevelt ordered libel suits against the newspapers under an old statute which had nothing to do with libel, being for the protection "of harbor defenses and fortifications," but which carried a criminal penalty. The government suits (justified by Roosevelt on the ground that "libel upon the United States government" was involved) accused the *World* and *News* of criminally libeling Theodore Roosevelt, J. Pierpont Morgan, William Nelson Cromwell and three other persons.[23] One Federal district attorney resigned rather than act, insisting the suit "strikes at the very foundations of our government." [24] The two suits were dismissed by the courts, one judge saying in his decision: "There are many peculiar circumstances about this Panama Canal business. I have a curiosity to know the real truth," adding that Cromwell's behavior before the Senate Committee "gave just ground for suspicion." [25] In 1911 the Supreme Court rendered unanimous decision in the *World's* favor. The question of "who got the money" is still unanswered.

After the Panama conquest President Roosevelt, interpreting the Monroe Doctrine as giving the United States the right of intervention in Latin-American states to "protect life and property," applied "Big Stick" tactics to Santo Domingo, upon which he imposed a treaty accepting American control over the Dominican customs, finances and the claims of all foreign creditors. The American Senate refusing to ratify the treaty, Roosevelt answered by making an "executive agreement" with Santo Domingo, and established another protectorate.[26] There was a storm of protest in Latin America, which felt itself menaced, as Roosevelt acted under the Monroe Doctrine which he converted from its original purpose of preventing European colonization in the Americas into an instrument for promoting the financial and political supremacy of the United States.

The most conscious expression of developing financial imperialism at this time was the International Banking Corporation organized in 1902 (later becoming a subsidiary of the National City Bank). It was a concentration of important interests, the board of directors including Henry C. Frick, Edward H. Harriman, Jules S. Bache, Edwin Gould and Isaac Guggenheim, moving within the Standard Oil orbit.[27] Securing the American fiscal agency of China, the corporation by 1910 had sixteen branches in China, Japan, India, the Philippines, Mexico, Santo Domingo and Panama.[28] It was no accident that Harriman, Morgan's old enemy, participated in the International Banking Corporation. He was interested in organizing a ship-and-rail line circling the world, by way of Manchuria, Siberia, the Baltic and New York, and securing railroad concessions in China with their large profits and mining privileges. During the war with Russia, Japanese loans aggregating $130,000,000 were floated in the United States by Kuhn-Loeb syndicates (in which Morgan's Bank of Commerce participated). Harriman used the prestige of this financing to make a tentative agreement with Japan for joint American-Japanese ownership of the South Manchurian Railway and equal participation in all its industrial enterprises, the American minister in Japan co-operating in the project. After the treaty of peace, however, Japan rejected the agreement, not desiring to share its Manchurian conquests with American finance.[29]

In 1905 the House of Morgan intervened in the Chinese situation by acquiring control of the American China Development Co. This company, organized by American capitalists (including Standard Oil interests) to operate railroads, steamships, telegraph and telephone lines in China, obtained in 1898 coal mining and industrial franchises and a concession to build a railroad from Canton to Hankow.[30] The Chinese government specifically retained the right to cancel the concession should it come under other than American ownership, the concession forbidding the Americans to "transfer the rights of these agreements to other nations or people of other nationality." [31] Some time before this a Franco-Belgian company organized upon the personal initiative of King Leopold of the Belgians, with which were associated other exploiters of the Congo Free State, secured a concession to build the railroad from Hankow to Pekin: "I'll get the choice cuts, all right," said Leopold in his characteristic butcher's jargon.[32]

Belgians tried to secure the Canton-Hankow concession also but failed, the Chinese not desiring them to become too strong, after which, in 1899, they secured stock control of the American China Development Co., although this did not become public until four years later. China now threatened to cancel the concession in accordance with its specific provisions. (Only twenty-eight miles of the road had been built.) The Belgians protested, arguing that the company was still American, and King Leopold begged President Roosevelt to intercede on behalf of the white race and, presumably, its profits.[33] The American government, by diplomacy, supported the Belgians, although the Chinese government was clearly within its rights. At this juncture J. P. Morgan & Co. bought control of the American China Development Co., complicating the situation.

The Chinese government still threatening cancelation, Washington informed it that the United States could not tolerate such "spoilation." [34] A former American minister to China advised President Roosevelt that "surrender of the concession means a serious blow to American prestige and interests." [35] The New York *Times* considered the concession of "vital concern" because of the "advantage it would afford American commerce and the prestige it would give the United States in a section of China where British, German and French capital is being poured in very largely in an effort to further certain political plans of those nations in the Far East.... The United States, with her growing trade and commerce in the Far East and her possession of the Philippines, will be called on to take a leading part in the readjustment of Far Eastern affairs if her interests are to be preserved." [36] With which the New York *Tribune* agreed, insisting that the concession was "very important and potentially valuable." [37] This was precisely the attitude of the American government as expressed by President Roosevelt, and the utmost diplomatic pressure was used to prevent China canceling the concession.

Apparently none of these far-flung considerations animated Morgan in acquiring control of the American China Development Co. He bought to sell—at a good profit, as did the stockholders. Important influences converged on Morgan not to sell. The Chinese government, compelled by American intervention to withdraw its legitimate cancelation, offered an indemnity of twice what the Americans had invested, which was acceptable to Morgan. He decided to sell. King Leopold visited Morgan when the financier's yacht was in European waters, and urged retaining the concession.[38] President Roosevelt invited Morgan to a conference and suggested the same thing, this being the decision of the Cabinet.[39] Morgan considered the suggestion, but at a subsequent conference informed Roosevelt that the stockholders insisted upon selling. China canceled the concession and paid $6,750,000 indemnity to the American China Development Co., representing 100 per cent profit on the original investment—extortionate but profitable. In announcing the decision to sell, President Roosevelt said: "Mr. Morgan has consulted with the administration, and shown every desire to do what American interests in the Orient demanded." [40]

Yet, according to Roosevelt himself, American interests in the Orient demanded retention of the Hankow-Canton concession. Immediate profit probably swayed Morgan in making the sale, but there were other considerations determining his action. The House of Morgan was not prepared to intervene in China on any large scale, the prevailing conditions not being favorable. China at the moment was determined to cancel all the concessions possible. Conditions were particularly unfavorable for American enterprise, the Chinese having declared a boycott on American goods in protest at "the barbarous methods that have been used in enforcing the Chinese Exclusion Act."[41] So strong was anti-American feeling in China that President Roosevelt sent Secretary of War William H. Taft as peacemaker.[42] Under the circumstances Morgan concluded that withdrawal was the safer policy, particularly as he was never interested in pioneering imperialistic adventures.*

As Morgan withdrew from China, Harriman plunged in again, renewing in 1906 his struggle to secure control of the South Manchurian Railroad. Efforts to revive the 1905 agreement failing, Harriman prepared to parallel the South Manchurian, a project requiring large capital and the American government's diplomatic support. The State Department granted the support while Harriman's bankers, the National City Bank and Kuhn, Loeb & Co., agreed to raise the capital. An agreement was concluded for the organization of an American-Chinese Manchurian Bank to finance railroad construction, and, with the approval of Secretary Root, Kuhn, Loeb & Co. agreed to underwrite a loan of $20,000,000. But the death of the Dowager Empress, which upset the political alignment in China, smashed Harriman's plans.[43]

Meanwhile American finance did not neglect Latin Amer-

---

* About a year later J. P. Morgan was among the signers (most of them clergymen, with three or four businessmen) of a memorial to Secretary of State Elihu Root asking that the American government, which had given moral support to establishment of the Congo Free State, act against delay in introducing reforms urged by King Leopold's own commission, including abolition of the oppressive labor tax, appropriating the natives' land, use of brutish sentries who murdered, pillaged and raped the natives, employment and maltreatment of children, judicial injustice and punitive expeditions. (New York *Tribune*, December 26, 1906.)

ica. J. P. Morgan & Co. issued a $2,250,000 loan for railroad construction in Panama.[44] The National City Bank and Speyer & Co. secured a contract from the Bolivian government for railroad construction and issued a loan of $18,500,000 on terms very onerous to Bolivia, while an American construction company (operating on a cost plus 10 per cent basis) secured large profits by wastefully piling up the costs.[45] In 1908 the House of Morgan issued a loan of $2,500,000 to Bolivia to stabilize its exchange (upset by the American panic of 1907).[46] The following year the Morgans secured $10,000,000 of an international loan to Argentina.[47]

Under Roosevelt's imperialistic interpretation of the Monroe Doctrine the United States now intervened in the financial affairs of Honduras. In 1908 European creditors urged Honduras to refund its foreign debt of $125,000,000 largely tainted with frauds, proven by British government investigation, after which Honduran bonds were bought up by speculators at a small price.[48] Considering the terms proposed onerous, the Honduran government appealed to Secretary of State Knox, who acted immediately in accord with his policy of promoting "Dollar Diplomacy" and keeping European nations from intervening in Latin-American affairs. Knox asked J. P. Morgan & Co. to undertake the Honduran refunding, which was done in 1911, the debt being adjusted downward and arrangements made for a $10,000,000 loan to Honduras.[49] The accompanying conditions imposed American financial control: the loan was to be guaranteed by a lien on the Honduran customs, the collector to be selected from a list of names submitted by J. P. Morgan & Co. and approved by the president of the United States, the government to sign the loan convention and act as guarantor.[50] The Nicaraguans felt that they had jumped from the frying pan into the fire, insisted the Morgan terms were "an imitation of the Santo Domingo plan—an American financial protectorate," and rejected the convention.[51] Objecting to the financial protectorate features the American Senate declined to ratify, although urged by President Taft and Secretary Knox, who argued customs control was necessary to induce capital to become "the instrumentality of peace and prosperity" in the "backward republics in the neighborhood of the Panama Canal." [52]

Two years later the National City Bank secured control of the National Bank of Haiti, which later led directly to American military occupation (followed by similar action in Nicaragua). [53]

In its penetration of Latin America the United States met the mercantile and financial competition of European powers. Imperialistic antagonisms sharpened, converging on China. While transforming the Monroe Doctrine into an instrument for the domination of Latin America, President Roosevelt pursued an equally aggressive policy in the Orient, particularly China, urging Morgan to retain control of the Hankow-Canton concession and granting diplomatic support to Harriman's projects.

"America's geographical position in the Pacific," said Roosevelt, emphasizing that the Panama Canal had made the United States more than ever a Pacific power, "is such as to insure peaceful domination of its waters in the future, if we only grasp with sufficient resolution the advantages of that position." [54] Financiers and manufacturers declared "it is increasingly necessary to find profitable outlets for our merchandise, and there is no more alluring field than the Chinese Empire." [55]

But European powers were monopolizing the Chinese markets (modified by Japanese penetration). "Spheres of influence," said Thomas W. Lamont, one of the Morgan partners, "served to divide up China commercially into almost water-tight compartments, and the nations like the United States which had no compartments could not do much trading." [56] Its old civilization upset by the pressure of industrialism and clashing imperialisms, in the agony of transition,

China was the prey of foreign (and native) adventurers, concessionaires, political job-hunters and rapacious financiers.

The struggle for an American "place in the sun" in China
flared up in 1909 in an organized contest with European financiers, in which the House of Morgan (the issue now being decisive) represented American financial and imperialistic interests.*

British, German and French bankers secured a Chinese loan
of $27,500,000 to finance railroad construction. Secretary Knox,
developing his plans for loans and concessions in China as sup-
plementary to the "Open Door" policy, decided to compel
American participation in the loan on a basis of equality with
the European powers. Prepared to use diplomacy in the struggle, Knox called upon the House of Morgan for financial co-
operation. Henry P. Davison, one of the Morgan partners, went
to Washington.

"Can we," asked Knox, "rely upon you to perfect the financing arrangements which are vital if our plan is to be com-
passed?"

In the person of Davison the House of Morgan answered,
"Yes." [57]

J. P. Morgan & Co. organized a syndicate including the First
National Bank, National City and Kuhn, Loeb & Co. The syndicate represented a mobilization of American financial power
for an international struggle directly instigated by the government, the purpose being to secure loans, concessions and equality with Europe in the exploitation of China.[58] Most of the
negotiations, for the Morgans, were handled by Davison.

Secretary Knox called upon China to admit the American
bankers to participation in the proposed loan. The Morgans
made a similar demand upon the European bankers. While
the American government issued "solemn" warnings to China

---

* In this year J. Pierpont Morgan, Jr., was elected to the board of directors and finance committee of the United States Steel Corporation. The stock
exchange "celebrated" by advancing Steel stock three points. (*Commercial and
Financial Chronicle*, May 29, 1909, p. 1340.)

and used diplomatic pressure, the Europeans ordered China not to yield. The Chinese government, helpless, was afraid to do anything: wherever it might raise its head, an American or European bludgeon prepared to descend. Backed by their governments, the European bankers rejected the demand of the American bankers backed by their government. Diplomacy and finance united in one of those struggles which constituted the background of the World War.

President Taft, who accepted all the imperialistic but few of the "progressive" policies of Roosevelt, had said in his inaugural address that the United States could not maintain her interests in the Orient "if it is understood that she never intends to back up her assertion of right and her defense of her interests by anything but mere verbal protest and diplomatic note." [59] Making clear the government's intention to back up the bankers, Taft personally and undignifiedly appealed to the Chinese regent for "equal participation" in the loan by the Morgan syndicate. Coerced China left the decision to the European bankers and their governments, who, afraid to force the issue, granted American participation on the basis of "absolute equality." [60] The powers obligingly raised the loan to $30,000,-000, more easily split four ways, the Morgan syndicate receiving $7,500,000—a "pittance," said the *Commercial and Financial Chronicle*, "but the principle is full of far-reaching possibilities." [61]

Now actively engaged in the Chinese struggle, the Morgan syndicate scored a coup by securing a Manchurian agreement for construction of a railroad, American bankers to furnish the money. Diplomatic representatives again drummed up business, the State Department using the Manchurian agreement in an effort to realize "neutralization" of the railroads, but the powers rejected the offer. Uniting against American finance, Russia and Japan now recognized each other's spheres of influence in Manchuria and protested to the Chinese government against the proposed American railroad as "inimical." [62] Not prepared to force the issue, the United States abandoned the scheme, while China looked helplessly on as clashing imperialisms wrangled over the booty.

Another and more important Morgan coup was the Chinese currency reform loan of $50,000,000, secured in 1910 through the efforts of the International Banking Corporation and American diplomacy.[63] The bankers of Britain, Germany and France now insisted on equal participation, as the Americans had done previously. The demand was rejected, but after another diplomatic war the Morgan syndicate and the government yielded. Deciding upon a truce, the American, British, French and German bankers concluded an agreement for "co-operation of the signatories in the matter of future loans to the Chinese government and mutual participation therein," China being compelled to agree that in the event of new loans "the contracting banks shall first be invited to participate." [64] An international financial protectorate over China.

In all its imperialistic operations in China the House of Morgan, as the concentration of American finance, had complete government support. President Taft in his message to Congress in 1910 declared the success of the Morgan syndicate in securing the currency loan was "gratifying," spoke of the government's "assistance," and concluded that the Chinese loans were "of the greatest importance to the commercial interests of the United States." [65] The older theory of the separation of government and industry was discarded in favor of "Dollar Diplomacy," of the imperialistic policy uniting government, diplomacy and finance for international struggle.

Assuming political initiative, government urged financial action upon the House of Morgan, spurred on by the other nations' imperialistic division of the world. American capitalism broke through its national barriers and penetrated the world's markets: by 1912 American foreign investments amounted to $2,000,000,000 (against $500,000,000 in 1900).[66] Expressing major industrial and financial developments, the House of Morgan now participated actively in the export of capital, as it had previously in the import of capital, imperialism becoming a definite phase of American industry and finance.

After the Chinese revolution, European opinion considered China on the verge of bankruptcy and foreign control, bankers foreseeing a "rosy future." [67] The Chinese Republic in 1913 decided to borrow $125,000,000 for reconstruction purposes, suggesting to the European and American bankers that Russia and China be included in the consortium. [68] The Morgans, again heading a syndicate including the First National Bank, National City and Kuhn, Loeb & Co., decided they would participate in the new Six-Power loan only "if expressly requested to do so by the government," and to withdraw unless the Wilson Administration pledged the support granted by previous administrations. Refusing the support, President Wilson said the "conditions of the loan seem to touch very nearly the administrative independence of China itself," mean the possibility of "forcible intervention" and are "obnoxious to the principles upon which the government of our people rests." [69] Refused government support, the House of Morgan and its associates withdrew from the Six-Power loan. Although rejecting imperialism in China, President Wilson pursued an aggressive policy in the Caribbeans, declared against Europeans receiving concessions in Latin America, and six years later asked the House of Morgan to re-enter the Chinese Consortium.

CHAPTER XXIX

THE 1907 PANIC

> *"Ahem!" said the Mouse with an im-*
> *portant air. "Are you all ready?"*
> *"Ugh!" said the Lory, with a shiver.*
> *"I beg your pardon!" said the Mouse,*
> *frowning, but very politely. "Did you*
> *speak?"*
> *"Not I!" said the Lory hastily.*
> *"I thought you did," said the Mouse.*
> *"I proceed."*
>
> ALICE IN WONDERLAND

IN 1907 J. Pierpont Morgan was seventy years old, and many believed he had retired. They misjudged Morgan. Almost up to the moment of his death he was aggressively active, dominating the House of Morgan. Of a friend who retired from business and shortly died, Morgan was reported to have said: "If he'd kept at work he'd have been living yet."[1] The story is probably apocryphal; in one form or another it appears in the biography of every American captain of industry and finance. Yet it characterizes Morgan and the businessmen of whom he was the ideal, and the type. The man expressed a cycle of civilization, with his absorption in business (which meant power, the chance to impose himself on others), his glorification of things, and his eternal big black cigar. Then came the great panic of 1907, yielding Morgan the supreme moment of his power.

Although actively in the financial whirl, Morgan, along with other important financiers, was unaware of the developing panic. After the depression of 1904 business developed unprecedented activity and prosperity flourished. Financiers rationalized the "boom" and insisted panics could not arise any more owing to the control imposed by industrial and financial concentration² (as they did after the depression of 1921). But they miscalculated, and Morgan with them.

Industry was still unregulated, there being no machinery to adjust production and consumption and prevent industrial crises. Prosperity, as usual, by concentrating profits and income, produced reckless speculation, particularly in rail stocks. E. H. Harriman, with the money secured from the sale of Union Pacific's holdings in Great Northern and Northern Pacific, plunged into the market buying immense blocks of rail stocks (to enlarge his railroad empire) and inflating prices. The Standard Oil oligarchy again busily manipulated the market, concentrating on Amalgamated Copper the price of which rose to 115 and then crashed to 52, the turnover being 30,000,000 shares in one year.³ Increasingly large issues of new securities, of more and more doubtful types, aggravated the speculative mania. Financial strain developed. The "undigested securities" of which Morgan spoke soon became indigestible. Unscrupulous financiers used the resources of banks and insurance companies in stock-jobbing schemes and speculation.

The whole financial situation was unsound. An aggravated, but characteristic, expression of the situation was the Morse-Heinze group. Charles W. Morse (afterward sent to prison) accumulated a large fortune out of the American Ice Co., charging extortionate prices, manipulating its stock and bribing public officials.⁴ Morse organized an overcapitalized and unsound combination of Atlantic coastal lines (buying from J. P. Morgan & Co. a railroad in order to get control of one steamship company) and then acquired a series of banks in New York City, using the collateral of one bank for loans to buy other banks.⁵ An ally of Morse, F. Augustus Heinze, had large industrial and financial interests, in control of United Copper and the Aetna Indemnity Co.⁶ This Morse-Heinze group was in the forefront of the speculative movement using the resources of financial institutions for stock-jobbery and speculation, but it was powerful, amassing millions, and the envy of lesser magnates.

In March, 1907, the approaching financial storm threw out warnings. Prices broke severely on the New York Stock Exchange—"frightful" declines, according to Wall Street.[7] Production and earnings were slackening, and this necessarily affected the inflated prices of stocks. The situation was aggravated by large financiers being forced to liquidate owing to their many issues of "indigestible securities."[8]

The financial community refused to recognize the facts and insisted that President Roosevelt's "policy of hostility against all corporations and their securities, particularly railroads," was responsible for the disturbances in the stock market.[9] Morgan and three other important financiers called upon the President to discuss the situation, the conference being interpreted as "satisfactory" by Wall Street.[10]

But the industrial and financial situation was inherently unsound, and neither Roosevelt nor Morgan could change it. Stock prices broke again in August, seriously affecting banks that had bought stocks in the March disturbance, expecting to sell at higher prices but could not. To ease the money situation the Treasury distributed $28,000,000 to banks in the smaller cities.[11] Business failures increased and many corporations crashed.[12] In October United Copper shares collapsed and cleaned out F. Augustus Heinze. The Mercantile National Bank, under Heinze's control and which financed his speculations, was seriously affected by the break in United Copper. Help was given by the other banks only on condition that Heinze and the directors retire. This was done and the Mercantile National reorganized.[13] By now the situation was uncontrollable. The Knickerbocker Trust Co., under Morse control, financing his speculations and an affiliate of Heinze, was in an insolvent condition. Its suspension threatened when the National Bank of Commerce refused to act any longer as its

Clearing House agent. There was a run on the bank—"one young woman, it was observed, paced nervously up and down until the bank opened." [14] At a conference in Morgan's office, representing a concentration of financial forces, the ultimatum went forth that the Heinze-Morse interests must withdraw from all financial institutions before they could expect aid. This was done, and Knickerbocker's new president appealed personally to Morgan for help, who answered: "I can't go on being everybody's goat. I've got to stop somewhere." [15] At another conference the decision was "thumbs down" on Knickerbocker Trust. After the conference Morgan said:

"We are doing everything we can, as fast as we can, but nothing has yet crystallized."

Asked about Knickerbocker Trust, Morgan replied:

"I don't know anything about that; I am not talking about that." [16]

Under Morgan's direction organization and plans were being developed to meet the crisis. On October 20, in spite of underlying uneasiness, Wall Street was confident, Jacob H. Schiff saying: "The trouble is over and the general situation sound." [17] Within three days banks began to crash and panic broke loose on the Stock Exchange.

Secretary of the Treasury George B. Cortelyou rushed to New York and held conferences with Morgan, Perkins, Baker, Stillman and others. Government accepted the Morgan dictatorship—an inescapable decision. There was no central banking institution under government control to mobilize the banks' resources in the crisis. In spite of financial centralization by Morgan and others, the nation's banking system was incompletely co-ordinated, reserves being scattered in the vaults of thousands of banks which distrusted each other and did not or could not effectively co-operate. There was a scramble for money by the banks and no central institution to provide and distribute the money. Co-operation and centralized organization had to be improvised in the midst of the panic, while banks crashed, necessarily by the House of Morgan, the most powerful of financial institutions, and under control of the only man with sufficient financial authority, J. Pierpont Morgan. What a properly organized banking system would have done automatically Morgan had to do in an improvised and dictatorial style. Cortelyou accepted Morgan's dictatorship, testifying in the Money Trust investigation:

UNTERMYER: What was Mr. Morgan's relation?

CORTELYOU: Mr. Morgan's relation to it was that, by the consensus of opinion, he was regarded as the leading spirit, I think, among the businessmen who joined themselves together to try to meet the emergency.

UNTERMYER: He was the representative of the banks, was he, in a sense?

CORTELYOU: He was the representative of the general business of the community.

UNTERMYER: Mr. Morgan was the general in charge of the situation?

CORTELYOU: He was generally looked to for guidance and leadership.

UNTERMYER: And the banks acted under his directions and took his instructions?

CORTELYOU: For the time being, I suppose that was true.[18]

The Treasury deposited $42,000,000, without interest,[19] in banks under control of or affiliated with the House of Morgan, the disposal of which for purposes of relief was determined by a series of conferences under final authority of Morgan himself.

J. P. Morgan & Co. were in shipshape condition to meet the crisis, having learned from the experience of 1903-4 to maintain a high degree of liquidity in their resources. In the persons and institutions of Morgan and his chief lieutenants, George F. Baker of the First National Bank and James Stillman of the National City, was concentrated an immense money power which dominated all the other banks and the general situation. They necessarily determined measures to meet the crisis, and

Baker and Stillman unquestioningly accepted Morgan's authority. With royal generosity Morgan afterward said to his son (who was not in New York during the panic): "Of course, you see, it could not have been done without Mr. Baker; he is always ready to do his share—and more." [20]

It was Morgan's supreme moment, the final measure of power and its ecstasy. President Roosevelt, the scourge of "malefactors of great wealth," accepted Morgan's financial dictatorship through the Secretary of the Treasury. One after another Morgan's antagonists came to him, offered their resources and asked his orders—John D. Rockefeller, Edward H. Harriman, Jacob H. Schiff, Thomas F. Ryan, and after them came presidents of banks, railroads and industrial combinations. To a reporter Harriman said: "This is no time for words. It's action now." [21] All of them asked Morgan's orders, which he issued in his sharp, abrupt manner. Conference after conference was held, usually in Morgan's library. While the lesser masters of money discussed plans in the library, in a small adjoining room Morgan sat in massive truculent silence, playing solitaire and smoking his eternal big black cigar. Aloof, masterful, majestic. The lesser masters of money coming to some decision, Morgan would stroll in, listen, usually answer "yes" or "no." Or they gave him a sheet of paper upon which they had set down their resources or needs, which Morgan might tear up, silently. Then the master of money went back to his solitaire and eternal big black cigar, until called again. [22] Or, in more important conferences, Morgan sat with the others, silent, listening, usually speaking only to impose his will. Yes, it was Morgan's supreme moment.

Call money on the Stock Exchange shot skyward and its president, R. H. Thomas, discussed the situation with Stillman. Thomas testified in the Money Trust investigation:

UNTERMYER: You spoke to Mr. Stillman of the money stringency?

THOMAS: Yes.... He recommended me to go to Mr. Morgan and tell him the exact story I had told him, Mr. Stillman.

UNTERMYER: Did you go to Mr. Morgan's office?

THOMAS: Yes. . . . Mr. Morgan said, "We are going to let you have"—I think these are his words—"$25,000,000. Go over to the Exchange and announce it." I said, "One suggestion, Mr. Morgan, I would like to make." He said, "What is it?" I said, "It is this: That you divide this money up among several people, as I think it would have a better effect in bringing in money and meeting the emergency." He said, "That is a good suggestion. Perkins, divide that up in lots among several people." And I proceeded to the Stock Exchange.[23]

Morgan's decisive influence in the crisis was determined by personality plus the financial dominance of the House of Morgan. There were, first of all, the banks, railroads and industrial corporations under direct Morgan control or influence, the officers of whom were accustomed to accept Morgan's orders. This largest of the financial groups was bound with other groups by the community-of-interest system which operated under overlordship of the House of Morgan, the whole representing an amalgamation of financial forces dominated by J. Pierpont Morgan. Then there was the factor of personal prestige. Morgan was the businessman's ideal, solid, substantial and successful, silent and masterful, inspiring confidence in men who might dislike and fear him. Once the panic assumed the dimensions of unreasoning stampede, inspiring confidence in lesser men constituted much of Morgan's contribution to the restoration of normal conditions.

While banks crashed and the cries for help multiplied, the improvised organization directed by Morgan mobilized the available money and distributed it to banks and other financial institutions. J. P. Morgan & Co. announced they would anticipate all interest and dividend payments payable through the firm, particularly the Northern Pacific dividend of $2,700,-000, in furtherance of the movement to relieve the monetary tension.[24] John D. Rockefeller deposited $10,000,000 in one trust company and pledged fifty more.[25] The banks imported gold from Europe. Money was poured into the Stock Exchange, Morgan ordered the bears not to sell, and James R. Keene was engaged to prevent another market crash.[26] By October 28 the newspapers reported the situation "getting back to normal." [27]

In these operations first consideration, of course, was given to institutions under the control or influence of the House of Morgan, its affiliates and allies. There were protests from some of the smaller trust companies that money placed in Morgan's hands was being withheld, that they were receiving no relief. There was a run on the Trust Company of America, but its president's appeals for help were brushed aside by Morgan, whose attitude was: "There are too many: wipe them out." At one of the conferences where trust-company relief was discussed Morgan said, bluntly:

"Why should I get into this? My affairs are all in order. I've done enough. I won't take all this on unless—" and then a gesture signifying *"unless I get what I want out of it."* [28]

James Stillman disagreed, favoring immediate trust-company relief. But the situation was delicate: none dared challenge Morgan directly, except Stillman, who knew, however, that if Morgan definitely said "no," the decision was final, the others being compelled to accept. Stillman knew his Morgan, the man's arrogant pride and dislike of yielding. Diplomacy was necessary to placate Morgan's pride, or it might prevent him changing his opinion. After an all-night struggle, in which finesse matched itself against massive power, Stillman conquered. The trust companies were promised relief.[29]

The panic was almost over when it was reported to Morgan that one of the most important brokerage firms in the city would go bankrupt unless aided immediately. The brokers, Moore & Schley, held a large block of stock of the Tennessee Coal, Iron & Railroad Co., pledged as collateral by a syndicate including John W. Gates and Oliver H. Payne, and which could not be easily sold as the stock's market was limited.[20] It was suggested that relief might assume the form of the United States Steel Corporation buying Tennessee Coal & Iron, issuing in payment its own bonds which were more negotiable than the stock. A midnight conference in Morgan's library considered the suggestion. Gary and Frick opposed purchase, Frick proposing instead that they loan Moore & Schley $5,000,000.[31] Morgan insisted on purchase. There being a problem of legality under the anti-trust laws, Gary and Frick were sent to Washington to secure President Roosevelt's approval, which was granted.[32]

United States Steel's purchase of Tennessee Coal & Iron was justified on the ground that it checked the panic, Roosevelt maintaining that "my action" in approving the purchase produced "stoppage of the panic."[33] But did it? The panic was practically over. Moore & Schley could have been saved by other means, by a direct loan, by some of the millions which had appeared to help the banks and stock market. At the government investigation of the Steel Trust in 1911 Gary testified:

LITTLETON: Suppose, instead of buying Tennessee Coal & Iron, you had loaned United States Steel bonds to Moore & Schley for the purpose of saving the situation, would you not have effected the same result?

GARY: It is possible. That was not suggested, however. We offered to lend them five or six millions and take stock of Tennessee Coal & Iron as collateral security. But they came back with the statement that that would not answer the purpose.

LITTLETON: You could have loaned the bonds without any embarrassment to the Steel Corporation?

GARY: We could.

LITTLETON: And if the bonds, when exchanged, were the means of saving Moore & Schley they would have been just as efficient means when loaned, would they not?

GARY: They would.[34]

Relief for Moore & Schley was necessary: other purposes determined the *form* of the relief. Tennessee Coal & Iron, the leading iron and steel concern in the South, owned immense reserves of coal and iron ore in Alabama. It was the potential basis for another large steel combination; in fact, plans had been made to combine with two other companies but were never completed.[35] In buying Tennessee Coal & Iron, United States Steel acquired an important competitor and became the most powerful single factor in the Southern iron industry. In normal times the purchase would have been impossible, considering the attacks being made on United States Steel as a monopolistic combination. The panic provided the opportunity for an unusually sharp business stroke on the great value of which Gary expatiated within a few months and which added 600,000,000 tons of iron ore and 1,000,000,000 tons of coal to the reserves of the United States Steel Corporation.[36]

The panic was over.... Revelations appeared of the dishonest use of trust-company funds by officers and directors.[37] ... There was a crop of arrests, and another crop of suicides.... President Charles T. Barney, of Knickerbocker Trust, although himself solvent, committed suicide owing to "loss of prestige." [38] ... Howard Maxwell, another trust-company president, slit his throat. Arrested on a charge of grand larceny for using trust funds in stock deals, Maxwell, penniless, was abandoned by all his friends, who declined to help raise bail. These friends offered to pay the funeral expenses, but the widow scornfully rejected their offer: "I do not want the help they now offer— too late." [39] ... In New York City there were 100,000 unemployed and probably 3,000,000 in the nation. "Men are eager to work for 35c. a day," and bread lines were overwhelmed by the needy.[40] ... In the midst of the panic Andrew Carnegie, seventy years old and enjoying his golf, said: "All is well, since all grows better." [41] ... Morgan and Baker went to Washington to confer with President Roosevelt and report the end of the panic.[42] ... Industrial depression continued for almost two years. Clever businessmen organized the "Sunshine Movement," urging people to think prosperity as a means of restoring prosperity.[43] But in spite of the magic potency of sunshine prosperity declined to prosper.

J. Pierpont Morgan received the formal thanks of the financial community for his work during the crisis. "The man of the hour," said the press, praising his "genius for dealing effectively with intricate problems of business and finance."[44] Lord Rothschild issued a bulletin: "Morgan's latest action fills one with admiration and respect."[45] The panic produced many failures and changes in financial power and alignments, but— "Morgan still reigns!"[46]

CHAPTER XXX

MORGAN'S SYSTEM

How cheerfully he seems to grin,
How neatly spread his claws,
And welcomes little fishes in,
With gently smiling jaws!
ALICE IN WONDERLAND

DURING and after the 1907 panic it was freely charged that dominant financial interests, particularly the House of Morgan and its affiliates, deliberately engineered the crisis in order to crush competitors and magnify their own power by larger centralization and control. Denunciations flamed forth in Congress and the press, intensifying popular discontent and strengthening the developing movement for government regulation of corporate combinations.

While the criticism was unjustified, economic forces beyond the control of the financial magnates producing the panic, the magnates facilitated its coming and sharpened the disaster by their reckless promotions, unscrupulous use of other people's money and frenzied speculation.

And when the panic broke loose most of the magnates were frightened, helpless, their morale shattered. Men formerly dominant, austerely aloof, as if carved of granite, now ran like a flock of sheep after the Morgan bell-wether.

The panic, moreover, revealed the incapacity of finance, as the unifying expression of business, to insure economic security. Fooling themselves and the public, the magnates believed they were creating a system in which panics could not occur. After the Steel Trust organization John B. Claflin said at a bankers' dinner where J. Pierpont Morgan was an honored guest: "With a man like Mr. Morgan at the head of a great industry, as against the old plan of many diverse interests in it, production will become more regular ... and panics become a thing of the past." [1] But the 1907 panic, only six years later, was as bad as the panics of 1857 and 1873 when Morganization was still in the future. Morganization, the centralization of industry and finance imposing financial control over industry, introduced co-ordination and regulation, but it was largely co-ordination of control and regulation of profits, and only partly unification of the nation's economic life.* The production and distribution of goods was still determined loosely by markets, prices and profits, still unregulated in terms of balancing production and consumption, still competitive in the struggle after larger and larger profits—booms, depressions and panics being the consequences. Morganization, the community of interest and control, measurably prevented business disturbances produced by buccaneers waging war on each other and by unrestrained competition, but it did not and could not prevent the more serious cyclical disturbances of business.

This limitation on the power of financial centralization, and of finance itself, appears in the "stoppage" of the panic. Morgan and other bankers stabilized the financial situation: by the end of 1907 Wall Street was again "normal" and security prices rallied. But financial stabilization did not revive business prosperity; during the first nine months of 1908 commercial failures increased and production declined. [2] The dynamics of business revival and prosperity lay in the creative force of production and consumption, not in financial centralization and control.

The great bankers, in whom financial control was centralized, neither originated nor introduced fundamental economic changes, most of which developed without their aid. They

* During 1915-30 the centralization of industry and finance assumed immensely larger proportions, yet prevented neither the 1921 panic (equal to the worst in American economic history) nor the severe business depression of 1929-30.

scarcely participated in the development of railroads and steamships, the first telegraph line was constructed by Congressional appropriation, and they only slightly assisted the development of the steel, telephone, electric and automobile industry.[3] Bankers, by the very nature of their institutional function, usually appear in an enterprise *after* it is established and successful. Finance is regulative, not creative. The creative force is in industry itself. Money, which is finance, conveniently expresses the relationships between one industry and another, between production and consumption. Under business enterprise money becomes the supreme power, usurping the function of determining production and consumption; and Morganization, by the control of money, usurped financial control of industry. In this control inhered a measure of regulation, but it neither insured prosperity nor prevented panics. For that, larger unification and social control of industry are necessary.

While the financial magnates did not engineer the 1907 panic to crush competitors and magnify their own power by larger centralization and control, that was, however, exactly what happened.

The panic crushed many financial combinations, such as Morse-Heinze, their holdings being acquired by the survivors. Banks consolidated to increase their resources, prestige and power. Although James Stillman retired from active control of the National City Bank, his successor, Frank A. Vanderlip, continued its aggressive policy of expansion, extending the Bank's control of trust companies and increasing its affiliations with large institutions in other cities.[4] Harriman, apparently bent upon creating a money power capable of competing with J. P. Morgan & Co., used the immense resources of Union Pacific to develop his own system of financial centralization and control. He spent $130,000,000 buying stock in other roads, becoming a director in twenty-seven railroads with a mileage of 39,354, including control of two lines to the

Atlantic.[5] He then snatched Erie from the House of Morgan.[6] Developing his plans, Harriman acquired large interests in the Guaranty Trust Co. and the Equitable Life Assurance Society.[7] Now the mightiest single factor in railroads, pursuing imperialistic plans in Asia and developing formidable financial power, Harriman loomed as a direct and threatening competitor of Morgan. But Harriman's end approached. His railroad manipulations aroused investigation and action by the national government—"actively and openly aided by apparently invincible Wall Street alliances, and secret enemies in his own camp almost as strong."[8] Moreover, Harriman was incapable of institutionalizing his system, as Morgan did: everything, with him, seemed to require the personal touch. Worn out, he died in 1909, and the Harriman system collapsed.

Meanwhile the House of Morgan, emerging triumphant out of the panic, consolidated its system. Immediately after the panic Morgan's Bankers Trust Co. absorbed the Trust Company of America (and the Mercantile Trust in 1911).[9] Within three months of Harriman's death Morgan and his associates bought his stock in the Guaranty Trust along with Mutual Life's holdings.[10] Tightening his control of New York Life, Morgan proceeded, in 1910, to buy control of Equitable Life,[11] becoming dominant in the three largest insurance companies. Under complete control of the House of Morgan, with Henry P. Davison and William H. Porter (both Morgan partners) and George F. Baker as voting trustees and Davison and Thomas W. Lamont as directors, Guaranty Trust absorbed six other trust companies.[12] The Guaranty and Bankers Trust companies were the first and second largest in the country, with combined resources of $357,000,000.[13]

Control of larger financial resources meant larger financial control over industry. In 1909 J. P. Morgan & Co. reorganized the Chicago Great Western Railroad, Morgan and Baker becoming two of the three voting trustees and Charles H. Steele a director.[14] Another Morgan partner became a director in the

Westinghouse Electric Co. (reorganized by the Morgans after
the 1907 panic), the competitor of General Electric, community of interest being established.[15] The House of Morgan extended its influence in the American Telephone & Telegraph
Co., Davison becoming a director and the Morgans marketing,
between 1906 and 1912, $299,000,000 of the company's securi-
ties, largely used to buy up independents and secure control of
Western Union.[16]

But the years immediately after the 1907 panic, which
marked the end of a period, were characterized by stabilization, not expansion. Speculation and manipulation broke loose
again on the Stock Exchange, for a time forcing the prices of
many stocks above the levels of 1907 and 1906,[17] but business
depression prevented any considerable speculative movement.
Financial adventures almost ceased, there being scarcely any
large combinations or promotions (except the attempt of the
New York, New Haven & Hartford Railroad, under Morgan's
direction, to monopolize New England's transportation facilities). Sobered by the panic and its aftermath, and by Theodore Roosevelt's campaign against the "malefactors of great
wealth," finance and Big Business concentrated on consolidating their conquests. The death of Harriman, the only man
capable of disputing Morgan's supremacy (the rapier and the
broadsword!) eliminated the only threat to the system of
community of interest which now flourished undisturbed under
overlordship of the House of Morgan.

The National City Bank merged in larger community of
interest with the House of Morgan, while Standard Oil, its
former aggressive masters retiring and put on the defensive
by government action, was in no mood to struggle for larger
power, satisfied to maintain itself. Morgan, apparently eternal,
was still active, but most of the other magnates of an embattled
age were either dead or retired. There was none to dispute J.
Pierpont Morgan's supremacy in the system of financial centralization and control, over which towered the House of

Morgan, now unchallenged in its mastery (except by the government).

By 1912 Morgan s system of financial centralization and control appeared definitely in all its essentials.

At the basis of the system was institutionalized control of financial resources, of money and credit. By means of voting trusts, stock ownership and directorships J. P. Morgan & Co. controlled or dominated three national banks (exclusive of First National), three trust companies and three life-insurance companies, with large aggregate resources. (J. P. Morgan & Co. held deposits of $162,491,000, one-half by seventy-eight interstate corporations in thirty-two of which the Morgans were represented by directorships, marketing $1,950,000,000 of their securities between 1902 and 1912.) [18]

By means of stock ownership, voting trusts and directorships J. P. Morgan & Co. dominated ten great railroad systems, with mileage of 49,000, and had close financial affiliations with eighteen other railroads, three street railway corporations and one express company (besides control of the International Mercantile Marine Co.).[19]

By means of voting trusts, stock ownership and directorships J. P. Morgan & Co. dominated five great industrial corporations—United States Steel, General Electric, American Telephone & Telegraph, International Harvester and Western Union. In addition the Morgans held directorships in nine more industrial corporations and had close financial relations with eleven others (including Western Electric and American Fruit).[20]

In all, the Morgan partners held seventy-two interlocking directorships in forty-seven of the largest financial and other corporations with more than $10,000,000,000 in resources or capitalization. The House of Morgan, moreover, completely dominated the Bankers Trust, Guaranty Trust and National Bank of Commerce, whose officers and directors held upward of 300 interlocking directorships, many of them in corporations not under direct Morgan control or influence.[21]

This control of the House of Morgan was enlarged by its affiliate, the First National Bank, four of whose officers held forty-six directorships in thirty-seven corporations, some interlocked with and others independent of direct Morgan control.[22] The Morgans and their affiliates constituted the supreme financial combination and power, upward of $18,000,000,000 in corporate resources or capitalization being under their control or influence.

George F. Baker, president of the First National Bank, an efficient money-making machine probably twice as rich as Morgan, was one of the dominant factors in the system of financial centralization and control. The most secretive of the masters of money, his contempt of public opinion was equal to Morgan's. "It is none of the public's business what I do," said Baker.[23] Of First National's 100,000 shares of capital stock, Baker and his son owned 25,000, J. P. Morgan & Co. 14,500, Henry P. Davison and Thomas W. Lamont 1,000 shares each, and James J. Hill 3,900, making the Morgan interest almost as large as Baker's. Morgan, Davison and Lamont were First National directors and Morgan a member of the executive committee.[24] In spite of being unknown to the public, Baker was almost as powerful as Morgan, under whose direction, however, he always worked willingly and harmoniously.

Trailing the House of Morgan and its affiliates was the National City Bank, five of whose officers held thirty-two directorships in twenty-six corporations.[25] After the 1907 panic rivalry between Morgan and Stillman largely ceased, more intimate community of interest being established: J. P. Morgan & Co. in 1909 acquired large holdings of National City stock (becoming the largest stockholder next to Stillman and his son), and two years later National City acquired large holdings in Morgan's National Bank of Commerce.[26] Competitive struggle for supremacy merged in institutionalized co-operation under over-lordship of the House of Morgan.

The interlocked Morgan-Stillman-Baker combination held a total of 341 directorships in 112 of the dominant financial and other corporations with aggregate resources or capitalization of $22,245,000,000, as follows:

Thirty-four banks and trust companies—118 directorships; resources, $2,679,000,000 (13 per cent of all banking resources).

Ten insurance companies—30 directorships; resources, $2,293,000,000 (57 per cent of all insurance resources).

Thirty-two transportation companies—105 directorships; capitalization, $11,784,000,000; mileage, 150,000.

Twenty-four industrial and commercial companies—63 directorships; capitalization, $3,339,000,000.

Twelve public-utility companies—25 directorships; capitalization, $2,150,000,000.[27]

Other investment houses, banks and trust companies were creating minor combinations of their own. In all, 180 individuals representing eighteen financial institutions in New York, Boston and Chicago (including J. P. Morgan & Co., the Morgan affiliates and allies, Kuhn, Loeb & Co., Lee Higginson & Co., Speyer & Co. and Kidder, Peabody & Co.) held 746 directorships in 134 corporations with aggregate resources or capitalization of $25,325,000,000 [28]—dominating the economic life of the nation.

In this centralization of industry and finance the House of Morgan was the dominating factor. There were shades of control in the system. Not all affiliated corporations were dominated as completely as Morgan dominated United States Steel. But within the system as a whole, of which the pivot was the House of Morgan, definite and complete control prevailed in its larger aspects.

There was nothing peculiarly American in financial centralization and control. In Europe, particularly Germany, the centralization was infinitely larger. Five or six German great

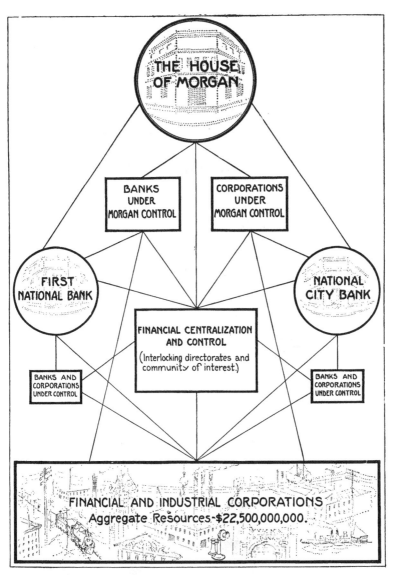

THE HOUSE
OF MORGAN

BANKS
UNDER
MORGAN CONTROL

CORPORATIONS
UNDER
MORGAN CONTROL

FIRST
NATIONAL BANK

NATIONAL
CITY BANK

FINANCIAL CENTRALIZATION
AND CONTROL
(Interlocking directorates and
community of interest.)

BANKS AND
CORPORATIONS
UNDER CONTROL

BANKS AND
CORPORATIONS
UNDER CONTROL

FINANCIAL AND INDUSTRIAL CORPORATIONS
Aggregate Resources-$22,500,000,000.

FINANCIAL CENTRALIZATION AND CONTROL, 1912

Brown Bros.

CHARLES S. MELLEN

banks institutionalized an almost complete control of financial resources, regulating industry, determining general policy, national and international, and dominating the government with which they worked in full agreement. Larger financial centralization in Germany, France and England was a result of three factors: industrial and financial combination did not meet with any substantial resistance, the struggles of imperialism demanded unification and centralized manipulation of financial resources, and governments encouraged the centralization of industry and finance.

In the United States, on the contrary, industrial combination and its accompanying financial centralization and control aroused intense resistance. The Granger, Populist and Bryan movements glorified small-scale industry and insisted on restoring competition, while European revolt usually assumed the form of socialist acceptance of large-scale industry and proposals for its socialization. American resistance did not prevent the development of financial centralization and control, but compelled the adoption of comparatively loose and incompletely institutionalized forms.

The system of community of interest, and the emphasis on financial centralization and control operating by means of 180 interlocking directors, disproportionately stressed the personal factors, making centralization appear as if simply the work of predatory financiers. But community of interest meant much more than that. Centralization was the inevitable product of large-scale, concentrated capitalism, developing new institutions and functions; class resistance and government prohibitions interfered with centralization assuming completely institutional aspects, compelling it in many cases to adopt the looser forms of community of interest and personal relationships in order to evade legal restrictions and avoid public antagonism.

These conditions provided an opportunity for the personal dictatorship of J. Pierpont Morgan. In any system where relationships are not completely institutionalized authority becomes more personal than institutional, favoring the emergence of dictatorship. While an institutional development, the system of financial centralization and control was compelled to function partly on the personal basis of community of interest, in which Morgan usurped dictatorship. He was not the most constructive of the captains of industry and finance, Wall Street placing him below Harriman and Hill in that respect,[29] but Morgan had the advantage of being a financier, and finance was the concentration point of the system. He was not the most brilliant of financiers, as such, Baker and Stillman being at least his equals, but Morgan had the advantage of being more of a ruler, supremely capable of imposing himself by personal authority where the others depended largely upon institutional power. And, finally, Wall Street trusted Morgan where it would not trust anybody else. Dependability is a necessary quality of sustained dictatorship.

The basis and distinctive financial feature of Morgan's system of centralization and control was the development by banks and other financial institutions of investment functions and their penetration of industry. The critics of centralization urged separation of functions, insisting that a bank should limit itself to commercial business, not realizing that integration of industry and finance compelled banks to assume investment functions.

National banks were not directly authorized by law to engage in investment-banking operations, but they did just the same. When the government challenged the practice, the First National Bank (in 1908) organized a separate company, the First Security Co., to carry on investment operations. First National declared a dividend of 100 per cent which was issued to stockholders in the form of stock ($10,000,000) in the new security company, the two institutions having the same directors, the president, vice-president and cashier of the bank being trustees of the security company. The organization agreement, between George F. Baker representing the trustees and J. Pierpont Morgan representing the stockholders, made bank and security company inseparable. Within four years the First Security Co., in addition to paying regularly 12 to 17 per cent dividends, accumulated surplus equal to 40 per cent of its capital.[30] The idea of a security company owned by and inseparable from the bank, carrying on investment operations forbidden under the National Bank Act, was adopted in 1911 by the National City Bank in its organization of the National City Co., the $10,000,000 stock of which was secured by the bank paying a 40 per cent dividend to stockholders.[31]

The organization of security companies constituted evasions of legal restrictions upon national banks, imposed, however, by the needs of developing industry and finance. Large-scale industry required larger, more unified banking facilities, and erased the old distinctions between commercial and investment operations. Corporate combinations, their ownership and management separated by the multiplication of stockholders, required contacts and unity with each other, which financial centralization and control provided. Morgan's system, operating by means of a complex (if incomplete) institutionalized mechanism for the control of financial resources and corporate industry, was the expression of a new economic order, of concentrated capitalism, and its need of a measure of unity and regulation. As the sensitive expression of the new order, finance imposed unity and regulation upon corporate industry (since society in the shape of its government almost completely rejected the task).

But while necessary under the conditions of concentrated capitalism, the system of financial centralization and control had its predatory aspects and abuses, while it limited the scope of small-scale competitive enterprise. Revolt against the system developed, and against the House of Morgan and its affiliates as the system's most characteristic representatives.

PART EIGHT

REVOLT—AND CONQUEST

CHAPTER XXXI

REVOLT: MORGAN AND ROOSEVELT

> *"Thinking again?" the Duchess asked, with*
> *another dig of her sharp little chin.*
> *"I've a right to think," said Alice*
> *sharply.*
> *"Just about as much right," said the*
> *Duchess, "as a pig has to fly."*
>
> ALICE IN WONDERLAND

CONSOLIDATION by the House of Morgan of its system of financial centralization and control (between 1902 and 1910) proceeded in the midst of social revolt against corporate combinations. Out of this revolt developed readjustment and conquest, unification of trustified capitalism and its acceptance by business and government. Meanwhile combinations were threatened by the revolt which challenged the dominance of the House of Morgan at the moment of its acceptance by the financial community.

Although Morganization emerged by waging war upon the buccaneers who disturbed business, J. Pierpont Morgan was himself measurably animated by the buccaneer spirit of contempt of larger social interests.

"Law?" exclaimed "Commodore" Cornelius Vanderbilt, the manipulator of railroads. "What do I care for law? Hain't I got the power?"

And Morgan, the master of money, said:

"Men owning property should do what they like with it."

"I owe the public nothing."

Supplemented by the gesture signifying, "unless I get what I want out of it."

Coming to power in an age of buccaneering, Morgan retained the spirit of the age while partly changing its methods: the difference between him and Vanderbilt lay not in their sentiments but in the systems under which they operated. Neither the one nor the other considered larger social interests. Both resented the interference of law, public opinion and government. The two men, however, were separated by the difference between buccaneering and dictatorship—Vanderbilt's impulse was to grab, Morgan's to rule. By its very nature as a sort of financial government, Morgan's system suppressed the more flagrant buccaneering practices. But while the system of centralized financial control necessarily excluded Vanderbilt-Gould methods of plunder by lessening competitive struggles, limiting the magnates in waging war upon each other and imposing more responsibility and unity within the limits of Big Business, these changes did not prevent the combined magnates waging war upon the people. In this sense Morganization was as predatory as the buccaneers of the preceding stage in the development of American capitalism.

Of impeccable honor in dealing with associates (an important factor in his supremacy in the community-of-interest system), Morgan had little sense of responsibility beyond his immediate associates and enterprises. "I owe the public nothing," he said, expressing class arrogance, aristocratic bias and the logic of the financier impatient of restraint by the rabble and government. Logic insisted that corporations should not cut each other's throats, that financial control meant more stabilized, efficient and profitable business. But logic is relative and much depends upon its premises. Morgan's premise was that "men owning property should do what they like with it"—the conclusion being that the financier may combine and manipulate as he pleases within the limits of the system in which the financier operates. No interference by larger social interests!

Morgan was the complete reactionary, his contempt of politics being largely contempt of democracy (where it was not the businessman's snobbish assumption of superiority over the politician). In this contempt of social progress Morgan was the model of his class, as he was also the model in his mannerisms —the arrogance, the eternal big black cigar, the massive truculent silence.

The magnates of industry and finance looked upon their world and called it good. Naturally. It met their needs and accepted their power. The defeat of Bryanism in 1896 and the revival of prosperity a few years later introduced an era of aggressive expansion and consolidation of industry—and immense accumulation of profits. By 1900 triumphant plutocracy appeared supreme, largely unregulated, contemptuous of interests other than its own. Industrial and financial expansion then overshot itself and crashed in 1902-3, initiating a series of reverses for the House of Morgan, temporarily halting the march of combination, and intensifying popular discontent at the abuses of concentrated capitalism. Social revolt flared up again.

This revolt Morgan and the other magnates disdainfully dismissed as demagogic impudence upon which they waged merciless war.

While expressing all the older grievances (limiting of business opportunity by industrial combination, corporate oppression of competitors, railroad rebates, feudal conditions of labor), the new revolt assumed decisive social aspects. The pre-1900 generation struggled for the largest share of the spoils of developing industrialism but did not seriously concern itself with the accompanying evils. Now these evils were exposed and condemned by men and women of another generation who were stigmatized as Muckrakers, from the Man with the Hoe in *Pilgrim's Progress* who was so absorbed in filth that he rejected a celestial crown. But the Muckrakers insisted celestial crowns were conjectural while social filth was real, and proceeded to expose the evils of slums, child labor, low wages, industrial hazards, business buccaneering, political corruption and financial malpractices. They charged frauds, thefts, corruption, and named names. Yet convictions for libel were extraordinarily scarce. Popular discontent was intensified by the exposures and agitation of the Muckrakers, snipers in the new movement of social revolt. Labor was organizing and becoming more articulate, socialism acquiring considerable strength (proposing government ownership of corporate combinations instead of suppression or regulation). Out of the middle class came men and women animated by much of the idealism of John Pierpont's generation, urging reforms. The social sap was stirring, stirring, compelling serious consideration of social legislation to remedy abuses and more equally distribute the gains of economic development.

This movement infuriated the magnates. They insisted on the final measure of their privileges and power, scorning concessions to the rabble. Morgan was equally arrogant and contemptuous of progress, disposing of the movement of revolt with the words:

"A few men in this country are charged with the terrible offense of being very rich. The fact is that the wealth of this country is less 'bunched' than at any time in its history. I mean that wealth is more equally distributed among the people than ever before." [1]

Morgan was completely wrong, his opinion being determined by reactionary impulses and not by the facts. After the Civil War and up to 1896 the concentration of wealth and income decreased, but then a continuous increase set in until by 1910 the richest 1.6 per cent of the population were receiving 19 per cent of the national income—twice their 1896 share. [2] Rising wages were offset by rising prices: real wages, the purchasing power of money wages, were comparatively stationary between 1897 and 1914. [3] Labor discontent developed, aggravated by the depression prevailing after the 1907 panic (up until the World War). The multiplication of wealth meant concentration of wealth, admitted and lamented by the New York

Journal of Commerce: "Concentration of wealth and power in a few hands is undesirable, even though the aggregate of wealth and of economic power is thereby enhanced. Equitable distribution is even more important than abundant production."[4] This was the cry of small businessmen borne down upon by monopolistic combinations (and business depression).

The American social revolt was matched by another revolt in Great Britain, where Lloyd George, Chancellor of the Exchequer, introduced the comprehensive system of social legislation which the privileged classes condemned as "confiscatory." Morgan detested Lloyd George and his "socialistic legislation," expressing the fear that the United States might imitate the British.[5]

Morgan's detestation of social legislation was shared by his class. The magnates arrogantly repudiated reform, clamoring that "paternalistic legislation" would wreck the American people's "sturdy individualism." But the magnates conveniently forgot that monopolistic combinations crushed economic individualism, and that they never rejected "paternalistic legislation" favorable to their own interests. Accustomed to politics as the giver and protector of privileges and spoils, the magnates of industry and finance were aghast at politics being used to promote larger social interests. They bitterly opposed economic and political reforms. The Federal taxation of corporate and personal incomes, now accepted in our fiscal system, was characteristically condemned as "confiscatory" and the precursor of socialism, one banker saying: "The government, instead of taxing incomes, ought to pay premiums to men achieving financial success."[6] In Scriptural terms—"To him that hath shall be given and from him that hath not shall be taken." Change was resisted, except change in the interest of the plutocracy. Morgan and the other magnates were not simply guilty "of the terrible offense of being very rich," but of the more serious offense of refusing to recognize social maladjustments and callously repudiating remedial legislation.

But while important, the struggle for social legislation and reforms simply provided the steam for the more decisive struggle—government regulation of corporate combinations, upon which the revolt concentrated itself. Politics expressed the struggle. Although Morgan despised politics, most of his affiliates engaged in politics (often corrupt politics) to promote the interests of enterprises under control of the House of Morgan. Moreover, as the balance-wheel of developing economic forces and antagonistic class interests, politics could not afford to despise Morgan and his system which in many aspects challenged government and its authority.

Concentrated capitalism had built up an immense industrial and financial structure almost wholly independent of government control. The complexity of this structure compelled regulation. Morganization imposed a measure of regulation by the institutionalized control of financial resources and industry, by limiting competition and by the community-of-interest system. But this regulation was incomplete, and it operated largely in terms of the interests of particular groups. (Moreover, in spite of Morgan's belief to the contrary, financial and social problems are inseparable.) It was necessary to unify capitalism, to adjust economics and politics to each other in terms of the new system of centralized industry and finance. This meant the larger unity and regulation of government control over corporate combinations, including Morganization itself. In the struggle to impose this regulation government necessarily clashed with the House of Morgan, the most important expression of centralized industry and finance acting almost wholly independent of government control.

While this new movement for the regulation of corporate combinations accepted industrialism and Big Business, distinguishing it from Bryanism, there were many proposals for the destruction of combinations and some suggestions that magnates like J. Pierpont Morgan be put in jail "to help the law and make it respected." [7] In the movement, essentially one of readjustment in the interests of concentrated capitalism itself, lurked the threat that discontent with corporate abuses might become destructive action against capitalism unless Big Business "cleaned house."

President Theodore Roosevelt, who vocalized the revolt while moderating its temper, declared the magnates' "idiotic folly" and reactionary arrogance encouraged radicalism, insisting that the "serious social problems" produced by industrial develop-ment required appropriate legislation, adding, however: "We are not trying to strike down the rich man; on the contrary, we will not tolerate any attacks on his rights."[8] Animated by middle-class horror of class war, Roosevelt proposed to regulate both the plutocracy and the proletariat to secure social peace, condemning socialists and radical union agitators as savagely as the "malefactors of great wealth."

Roosevelt was a political realist, not a radical.

"The great development of industrialism," the President said, "means that there must be an increase in the supervision exer-cised by the government over business enterprise."[9] Roosevelt urged Federal regulation of corporate combinations to eliminate abuses and unify the larger interests of capitalism, which meant strengthening industrial and financial centralization by adjust-ing Big Business (which Roosevelt accepted) to government in an irresistible unity for larger economic dominion, particularly in the markets of the world.

But the magnates of industry and finance, led by J. Pierpont Morgan, resisted corporate regulation as much as social legis-lation, the cry being "Let us alone!" Big Business objected to "increasing the powers of government" (although making no objection to increasing the powers of industry and finance) and maintained that Roosevelt's campaign to regulate corporate combinations "disturbed business." The legend developed that it caused the panic of 1907, the *Commercial and Financial Chronicle* repeating as late as 1911 that "the panic was really the work of Roosevelt himself."[10] During the panic Charles S. Mellen, president of the New York, New Haven & Hartford Railroad (under control of the House of Morgan, Mellen being known as "Morgan's office-boy") attacked Roosevelt's regulation campaign as a "drunken debauch" producing business disturbance.[11] Roosevelt replied that his policies, "representing the effort to punish successful dishonesty," did not cause the panic, "but if they have, it will not alter in the slightest degree my determination that they shall be persevered in unswervingly."[12] So bitter was the feeling that the directors of the United States Steel Corporation considered a resolution (which was tabled, however) forbidding Chairman Gary to visit President Roosevelt.[13]

Much of the antagonism was determined by personal animus. Accustomed to buying political subservience with campaign contributions, the magnates resented Roosevelt accepting their money and then denouncing them. In the 1904 election the magnates contributed $2,100,000 to Roosevelt's campaign fund, including $500,000 by George J. Gould, $150,000 by J. P. Morgan & Co. and $100,000 by Standard Oil.[14] The usually astute Roosevelt misread the public mood, and, afraid of defeat, sent for a delegation of magnates (men he had been denouncing as "malefactors of great wealth") to ask for financial help. Among them was Daniel S. Lamont of Northern Pacific and Henry C. Frick of United States Steel. The delegation went secretly to the White House. Roosevelt, according to Lamont, made "distinct promises," while Frick said of the conference, in his usual cynical strain:

"Why, Roosevelt fairly went down on his knees to us in his fear of defeat, and said that he would be good and would leave the railroads and the corporations alone if we would only give him this financial help. We did, but he didn't stay put in his second term. We got nothing for our money."[15]

"He didn't stay put." This infuriated the magnates, unused to "getting nothing for their money." Other things infuriated the magnates still more. They were accustomed to interview the

President (of whom they spoke sarcastically as "the Little Father") [16] and ask what they could or could not do in particular situations; if political exigency demanded contradiction of the advice given, Roosevelt issued denials and called the magnates liars. Which was sometimes true, but not always. This Rooseveltian idiosyncrasy aroused particular resentment. In the financial community they sang this parody of a popular song:

> *Everybody lies but Roosevelt*
> *And he lies around all day.*
> *They think he's made of iron,*
> *But he's only common clay.*[17]

The campaign to impose government regulation on corporate combinations aroused the unrelenting hostility of Morgan, who was the focus of resistance. Regulation struck at his own arbitrary power, at enterprises under control or influence of the House of Morgan, and appeared to threaten the system of financial centralization and control. The man who had introduced dictatorial regulation in industry and finance by combination and community of interest resented the larger regulation of government supervision. Morgan's reactionary impulses were shocked by proposals of progressive legislation, and his arrogant, masterful nature was outraged by government intervention and regulation. He completely missed the significance of Rooseveltian regulation as a means of consolidating the system of industrial and financial centralization. Roosevelt and Morgan agreed on fundamentals, both accepting Big Business; they disagreed on the necessity and the means of readjustment, of making concessions to public opinion. Roosevelt interpreted regulation in terms of class, of unified capitalism, Morgan in terms of personal power: the dictator often sacrifices class interests to maintain his dictatorship. Arrogant and reactionary, declining to make concessions and readjustments, Morgan and the other magnates inflamed public opinion, endangering their system and class supremacy. "The corporations," said George W. Perkins in 1911, after his retirement from J. P. Morgan & Co., "should be under Federal regulation ... or else public ownership will be forced upon us, and public ownership will open the gate to socialism." [18] What probably hurt the magnates most of all was Roosevelt's contempt for their wealth. In 1908 he wrote a friend:

"I am simply unable to make myself take the attitude of respect toward the very wealthy men which such an enormous multitude of people evidently really feel. I am delighted to show any courtesy to Pierpont Morgan or Andrew Carnegie or James J. Hill, but as for regarding any one of them as, for instance, I regard Prof. Bury, or Peary, the Arctic explorer, or Admiral Evans, or Rhodes, the historian—why, I could not force myself to do it even if I wanted to, which I don't." [19]

Roosevelt and Morgan being the chief antagonists in the struggle, the Gridiron Club once invited them to a dinner in an effort at reconciliation. In his speech Roosevelt said the people were in an unstable temper, and that steps must be taken to restore confidence and security. Suddenly Roosevelt turned, walked along the table to where Morgan sat impassively, and, shaking his fist in the financier's face, shouted:

"And if you don't let us do this, those who will come after us will rise and bring you to ruin!" [20]

It was useless. Regulation affected Morgan as a personal affront. Probably the most humiliating moment of Morgan's life was the interview with Roosevelt after the institution of government proceedings against the Northern Securities Co. Morgan's temperamental dislike of Roosevelt became violent, unreasoning hatred, which fed on itself and on events. When Theodore Roosevelt retired from the presidency in 1909 and went on a hunting trip to Africa, J. Pierpont Morgan said feelingly to a friend: "I hope the first lion he meets does his duty." [21]

CHAPTER XXXII

THE STRUGGLE FOR REGULATION

The cook took the cauldron of soup off the fire, and at once set to work throwing everything within her reach at the Duchess and the baby.
"Oh, please mind what you're doing!" cried Alice, jumping up and down in an agony of terror. "Oh, there goes his precious nose"—as an unusually large saucepan flew close by it, and very nearly carried it off.

ALICE IN WONDERLAND

GOVERNMENT regulation of corporate combinations meant imposing definite (if essentially unimportant) limitations upon industrial and financial magnates; but the magnates resented limitations, accustomed to doing largely as they pleased with money, investors, corporations and government itself. This attitude was uncompromisingly expressed by Henry O. Havemeyer, of the Sugar Trust, under examination by T. W. Phillips of the Industrial Commission:

PHILLIPS: Do you believe that trusts should be put more specifically under government control than they are?

HAVEMEYER: Not at all. I think the government should have nothing to do with them in any way, shape or manner.

PHILLIPS: You think, then, that when a corporation is chartered by the state, offers stock to the public, and is one in which the public is interested, that the public has no right to know what its earning power is or to subject them to any inspection whatever?

HAVEMEYER: Yes; that is my theory. Let the buyer beware: that covers the whole business. You cannot wet-nurse people from the time they are born until the time they die. They have got to wade in and get stuck, and that is the way men are educated and cultivated.... I say, hands off.[1]

While having more to hide than most other trusts (except Standard Oil), the American Sugar Refining Co. being guilty of monopoly, extortion and corruption, and insisting, consequently, on corporate secrecy, Havemeyer's sentiments were shared by the other magnates. This was not simply class arrogance. It was the malign stupidity of men clinging to old buccaneering customs in spite of their being a danger to the new system they had built up and represented. Corporate combinations were assailed from all sides, in the press, the legislatures, by the national government itself. Measures of regulation were necessary, if only to still the storm of popular revolt —which was Theodore Roosevelt's strategy. Regulation, moreover, was in the interest of corporate combination itself (amply proven by the fact that under government regulation combinations were accepted by the public, becoming larger and more prosperous).

Although J. Pierpont Morgan resisted government regulation, true to his creed that "men owning property should do what they like with it," Morganization, in the enterprises dominated by the House of Morgan, limited the right of "men owning property" to "do what they like with it." This limitation was largely in the interest of control by the House of Morgan: Rooseveltian regulation was in the interest of unified capitalism. Most of Morgan's satraps accepted his rejection of government regulation, an exception being E. H. Gary who favored "strict governmental supervision."[2]

While restraining competition among affiliated enterprises, Morganization did not limit their unrestrained power over competitors and the public. The Anthracite Combination, in control of 90 per cent of the output, ruthlessly crushed independent coal operators and oppressed consumers by extortionate prices. This combination was operated by a group of railroads through ownership of subsidiary coal companies (often illegally) working together in the community-of-interest system, most of the railroads being dominated by the House of Morgan.[3] As the anthracite strikes clearly revealed, Morgan dominated the coal combination, his mastery being definite and unchallenged. The new revolt against corporate combinations broke loose in 1902, when an unsuccessful effort was made to dissolve the coal combination, and the following year the Interstate Commerce Commission started an investigation. Three years later Congress made it unlawful for railroads to transport any commodity (except timber) which they manufactured, mined or produced. If obeyed, the law meant breaking up the anthracite coal combination, compelling the railroads to dispose of their coal properties, but Morgan's satraps did not comply with the law. The government started suit, an extremely limited victory being secured after much litigation: certain practices were forbidden and the anthracite railroads compelled to make minor readjustments.[4] One coal company, ordered separated from its railroad ownership, earned 90 per cent on its stock and paid a 52 per cent dividend.[5]

Meanwhile, in 1905, investigation revealed gross mismanagement and corruption among life-insurance companies. Factions struggling for control of the Equitable Life Assurance Society "spilled the beans," making accusations against each other revealing systematic plundering of the company by its officers. Life-insurance thievery endangered the interests of the very widows and orphans whom the magnates were always tearfully invoking in their diatribes against government regulation. Public wrath compelled action, and the New York State Legislature appointed an investigating committee. After much difficulty (prominent lawyers having "been seen" and refusing to serve) [6] the committee secured Charles Evans Hughes as counsel, and proceeded to investigate thoroughly.

The investigation revealed that unsavory conditions had for years prevailed among life-insurance companies, particularly

the Mutual, Equitable and New York Life. There were some
legal restrictions on the use of the companies' immense resources, but they were insufficient and easily evaded. By organizing new banks and trust companies or acquiring an
interest in old ones life-insurance directors and officers engaged
in all sorts of speculative (often shady) enterprises. Insurance
money was "placed in affiliated banks and trust companies
by maintenance of inactive deposit accounts at low interest." [7]
"Irresponsible power" produced "extravagance and disregard of
the interests of policyholders," the "officers and members of the
finance committees being in positions of conspicuous financial
power" and able "to greatly advance their personal fortunes." [8]
Officers and directors secured stock in banks and trust companies, pledged it as collateral for loans in their own insurance
company and used the money to pay for the stock; passing
upon their own loans, they borrowed on poor collateral or no
collateral at all, and they "began to grow rich, in many cases
where at the start they had no capital whatever." [9] These
manipulations "weakened the official sense of responsibility,
multiplying the opportunities for gain, both direct and indirect,
to officers and directors through the use of the company's
funds." [10] Investment bankers secured influence or control in
life-insurance companies, manipulating their resources in promotions and unloading on them masses of overcapitalized
issues, most of which declined heavily in the period of "undigested securities" in 1902-4. Kuhn, Loeb & Co. and E. H.
Harriman drew heavily upon Equitable's resources, while in
four years the New York Life (dominated by Morgan through
its president and George W. Perkins, chairman of the finance
committee) bought $38,804,000 in securities from J. P. Morgan
& Co. [11] How syndicate participations were determined was
described by Edmund D. Randolph, treasurer of New York
Life and member of its finance committee:

RANDOLPH: J. P. Morgan & Co. send you over an agreement
which you sign.

HUGHES: A formal agreement?

RANDOLPH: A formal agreement. Their method is more exact in that particular than most of the others.

HUGHES: Then do you get from them at the final conclusion of the matter a detailed statement showing what profits have been made?

RANDOLPH: No.

HUGHES: You don't know who your associates are?

RANDOLPH: No, not always.

HUGHES: Don't you take any steps to assure yourselves that a proper accounting is made?

RANDOLPH: We do not, nor does anyone else.[12]

Dishonest expedients were often used to hide the facts from the Superintendent of Insurance. In connection with certain transactions in Morgan's International Mercantile Marine Randolph testified:

HUGHES: On December 31, 1903, under head of sales you find the "Navigation Syndicate [International Mercantile Marine] $800,000." To whom did you sell?

RANDOLPH: To J. P. Morgan & Co.

HUGHES: On January 2, 1904, there is an entry of a purchase of Navigation Syndicate $800,000 at par. From whom did you buy?

RANDOLPH: J. P. Morgan & Co.

HUGHES: That statement [to the Superintendent of Insurance] showed that you held only $3,200,000 of International Mercantile Marine?

RANDOLPH: Yes.

HUGHES: But as a matter of fact down to December 31 you had $4,000,000?

RANDOLPH: Yes, sir.

HUGHES: And as a matter of fact, immediately after the day that report was made you took back the $800,000?

RANDOLPH: Yes.

HUGHES: The whole purpose was to be able to state in your

report to the Superintendent of Insurance that you had only
$3,200,000?

RANDOLPH: Yes.[13]

In this transaction George W. Perkins acted both for New
York Life and J. P. Morgan & Co., being the go-between in
syndicate participations and security purchases.[14] In another
transaction, buying for New York Life and selling for J. P.
Morgan & Co., Perkins insisted he had secured a bargain:

HUGHES: Did you bargain with any person other than yourself?

PERKINS: I think I did it with myself, probably.[15]

So mixed up in the insurance scandals was Perkins that
newspapers reported he might retire as one of the Morgan
partners,[16] but that did not happen until some years later.

The insurance companies contributed generously to the
campaign funds of the Republican and Democratic parties,
although favoring the Republican, the contributions being
charged to "legal expenses." They "systematically attempted to
control legislation in New York and other States which could
affect their interests directly or indirectly," and insurance de-
partments of State governments were placed on the companies'
payrolls.[17] To "avoid waste of effort" Equitable, Mutual and
New York Life divided the country among themselves and
their "legislative representatives," each company "looking after
its chosen district and bearing its appropriate part of the total
expenses." In 1904 Perkins contributed $48,700 to the Roose-
velt campaign, being subsequently reimbursed by New York
Life; and one of the New York Life "legislative representatives" received $1,167,000 in ten years, part of the payments
being made through Perkins and J. P. Morgan & Co.[18] The
Mutual political payments were approved by George F. Baker,
one of the company's trustees.[19] By this and other means
the policyholders' money was squandered.

These revelations compelled action. Many life-insurance officers and directors retired, although none was punished. Regu-

lation was tightened by the New York Legislature, campaign contributions and ownership of bank and trust-company stocks being prohibited, absolute publicity insisted upon, and other measures adopted to protect policyholders against financial malpractices.[20]

Among the protective legislative measures was one prohibiting participation in syndicates by life-insurance companies. But these companies had to make investments. They continued buying large amounts of securities, although they could not participate in syndicates, and their control was still important to promoters and investment bankers. Thomas F. Ryan, an active speculator and promoter, bought the majority stock in Equitable Life (the investment value of which was nil, its value being control of Equitable's resources). Then E. H. Harriman, after persistent efforts and threats, secured part of Ryan's holdings.[21] Upon Harriman's death in 1909 Morgan bought his Equitable stock and compelled Ryan to sell. Ryan sold, unwillingly: he *had* to. If Morgan wanted something he usually got it, and Ryan was helpless in spite of his resources and power. At the Money Trust investigation Morgan testified:

UNTERMYER: Did Mr. Ryan offer this stock to you?

MORGAN: I asked him to sell it to me.

UNTERMYER: Did you tell him why you wanted it?

MORGAN: No; I told him it was a good thing for me to have.

UNTERMYER: Did he tell you that he wanted to sell it?

MORGAN: No; but he sold it.

UNTERMYER: What did he say when you told him you would like to have it, and thought you ought to have it?

MORGAN: He hesitated about it, and finally sold it.[22]

Only after years of persistent effort did Harriman succeed in making Ryan sell part of his Equitable holdings, but the sale of all of Ryan's holdings was much more simple: Morgan insisted, Ryan sold, although he did not want to sell. One may imagine the scene: The shrinking, baffled Ryan considering Morgan's ultimatum, observing the threat in Morgan's fierce eyes glaring beneath the shaggy eyebrows, the overwhelming merciless arrogance. "It is a good thing for me to have that stock, Mr. Ryan," said Morgan. Ryan wilted and sold, although he did not want to sell.

The Equitable majority stock Morgan bought had a par value of $51,000 for which he paid $3,000,000; dividends being limited, the yield was only one-eighth of one per cent—an unbusinesslike investment transaction.[23] Asked what his motive was in buying the Equitable stock, Morgan said it was "good business," the "desirable thing for the situation," the stock was better in his ownership than in Ryan's, he did not want the stock to get "into hands that might prove injurious."[24] Try as the inquisitor might, no more satisfactory answer was forthcoming. But since the Money Trust was being investigated, Morgan could not admit that the Equitable purchase was another development in the system of institutionalized control of investment resources: Equitable's assets amounted to $400,000,000, and by 1912 the company owned $48,000,000 of securities issued or sold by J. P. Morgan & Co.[25] While life-insurance companies were prohibited from participating in syndicates, control could still influence them to buy particular securities issued by particular investment houses as against others. Morgan appointed three voting trustees for his stock, including himself, and offered to sell the stock to Equitable if it decided to mutualize. But the directors considered Morgan's price of $5,000 a share too high, the stock fetching only $300 in the market, and decided it was not "possible, either legally or in common fairness, to pay $5,000 for Mr. Morgan's majority shares and leave the minority shareholders to shift for themselves."[26] Upon his death two years later Morgan's estate received the stock, in spite of expectations that he might will it to Equitable Life, and in 1915 the stock was sold (at a profit) to T. Coleman du Pont.[27]

Revelation of life-insurance mismanagement and corruption aggravated the revolt against corporate abuses and strengthened the campaign for government regulation, in which the railroads constituted an active front.

Morganization and community of interest among the railroads eliminated rate wars but not other evils. The Interstate Commerce Act of 1887 had broken down, owing largely to judicial hostility (judges often being interested in railroads whose cases they tried), rendering the Interstate Commerce Commission helpless. There were growing complaints at the great and almost continuous rise in freight rates,[28] which, while partly due to the general upward movement in prices, was also partly due to consolidation. Most of the old abuses persisted. The Commission's great weakness was lack of power to fix rates. Rate discriminations and secret rebates still flourished, Standard Oil, again, receiving favors from the railroads, among them the New York, New Haven & Hartford (under control of the House of Morgan).[29] Helpless in the hands of powerful industrial combinations, who often extorted absolutely unfavorable rates, the railroads began to realize they were losing money and favored government action. Congress in 1903 adopted more stringent measures against rebating. Within three years the Interstate Commerce Commission collected $586,000 in fines for rebating, half of which was levied on the American Sugar Refining Co.[30] Abuses persisting and encouraged by the government's victory in the suit to dissolve Morgan's Northern Securities Co., President Roosevelt declared railroad regulation the "paramount issue" and urged that the Interstate Commerce Commission be given power to prescribe rates to "put the big shipper and the little shipper on an equal footing."[31] Although favoring legislation against rebating, the railroads resisted larger regulation and control of rates by the government.

Combining to fight Roosevelt's proposed legislation, the railroads organized publicity bureaus in all the larger cities with headquarters in Washington headed by Samuel Spencer, president of the Southern Railroad (under control of the House of Morgan).[32] Spencer, an intimate business associate of Morgan's for twenty-five years, agreed that "secret and discriminatory rates are wrong and must be stopped," but insisted that government control of railroad rates was "commercial lynch law" and "necessarily unjust to the railroads and opposed to the fundamental principle of Anglo-Saxon jurisprudence." [33] In other words, Spencer approved legislation protecting the railroads but objected to legislation protecting the public. Among the means, legitimate and illegitimate, used by the Spencer bureaus to influence public opinion against legislation to regulate rates was business, financial and social pressure on newspaper editors, whose affiliations and characteristics were card-indexed: "Weak and bibulous man. Tractable to railroad suggestions. Pro-Roosevelt." [34] Railroad propaganda flooded the nation, in spite of which Congress in 1906 passed the Hepburn Act increasing the scope of railroad regulation and giving the Interstate Commerce Commission power to nullify unreasonable or discriminatory rates.*

The government now developed more aggressive action against the railroads and the magnates in control, particularly E. H. Harriman. Yearning after larger power, Harriman was the most disturbing factor in the railroad situation (although probably the most constructive of the magnates). Investigating the Harriman system, the Interstate Commerce Commission stigmatized the Chicago & Alton reorganization as "looting" by "unscrupulous financiers," but reported no violations of law. In 1908, under the Sherman anti-trust act, the government started suit to compel Harriman's Union Pacific to divest itself of stock in Southern Pacific and four other railroads. [35]

There was considerable personal animosity in the campaign against Harriman (encouraged, also, by Harriman's business

---

*The Hepburn Act compelled railroads to divest themselves of interests in mining and manufacturing concerns—aimed particularly at the Anthracite Coal Combination under control of the House of Morgan. This provision was nullified by a railroad organizing a separate company and distributing the stock among its own stockholders. (*Commercial and Financial Chronicle*, August 17, 1907, p. 373.)

rivals). Not overscrupulous politically, Theodore Roosevelt denounced the "malefactors of great wealth" but eagerly accepted
their campaign contributions: in 1904, there being danger of
Republican defeat in New York State, Roosevelt asked Harriman to raise money for the campaign there ("you and I are
practical men," the President wrote). Harriman responded, to
the tune of $250,000, of which he contributed $50,000, J. P.
Morgan $10,000, Equitable Life $10,000, George W. Perkins
$10,000 and the Rockefeller interests $30,000.[36] But to protect
himself when the facts became public, Roosevelt insisted Harriman's help was unsolicited and denounced him as "an undesirable citizen" of "deep-seated corruption" and "an enemy of
the republic." [37]

The break with Harriman undoubtedly sharpened Roosevelt's attacks and probably hastened action against the Harriman system but did not determine the regulation policy. Being
the immediately aggressive and disturbing factor, Harriman
was more vulnerable than other railroad magnates, particularly
as his system was built up largely by direct stock ownership
and combination in contrast to Morgan's system of financial
control, interlocking directorates and community of interest.
Union Pacific was forced to give up control of other roads, the
Pennsylvania to disgorge Baltimore & Ohio, there were other
readjustments, and government regulation tightened.[38]

J. Pierpont Morgan resisted this tightening of government
regulation. At a banquet to Morgan in Chicago B. F. Yoakum
declared the country "now needs a rest from further regulative
laws," the declaration receiving the "particular approval" of
Morgan,[39] who acquiesced in the resistance to regulation offered
by his satraps. In spite of his intense dislike, Morgan called on
President Roosevelt a number of times to express his opinion
against railroad legislation; and in 1910 Morgan was instrumental in having a delegation of five railroad presidents (three
of them under control of the House of Morgan) call on President Taft to dissuade him from further regulative legislation,

but failed.[40] Federal regulation of railroads tightened, larger
powers were granted the Interstate Commerce Commission, including the power to suspend rates and jurisdiction over telegraph and telephone systems, and by 1913 Commissioner
Charles Prouty could say:

"The government cannot rightfully grant an increase of
railroad rates until it knows that the money so raised shall be
properly expended. That will be when railroads cannot spend
money except for railroad purposes, when they cannot buy the
securities of other railroads, when they cannot issue securities of
their own without the consent of the Federal government, and
when they cannot put the securities to any use except those
specified." [41]

These sentiments must have sent shivers down the ghostly
spines of Vanderbilt, Gould and Harriman, and they were
almost equally repugnant to Morgan, who, while crushing
flagrant buccaneering practices, still considered railroads as
pieces in the chess game of financial manipulation and control.

In the development of more stringent regulation much was
contributed by the spectacular expansion and crash of the New
York, New Haven & Hartford Railroad system (under control
of the House of Morgan).

J. P. Morgan became a New Haven director in 1892, and
within seven years consolidation increased the road's mileage
from 508 to 2,017, prospering exceedingly. Between 1903 and
1912 New Haven increased its capitalization from $93,000,000
to $417,000,000, mostly bonds, $200,000,000 of the increase
being used to acquire control of other railroads, steamships and
street railways in a systematic campaign to monopolize New
England's transportation.[42] The storm of protests by businessmen and others was ignored. Legislation was circumvented:
when Legislatures objected to its ownership of trolley lines
New Haven simply organized a separate company under its
control. Large amounts of money were spent to buy roads
simply for their "nuisance value" to monopoly, and in one

case $1,500,000 per mile was paid for a railroad which yielded a large yearly loss.[43] In spite of protests by Legislatures, business interests and the public, New Haven proceeded unswervingly on the road to monopoly—and ruin.

This policy of expansion was directed by Morgan himself. George F. Baker, William Rockefeller and Morgan dominated the New Haven directorate, and Morgan dominated the other two. It was upon Morgan's own motions that large increases in capitalization were voted for monopolistic expansion.[44] Intense protests met New Haven's absorption of the Boston & Maine Railroad (necessary for the monopolization of New England's transportation), directly maneuvered by Morgan, who became a member of Boston & Maine's directorate and of its executive committee.[45] The New Haven's president, Charles S. Mellen, was known as "Morgan's office-boy." Mellen was with the Morgan-Hill Northern Pacific when Morgan made him president of New Haven. It was by long-distance telephone that Mellen secured the Northern Pacific job:

MORGAN: Is that you, Mr. Mellen?

MELLEN: Yes.

MORGAN: Anybody hear what we say?

MELLEN: No.

MORGAN: Will you take the Northern Pacific?

MELLEN: Yes.

MORGAN: Will you leave it all to me?

MELLEN: Yes.

MORGAN: Good-bye.[46]

It appears that Morgan acted pretty much as he pleased with New Haven. Once the directors considered an agreement with a banking house other than J. P. Morgan & Co. Morgan frowned: there was no further consideration. In another case Morgan informed Mellen by telephone that he had bought a railroad for New Haven, but did not give the price; when Mellen looked up the price it was so large it wrung an exclamation of astonishment, "Jerusalem!" At an investigation by the Interstate Commerce Commission Joseph Folk was particularly interested in this transaction:

FOLK: Why didn't you tell Mr. Morgan—"By what right did you buy that stock?"

(*Outburst of uproarious laughter from the lawyers present, convulsed by the idea of putting such a question to Morgan.*)

MELLEN (*smilingly*): Well, it did not seem that that was just exactly the right way to approach Mr. Morgan.[47] *

To cut short discussion and opposition at New Haven board meetings Morgan would fling his box of matches from him, smash his fist on the table and say:

"Call a vote! Let's see where these gentlemen stand." They always stood where Morgan wanted them to stand.[48]

When the New Haven directors voted money to buy the road which cost $1,500,000 a mile they knew neither the why nor the wherefore. After adjournment they flocked to Mellen to protest they did not know what the money was for and "had been made to act like dumb puppets by Morgan," there being no report of "what they were buying at such a big price." Mellen decided to approach Morgan and testified to a "very humiliating" experience:

MELLEN: Can you give me a few moments?

MORGAN: Certainly.

MELLEN: This note is not in the form it should be—there should be additional information given.

---

* While directing New Haven's unsound expansion, Morgan missed a great business opportunity. In 1908 J. P. Morgan & Co. were asked to underwrite $500,000 of $1,500,000 to promote the W. C. Durant automobile consolidation which afterward became General Motors, but declined. F. L. Stetson had no confidence in Durant. George W. Perkins considered Durant crazy for saying the day was coming when 500,000 automobiles would be sold yearly. "If he has any sense," said Perkins, "he'll keep such notions to himself if he ever tries to borrow money." Instead the Morgans backed the wrong horse in Benjamin Briscoe, in whose firm they had secured a half-interest as the condition for a loan of $100,000 when Briscoe was financially pressed. The stock Durant offered J. P. Morgan & Co. was worth over $200,000,000 in 1928 and had paid $35,000,000 in dividends. (T. F. McManus and Norman Beasley, *Men, Money and Motors*, pp. 5, 105-16.)

MORGAN (*excitedly, ominously*): Did not Mr. Stetson draw that note?

MELLEN: Yes, I suppose so.

MORGAN: Do you think you know more how it ought to be done than he does?

"I allowed I did not," said Mellen, "and dropped it." Violently taking up his hat and stick, Morgan left.[49] Mellen was New Haven's president but not its master.

In his testimony Mellen probably tried to place himself in as favorable a light as possible by shifting responsibility on Morgan for New Haven's disastrous policy of expansion, but in its larger aspects the policy was undoubtedly Morgan's. Mellen testified much as if he was unburdening himself by confession, there being a strain of religious resignation in his testimony: "I left undone the things that I ought to have done and have done the things I ought not to have done—you know the way the Prayer Book runs." [50] The fiat of Morgan made Mellen New Haven's president and the underling obeyed the master even when obedience was humiliating and disastrous. "I stood in greater awe of Mr. Morgan than of any other man I have ever met and the other directors probably shared my feeling," testified Mellen, admitting the "cowardice" of himself and the directors:

FOLK: Were you Mr. Morgan's man as president of the New Haven?

MELLEN: I have been called his office-boy. I was very proud of his confidence. I regard the statement that I was his man as a compliment.

FOLK: Who dominated the board of directors?

MELLEN: They used to vote as a rule pretty near where Mr. Morgan voted. There were strong men on the New Haven board other than Mr. Morgan, but I do not recall anything where Mr. Morgan was determined, emphatic, insistent—I recall no case in which he did not have his way....

FOLK: Was it through fear of Mr. Morgan's anger?

MELLEN: No, sir; I do not think I was afraid of Mr. Morgan, but I had the greatest respect for him. I yielded my judgment to him. He was a man of such tremendous force and success that I did not feel—or, rather, I felt that I was in the wrong in nine cases out of ten when I disagreed with him.[51]

Mellen's testimony, the essential integrity of which is unimpeachable (although J. Pierpont Morgan, Jr. denied his father had kept Mellen in ignorance of important facts),[52] reveals the relations between Morgan and his satraps—he overwhelmed them with his force and authority, compelled obedience, ruled with an iron hand. There was the institutionalized power of the House of Morgan, and there was the domineering personality of Morgan himself which imposed ruthlessly upon lesser men. Morgan brooked no interference, no opposition within his empire: his mastery was dictatorship in all its essentials and procedure.

"Men have told me," said Mellen, "that in my relations with Mr. Morgan I came off with fewer scars than others did." [53]

The New Haven's monopolistic expansion ended in disaster, government action and recrimination. Clamor against the management multiplied. Wrecks increased, in one case President Mellen being indicted for manslaughter. For three years dividends were paid out of surplus and by short-term borrowing, which increased seven-fold. In 1913 the dividend was reduced, the stock declined from 130 to 87, and stockholders organized a protective committee.[54] Of New Haven's 25,000 stockholders 10,220 owned only one to ten shares [55]—and there were large losses among these small investors, among the widows and orphans whose interests the magnates always tearfully invoked in the pleas against government regulation. In 1912 Mellen was indicted for criminal restraint of trade, and the following year he was forced out of the presidency by the stockholders' protective committee (and J. P. Morgan, Jr.). Events now moved swiftly. Stormily attacked by stockholders for its "excessive profits" in financing New Haven, particularly on a proposed new issue of convertible debenture bonds, J. P. Morgan & Co. withdrew as fiscal agents and from all director-ships, revealing that in three years they had raised $168,-627,000 for New Haven on which the commissions were $889,000 and the profit only $441,000.[56] The New Haven system was dissolved, dividends suspended, and many years passed before it recovered from the after-effects of its monopolistic spree.

One of the New Haven episodes was Morgan's indictment for conspiracy in a particular railroad transaction. "He wept," according to one chronicler, "and from an aching heart wailed:

" 'To think that after all these years I have been branded by my own government a criminal, fit only to be thrown into jail.' " [57]

In the end, as at the beginning, when during the Civil War a Congressional Committee said of Morgan (among others): "He cannot be looked upon as a good citizen." ...

In promoting the New Haven Railroad's monopolistic ex-pansion J. P. Morgan made the same mistake as in the case of International Mercantile Marine—combination apparently for the sake of combination, disregarding decisive economic (and political) considerations. By combining everything in sight, good, bad and indifferent, New Haven wasted money and sacrificed efficiency. Under other conditions monopolizing New England's transportation might have proven profitable by the power to extort monopoly rates, but now government regula-tion prevented extortion. New Haven's expansion was simply adventurism, the expression of unrestrained personal power; and there was more than the suggestion of megalomania in Morgan's ruthless pursuit of monopolistic combination. Disaster was inevitable. Out of this and other disasters centralized in-dustry and finance learned there are limits to combination in size, character and profits, that combination in itself is not necessarily a good thing, producing many important changes in structure and policy. The New Haven experience, moreover, provoked more stringent government regulation of railroads.

Meanwhile, on another front of the campaign, regulation was being imposed on the trusts. By 1904 there were 440 trustified combinations capitalized at $20,379,000,000, one-third under control of seven combinations over which towered the United States Steel Corporation.[58] The most important of these trusts were under control or influence of Morgan. In spite of intense corporate opposition the Federal Government organized a Bureau of Corporations, one of the first acts of which was to investigate United States Steel. In 1905 the Beef Trust was ordered dissolved, Swift & Co. and others being restrained from illegal combination in restraint of trade, from organizing to maintain prices, and from receiving discriminatory railroad rates.[59] This decision was considered a victory for Theodore Roosevelt, and he proceeded to press the regulation campaign more vigorously. President Roosevelt instituted twenty-five antitrust prosecutions and President Taft forty-five (although Taft was considered "conservative" in comparison with the "radical" Roosevelt).[60] The government's arm was steeled by exposures of trust iniquity: among them the revelation of tainted food sold by the Beef Trust and American Sugar Refining's long-continued system of customs swindles (in spite of its tariff favors and the enormous profits from monopoly prices), the company being compelled to make restitution of $2,134,000 to the government.[61]

But definite regulation developed slowly, antagonistic interests driving at different tangents. Two extremes jostled each other: "Off with their heads!" and "Let us alone!" Industrial combination represented economic progress, in spite of abuses and occasional inefficiency. Production by machinery inevitably led to larger technical units, more capital investment and combination, multiplying the output of goods. The abuses of combination were not in itself but in ownership and manipulation. Critics spoke of "restoring competition" as if nothing had happened in the economic world since the introduction of machinery, and as if it was the prescriptive right of the small businessman to compete (although himself trying to become big) by crushing combination, if necessary. The government itself had no settled trust policy, much depending on the public temper and political considerations. Judicial decisions conflicted with each other, expressing fallibility of legal wisdom and immaturity of regulation. In one case a judge decided the combination of two express drivers was illegal combination in retraint of trade![62] The situation was clarified by the Supreme Court decision ordering dissolution of the Standard Oil Co.

Attacks upon Standard Oil multiplied, in spite of John D. Rockefeller's increasing philanthropy. The public gloated when the company was heavily fined upon conviction of receiving discriminatory rates from the Chicago & Alton Railroad.[63] Almost universal approval greeted the government's suit to dissolve the Oil Trust. When the Supreme Court ordered dissolution in 1911 the *Commercial and Financial Chronicle* declared the decision inevitable: "The government had piled up such a mass of evidence, step by step, covering a period of forty years, all tending to support the allegations of a consistent and persistent purpose to restrain commerce and monopolize trade and production, that absolutely no way of escape was left open."[64] Moreover, Standard Oil was guilty of ordinary crimes independent of the technical issue of combination: "It seems as if the combination must have been held illegal under the principles of the common law—so overwhelming was the evidence against it." The *Chronicle* added: "Of course the astute managers of Standard Oil may safely be trusted to work out its salvation through other and lawful forms of organization."[65] Which was precisely what they did. At the basis of Standard Oil was an integrated economic efficiency which court decrees could not destroy.

The financial community considered the Supreme Court decision "reassuring."[66] "It is very satisfactory," said J. P. Morgan, although President Taft was "disappointed" and the radicals

in Congress "bitter." [67] This difference was created by the
Supreme Court's opinion that Standard Oil was guilty of
unreasonable restraint of trade, repudiating the government's
contention that any restraint of trade was illegal, whether reasonable or unreasonable. The Court insisted that application of
the anti-trust laws must be guided by "the rule of reason." [68]
Bigness in itself was not illegal. Government might supervise
and regulate but could not destroy combinations.

Under the decree's terms competition was not restored in the
oil industry. The Standard Oil dissolved into separate companies which divided territory and worked together harmoniously, community of interest being maintained by majority
stock ownership among the same small group previously dominating the corporation.

Clamor for the restoration of competition persisted, although
this restoration was economically impossible. But while the
struggle was not over by any means, the Standard Oil decision
prepared the basis for an adjustment of government and Big
Business by practically merging them in terms of monopolistic
capitalism, of supervision and regulation accepting industrial
and financial centralization in the larger unified capitalism. The
issue was finally settled in favor of Big Business by the Supreme
Court decision, almost ten years later, dismissing the government's suit to dissolve the United States Steel Corporation.

Early in 1911 Congress ordered an investigation of United
States Steel. Its dominance aroused suspicion, intensified by
absorption of Tennessee Coal & Iron during the 1907 panic.
United States Steel controlled 50 per cent of the industry's
output and five more corporations another 40 per cent. [69] Under
these conditions suppressing or regulating competition was
easy. The six corporations maintained harmonious relations,
Chairman Gary actively organizing "dinners," "institutes" and
friendly relations generally to maintain prices. [70] Dominating
the American foreign trade in iron and steel, having tripled its
exports, United States Steel was powerful enough to convene a

world conference of the steel powers to keep competition, in the words of Gary, "within bounds" by adopting the Golden Rule.[71] But Gary's lofty moral sentiments (this being a wicked world) sharpened instead of allaying public suspicion and hostility, and five months after the Supreme Court's Standard Oil decision the government started suit to dissolve the United States Steel Corporation.

This action aroused Morgan. It struck at the most important of the House of Morgan's affiliated enterprises. President Taft having urged "voluntary breaking up" of combinations in restraint of trade, the financial community was alarmed by rumors that United States Steel contemplated voluntary dissolution to avoid trial. It meant making size in itself illegal, since the Corporation was not guilty of Standard Oil's unsavory practices. The *Commercial and Financial Chronicle* asked:

"Will J. P. Morgan, to whom the country is indebted for so much, again take a stand in defense of its business interests?" [72]

Morgan did. He brushed aside counsels of despair in his own camp, many of his associates insisting on voluntary dissolution. Capitulation not only meant self-stultification but abandonment of Morgan's most cherished industrial enterprise. It meant, moreover, imperiling the principle of combination. In the name of the directors of the United States Steel Corporation Morgan said:

"The Corporation was organized for business reasons ... not to restrain trade or obtain a monopoly. In all its operations the company has scrupulously observed the law and recognized the just rights of its competitors.... The directors feel that their duty to their stockholders, their employees and the public requires that they set at rest all rumors that they are contemplating any voluntary dissolution or disintegration of the Corporation." [73]

More than the issue of combination was involved. Organized labor, which within ten years had tripled its membership and become a definite power, was waging an active campaign against United States Steel, the American Federation of Labor being partly responsible for the investigation and dissolution proceedings. Although insisting that "the men *wanted* to work seven days a week," [74] the Corporation under pressure limited the seven-day week, but not other oppressive conditions of labor. Moreover, while unionism increased generally it did not increase in the plants of large corporations, and among these United States Steel was the center of resistance to unionism. "I am of the opinion," said Elbert H. Gary in 1906, "and always have been, that labor unions, properly managed, are a benefit to the workingmen. But—" [75] That "but" included reservations striking directly at unionism and covering denial of the right to organize, espionage and using the municipal police to prevent unions and strikes, and the paternalism of "welfare" in place of independent unionism. United States Steel set the pace for other combinations. The American Federation of Labor multiplied its attacks upon the Steel Trust as a strategic maneuver in the campaign to unionize the iron and steel industry. United States Steel's resistance to dissolution was almost as much resistance to unionism as defense of the principle of combination.

The combined labor and middle-class attack seriously threatened United States Steel. But it weathered the storm. In 1915 there was a District Court decision in favor of the Corporation, and the Supreme Court in 1920 affirmed the decision (six to three) by ruling that United States Steel represented "not monopoly, but concentration of efforts with resultant economies and benefits." [76] Industrial and financial centralization conquered, initiating still more corporate combinations.

But conquest was preceded by an intensified drive against combinations, signalized by government proceedings against the International Harvester Co., American Telephone & Telegraph Co. (which was forced to give up control of Western Union) [77] and other combinations, compelling modifications and readjustment in structure and policy.

GEORGE F. BAKER

HENRY P. DAVISON

Although affecting affiliated enterprises, the campaign for government regulation of corporate combinations did not at first directly affect the House of Morgan itself. But a direct offensive was inevitable, as the House of Morgan represented the system of financial centralization and control of industry, and the offensive materialized in the Money Trust investigation of 1912.

By this time the public mood was much more radical than when Theodore Roosevelt initiated his regulation campaign. In spite of government action, combinations were still arrogant and oppressive, while business depression sharpened labor and agrarian discontent, developed a decided drift toward socialism, and created a substantial middle-class liberal movement largely under Robert M. La Follette's inspiration. Every social transition sharpens class antagonisms and discontent. The campaign to regulate corporate combinations, necessary in the transition of Big Business to supremacy, merged in more radical proposals to democratize industry and government. Even Roosevelt, essentially conservative, was swept off his feet by the spirit of radical protest, aggressive reform and social idealism among the Progressives whose program he adopted to the strain of "We stand at Armageddon and we battle for the Lord!" (Roosevelt recovered after the campaign.) Increasing radicalization produced Republican defeat in the 1910 Congressional elections, the Roosevelt Progressive revolt, and Woodrow Wilson's election to the presidency in 1912.

This upflare of progressivism, representing the interests of small businessmen, the farmers and labor, emphasized the more radical aspects of the revolt against centralized industry and finance, proposing government action on corporate combinations to restore, in Wilson's words, "our old variety and freedom and individual energy of development." [78] Wilson urged the punishment of officers and not corporations in convictions of illegal practices, favored "liberating business" by restoring competition, and said in 1911: "The great monopoly in this country is the money monopoly.... A great industrial nation is controlled by its credit. Our system of credit is concentrated ...in the hands of a few men...who chill and check and destroy economic freedom." [79] The revolt against corporate combinations now converged on the "Money Trust."

Early in 1912 the House of Representatives decided to investigate the Money Trust, which primarily meant J. P. Morgan & Co. Again Morgan became a dominant campaign issue (as in 1896). At the Democratic convention William Jennings Bryan put through a resolution against "the nomination of any candidate for president who is the representative of or under obligations to J. Pierpont Morgan, Thomas F. Ryan, August Belmont, or any other member of the privilege-hunting or favor-seeking class" (instigating denunciation of Bryan by one delegate as a "money-grabbing, favor-seeking, office-chasing marplot"). [80] The Money Trust investigation and its aftermath decided the forms and limitations of corporate regulation, readjustment and final conquest.

CHAPTER XXXIII

MONEY TRUST TESTIMONY

*The Knave was standing before them, in
chains, with a soldier on each side to
guard him; and near the King was the
White Rabbit, with a trumpet in one hand
and a scroll of parchment in the other.
"Call the witness," said the King.*

ALICE IN WONDERLAND

THE Pujo Committee's investigation of the Money Trust,
directed by Samuel Untermyer, although it failed to prove the
existence of a money trust, revealed an immense concentration
in the institutionalized control of financial resources, of money
and credit.* This control operated by means of stock ownership, interlocking directorships, financial control of corporations, and the community-of-interest system. J. Pierpont
Morgan, George F. Baker and James Stillman (who had practically retired at this time and did not testify) were the dominant forces in the centralization of finance and industry. But
these financiers denied any possession or consciousness of
power: indignantly they thrust away the crown. Testifying on
the control of the First National Bank by himself, J. P.
Morgan and other interests Baker said:

BAKER: There has never been any dispute about the control.

UNTERMYER: About your control?

BAKER: About mine any more than anybody's.

UNTERMYER: Nobody has disputed your control?

BAKER: No, sir; and I have not disputed any one else's
control.... We are a very harmonious family, I am happy to
say, and we cannot get up any quarrels.[1]

* The Pujo Committee's findings on financial centralization are summarized
in Chapter XXX, "Morgan's System," pp. 354-56.

The family was undoubtedly harmonious, with Baker and Morgan in control and never disagreeing—Baker being a sort of Father Joseph to Morgan's Richelieu. Repeatedly, almost naïvely, the seventy-three-year-old witness denied his own power:

UNTERMYER: Is Mr. Morgan recognized as the great general in this financial army down in Wall Street?

BAKER: I think so.

UNTERMYER: And you and Mr. Stillman are recognized as his chief lieutenants?

BAKER: I do not think so; no, sir.

UNTERMYER: Try to overcome your modesty, Mr. Baker. Mr. Morgan, Mr. Stillman and yourself are the three dominant powers, are you not?

BAKER: I will not confess to that.

SPOONER: He is not obliged to incriminate himself, is he?

BAKER: I will confess it during the panic of 1907.

UNTERMYER: That is what happened during the panic—that Mr. Morgan was the general and you were the chief lieutenants?

BAKER: Yes.

UNTERMYER: He has not surrendered that post, has he?

BAKER: No; I guess it has expired—

UNTERMYER (*interposing*): By limitation?

BAKER: Yes.[2]

But in spite of denials of his own power, Baker, in the course of the severe examination by Untermyer, made clear his desire to avoid controversy, gave the information asked (often against counsel's protest), his testimony being characterized as "much more illuminating and important" than Morgan's. Baker admitted danger lurked in the increasing centralization of the control of money and credit:

UNTERMYER: Do you think that [further concentration] would be dangerous?

BAKER: I think it has gone far enough.

UNTERMYER: You think it would be dangerous to go further?

BAKER: It might not be dangerous, but still it has gone about far enough. In good hands, I do not see that it would do any harm. If it got into bad hands, it would be very bad.

UNTERMYER: If it got into bad hands it would wreck the country?

BAKER: Yes, but I do not believe it could get into bad hands.

UNTERMYER: So that the safety, if you think there is safety in the situation, really lies in the personnel of the men?

BAKER: Very much.

UNTERMYER: Do you think that is a comfortable situation for a great country to be in?

BAKER: Not entirely.[3]

Being almost as important a factor in financial centralization as Morgan himself, George F. Baker's testimony aroused intense interest. There was equal interest in the testimony of Henry P. Davison. Formerly vice-president of the First National Bank, Davison had become a partner in J. P. Morgan & Co. some years previously. Active in the Guaranty Trust mergers, having handled the negotiations for American participation in the Chinese loan, and now a director in the American Telephone & Telegraph Co.,[4] Davison was more and more becoming the most important Morgan partner. Antagonistic in his testimony, Davison made no concessions, more royalist than the king. He did not yield on the issue of financial centralization, limiting himself to admitting there should not be any more "until commerce and industry require it."[5] In spite of his own interlocking directorships and the House of Morgan's activity in imposing its control on banks, life-insurance and trust companies, Davison denied there was any advantage for his firm in the interlocking of directorates:

UNTERMYER: You recognize, do you not, that there is a great advantage in having the entrée and the interest in these banks and representation on the board; or do you think there is no advantage whatever?

DAVISON: Absolutely no advantage at all.

UNTERMYER: None whatever?

DAVISON: In the placing of securities.

UNTERMYER: You think it is a disadvantage?

DAVISON: At times. Not always.[6]

Curious testimony, in spite of its modification! Sheer benevolence, apparently, animated Morganization in its imposition of control over banks and other financial institutions. Interlocking financial directorships *were* an advantage in syndicate and other investment operations, an expression of financial interdependence and complexity, necessary in spite of abuses. There was some truth in Davison's contention, however, many of the interlocking directorships of the House of Morgan being justified not in terms of business profit but in terms of Morgan's system of financial control, of financial government.

Davison clearly conveyed his belief that whatever J. P. Morgan & Co. did was justified and right:

DAVISON: If any transaction was done at the request of J. P. Morgan & Co. the minority holders were protected, if they could protect them, because that is the policy of the house. That I know and that is all I know.

UNTERMYER: That you know back in 1903, although you did not come into association with them until 1909?

DAVISON: Yes; I know that back for fifty-five years, which is ten years older than I am.

UNTERMYER: I see. Why not go back a little further?

DAVISON: Well, that was the beginning of the house. That is the reason.

UNTERMYER: In other words, you know that J. P. Morgan & Co. can do no wrong?

DAVISON: I know that J. P. Morgan & Co. could do no wrong if their endeavors and the circumstances permitted them to do as they wanted to do.[7]

Of one transaction Davison said: "I do not know why the House did it, but if the House did it, it is most defensible." He insisted the "blessings" of the trusts "are not as great as they were before they were disturbed," although, he added, "I do not believe in monopoly or oppression." Asked if, in his judgment, it was wrong for the government to interfere with the trusts, Davison replied: "No, if they were illegal and violating the law. I think it would have been better, I decidedly think it would have been better, to have approached it the other way and correct the law and put supervision and control over the trusts." [8]

The testimony of J. Pierpont Morgan, naturally, aroused the most interest. Almost every investigation or prosecution of the more important industrial combinations revealed relationships with the House of Morgan, dominant and pervasive. Now the usually silent master of the House of Morgan was to speak, compelled to speak by the government whose interference in industry and finance he resented. But if they calculated on butchering Morgan to make a Roman holiday, the calculation was mistaken. This appearance before the Pujo Committee marked the culmination of public denunciation which Morgan contemptuously ignored, of government interference which Morgan considered in terms of personal affront. Anger raged in the master of money—anger, and outraged pride, and the baffled power of dictatorship compelled to recognize (even if temporarily) the mightier force of another power. Probably the aristocratic Morgan's strongest feeling was indignation at becoming a public spectacle for the masses whom he despised. But the old man, seventy-six years old, had himself under absolute control: he was suave, courteous, almost expansive, neither arrogant nor condescending. Nor was there any *apologia pro vita sua:* Morgan yielded nothing to his inquisitor.

Morgan appeared to testify, accompanied by his son, several partners and eight attorneys, whose fees for two days were estimated at $45,000.[9] (The money was wasted, Morgan ignoring the attorneys and deciding on his own answers.) While waiting to be called Morgan dozed; a stenographer, in passing, brushed the old man who sat up belligerently, his eyes menacing.[10] "I am getting old," said Morgan, smilingly, in asking for a seat on the dais reserved for the investigating committee, "and my hearing is not as good as it used to be." [10]

At first slightly nervous, which worried his attorneys, Morgan answered "yes" or "no," suspiciously. But after observing there was no intention to badger him, and becoming interested in the battle of wits between himself and Samuel Untermyer, Morgan answered more freely and elaborately. But Untermyer did not succeed in getting him to make any damaging admissions. Morgan fascinated the spectators: dominating but not domineering, he sometimes banged the table while answering but was usually cordial and often amusing. His years showed in occasional lapses of memory, not in anything else— except, perhaps, in the mellow tone of some of his answers and an old man's inclination to mischievous (not antagonistic or venomous) retorts. At every chance Morgan shot a bolt at his inquisitor, laughing hilariously at the sally; but if the spectators laughed, his own smile faded.[11]

Like Davison, Morgan declined to admit that anything wrong had ever been done by the House of Morgan, granted that centralized money power could be used harmfully but denied it was dangerous, and insisted there was no money trust:

MORGAN: You cannot make a trust on money.

UNTERMYER: There is no way one man can get a monopoly of money?

MORGAN: No, sir; he cannot. He may have all the money in Christendom, but he cannot do it.

UNTERMYER: If you owned all the banks of New York with all their resources, would you not come pretty near having a control of credit?

MORGAN: No, sir; not at all.

UNTERMYER: You admit, do you not, that men may get control of railroads, or business enterprises, and monopolize them and abuse their privileges?

MORGAN: Yes, anybody—

UNTERMYER: And retain control?

MORGAN: Yes.

UNTERMYER: And you say that so far as the control of credit is concerned, they cannot do the same thing?

MORGAN: Of money, no; they cannot control it.[12]

Admitting nothing, Morgan indulged in denials of too sweeping a character. There was no money trust, but there was measurable and undeniable institutionalized control of financial resources and credit. But still more sweeping was Morgan's denial of his own power, outdoing George F. Baker:

UNTERMYER: When a man has got vast power, such as you have—you admit you have, do you not?

MORGAN: I do not know it, sir.

UNTERMYER: You do not feel it at all?

MORGAN: No, I do not feel it at all.

UNTERMYER: Your firm is run by you, is it not?

MORGAN: No, sir.

UNTERMYER: You are the final authority, are you not?

MORGAN: No, sir.

UNTERMYER: You have never been?

MORGAN: Never have.

UNTERMYER: Your power in any direction is entirely unconscious to you, is it not?

MORGAN: It is, sir; if that is the case.

UNTERMYER: You do not think you have any power in any department of industry in this country?

MORGAN: I do not.

UNTERMYER: Not the slightest?

MORGAN: Not the slightest.[13]

The spectators gasped, or laughed, or smiled sardonically, according to their bent, at this financial Cæsar declining the im-

perial crown of power. Thrust and parry, thrust and parry, all
the thrusts being parried by Morgan's impenetrable resolve to
admit nothing. In accordance with this resolve the master of
the House of Morgan denied that directors serving under vot-
ing-trust agreements were either controlled or influenced by the
trustees selecting them:

UNTERMYER: Do you not realize that a board thus selected is
under the domination of the people who name it?

MORGAN: My experience is quite otherwise, sir.

UNTERMYER: Is it your experience, then, that the people who
name a board of directors and have the right to rename them,
or to drop them, have less power with them than people who
have no concern in naming them?

MORGAN: Very much so, sir.

UNTERMYER: Assuming you were the voting trustee for all
of the great systems of railroads in the United States, it would
concentrate control in your hands, would it not?

MORGAN: No, sir; it would not.[14]

Again—admit nothing! Untermyer was baffled by the overwhelming insolence of Morgan's denial of elementary facts.
The old man simply chuckled, apparently enjoying himself
hugely, although the strain of evading the inquisitor's thrusts
produced some agonizing moments. But he rejected offers of
respite and insisted on going ahead. Admitting his preference
for combination, Morgan testified that he did not object to competition:

UNTERMYER: You are opposed to competition, are you not?

MORGAN: No; I do not mind competition.

UNTERMYER: You would rather have combination, would you
not?

MORGAN: I would rather have combination.

UNTERMYER: Combination as against competition?

MORGAN: I do not object to competition, either. I like a little
competition.[15]

Laughter greeted this sally. Undoubtedly he did "like a *little* competition." Morgan admitted his dislike of stock-market manipulation (which was true, although manipulation was used in 1901 to make a market for United States Steel stock):

UNTERMYER: Manipulation is a bad thing, is it not?

MORGAN: I think manipulation is always bad.

UNTERMYER: You disapprove of it?

MORGAN: I do, sir.

UNTERMYER: Do you approve of short selling?

MORGAN: I never did it in my life, that I know of.... I do not like it—not that I wish to criticize it at all, because I do not see how you can get along without it.

UNTERMYER: Why can you not get along without a man's selling something he has not got in the way of stocks?

MORGAN: That is a principle of life, I think.[16]

"That is a principle of life." Morgan justified prevailing financial practices as inevitable, as identical with life itself, although he had shown the limitations of practices and institutions by participating in revolutionizing the nation's financial structure. Morgan, moreover, identified financial policy with the larger aspects of public policy, apparently incapable of separating them: he declined to admit that public policy might determine or modify financial practices. In discussing whether it was good public policy for interstate corporations to make deposits with private bankers over whom there was no government supervision, Morgan testified:

MORGAN: It is a mere matter of judgment, I should say.

UNTERMYER: As a matter of policy—

MORGAN: As a matter of judgment, I should say—

UNTERMYER: As a matter of public policy, concerned with the regulation of interstate corporations that are owned by the public and whose shares are widely scattered, you are of the opinion that they should be permitted, without restriction, to make their deposits with private bankers just as readily as with banks that are chartered?

MORGAN: If their directors so decide.

UNTERMYER: Do you not think that anybody other than the board of directors has an interest in that subject?

MORGAN: If it is a company, it can be examined at any time.

UNTERMYER: But the question is whether they ought to have the right to do such a thing?

MORGAN: I should think that was left to the board of directors.[17]

The directors should do as they like, in accordance with their own judgment. Public policy, as the expression of the unification and maintenance of class interests and supremacy, should not interfere with particular directors or financial institutions. As a logical consequence, Morgan identified the interests of his financial dictatorship with the interests of the nation:

UNTERMYER: Is not a man likely, quite subconsciously, to imagine that things are for the interest of the country when they are good business?

MORGAN: No, sir.

UNTERMYER: You think you are able to justly and impartially differentiate, where your own interests are concerned, just as clearly as though you had no interests at stake, do you?

MORGAN: Exactly.

UNTERMYER: Of course, there is a possibility of your judgment being mistaken, is there not?

MORGAN: Oh, I may be wrong in my judgment, but I do not think it lies in that direction.[18]

Out of the ordeal, according to contemporary opinion, Morgan emerged with flying colors. The investigating committee was unable to pin on him personally anything of dishonest, scandalous or disreputable nature. Morgan's testimony, however, revealed him as a man of immense arbitrary power, of reactionary impulses, of the stuff dictators are made. His very denials emphasized his power. There was an approach to megalomania in the insistence on being capable of differentiating "justly and impartially" between his own interests and the interests of the nation, but this was characteristic of Morgan's class which conceives itself as the nation. The inquisitor thrust at an ogre and revealed simply the financial despot, the master of money.

This master of money represented the system of financial centralization, and the system offered its defense through a statement by J. P. Morgan & Co. (at the Pujo Committee's request, prepared by Henry P. Davison). The statement denied, rightly, that financial centralization gave its representatives the power to "regulate interest rates, and to create, avert and compose panics." It branded as "preposterous" the idea that "every interlocking director has full control in every organization with which he is connected," and insisted it was "a duty, not a privilege" for the investment banker to hold directorships "because of his moral responsibility as sponsor of the corporation's securities." Financial concentration, the Davison-Morgan statement declared, is "due simply to the demand for larger banking facilities to care for the growth of the country's business.... As it is, American banks have not kept pace with the development of American business.... Even our largest banks are seldom able separately to extend the credit which large undertakings require, no one national bank being permitted by law to loan in excess of 10 per cent of its capital and surplus to any one individual or concern." [19]

There were two aspects of the offensive against financial centralization: objection to centralization as such and objection to its abuses and largely unregulated character.

The Davison-Morgan statement answered only the first objection, the easiest to answer because indefensible. Financial centralization was the logical development of capitalism, the response to industrial concentration. By its control of credit and investment capital upon which industry depends, financial centralization usurped the supreme power of determining the flow of capital and labor, of measurably regulating corporations, of imposing definite mastery upon economic life. This centralized mechanism of control was indispensable, consider-

ing the complex character of concentrated capitalism, but it
represented the accumulation of formidable and dangerous
power. J. P. Morgan & Co. denied the danger:

"All power—physical, intellectual, financial or political—is
dangerous in evil hands. If Congress were to fall into evil hands
the results might be deplorable. But to us it seems as little likely
that the citizens of this country will fill Congress with rascals
as it is that they will entrust the leadership of their business
and financial affairs to a set of clever rogues." [20]

The comparison limps. There was some popular control over
Congress but none over the centralized financial mechanism
presided over by J. Pierpont Morgan.

Moreover, Morganized financial centralization was lopsided.
It was lopsided not merely because it was measurably the dictatorship of one man, but because the system was not sufficiently inclusive and institutionalized: it yielded control over
investment resources and corporations but not over general
business conditions, being largely helpless in panics. The financial magnates centralized in order to co-operate and unify their
own resources and power, but rejected larger unity and co-
operation as their antagonists rejected centralization altogether.
Only the intervention and regulation of government could produce the larger centralization required by concentrated capitalism and by developing imperialism.

The Pujo Committee objected to financial centralization, but
their recommendations were incapable of breaking the system.
They proposed the abolition of interlocking directorates, of voting trusts in banks and of interstate corporations making deposits with private bankers (aimed specifically at J. P. Morgan
& Co.), approval of bank consolidations by the Comptroller of
the Currency, and prohibition of national banks engaging in
underwriting operations.[21] None of these recommendations
menaced financial centralization itself, but only comparatively
unimportant personal aspects (except the prohibition of national banks engaging in underwriting operations, which was

against the tendency of unifying economic functions). The recommendations urged government regulation. Out of government regulation financial centralization was to emerge stronger, more unified and institutionalized, but minus the aspect of personal dictatorship represented by J. Pierpont Morgan.

> *There will be no successor to Morgan.*—
> Wall Street Journal, *April 1, 1913.*
> *Now Wall Street is beyond the need or*
> *the possibility of one-man leadership. There*
> *will be co-ordination of effort, union of re-*
> *sources, but Morgan will have no successor.*
> —*New York* Times, *April 1, 1913.*
> *He was the last of his line. Never again*
> *will there be another J. Pierpont Morgan.*
> *...No man clothed with irresponsible,*
> *autocratic power could be expected to*
> *wield it more honorably or ably or patri-*
> *otically than he. But the system itself is*
> *impossible....The Morgan empire is one*
> *that the satraps cannot govern and will*
> *not be permitted to govern.*—*New York*
> World, *April 1, 1913.*

SHORTLY after testifying in the Money Trust investigation, in
January, 1913, J. Pierpont Morgan went to Europe. This was
an old custom. While on these trips he received reports on all
transactions of the House involving more than $5,000,000 and
on all matters of policy.[1] The master retained his mastery. Now,
for the first time, Morgan severed all business relations and
gave full responsibility to his partners, retiring in quest of
health. Three months later Morgan died.

All through February and March there were many newspaper reports and denials of Morgan's illness. The sick man
flitted from Cairo to Naples to Rome, surrounded by members
of his family, intimate friends and an army of valets and cour-
iers, pestered by swarms of predatory vendors of art. On March
30 it was admitted that Morgan was critically ill—he had been
in bed for seven days, refusing food, losing strength. Almost

up to the end he retained his intelligence and spirit: "Don't
baby me so!" he cried. Then Morgan's mind collapsed, delirium
set in, and he died on March 31.[2]

Newspapers featured the death as they had the illness. There
was a flood of condolences and tributes from the mighty of
earth. "He was a great and good man," said Pope Pius, who
once, after an interview with Morgan, had regretted not discussing with him the Vatican finances.[3] The master of souls
blessed the master of money. William Jennings Bryan, as
Secretary of State, ordered the American Ambassador in Italy
to make arrangements for Morgan's funeral, and Mrs. Bryan
wrote in her diary: "If Mr. Morgan knew that Mr. Bryan was
dallying with his funeral arrangements...!"[4] (Eleven years
later Bryan was compelled to accept John W. Davis, a former
attorney of J. P. Morgan & Co., as the Democratic candidate for
president.)

There were preliminary funeral services in Rome, final
services in St. George's Protestant Episcopal Church, New York
City, and burial in Hartford, Morgan's birthplace. The aristocracy of money and the aristocracy of blood united in their
tributes. While the New York funeral service was in progress,
the New York and Chicago Stock Exchanges closed. Simultaneously the English held services in Westminster Abbey,
where the choir sang "Lead, Kindly Light," Morgan's favorite
hymn. St. George's Church was swamped with floral wreaths—
from Kaiser Wilhelm II, the Kings of Italy and Britain, the
French Government. There were wreaths from American
magnates of industry and finance, most of whom were in the
church: Vanderbilts, Rockefellers, Gen. Horace Porter. Among
the pallbearers were George F. Baker, Elbert H. Gary and
Elihu Root. The choir sang, "Asleep in Jesus," requested by
Morgan in his will. Business in Hartford stopped while its
foremost citizen was being buried.[5] J. Pierpont Morgan departed in a final burst of the splendor and magnificence he so
intensely loved.

While making generous donations to his church, Morgan was not particularly pious, but the first article of his will was a confession of faith which evoked clerical enthusiasm:

"I commit my soul into the hands of my Saviour, in full confidence that having redeemed it and washed it in His most precious blood He will present it faultless before my Heavenly Father; and I entreat my children to maintain and defend, at all hazard and at any cost of personal sacrifice, the blessed doctrine of the complete atonement for sin through the blood of Jesus Christ, once offered and through that alone." [6]

Discussing this confession of faith one clergyman said: "The good that Mr. Morgan has done Christ's cause is incalculable, and Christ's cause is the nation's and the world's welfare." [7]

Morgan's Fundamentalist faith is often characteristic of strong, silent men whose natures are simple and direct, tinged with naïveté. There were traces of a sentimental, almost romantic quality in Morgan, which during his youth expressed itself in love of a woman approaching death. In later years he suppressed this quality, unbecoming in the financier, and it survived only in the overwhelming love of the splendor and magnificence of power and religion. (Probably much of Morgan's arrogance, domineering masculinity and reserve constituted a defense mechanism against emergence of the sentimental quality he despised: the strong man had his moments of weakness, cloaked by an impenetrable arrogance and reserve.) The Fundamentalist God is a god of power and magnificence, created in the image of strong, simple men of elemental force and aspirations. This God is arrogant, arbitrary, merciless, lusting after power, obedience and splendor—the image of Morgan. They recognized and understood each other.

Morgan's ideal was power—power, not money. His estate was comparatively small: $69,450,000, exclusive of art treasures valued at $50,000,000. (After bequests of $700,000 to charity, $16,000,000 to members of the family and one year's salary to employees of the House of Morgan, the balance was

left to J. Pierpont Morgan, Jr., as residuary legatee.)[8] There
were scores of wealthier magnates, including men who were
mere underlings of Morgan. He had striven after power, not
simply after money.

When cables flashed the report of J. Pierpont Morgan's death
the flag on the building of his firm in Wall Street was lowered
to half-mast, and all the other flags responded sympathetically.
(The death did not affect prices on the Stock Exchange.) In
Morgan's own office the shades were drawn, the door closed,
the traditional corner and desk of authority unoccupied. Business proceeded amid comparative silence. Then the old bustle
revived and business was as usual.[9]

J. Pierpont Morgan died in an uneasy and fretful world
approaching catastrophe. . . . Revolution convulsed China and
Mexico, directed against feudal conditions of oppression and
foreign imperialistic domination. . . . The Balkans and Turkey
(itself in the midst of democratic transformation) waged war
on each other, the prelude to another and more catastrophic
war. . . . Russia, in all the trappings of imperial splendor and
magnificence, celebrated the tercentenary of the Romanoff
dynasty (overthrown only four years later), the Czar graciously
granting amnesty to minor political offenders and attending
the theater accompanied by 40,000 soldiers, police and gen-
darmes.[10] . . . An English court dissolved the Peruvian Amazon
Co., convicted of abominable atrocities on native workers in the
Putumayo.[11] . . . British and German rivalry flared up in China.
Germany decided on expenditures, "far in excess of the most
extravagant conjectures," to increase the "striking force" of the
army. France retaliated by strengthening its own army. A war
scare caused stocks to slump on the Berlin Boerse, compelling
the Imperial government to issue a reassuring declaration:
"Peace is sure."[12] . . . Major-General Leonard Wood declared
the United States was "sadly unprepared" for war: "There is
no especial reason to expect an early war, but wars come suddenly in these days."[13] . . . Tammany was again assailed for

graft and vice in New York City.[14] ... The Illinois Vice Commission reported low wages were an important cause of prostitution. One philanthropic employer insisted $8 a week was enough for girls living away from home, but admitted that paying them $5 more would not wipe out dividends. Under pressure of agitation the International Harvester Co. increased its girls' wages from $5 to $8 weekly.[15] ... The lynchings of Negroes declined over 1890, from 2.88 per 1,000,000 population to 0.67.[16] ... Congress considered measures to tighten government regulation of industrial and financial combinations, particularly financial. ... President Woodrow Wilson received a petition to pardon John H. Patterson, president of the National Cash Register Co., convicted of criminal violation of the antitrust law (the conviction being subsequently set aside) and sentenced to one year's imprisonment.[17] ... In his inaugural address President Wilson said:

"We have been proud of our industrial achievements, but we have not hitherto stopped thoughtfully enough to count the human cost, the cost of lives snuffed out, of energies overtaxed and broken, the fearful physical and spiritual cost to the men and women and children upon whom the dead weight and burden of it all has fallen pitilessly the years through. The groans and agony had not yet reached our ears, the solemn, moving undertone of our life, coming up from the mines and factories, and out of every home where the struggle has its familiar and intimate seat. ... Our duty is to cleanse, to reconsider, to restore, to correct the evil without impairing the good, to purify and humanize every process of our common life without weakening or sentimentalizing it." [18]

CHAPTER XXXV

THE HOUSE OF MORGAN: 1913-1929

> *"Would you tell me please, which way I*
> *ought to go from here?"*
> *"That depends a good deal on where*
> *you want to go," said the Cat.*
> *"I don't much care where—" said Alice.*
> *"Then it doesn't matter which way you*
> *go," said the Cat.*
> *"—so long as I get* somewhere," *Alice*
> *added as an explanation.*
> *"Oh, you're sure to do that," said the*
> *Cat, "if you only walk long enough."*
> ALICE IN WONDERLAND

DURING his lifetime J. Pierpont Morgan *was* the House of Morgan, almost inseparable. The whole system of industrial and financial centralization and control, in fact, appeared to be maintained by personal prestige and power, particularly as it operated so much in terms of community of interest instead of on a completely institutionalized basis. But Morgan's death revealed that, aside from his peculiar quality of dictatorship, the system expressed the requirements of concentrated capitalism. His death produced no effect on the system of centralization nor in the House of Morgan, creating scarcely a ripple. J. Pierpont Morgan, Jr., dynastically succeeded his father and the House of Morgan functioned smoothly. Changes were the consequence of other developments.

What Morgan's death ended was his own personal dictatorship, nor was there any succession to the dictatorship. Other times, other manners. Morgan's dictatorship did not express the system of industrial and financial centralization itself, simply the system's *development* (which provided the opportunity for dictatorship). This development constituted a transition period accompanied by immense economic and political changes, and social war. Transitions produce dictators, who are usually the mathematical concentration point of changes which have not yet become institutional and accepted. The turmoil of transition offers the "strong man" the opportunity to seize power. Strong businessmen after the Civil War seized power in the midst of changing economic relationships and institutions, loosely integrating their system by means of community of interest within which Morgan seized supreme power. Becoming completely institutionalized and accepted, the system cast off personal dictatorship. There was no successor to J. Pierpont Morgan—not owing to a scarcity of potential dictators, but because the system of industrial and financial centralization and control no longer required personal dictatorship, functioning now in terms of the dictatorship of an institutional oligarchy.

Personal dictatorships, moreover, usually go beyond the legitimate requirements of the system and class they represent, readjustments becoming necessary. These readjustments introduced changes and modifications, including more government regulation, but industrial and financial centralization and control conquered as a system, assuming larger scope and power. The House of Morgan retained its financial supremacy, expressing the most important aspects of concentrated capitalism, emphasizing the more constructive aspects of finance, becoming less of a promotion house and more of a great bank on the European model (but without government control).

Readjustment was largely imposed upon the industrial and financial magnates, although some of them qualifiedly accepted the new dispensation. The House of Morgan, within limits, recognized that concessions and adjustments were necessary. At the dinner of the Pennsylvania Society in December, 1913, Henry P. Davison, the dominant Morgan partner, said:

"For some years past this country, in common with other

nations, has been feeling the movement of new forces, new utterances and strivings.... Changes have taken place.... The man of affairs of the present day must realize the movement of the last twenty years is not the blind expression of dissatisfaction and unrest that many consider it to be. Its purpose is not, as surface appearances seemed to indicate, to tear business down or to thwart and ruin industry. It has been rather to force all business corporations that are of such great magnitude or importance as to affect directly the great body of the people to be conducted more openly, with more scrupulous fidelity to the interests of both the public and the thousands of small investors who are really the owners of these corporations." [1]

There was much more in the movement of revolt than Davison admitted, but his utterances indicated lessening of opposition to readjustment.

Under President Woodrow Wilson readjustment proceeded systematically, Congress adopting an important program of industrial, financial and social legislation. While his utterances were couched in lofty strain, Wilson's proposals were remarkably practical, using government to make concessions to different class interests and unify capitalism. The Jeffersonian Wilson enlarged the powers of government beyond the limits imposed by the ideals of agrarian democracy, unavoidable in the readjustment of government and a complex industrial system. Out of readjustment industrial and financial centralization and control emerged stronger, although stripped of some of its worst (and unessential) abuses.

Since its initiation the struggle against industrial combinations, while temporarily disturbing, strengthened them by compelling the adoption of more legal and efficient forms of organization.[2] Wilson proposed to restore competition, but instead imposed larger regulation, abolishing Roosevelt's commissioner of corporations and substituting the Federal Trade Commission, which served industry as the Interstate Commerce Commission served the railroads. While regulation by the Fed-

eral Trade Commission restrained "unfair" competitive practices, corporate combinations became still larger. They were,
moreover, spiritualized: instead of "The public be damned!"
they adopted the motto, "The public be served!" Since government regulation limited buccaneering practices, the magnates
of industry pursued the spiritual consolation of service.

Out of the Money Trust investigation developed reforms in
the banking system, long notoriously defective. Under Wilson's pressure, the Federal Reserve Act was adopted in December, 1913, in spite of opposition among the large bankers, who
condemned the system as "political banking" and insisted upon
one central institution under banker control.[3] Instead the Federal Reserve System operated under government control, the
Reserve Board consisting of two permanent government officers
and five others appointed by the President. Financial opinion
was gloomy, maintaining that "practical considerations standing in the way of successful establishment of the System over-
shadow everything else."[4] Although it did not accomplish
one of the objectives, the elimination of panics, the Federal
Reserve System measurably unified and stabilized the banking
system, eliminating many abuses and the conditions making
necessary dependence during panics upon financial dictatorship
(such as was exercised by J. Pierpont Morgan in 1907).

Another result of the Money Trust investigation was the
prohibition (in the Clayton Act, adopted October, 1914) of
interlocking directorships in banks, private bankers being forbidden altogether to serve as directors. Immediately J. Pierpont
Morgan, Jr., withdrew as director in the National City Bank
and the National Bank of Commerce, and his partners from
other banks. The House of Morgan went further. Announcing
that directorships were a "serious burden on our time" and
considering the "change in public sentiment in regard to directorships," Morgan and his partners resigned thirty of their
directorships in non-financial corporations, eighteen by Morgan
himself, withdrawing completely from the New Haven, New

York Central and American Telephone & Telegraph (all three under investigation by the Interstate Commerce Commission). But J. P. Morgan & Co. retained thirty-three directorships, so arranged that one representative remained on boards of the more important corporations under control or influence of the House of Morgan.[5]

These changes altered slightly the form but not the substance of financial centralization and control. The House of Morgan still maintained its affiliations with First National, Bank of Commerce, National City, Chase National and other banks and financial institutions. Instead of the comparatively loose system of community of interest and interlocking directorates, now illegal, the banks were to consolidate and combine, producing an institutionalized centralization of financial resources much greater than in the elder Morgan's day. Nor was there any lessening of financial control of corporate enterprises; on the contrary, as new and larger combinations appeared the scope of financial control broadened and deepened.

All Wilson's legislation, in the final result and in spite of his proposal to restore competition, strengthened the system of Big Business. The representatives of Big Business, however, bitterly assailed Wilson, accepting readjustment only under compulsion. The new master of the House of Morgan, in spite of Davison's partial recognition of the constructive aspects of the revolt against corporate business, was completely reactionary in his sentiments. The son of the father spoke when J. Pierpont Morgan, Jr., said in a private discussion:

"Politicians don't want to help business in this country, and the people don't want them to help business. That is the boast in Washington and that is the major sentiment in the country.

"If Mr. Wilson or the politicians thought that 80 per cent of the people wanted business helped, they would help business. But do the people of this country want business helped? I think public sentiment has been against business since 1890, when the Sherman Anti-Trust Act was passed. There is no difference

between the political parties, except there is less sectionalism in
the Republican party. Who did more than Theodore Roosevelt
to smash business? It is no use trying to educate the people.
They will only learn when they see the results, and then they
will turn upon their leaders and say: 'Yes, we agreed with you
on attacking business, but you should have told us that we were
wrong, and now out you go!'

"Legislation is aimed, and boastfully aimed, against business
and the destruction of values. But nobody can say anything or
do anything at the present time. Sentiment has got to run its
course." [6]

The business Bourbons neither forgot nor learned anything.
Their answer to Wilson was the answer they gave Roosevelt:
"Let us alone!" But they could not be left alone. They were
incapable of eliminating gross abuses, of readjusting and unifying their system. Revolt persisted, and might become dangerous. The Wilson Administration, attuned to the public temper,
adopted legislation in the interest of farmers and labor, which
Big Business resisted bitterly, particularly the exemption of
agricultural and labor organizations from the provisions of the
anti-trust laws. In 1915 the Industrial Relations Commission
investigated industrial unrest, in answer to the mounting wave
of labor dissatisfaction and strikes. Morgan was called to testify,
and insisted, "with a nonchalant, engaging laugh," that he
knew nothing whatever about how long employees should
work, at what age children should go to work, the relations
between capital and labor, or the unequal distribution of
wealth. The questions exasperated him. Under examination by
Chairman Frank P. Walsh, Morgan testified:

WALSH: How far do you think stockholders and directors
are responsible for labor conditions?

MORGAN: I don't think stockholders have any responsibility in
that matter.

WALSH: How about directors?

MORGAN: None at all.

WALSH: Who are responsible?

MORGAN: The officers, the executive officials or people whom they appoint to take charge of the plants. The officers are responsible, as they have to see that those they appoint carry out their instructions.[7]

This indifference to labor, characteristic of indifference to larger social interests, was emphasized by Morgan when, asked whether $10 a week was the proper wage for a workingman, he burst forth: "If that's all he can get and takes it, I should say that is enough."[8]

The junior Morgan resembled his father temperamentally as well as physically—the same indifference to public opinion, the arrogance become slightly supercilious, the silence (giving even less interviews), not anywhere as much of a dominating personality as the old man but still mastering the House of Morgan and its affiliates. His "ethical code" of business was practical: "Never do something you do not approve of in order more quickly to accomplish something that you do approve of."[9] Serenely Olympian, he never engaged a press-agent to cultivate popularity, as the Rockefellers and others do. The storm of criticism let loose by the collapse of the New Haven Railroad exasperated J. P. Morgan, Jr., and he said (in the spirit of his father's, "I owe the public nothing"):

"I have lost all hope of receiving fair consideration from the people of Massachusetts. Don't talk to me about appealing to the public. I am done with the public, for the present anyway."[10]

Yet the Roosevelt-Wilson movement, which so aroused Morgan's exasperation, strengthened American industry and finance by reconciling antagonisms and creating more unity, preparing the United States for war and world power (out of which arose the financial world power of the House of Morgan).

All the imperialistic antagonisms, the export of capital, the competition for markets, the seizure of natural resources and the little colonial wars flared up in the agony of the World

War. "The struggle for commercial supremacy," said Elbert H. Gary, "was the underlying cause of the war, or at least had a decided influence upon its precipitation." [11] Fifty years of astonishing economic conquests, of marvels of science, engineering and technique, of man's mastery over nature—all mobilized to produce and wage the largest, most destructive and brutal war in history. Civilization sprawled in the bloody muck of nightmare battlefields where men died to decide the issue of imperialistic world power and profits, producing the collapse of a cycle of civilization....

When war appeared inevitable, on July 30, 1914, a conference met in the offices of J. P. Morgan & Co. over which Morgan presided. Officers of the most important banks and of the Stock Exchange discussed financial action in the event of war, particularly whether to close the Exchange in view of heavy liquidation by European owners of American securities. The decision was not to close. [12] Then larger liquidation and the disastrous break in prices forced the Exchange to close for four months in self-defense—the American money market was still dependent upon Europe.

After the declaration of war, in August, the majority of bankers favored suspension of gold payments to Europe. Insisting that suspension would prove dangerous to American international credit, the House of Morgan mobilized the investment bankers and forced a decision in favor of maintaining gold payments. Where closing the Stock Exchange indicated America's dependence upon Europe, the decision to maintain gold payments expressed the underlying strength of the American financial structure. J. P. Morgan & Co. then arranged a $100,-000,000 gold loan for New York City to meet maturing municipal obligations in London and Paris. Maintenance of international gold payments was an important factor in floating loans for the Allies and making New York the world's leading money center (plus the immense productive capacity of American industry). [13]

The war's immediate effect was to aggravate business depression in the United States, foreign trade slumping disastrously. One month before the war the National City Bank adopted "comprehensive plans" for developing foreign trade by opening branches abroad (permitted by the Federal Reserve legislation), particularly in South America, but the plans now held fire.[14] Depression continued until early in 1915, when large loans to the Allies, arranged by the House of Morgan, produced business revival and prosperity.

In August, 1914, Morgan, Harjes & Co. received $6,000,000 in gold from the Bank of France to open a credit with J. P. Morgan & Co. for purchases in the United States, preliminary to a loan of $100,000,000.[15] Asked by the Morgans if the loan was within the scope of President Wilson's neutrality declaration, the State Department replied through Secretary Bryan that loans to belligerents were "inconsistent with the spirit of true neutrality."[16] Business overruled Bryan. Britain and France made large purchases in the United States, mostly paid for in cash secured from the sale of American securities. The situation financially was impossible, limiting the Allies' purchases and straining their resources. Unless American loans financed the Allies the flood of orders might dry up at its source, and drying up the flood meant persistence of business depression.

An Anglo-French Commission discussed the problem with J. P. Morgan & Co., the government ceased frowning on loans to belligerents, and in October, 1915, the House of Morgan arranged a loan for the unprecedented amount of $500,000,000, to be spent by the Allies exclusively in American purchases. No compensation was received by the Morgans as negotiators of the loan or as managers of the underwriting syndicate, the profits of which were large. The proposed loan, said Morgan, "is imperative to preserve trade under existing conditions," identifying the loan with business prosperity.[17]

Britain and France approached the House of Morgan as a matter of course: it was financially supreme in the United

States and it had always maintained confidential relations with the British government through its British branch (now Morgan, Grenfell & Co.).

Upon the suggestion of Henry P. Davison, Great Britain made J. P. Morgan & Co. its commercial agents in the United States with exclusive control over all purchases, Morgan himself negotiating the contract.[18] The arrangement met considerable British criticism on the ground that "J. P. Morgan & Co. favored concerns in which they were interested to the exclusion of others." Lloyd George defended the Morgans in parliament and Davison went to London to answer criticisms, which were inspired by businessmen who did not appreciate the magnitude of the war and insisted on competitive relations with American industry.[19] Concentration of purchases in the Morgan agency saved millions to the British government, facilitated ordering and delivery, and prevented frauds by a horde of speculative contractors.

J. P. Morgan & Co. organized a separate purchasing department under Edward R. Stettinius (afterward a Morgan partner), the largest commercial agency in the world. Most of the orders were kept "in the family," going to corporations under control or influence of the House of Morgan in the system of financial centralization and control. There were single orders as high as $67,000,000; within one year purchases amounted to $500,000,000 and $3,000,000,000 by September, 1917.[20] In addition to these purchases, large loans and credits to the Allies, the Morgans marketed at least $2,000,000,000 of American securities formerly owned in Europe.[21]

The Morgan loans and purchases revived American industry and started an upward movement of prosperity. "Owing to the pressing demands of foreign nations at war," said Samuel Vauclain of the Baldwin Locomotive Works, "and the tremendous executive efforts of the banking house of J. P. Morgan & Co., every avenue of trade was stimulated by them, and rapidly, but safely, the pall of depression was lifted. The question for

months was, 'How to do it?' Until this question was answered
by J. P. Morgan & Co. and the answer accepted as a finality, a
chaotic condition existed." [22] Since many of the articles purchased for the Allies by the House of Morgan were previously
not manufactured in the United States or in very small quanti-
ties, new industries were created and scores of new plants built,
particularly in the manufacture of munitions. The war had
become a war of munitions, of machinery. Absorbed in the
manufacture of death, the belligerents could not meet the demands of foreign markets while England and France placed
an embargo on foreign loans. American industry and finance
met the world's cry for goods and money. During 1916 business prosperity reached dizzying heights, United States Steel's
profits were $272,000,000, other profits were almost as fabulous,
millionaires multiplied overnight, labor was fully employed
(although real wages were stationary),[23] exports increased two-
fold, and commercial world power beckoned.

Never was the House of Morgan's prestige and power larger
than during 1915-16, directly affecting industrial activity, its
financial leadership unquestioningly accepted, developing still
closer relations with the First National and National City
Banks. Then came American entry into the war and the comparative eclipse of the Morgans.

Complicated by all sorts of cross motives, racial and national-
istic, the World War was determined by the struggle for imperialistic supremacy, flaring up in Asia and Africa, and in the
Americas. While urging their peoples on to the supreme sacrifice in the name of Liberty and Kultur, European statesmen
by secret agreements revealed the real purposes by dividing
up colonies, markets and "spheres of influence," redistributing
the world's economic power. Fatedly the United States plunged
into the war, and here also cross motives appeared: Anglo-
Saxon racial sympathy dominant in the seats of the mighty,
vested interests created by the loans to the Allies threatened
by German victory, national pride straining at the leash, Wood-

row Wilson's desire to act as peacemaker, the belief that victorious Germany would be more powerful and menacing than victorious Britain, and the sheer glacial drift of events. The decisive force, however, was that the United States, for twenty years slowly but implacably developing as an international force, could not remain indifferent to the issue of redistributing world power involved in the war. Itself directly coveting no territory, the United States intervened to maintain the balance of power between Germany and Britain ("peace without victory," Wilson's policy before intervening in the war): the balance, as in the case of the "Open Door" in China, being the form of expression of American interests.

The House of Morgan dominated the financial and industrial situation until America's entry into the war produced new alignments. Measures of war-time "social controls" limited the Morgan functions and importance.

Prepared to wage war to the limit, the United States government organized itself as a practical economic dictatorship. The War Industries Board, under chairmanship of Bernard M. Baruch, was given almost unlimited powers by President Wilson over industry, determining prices, distributing raw materials and deciding between essential and non-essential goods, while the government itself assumed control of the railroads, supplemented by the Food and Fuel Administrations. Mobilizing the Federal Reserve banks the Treasury raised $21,326,000,000 in war loans, the whole nation being organized to sell the bonds by means of pressure on small investors and the manufacture of bank credit.[24] In this task the investment bankers played a minor rôle: while they subscribed to the Liberty loans, the Morgans were not important in financing the war.

The Allies now dealt directly with the United States government in securing loans and making purchases, dispensing almost completely with the Morgan services. When the American government felt indisposed to lend Canada money, J. P.

THOMAS W. LAMONT

J. PIERPONT MORGAN, JR.

Morgan & Co. issued a loan of $100,000,000, and they continued to buy sterling to stabilize British exchange,[25] but during the American phase of the war the House of Morgan was largely limited to routine banking business.

Another phase of the Morgans' comparative eclipse was President Wilson's reluctance to use the personnel of the House of Morgan in government service. The neglect rankled, and J. Pierpont Morgan said in a private discussion:

"It is true that I went to Wilson and offered my services, but he did not refer me to Mr. Baruch. He was very nice, and said he would send for me when wanted.

"I and every member of this House are ready to be commandeered by the government. We will do anything that is right, honorable and not to the injury of our credit. But at the present time what can we do but sit and wait on the sidelines until we are called? All this machinery is here for any service the government wishes, and there is no question of compensation, commission or profits. As to why our men are not summoned, you must ask Washington. It is not proper for me to ask."[26]

"Not to the injury of our credit"—identical with Junius Morgan's attitude during the Civil War. But the conscript was not permitted to say: "You may commandeer me for anything that is right, honorable and not to the injury of life or limb." ...

President Wilson did not wholly neglect the House of Morgan's personnel. Thomas W. Lamont was frequently called to Washington to discuss financial matters and he was a member of the delegation accompanying Wilson to Paris, serving on the Reparations Commission of the Peace Conference.[27] Before this, in 1918, the State Department approached the House of Morgan to protect American interests in Mexico. Since the revolution there had been no payments of interest on the $350,-000,000 Mexican foreign debt. An international bondholders' committee being organized to compel payment, the American bankers insisted on half the representation. Britain and France objected, declaring their joint interests were three times as large as the American, to which the State Department replied that the United States was paramount geographically in Mexico [28]— a doctrine upheld for the whole of Latin America by President Wilson in the recognition granted the Monroe Doctrine by the Covenant of the League of Nations. As formed, the international committee on Mexico, under Lamont's chairmanship, consisted of ten American, five British and five French representatives, the American members representing the Morgans and their affiliates (while one British member represented Morgan, Grenfell & Co.).[29]

Imperialistic antagonisms flared up again in China immediately after the armistice, and to protect American interests there the Wilson Administration in 1919 asked the House of Morgan to re-enter the Chinese Consortium (reversing the decision of 1913 which forced the Morgans' withdrawal). The move was directed primarily against Japan, preparing to tighten its grip upon Manchuria. Lamont, chairman of the American group in the Consortium, went to Tokio and Peking, and succeeded in making a settlement favorable to the United States. The Chinese Consortium is dominated by American finance, which pursues an almost independent policy in China (limited by rapprochement with Japan).[30]

Out of the war came the international financial supremacy of the United States: the dream of 1900, of making New York the world's chief money market, was now reality. While Britain and Germany clashed over world power, the American interloper snatched the prize which it might otherwise not have secured for decades.

Within this American financial supremacy the House of Morgan was supreme, indicated soon after the declaration of peace.

J. P. Morgan & Co. acted as financial agents of the Belgian government: in 1919 a rival American banking group tried to get the business, but their offensive was easily beaten down.[31]

American finance now mobilized its forces for international

action. The House of Morgan, active during the war in organizing the American International Corporation which had large
foreign interests, particularly in China, now organized the
Foreign Finance Corporation. This corporation, a concentration of financial forces, included J. P. Morgan & Co., Guaranty
Trust, Bankers Trust, National Bank of Commerce (all three
under Morgan control), First National Bank (Morgan affiliate), National City and Chase National Banks (Morgan allies).
Arthur M. Anderson, a Morgan partner, was president of the
Foreign Finance Corporation.[32] Another concentration of financial forces (including W. R. Grace & Co.) was the organization
by the Morgans, in 1922, of the Bank of Central and South
America, with twenty-two branches in Venezuela, Peru,
Colombia, Nicaragua and Costa Rica.[33] By 1926 eight American
banks owned 107 foreign branches in the world's strategic
centers, of which National City owned seventy-three—fifty-one
directly and twenty-two by its subsidiary, the International
Banking Corporation.[34] While their activities overlapped, the
Morgans concentrated on loans and investments and National
City on trade and the conquest of markets, actively broadening
the imperial scope of American financial interests.

During the war, before American participation, the Allies
borrowed $1,900,000,000, largely through the House of Morgan;
in the period of American participation the government
directly loaned $7,319,000,000 to the Allies, private houses lend-
ing only $1,500,000,000.[35] This immense export of capital was
exceeded after the peace, the largest foreign loans being floated
by J. P. Morgan & Co. Among the more important Morgan
issues between 1919 and 1926 were government loans to Belgium, France, England, Italy, Switzerland, Norway, Austria,
Germany, Japan, Australia, Chile and Cùba, the total approaching $1,500,000,000. Most of these loans were not simple finan-
cial transactions, but expressed the developing power of American imperialism.

The $50,000,000 loan to Cuba (the Morgans in 1914 floated a

Cuban issue of $10,000,000) strengthened the American protectorate over the island republic, the House of Morgan intervening in Cuban fiscal legislation on the ground of its adverse effect on the loan.[36]

Morgan pressure on the Belgian government, an aftermath of the 1925 loan of $50,000,000, aroused a storm of criticism.[37]

In the $110,000,000 loan to Germany in 1924 the German railroads were put under control of an American commission and three trustees, one of whom represented Morgan & Co. of Paris.[38]

A competing New York syndicate offered a higher bid for the Argentine loan of $45,000,000 in 1925, but the Morgans secured the issue in spite of their bid increasing the Argentine government's costs by $450,000.[39]

The $75,000,000 Morgan loan to Australia in 1925 aroused British fears that Australian trade might be diverted to the United States—expressing the bitter clash between British and American finance. It was the first Australian loan ever floated outside London, which could not supply the money.[40]

In 1925 Britain decided to stabilize its currency and secured large American credits—$200,000,000 from the Federal Reserve and $100,000,000 from J. P. Morgan & Co., on which the Morgan commission was $2,500,000.[41] Another indication of American financial supremacy, at which the Old Lady of Threadneedle Street sorrowfully shook her head.

After an interview between Thomas W. Lamont, Benito Mussolini and his finance minister, the House of Morgan in 1925 floated an Italian loan of $100,000,000 and extended $50,000,000 credits for stabilization. The profit margin on the loan was $4,500,000, J. P. Morgan & Co. receiving in addition $250,000 as negotiators of the loan and syndicate managers.[42] American loans and direct investments in Italian enterprises immeasurably strengthen the dictatorship of Mussolini, whom bankers, in Otto H. Kahn's words, consider "the strong man of Europe." [43] (The bankers were also very fond of Porfirio

Diaz, the Mexican "strong man" whose oppressive dictatorship was only broken by revolution.)

In these loan operations the Morgan syndicates included the National Bank of Commerce, Guaranty Trust, Bankers Trust, First National, National City, Chase National and Kuhn, Loeb & Co., a combination which dominates the field of foreign financing under Morgan overlordship.

American financial supremacy, of which the House of Morgan is the concentration point, expressed itself clearly in the various conferences to untangle the snarl created by the problem of German reparations.

Flushed with victory, breaking their Armistice pledges, and disregarding economic facts, the Allies imposed upon Germany (and Europe and the world) the burden of impossible reparations. The burden was aggravated by American refusal to accept the British proposal for general cancelation of war debts. J. P. Morgan favored cancelation. "They can never be paid," he said, declaring the loans were the "same sort of contribution to victory as soldiers." [44] Morgan apparently feels that the war debts and reparations seriously interfere with Europe's economic recovery and endanger the other European debts to American investors in which the House of Morgan is primarily interested.

In the final analysis reparations are determined by the United States. Two-thirds of Germany's reparations payments would be wiped out by American cancelation of war debts. Most of the German payments have been made possible by foreign loans floated largely in the United States by the House of Morgan—borrowing from the American Peter to pay the Pauls of England, France, Italy and Belgium. The Morgans are consequently a decisive influence in reparations, having the power of financial veto over almost any settlement (except cancelation).

Conference after conference met to discuss reparations, steadily lessening the fantastic claims upon Germany for $125,-000,000,000, reduced by the Reparations Conference of 1929 to $9,000,000,000.[45] At this conference the American representatives were J. P. Morgan and Owen D. Young (of the General Electric Co., an affiliate of the House of Morgan), Thomas W. Lamont and T. N. Perkins being alternates. Morgan was the "driving force" of the conference—the driving force of American financial supremacy.[46] German reparations payments were fixed on an annuity basis to run sixty years, although the plan will in all probability be revised again as in the case of previous settlements. The 1929 settlement provided for reducing German payments two-thirds in the event of cancelation of war debts.[47] Meanwhile the world staggers under the consequences of war debts and reparations, which thwart European economic recovery, restrict foreign trade, and are almost as disastrous to the victors as to the vanquished.

The 1929 Reparations Conference decided to take the problem out of politics (as if that could be done!). It created a Bank for International Settlements to handle the German payments, in which are represented the central banks of Germany, Britain, France, Italy, Belgium and Japan. The State Department forbidding Federal Reserve participation, American finance is represented directly by J. P. Morgan & Co. There are two American directors in the Bank (against one each for the other countries) chosen by Morgan, and the president, another American, was chosen upon Morgan's advice.[48] The House of Morgan dominates the Bank for International Settlements.

Of the Bank Morgan said: "It is the one thing which the conference was able to discover which would solve the problems of international settlements arising out of the war."[49] But the Bank is much more than that. Its task of handling German payments is only temporary, since reparations sooner or later will be wiped out. They are an economic monstrosity. They are used by France to prevent German recovery and by Britain as a means of pressure for American cancelation of debts. Meanwhile Europe totters under the burden, the burden being an important factor in the world-wide business depression of

1929, characterized by a general slump in foreign trade. In addition to the disastrous economic consequences, American finance will not make loans forever to enable Germany to pay reparations, endangering its other European loans. As the House of Morgan favors cancelation of war debts, it would accept wiping out reparations—and for the same reasons. American policy shapes itself in favor of a restored Germany— for economic reasons, and for the political reason of maintaining a balance of power in Europe (and the world) as against Britain in the struggle for imperialistic supremacy.

Since reparations are a temporary function of the Bank for International Settlements, its purely financial functions will become most important. It can and probably will facilitate foreign trade, using its resources for international financial stability. By its investment powers the Bank can influence developments in particular countries, impose financial pressure on the smaller and "backward" countries in the matter of loans, investments and foreign enterprises, become the centralized expression of the financial aspects of imperialism. The Bank for International Settlements clearly expresses the necessity of larger world unity, and accomplishes larger unity. But within the unity there are antagonisms and contradictions—struggle between the United States and Britain, between Germany and France, between Britain and France, Europe and the United States. Already there is considerable American objection, while an influential section of British financial opinion is unfavorable to the Bank as meaning American and European domination.[50] The Bank may temporarily reconcile antagonisms and contradictions, but it is the tragedy of imperialism to produce larger unity among the nations only, at the same time, to aggravate antagonisms, driving fatedly to war.

Behind the Morgan loans and Morgan dominance in the Bank for International Settlements is the steady outflow of American capital to all parts of the world. American foreign investments in 1914 amounted to $2,600,000,000 and to $16.600,-

000,000 in 1929 (exclusive of $12,000,0000,000 war debts).[51] One aspect of these investments are loans to foreign governments and corporations, another direct investments in foreign enterprises, and still another the establishment of enterprises under American ownership and control.

At the basis of American world power is a substantial colonial and semi-colonial empire, in the Philippines, Cuba, Liberia, and Central America—450,000 square miles and 25,000,000 inhabitants. The empire broadens to include countries bordering on the Caribbeans. Venezuela, Colombia and Peru are either financial or political protectorates of the United States. Investments of $1,389,000,000 make Mexico an American economic colony confirmed by political tutelage. By means of the imperialistic interpretation of the Monroe Doctrine and investments of $5,722,000,000, the United States is rapidly driving European trade and capital from Latin America.[52]

The United States, Britain, France and Germany wage a bitter struggle for control of Latin-American markets, investments and natural resources. This struggle flares up in Europe itself. In addition to large government loans, there is at least $2,500,000,000 of American capital in European industrial enterprises, of which about $700,000,000 is directly invested in enterprises under American ownership or control.[53] European capital is adopting measures against this invasion, facilitated by American investment of $492,729,000 in foreign financial institutions, mostly in Europe. The same situation exists elsewhere, there being probably 2,000 industrial enterprises in all parts of the world under American control.[54]

Dominant in the field of foreign loans, the House of Morgan is also a dominant factor in the direct investment of American capital in foreign enterprises, being interlocked with most of the giant corporations which are carrying on the struggle for international supremacy.

Characteristic of these developments is the General Electric Co. which, since 1892, has moved within the Morgan orbit.

General Electric, by means of stock ownership, interlocking directorates and community of interest, is interlocked with other corporations constituting an electric power trust with far-flung international affiliations. It controls International General Electric, General Electric of Canada and the largest electrical combination in Britain, has heavy investments in the German electric industry and other investments all over Europe.[55] The General Electric affiliate, Electric Bond & Share (in which J. P. Morgan & Co. have large interests through United Corporation and other enterprises) through its subsidiary, American & Foreign Power, controls utility corporations in twelve countries and has large interests in five others, its assets being $488,072,000.[56] It is dominant in Latin America, owning concerns formerly under British control, is a power in Europe, linked with the Adriatica-Volpi combination, and in China where it is preparing to acquire larger Asiatic interests through a subsidiary, the Far East Power Corporation.[57]

The American power trust, which becomes international, is developing a trust in communications. Radio Corporation of America, another Morgan affiliate, is interlocked with General Electric, International Telephone & Telegraph, Westinghouse Electric, American Telephone & Telegraph, General Motors and United Fruit. After slaking its Gargantuan appetite on all sorts of American enterprises, Radio Corporation is reaching out for world power in communications through its subsidiary, R. C. A. Communications, active in Latin America and the Philippines.[58] International Telephone & Telegraph, interlocked with Radio Corporation and the House of Morgan, controls All-America Cables and telephones, cables, telegraphs, radio and electric manufacturing corporations in thirty countries.[59]

All of these giant corporations are interlocked with each other and the House of Morgan in the struggle for control of strategic international communications, including railroads and airways, which is approaching supremacy in Latin America.

Another international struggle is over control of natural resources. The struggle for petroleum flares up everywhere, since 70 per cent of reserves are in countries which are the prey of imperialism. All the large American oil corporations have huge foreign interests, aggressively struggling for the control of oil— in Latin America, in Mesopotamia and Asia. The Continental Oil Co., a Morgan affiliate, has large oil concessions in Mexico.[60] In spite of interference by the government, the Mellon interests control the world supply of aluminum.[61] There is considerable American capital in Bolivian tin. The Guggenheims, inter-locked with the Morgans by community of interest, control 35 per cent of Chile's nitrate business, are the chief part-ners of the Chilean government in the $375,000,000 nitrate com-bination, have large mining interests in Mexico, South America, Africa, Europe and Asia, and are influential in Mining Trust, Ltd., which in Australia owns the world's richest silver, zinc and lead mines.[62] American copper interests control 95 per cent of the world's output. Kennecott Copper and its affiliates, un-der Morgan control, own copper and coal mines, power plants, haciendas, railroads and town sites in Peru and Chile.[63] The United States, in spite of its own immense natural resources, invests capital wherever there are natural resources to control.

Governments intervene in this struggle for the control of minerals and other natural resources, supporting their own business interests and aggravating international antagonisms. When President Hoover was Secretary of Commerce he en-gaged in a struggle against price-fixing by British rubber inter-ests (although he is now experimenting with fixing the price of American export wheat). It led directly to attempts to de-velop sources of rubber under American control, independent of and competing with the British. Henry Ford acquired a rub-ber plantation in Brazil and the Firestone interests a conces-sion in Liberia, an American protectorate, the State Department being active in the negotiations. The concession consists of 1,000,000 acres (at 6c. an acre), the plans implying forced native labor. Liberia at the same time was compelled to accept a $5,000,000 loan and an American financial commission under conditions which make Liberia a huge rubber plantation under Firestone control.[64]

American industry and finance, moreover, are active in international combinations, making alliances where they cannot conquer supremacy. There are three great international chemical combinations, American, German and British. Morgan, General Motors and Chase National Bank interests are influential in the British chemical combine and Rockefeller-Ford interests in the German, while the Morgans are also interlocked with the du Ponts and their far-flung chemical empire.[65]

General Motors, with its large foreign industrial investments, particularly in Europe, is characteristic of mass-production industries directly investing capital overseas to enlarge and control markets. American prosperity is interpreted in terms of larger and larger exports. "Trade follows loans," according to Thomas W. Lamont, emphasized by James Speyer: "A great export trade cannot be gained unless America loans its surplus capital abroad." [66] The order of the day is world expansion and power.

This export of capital has its constructive aspects. It knits the world together and creates larger unity, but at the same time provokes new antagonisms and contradictions. There is a philosophy of international understanding and peace by means of business which was excellently expressed by Dwight W. Morrow, the former Morgan partner:

"I have found that the business of international understanding is being carried on by business as it cannot be carried on by other means. Business is exchange of goods for goods and of goods for services. Though we speak of bargaining as sordid, when men first began to exchange, to trade or bargain, instead of using force to capture what they wanted, the first great challenge to barbarism had been made." [67]

But business still captures what it wants—by economic might

and the final resort to military force. Business competition is itself a form of war, and in international relations often compels the arbitrament of the sword. American bankers secure armed intervention in the Caribbeans, insisting on government protecting their investments. Political pressure is used to secure and maintain concessions in "backward" countries. Business combinations of one nation clash with the combinations of another over the division and control of world economic power. Governments intervene in the clash and antagonisms become political, ending in war. Business undoubtedly creates larger international unity and understanding: the forty years preceding the World War were characterized by developments unifying the world as never before. Out of that unity came the largest and most brutal war in history, provoked by the clash of competing imperialisms.

Financiers are sincere when they say they do not want wars —that is, any large war which upsets business, although they scarcely object to "little wars" against colonial peoples. But the financiers prepare the conditions of international competition and antagonism which make wars.

The great corporations interlocked with the House of Morgan (and others) pursue business objectives. Yet at every point they provoke antagonisms. The peace and quiet of the banker's office are not characteristic of the men in the field who fight for markets, investments, concessions and natural resources. They resort to tooth and claw. Business buccaneering is measurably restrained within the United States, but it flourishes joyously when American businessmen meet other businessmen in international rivalry. Our concessionaires in Latin America exploit the natives, manipulate governments, often instigate revolts. They despise the people out of whom they make money. In the balance, the antagonisms created outweigh the understanding.

More serious are the antagonisms created between American combinations and the combinations of other nations. The great

international competitors are the United States, Britain, France
and Germany, who are fighting each other for business—savagely, with nothing barred. At the moment the struggle is most
bitter between the United States and Britain, whose world
power is declining (although British foreign investments still
exceed the American by $4,000,000,000). American business is
driving the British from Latin America, converted Canada into
an economic colony, invaded the other Dominions, and substantially increased its share of India's trade while the British
share declines.[68] American capital has invaded Britain itself,
where measures are being taken to prevent American control
of great combinations.[69] The rivals lock horns in Europe, Africa
and Asia, over trade, investments, oil, rubber, metals, cables—
everything. On both sides the struggle is bitter and unscrupulous. While invading all the world's markets the United States
increases its tariffs to prohibitive heights, creating intense international ill-will and retaliations. Tariff wars do not produce
international understanding. The American tariff of 1930, according to the London *Times,* "makes necessary countermeasures as acts of self-defense." [70] Many British bankers and
industrialists who formerly favored free trade are now ardent
protectionists, urging imperial preference and imperial economic unity to strengthen the Empire, particularly for business
war with the United States.[71]

After analyzing the many antagonisms between Britain and
the United States one American writer says: "Either the
supremacy of America will be recognized by Britain in peace,
or that supremacy will be asserted in battles of blood." [72] In
other words—"Get out! The world is ours." But no great
nation willingly gives up the ghost, and Britain is still a formidable economic and naval power. The final resort of international rivalry is the arbitrament of the sword. There is much
peace talk between the United States and Britain, gestures of
understanding and friendship; but beneath it all the savage,
unrelenting struggle for economic world power goes on,

suggesting the pre-war peace talks and understandings between
Britain and Germany.

There are other antagonisms. France again exports capital,
and its imperialism now has a more solid industrial basis in
the great iron and steel industry created since the war. Germany rebels at the burden of reparations, and begins to long
again for a "place in the sun" of world power. Britain is desperate at its economic decline. Soviet Russia challenges the
capitalist world, which views suspiciously the creation of a new
economic order. There are continental antagonisms—between
Europe and Asia, Europe and the United States, the United
States and Latin America.

Colonial peoples are in revolt, and the imperialistic nations
wage "little wars"—as in the "peaceful" pre-war days. Britain
answers India's demand for independence with airplanes and
machine guns. France savagely crushes revolts in Indo-China,
and Holland in the East Indies. Belgium still misrules the
Congo. Italy thirsts after colonial peoples to exploit. The
United States intervenes with military force in the Caribbeans,
creating American Irelands, Indias and Egypts, and prevents
the overthrow of an oppressive régime in Cuba.

Into this devil's brew of multiplying international antagonisms the League of Nations distils a few drops of holy water
—but after all it *is* holy water. The growth of international
mistrust outstrips international understanding. There will be
more "wars to end war" and "make the world safe for democracy." *Le plus se change, le plus c'est la même chose.* The
while science produces more efficient weapons of destruction
and mechanized warfare becomes more menacing. It is a race
between catastrophe and social reorganization....

American world power is the fulfilment of the movement
started in 1898, helped by the World War and based on the
most efficient economic mechanism in the world. This mechanism, after the Supreme Court decision in 1920 denying dissolution of the United States Steel Corporation, began another

movement of consolidation, combination and centralization. In three months of 1929 there were forty-two mergers affecting $12,000,000,000 of corporate assets.[73] Concentration and centralization are now much larger than pre-war. Then concentration affected mostly basic industries, now it affects the whole of business, illustrated by the fact that chain stores are conquering the field of retail trade.

In 1925, 10,583 manufacturing establishments, 5.6 per cent of the total, employed 56.8 per cent of all factory workers and produced 67.8 per cent of the output.[74] But concentration is larger than appears in these statistics, many apparently independent enterprises being parts of larger corporate combinations. Concentration appears more clearly in the distribution of corporate profits. In 1923, 1,026 corporations, one-quarter of one per cent of the total, received 47.9 per cent of all corporate profits and 51.5 per cent in 1927. These dominant corporations represented one-third of all corporate capitalization.[75] They dominate American economic life.

As in the pre-war period, there are two aspects of concentration and centralization. One is the increase in productive efficiency. The other is financial control and the centralization of profits. Much of the concentration is justifiable only in terms of centralization of financial control and profits, not of productive efficiency. It represents the merging and consolidation of financial power.

Sensitive to major developments, J. P. Morgan & Co., although much less of a promotion house than in the elder Morgan's day, engaged actively in the new concentration movement.

With its affiliate, General Electric, the House of Morgan organized the giant Radio Corporation of America, interlocking dominant industrial and financial interests, arousing government anti-trust action.

In 1920 the Morgans and the du Ponts bought W. C. Durant's holdings in General Motors and acquired control, securing representation on the directorate along with the Morgan affiliates, Bankers Trust, First National Bank, General Electric and American Radiator. The du Ponts' investment represented part of their immense war profits and entry into the Morgan system of financial centralization and control. At the time the Morgan penetration of General Motors was interpreted as meaning a "more aggressive policy"—which developments more than justified.[76]

In 1929 the Morgans organized an important food combination, Standard Brands, Inc. Merging the Fleischmann Co., Royal Baking and other corporations, Standard Brands had assets of $67,500,000 and its stock a market value in excess of $430,000,000.[77] J. P. Morgan & Co., large stockholders, secured two representatives on the directorate. There were other important food mergers, among them the General Foods Corporation, with assets of $70,000,000, in which the Morgan ally, Chase National Bank, is a power.[78] Concentration among food manufacturers was stimulated by concentration among grocery-store chains, which in 1928 controlled 40 per cent of the trade.[79] More food mergers are in the making. Independent grocers wage war upon the chains, small manufacturers are squeezed by both the chains and the food-producing combinations. Apparently a few great corporations may come to dominate the food business (manufacturing and selling) and government may intervene and regulate, as in the case of the railroads.

The Standard Brands merger was preceded, in January, 1929, by the Morgans organizing the United Corporation, a public-utility holding company. Within one year the House of Morgan was a dominant factor in the utility and power business.

Almost another industrial revolution has been produced by the development of electric power. Twenty years ago a comparatively small industry, electric power has since had an immense expansion, particularly after 1922. There is in electric power the possibility of remaking the world, of decentralizing

industry without impairing its efficiency, of multiplying independence and the beauty of life. Yet by and large the development of electric power repeats the pattern of steam power—it
is used to pile up profits, increase waste and strengthen the
oppressive power of industrial and financial combinations, developing without conscious social controls.

Buccaneering flourishes in the power industry, as it did
among the railroads, although much more circumspectly. The
buccaneers carry a big stick, but they walk softly: instead of
thundering, "The public be damned," they graciously insist,
"The public be served." Yet the characteristic railroad buccaneering practices prevail: speculation, overcapitalization, extortionate rates, and combination determined by centralization
of control and profits. Since 1922 operating costs declined and
net revenues increased, the profits tempting the financier. Holding companies merged utilities bought at extravagant prices, increasing capital costs. These companies make high charges for
nominal services to the operating utility—"milking the patrons
of the utility and obtaining an enhanced return on investment," [80] according to one Public Service Commission. One
power holding company made 300 per cent profit and Electric
Bond & Share 105 per cent on "services" to operating utilities
under their control.[81] As in the case of the railroads, overcapitalization is used to justify high rates and the plea that lower
rates are "confiscatory."

More serious, the power industry, by consolidation, combination and financial centralization and control, develops dictatorship over industry and government. At the time of United
Corporation's organization, fifteen utility combinations and
their affiliates controlled 83 per cent, and five 47 per cent, of the
nation's electric output.[82] These combinations smashed effective
regulation by Public Service Commissions, owing to their own
strength and the fact that holding companies are not subject
to regulation under the law. The power industry and its
"counselors on public relations" (men who are using the tech-

nique of war propaganda in favor of corporate interests) control "the most extensive publicity bureau ever organized by private corporations in America" to fight government regulation of the power industry [83]—as Morgan affiliates organized to fight President Roosevelt's regulation of the railroads. When Congress considered regulating the utility industry, an army of power lobbyists descended on Washington. Investigation revealed millions spent on legislative manipulations, buying control of newspapers, hiring college professors to spread power propaganda and write textbooks in favor of utility corporations and against government regulation or ownership.[84]

The House of Morgan's organization of United Corporation meant that the power industry had come to maturity, since the Morgans seldom pioneer an industry. Through General Electric indirectly and Drexel & Co. directly J. P. Morgan & Co. were already important utility factors, the one controlling a large power holding company and the other being represented on the directorates of many power corporations. Starting with assets of $150,000,000, the Morgan United Corporation increased its assets to $750,000,000 within slightly more than one year, while its subsidiaries control assets of $5,123,000,000.[85] Under direct Morgan control, United Corporation interlocks many financial interests and still further interlocks the already interlocked directorates of nine subsidiary corporations.

United Corporation re-distributed public-utility control—the Morgans and their affiliates in the East, the Samuel Insull combination in the Middle West and another combination in the Pacific States. Moreover, the Morgan dependents, Bankers Trust, Guaranty Trust and First National Bank, and the Morgan allies, Chase National and National City Banks, are interlocked in the directorates of many power corporations not directly represented in United Corporation. The Morgan combination is the dominant utility power.

Itself the concentration of a series of mergers, United Corporation was active in the creation of the Commonwealth &

Southern Corporation, dominant in the South, and of the Niagara Hudson Power Corporation. Niagara Hudson, controlling a power system with assets of $450,000,000, bought control of the Frontier Corporation from Mellon, du Pont and General Electric interests (which interlocked in United Corporation). Frontier Corporation controls water-power sites on the St. Lawrence River capable of developing 2,400,000 horsepower, increasing Niagara Hudson's control of New York State's water-power to 80 per cent.[86]

The Niagara Hudson merger affected the issue of whether the development and control of water-power on the St. Lawrence, one of the largest potential sources of power, should be by the State or by private interests. Purchase of Frontier Corporation by Niagara Hudson (under control of United Corporation) being interpreted as a move against State control and development, Thomas W. Lamont issued the following statement:

"Neither J. P. Morgan & Co. nor, so far as they know, any one of the companies in which they have any interest, direct or indirect, have taken any position for or against public or private ownership of the St. Lawrence River water-power or the manner of its development. In our opinion, these are matters for the determination of the government of the United States and the government of the State of New York and by the Canadian authorities. In so far as we have any opinion in the matter, it is our belief that, speaking generally, these power companies are abstaining and should continue to abstain from intervention in the decision of this question and should loyally co-operate with the decision of the public authorities when that decision has been arrived at." [87]

A canny and shrewd statement, characteristic of the suave, diplomatic Lamont, but noncommittal. The power companies *are* opposing public ownership—even regulation. Lamont's statement was in accord with the House of Morgan's present policy of avoiding public antagonism—no longer the elder Morgan's arrogant (and often magnificent) flouting of public opinion. The system with which J. P. Morgan & Co. are identified will resist government regulation or ownership of the utility industry—as they did in the case of the railroads.

An increase of financial centralization and control accompanied the increase of industrial concentration. After 1923 banks merged rapidly, and by 1929 twenty banks and trust companies had combined resources of $16,225,000,000, equal to 27 per cent of all banking resources (exclusive of savings banks).[88]

Among the twenty dominant banks were Bankers Trust, Guaranty Trust and First National (Morgan dependents) with resources of $3,403,000,000. The Morgan allies, National City and Chase National Banks, had resources of $4,855,000,000. These five banks in the Morgan combination, with their combined resources of $8,258,000,000, are interlocked with other banks by means of directorships, the aggregate resources being almost $20,000,000,000, equal to 33 per cent of total banking resources (in comparison with 13 per cent in 1912). In addition the Morgan combination is interlocked by means of directorships with insurance companies the combined resources of which in 1929 were $12,500,000,000, or 65 per cent of all insurance assets.

The increase in financial centralization parallels an increase in the financial control of industry. Ownership and management are becoming more and more separated, owing to the great increase of stockholders who own but do not manage. In 1929 J. P. Morgan and his seventeen partners held 99 directorships in seventy-two corporations with combined assets of approximately $20,000,000,000, as follows:

Financial: 23 directorships in 19 banks and other financial institutions, including Guaranty and Bankers Trusts (4), Mutual Life, First Security Co., Chase Securities Corporation, Corn Exchange Bank, New York Trust, Discount Corporation and Aetna Insurance. Combined resources, $5,250,000,000.

Industrial: 47 directorships in 35 corporations, including

United States Steel (2), General Motors (2), Kennecott Copper (3), Standard Brands (2), Texas Gulf Sulphur, Continental Oil, Pullman Co. (3), International Harvester, General Electric, Philadelphia & Reading Coal & Iron, General Asphalt, Baldwin Locomotive, Associated Dry Goods, International Agricultural, General Steel Casting and Montgomery-Ward. Combined assets, $6,000,000,000.

Railroad: 11 directorships in 10 railroads, including Northern Pacific (2), Atchison, Topeka & Santa Fe, Western Pacific and Chicago & Erie. Combined assets: $2,500,000,000.

Utility: 18 directorships in 13 utility combinations, including United Corporation (2), Philadelphia Electric (2), International Telephone & Telegraph, All-America Cables and Postal Telegraph & Cable. Combined assets: $6,250,000,000.

The Morgan dependents, Bankers Trust, Guaranty Trust and First National Bank, have interlocking directorships of their own in corporations representing combined resources of $67,000,000,000, including American Telephone & Telegraph, International General Electric, Baltimore & Ohio, American Smelting & Refining, American International Corporation, Allied Chemical & Dye, American & Foreign Power, E. I. du Pont de Nemours, Equitable Trust, Erie, Goodrich Rubber, Houston Oil, Italian Superpower, New York Life, North American Aviation, New York, New Haven & Hartford, Radio Corporation, Aluminum Co. of America, Bethlehem Steel, Central Alloy Steel, Republic Iron & Steel, Cuba Co., Electric Bond & Share, Mellon National Bank, National City Bank, Western Union, Colombia Syndicate, Continental Illinois Bank & Trust Co. of Chicago, Curtiss-Wright Corporation, Equitable Life, Tidewater Oil and Goodyear Rubber & Tire. Eliminating duplications, J. P. Morgan & Co. and their dependents are represented in corporations with combined (net) assets of approximately $52,000,000,000.

In addition, the Morgan allies, Chase National and National City Banks, are represented by interlocking directorships

in corporations with gross assets of $51,000,000,000 and net of
$46,000,000,000, including Anaconda Copper, American To-
bacco, Cuban-American Sugar, American Power & Light, Cen-
tral Hanover Bank & Trust, Westinghouse Electric, American
Sugar Refining, Illinois Central, International Match, New
York Trust, International Power Securities, Consolidated Gas,
Union Carbide & Carbon, United Aircraft, American Locomo-
tive, Armour & Co., American Woolen, American Superpower,
Bankers Trust, General Foods, Metropolitan Life, Hudson
Coal, U. S. Industrial Alcohol, Republic Brass, Wickwire Spen-
cer Steel, New England Power, St. Louis & San Francisco and
Shell Union Oil.

The Morgan dependents and allies are interlocked in
many corporations. Eliminating duplications, the Morgan combination is represented by directorships in corporations with net
assets of approximately $74,000,000,000, equal to more than one-
quarter of all corporate assets.

In addition, the Morgan combination dominates investment
banking operations. During the first six months of 1930 J. P.
Morgan & Co. floated issues amounting to $628,000,000, more
than 18 per cent of the total.[89] The percentage becomes much
larger if the Morgan dependents and allies are included.
The system of financial centralization and control comprises
security issues as well as domination of corporate enterprises.

This immense power over American industry is concentrated
in 167 persons in the Morgan combination who hold more
than 2,450 interlocking directorships in corporations.[90] Immense as the power is in itself, it is all the greater considering
that it interlocks control and influence over those giant corporations which dominate their particular industries—and economic
life as a whole. Financial centralization and control are now
infinitely larger than in the elder Morgan's day.

Outside the dominant Morgan combination are minor combinations in the system of financial centralization and control
developed by other banking institutions, the whole represent-

ing an amalgamation of industry and finance. At the apex of the system of financial centralization and control is the House of Morgan. It does not directly control all the corporations in the system, nor the system itself, but acts as the balance-wheel owing to its dominance. J. P. Morgan, Jr. has not the power of his father—he wields large influence but not personal dictatorship. Nor is there any other dictator. The system itself dominates, institutionalized in the operations of the great banks, the dictatorship oligarchical, its manipulators being more glorified clerks than the flaming buccaneers and original constructive organizers of the preceding generation.

The Morgan system of centralization and control represents a concentration of financial forces, of finance capital imposing its control over industry. It is the heart of contemporary capitalism. There is no dispute over the power of the Morgans, the du Ponts or any other masters of money in the system, nor is there the struggle for supremacy waged by the elder Morgan, Stillman, Rockefeller and Harriman. There is now unity in the oligarchy of temporarily stabilized financial empire. If the system of centralization and control represents the financial integration and regulation of business made necessary by the complexity of modern corporate enterprise, it is equally an oppressive concentration of power beyond effective social control. Stabilization and government regulation eliminate some of the more flagrant abuses, but power overwhelming still inheres in the system's influence over economic life.

In sum, financial centralization and control comprise an industrial and financial government largely sufficient unto itself and responsible primarily to its oligarchical manipulators.

This immense concentration and centralization of industry and finance proceeded in the midst of unprecedented prosperity—measurably paralleling events after the Spanish-American War.

The post-war boom crashed in the panic of 1921. Centralized finance again proved its incapacity to insure prosperity, and marked time while the depression ran its course. Finance had little to do with the ensuing prosperity, which was the product of the combined efforts of labor, engineers and managements.

Wages are usually slashed in severe depressions. They were slashed in 1921, but not as much as prices declined, producing substantial increases in real wages. Managements might have slashed wages still more, but they hesitated: labor was in an aggressive mood. In 1919 more than 5,000,000 workers engaged in great strikes, including a strike in the plants of the United States Steel Corporation.* In 1920 there were more strikes, and a demand by the railway workers' unions for joint government-labor operation of the railroads. Instead of slashing wages to the bone, provoking labor resistance and strikes, employers turned to more efficient production, engineering and management and the elimination of waste to maintain profits. High wages combined with the upsurge in building, automobile production and instalment sales to revive business, the prosperity developing in 1923 being accompanied by the largest increase in real wages and productivity in American history. Finance's contribution was negative—the creative force lay in industry.

For six years prosperity flourished, in spite of agricultural depression and minor fluctuations. High wage levels were maintained (although the majority of wage-workers still could not afford minimum-comfort standards of living), corporate profits increased and business boomed, finance absorbing the largest relative share of prosperity.

---

* During the Steel strike J. P. Morgan wrote to Elbert H. Gary: "Heartiest congratulations on your stand for the open shop, with which I am, as you know, absolutely in accord. I believe American principles of liberty are deeply involved and must win if we all stand firm." (New York *Times*, September 23, 1919.) United States Steel's open shop is really a "closed shop"—closed against unionism. In 1923, under public pressure, the Steel Corporation promised to introduce the eight-hour day and abolish the seven-day week, but the changes were slight. In 1929 investigation revealed that while the number of men working twelve hours a day had been considerably reduced, at least 50 per cent worked ten hours a day or more, one-quarter were burdened by the seven-day week, and only 17 per cent worked five and one-half days. (*New Republic*, February 19, 1930, pp. 7-9.)

In the midst of this prosperity the system of financial centralization and control conquered larger power. Stockholders multiplied, more completely separating ownership and management. Holding companies and investment trusts were pyramided to concentrate control. Attacks upon corporate combinations almost ceased. The measures of regulation introduced by Roosevelt and Wilson perceptibly weakened, while business organized larger and larger combinations. Prosperity flourished. Business was accepted as omnipotent. Opposition collapsed. "Let us alone!" was the universal cry.

Government yielded priority to business. Millionaires preempted important posts in the national government. Post-war corruption, unequaled since President Grant's Administration, did not arouse any considerable public indignation, simply the petulant cry: "Don't disturb business!" One of the chief conspirators in the buccaneering raid upon the government's oil reserves was given a testimonial dinner by his associates, while another was overwhelmingly re-elected head of a great corporation by its stockholders—his régime meant large and regular dividends.[91] Prosperity multiplied goods, comforts, indifference and reaction. "Let us alone!"

Meanwhile speculation flourished riotously. Prices on the Stock Exchange shot to dizzying heights, discounting not only the future but eternity itself. Sober financiers acted as if the sky was the limit. Stock-market prosperity was identified with national prosperity. Business and speculation furiously speeded on, dislocating the balance of economic forces. Wages remained almost stationary, producing stagnation in purchasing power. Competition multiplied, provoking overproduction. Instalment sales reached their limit in the manufacture of purchasing power by mortgaging future income. Depression appeared in foreign countries. American industry began to droop in 1927, revived, drooped still more in the summer of 1929. Business showed all the signs of maladjustment and illness. But financiers and speculators, the masters of money, insisted all was

well. They implied that the old relation between stock prices
and corporate earnings had been suspended in the "new economic order." Investment markets were flooded by a mass of
"indigestible securities." Prices shot still higher while corporate earnings declined. More gas was pumped into the balloon
of speculation, and it burst. In October, 1929, came the great
collapse, the worst market crash in American history.

Once more, in spite of all claims to the contrary, industrial
and financial centralization proved its incapacity to insure
prosperity. Once more the economic mechanism, capable of
providing security, abundance and independence, broke down,
producing depression, disaster and unemployment—the old,
old story.

Again the House of Morgan came to the rescue. Under leadership of Thomas W. Lamont a pool was organized to maintain stock prices, composed of the Morgan banks and the
Guggenheim interests. The pool was most active in the stocks
of its affiliated enterprises, and probably prevented more dis-
orderly liquidation, but could not stop the melting away of
$25,000,000,000 in paper values.[92] The House of Morgan could
do no more, in spite of its immense power as the concentration point of American business.

This Morgan intervention was not as dramatic or important
as the elder Morgan's intervention in the panic of 1907. The
banks, owing largely to the Federal Reserve System (which
important bankers had opposed) were in much better condition to withstand the shock of crisis. There were no great bank
failures. But the market crash sharpened the business decline,
which developed into the worst depression since 1907, with at
least 4,000,000 workers scourged by the scourge of unemployment.

Another important difference in the 1929 depression was
government intervention under President Hoover. Where
President Roosevelt intervened to help the money market,
President Hoover intervened to revive prosperity. The Presi-

dent convened a conference of 400 "key" businessmen which formed a permanent organization to "stabilize business" and creatively act to end the depression.[98] There was much talk and many conferences, the government speeded up public-works construction, but the results were slight. Business kept on declining. The "scientific" efforts to revive prosperity were not much different from the "Sunshine Movement" after 1907.

While the measures adopted did not help much, they expressed emerging social action and control. Business in and by itself is unable to insure prosperity. The issue of social integration and control of business was much larger than President Hoover's experimental intervention in the business depression. There was implied in the action developing struggle for larger social control of industry, complicated by the oppressive power of financial centralization and control and its aggravation by imperialism. In this struggle for social reorganization and control of industry, as in the struggle of Roosevelt and Wilson to impose larger regulation on corporate combinations, the House of Morgan will again be the decisive representative of the forces objecting to changes not in the interest of financial centralization and control.

SOURCES CITED

BOOKS

Adams, Charles Francis: "Autobiography" (Boston, 1916). "A Chapter of Erie" (Boston, 1869). "Railroads: Their Origins and Problems" (New York, 1886). "The Crisis of Foreign Intervention in the War of Secession" (Boston, 1914). "The Interstate Commerce Act" (Boston, 1888).

Adams, Henry: "The Education of Henry Adams" (Boston, 1918).

Adams, James Truslow: "The Founding of New England" (Boston, 1921). "New England in the Republic" (Boston, 1926).

"Annual Meeting of the Proprietors of Hollis Street Church" (Boston, 1839).

Atkinson, Edward: "The Railway, the Farmer and the Public" (New York, 1885).

Barrett, Walter: "Old Merchants of New York" (New York, 1862).

Beard, Charles A. and Mary A.: "The Rise of American Civilization" (New York, 1928).

Beer, Thomas: "The Mauve Decade" (New York, 1926).

Bellows, Henry W.: "Historical Sketch of the Union League Club of New York, 1867-79" (New York, 1879).

Bishop, Joseph Bucklin: "Theodore Roosevelt and His Times" (New York, 1920).

Bliss, George: "An Address at the Opening of the Town Hall in Springfield" (Springfield, Massachusetts, 1826).

Bliss, J. A.: "The Problem: Shall Avarice Rule?" (New York, 1886).

Bodge, George M.: "Soldiers in King Philip's War" (Boston, 1906).

Bolles, Albert S.: "The Financial History of the United States" (New York, 1886).

Brandeis, Louis: "Other People's Money" (New York, 1914).

Burr, Anna Robeson: "The Portrait of a Banker: James Stillman" (New York, 1927).

Carnegie, Andrew: "Autobiography" (Boston, 1920).

Chase, Salmon P.: "Diary and Correspondence" (Washington, 1903).

Clark, Victor S.: "History of Manufactures in the United States" (Washington, 1928).

Clews, Henry: "Fifty Years in Wall Street" (New York, 1908).

Commons, John R. and Associates: "A Documentary History of American Industrial Society" (Cleveland, 1910-11). "History of Labor in the United States" (New York, 1918).

Cornwallis, Kinahan: "The Gold Room" (New York, 1878).

"Correspondence Between a Committee and the Pastor of Hollis Street Church" (Boston, 1840).

Cortesi, Salvatore: "My Thirty Years of Friendships" (New York, 1927).

Croffutt, W. A.: "The Vanderbilts and the Story of Their Fortune" (New York, 1886).

Curry, J. L. M.: "A Brief Sketch of George Peabody" (Cambridge, 1898).

Dacus, J. A.: "Annals of the Great Strikes" (Chicago, 1877).

Daggett, Stuart: "Railroad Reorganization" (Cambridge, 1908).

Denny, Ludwell: "America Conquers Britain" (New York, 1930).

Depew, Chauncey M.: "My Memories of Forty Years" (New York, 1924).

Dewey, Davis R.: "Financial History of the United States" (New York, 1924).

Dewing, Arthur S.: "Corporate Promotions and Reorganizations" (New York, 1921).

"Dictionary of National Biography" (London, 1917).

"Documents of the Hollis Street Society" (Boston, 1838).

Douglas, Paul: "Real Wages in the United States, 1890-1926" (New York, 1930).

Drake, Francis S.: "Dictionary of American Biography" (Boston, 1872).

Dunbar, Seymour: "History of Travel in America" (Indianapolis, 1915).

Dunn, Robert W.: "American Foreign Investments" (New York, 1926).

Duyckinck, Evert A.: "National Portrait Gallery of Eminent Americans" (New York, 1868).

Finger, Charles J.: "Frontier Ballads" (New York, 1927).

"First Century of the History of Springfield" (Springfield, Massachusetts, 1899).

Fitch, John A.: "The Steel Workers" (Pittsburgh Survey, 1911, Russell Sage Foundation).

Forbes, B. C.: "Men Who Are Making America" (New York, 1917).

Ford, Abbie A.: "John Pierpont" (Boston, 1909).

Gibson, Rowland D.: "Forces Mining and Undermining China" (New York, 1914).

Glück, Elsie: "John Mitchell" (New York, 1929).

Haddock, Charles B.: "An Address Delivered Before the Railroad Convention at Montpelier" (Montpelier, Vermont, 1844).

Hadley, Arthur T.: "Railroad Transportation" (Boston, 1886).

Hanaford, Phebe A.: "George Peabody" (Boston, 1884).

Harvey, George: "Henry Clay Frick, the Man" (New York, 1928).

Hibben, Paxton: "Henry Ward Beecher" (New York, 1927).

Hobson, C. K.: "The Export of Capital" (New York, 1914).

Hoggson, Noble Foster: "Epochs in American Banking" (New York, 1929).

Hovey, Carl: "The Life Story of J. Pierpont Morgan" (New York, 1912).

Hungerford, Edward: "The Story of the Baltimore & Ohio" (New York, 1928).

Hunt, Freeman: "Lives of American Merchants" (New York, 1858).

Jones, Eliot: "The Anthracite Coal Combination" (New York, 1914). "The Trust Problem in the United States" (New York, 1922).

Jordan, David Starr, and Kimball, Sarah Louise: "Your Family Tree" (New York, 1929).

Kennan, George: "Edward H. Harriman" (Boston, 1922).

King, W. I.: "The Wealth and Income of the People of the United States" (New York, 1915).

Lichtervelde, Louis de: "Leopold of the Belgians" (New York, 1929).

McElroy, Robert: "Grover Cleveland" (New York, 1923). "Levi Parsons Morton" (New York, 1930).

MacManus, T. F., and Beasley, Norman: "Men, Money and Motors" (New York, 1929).

Marsh, Margaret A.: "The Bankers in Bolivia" (New York, 1928).

Minnigerode, Meade: "Certain Rich Men" (New York, 1927).

Mitchell, Wesley C.: "History of the Greenbacks" (Chicago, 1903).

Moody, John: "Truth About the Trusts" (New York, 1905). "Masters of Capital" (New Haven, 1919).

Moody's "Manuals of Investments" (New York, 1930).

Morgan, Appleton: "A History of the Family of Morgan" (New York, 1897).

Morgan, Rev. Joseph: "The Nature of Riches" (Philadelphia, 1732).

Morgan, Nathaniel H.: "Morgan Genealogy: A History of James Morgan" (Hartford, 1869).

Myers, Gustavus: "History of the Great American Fortunes" (Chicago, 1908-10).

"National Cyclopedia of American Biography" (New York, 1893).

Nearing, Scott, and Freeman, Joseph: "Dollar Diplomacy" (New York, 1925).

Noyes, Alexander D.: "Forty Years of American Finance" (New York, 1909). "The War Period of American Finance" (New York, 1926).

Oberholtzer, Ellis P.: "Jay Cooke" (Philadelphia, 1907).

Paredes, Juan: "The Morgan-Honduras Loan" (New Orleans, 1911).

Parkman, Rev. Francis: "The Spirit of the Christian Ministry" (Boston, 1837).

Parrington, Vernon L.: "The Colonial Mind" (New York, 1927). "The Romantic Revolution in America" (New York, 1927).

Patten, Simon N.: "The Theory of Prosperity" (New York, 1902).

Peabody, George: "An Address at the Opening of the Eastern Railroad" (Salem, Massachusetts, 1838). "Three Letters" (Cambridge, 1910).

"Peabody Memorial": Maryland Historical Society (Baltimore, 1870).

Phelps, Clyde William: "The Foreign Expansion of American Banks" (New York, 1927).

Pierce, Franklin: "The Tariff and the Trusts" (New York, 1907).

Pierpont, John: "Airs of Palestine and Other Poems" (Boston, 1840). "A Discourse on the Covenant with Judas" (Boston, 1844). "Moral Resurrection: A Sermon Preached at the Ordination of the Rev. Oliver Everett" (Boston, 1837). "The Burning of the Ephesian Letters" (Boston, 1844).

Pittsburgh Chamber of Commerce: "The Insurrection Among the Railroads" (Pittsburgh, 1877).

Poor's "Directory of Directors" (New York, 1930).

Pyle, James Gilpin: "Life of James J. Hill" (New York, 1917).

Raushenbush, H. S., and Laidler, H. W.: "Power Control" (New York, 1928).

"Report of the Dinner to Junius Spencer Morgan" (New York, 1877).

Ripley, William Z.: "Railroads: Rates and Regulation" (New York, 1912).

Romero, Matias: "Railroads in Mexico" (Washington, 1882).

Roosevelt, Theodore: "Autobiography" (New York, 1926).

Schleuter, Herman: "Lincoln, Labor and Slavery" (New York, 1913).

Seitz, Don C.: "Joseph Pulitzer" (New York, 1924).

Sherman, John: "Recollections of Forty Years" (New York, 1895).

Smith, Matthew Hale: "Successful Folks" (Hartford, 1878). "Sunshine and Shadow in New York" (Hartford, 1868). "Twenty Years in Wall Street" (Hartford, 1870).

Stevens, Guy: "Selections from the Economic History of the United States" (Boston, 1909).

Stimson, A. L.: "History of the Express Companies and the Origin of American Railroads" (New York, 1858).

Stuart, Graham H.: "Latin America and the United States" (New York, 1928).

Tarbell, Ida: "The Life of Elbert H. Gary" (New York, 1925).

Tooke, Thomas: "A History of Prices" (London, 1838).

Tribolet, Leslie Bennett: "International Aspects of Electrical Communications in the Pacific Area" (Baltimore, 1929).

Trumbull, J. Hammond: "The Memorial History of Hartford County" (Boston, 1886). Editor, "The Public Records of the Colony of Connecticut, 1665-78" (Hartford, 1852).

Van Hise, C. R.: "Concentration and Control" (New York, 1912).

Ward, George W.: "The Early Development of the Chesapeake & Ohio Canal Project" (Baltimore, 1899).

Ware, Norman J.: "The Industrial Worker" (New York, 1924).

Washburn, Emory: "Argument Before an Ecclesiastical Council" (Boston, 1841).

Wells, David A.: "Recent Economic Changes" (New York, 1889).

Werner, M. R.: "Bryan" (New York, 1929).

White, Horace: "Money and Banking" (Boston, 1895).

Williams, Benjamin H.: "Economic Foreign Policy of the United States" (New York, 1929).

Wilson, James Grant: "Bryant and His Friends" (New York, 1886).

Wister, Owen: "Roosevelt, the Story of a Friendship" (New York, 1930).

PUBLIC DOCUMENTS

"Congressional Globe," 2nd Sess., 37th Cong., 1862; 3rd Sess., 37th Cong., 1862-3 (Washington, 1862-3).

Court of Claims, "Reports," 1866 (Washington, 1867).

New York State: "Official Testimony Taken Before the Legislative Insurance Committee of the State of New York." Same, "Report" (Albany, 1906).

——— "Report of the [Assembly] Select Committee to Investigate the Erie Railway" (Albany, 1873).

——— "Report of the Special Committee [Hepburn Committee] on Railroads" (Albany, 1880).

——— "Reports of Cases in the Supreme Court" (Albany, 1869 and 1871).

"Report of the Commissioner of Corporations on the Steel Industry" (Washington, 1911).

Reports of the Secretary of the Treasury (Washington).

"Statistical Abstract of the United States" (Washington, 1928).

"Investigation of Financial and Monetary Concentration in the United States," Testimony, Report (Washington, 1913). [Money Trust Investigation.]

"Statistics of Income," Bureau of Internal Revenue (Washington, 1923, 1927).

United States, House of Representatives: "Hearings Before the Committee on Investigation of the United States Steel Corporation" (Washington, 1912).

—— "Reports of Committees," 1861-2 (Washington, 1862).

—— "Reports of Committees, Court of Claims," 1862-3 (Washington, 1863).

—— "Reports of Committees," 1871-2, Report No. 7 (Washington, 1872).

United States, Senate: 54th Cong., 2nd Sess., Doc. No. 187, "Sale of Bonds" (Washington, 1896).

—— "Investigation of Panama Canal Matters" (Washington, 1910).

—— "Reports of Committees," 1871-3. Doc. No. 78. Crédit Mobilier (Washington, 1873).

United States Supreme Court: Decision in the Northern Securities Case (Washington, 1904).

United States Industrial Commission: Report and Proceedings (Washington, 1900-2).

PERIODICALS

Newspapers: New York "Journal," "Journal of Commerce," "Evening Post," "Herald," "Times," "Tribune," "Wall Street Journal," "World," London "Times."

Magazines: "Americana," "Bankers' Magazine," "Bradstreet's," "Century," "Commercial and Financial Chronicle," "Everybody's," "Forbes," "Forum," "Harper's Weekly," "Hunt's Merchants' Magazine," "Judge," "McClure's," "Nation," "New Age," "New Republic," "Railroad Gazette," "Railway World," "Saturday Evening Post," "World's Work."

NOTES

CHAPTER I

(1) Tribune, June 2, 1901; (2) World, May 26, 1901; (3) Times, July 12, 1912; (4) Century, July, 1913, p. 462; (5) World, April 1, 1913; (6) Barrett, I, p. 95; (7) Jordan, pp. 125, 208, 136; (8) ibid., p. 13.

CHAPTER II

(1) National Cyclopedia, VI, p. 184; (2) Appleton Morgan, pp. 17, 233; (3) ibid., p. 18; George Bliss, p. 5; (4) First Century of Springfield, I, pp. 305-7; (5) Appleton Morgan, p. 19; (6) Adams, Founding, pp. 341, 343; (7) Appleton Morgan, p. 235; (8) ibid., p. 235; (9) Adams, Founding, p. 353; (10) Trumbull, Public Records, p. 418; (11) ibid., p. 420; (12) Bodge, pp. 407, 442; (13) ibid., p. 443; (14) First Century of Springfield, II, p. 224; (15) Bodge, pp. 479-80; (16) Appleton Morgan, p. 48; (17) Clark, I, p. 145; (18) Nathaniel Morgan, p. 35; (19) Joseph Morgan, pp. 3-6, 14, 19.

CHAPTER III

(1) Hovey, p. 12; McClure's, Oct. 1901, p. 508; (2) Nathaniel Morgan, pp. 241, 243; (3) Hunt, II, p. 390; (4) Dunbar, III, p. 765; (5) ibid., p. 744; (6) Trumbull, Memorial History, I, p. 499; (7) ibid., pp. 500-2; (8) Hovey, p. 12; (9) Americana, April, 1919, p. 123; (10) Haddock, pp. 10-14; (11) Appleton Morgan, p. 77; (12) McElroy, Levi Morton, p. 237; (13) Smith, Successful Folks, p. 19; (14) McElroy, Levi Morton, p. 37; (15) Barrett, V, pp. 65-6; (16) Times, Aug. 21, 1865; (17) Adams, New England, p. 212; (18) Beard, I, p. 527; (19) Parrington, Colonial Mind, p. 365; (20) Appleton Morgan, p. 74; Hunt's Mag., Nov. 1839, pp. 461-2.

CHAPTER IV

(1) N. Y. Sun, March 3, 1913; (2) Hovey, p. 14; (3) Pierpont, Airs of Palestine, p. 2; (4) Dictionary of American Biography, p. 718; Ford, p. 18; (5) Pierpont, Moral Resurrection, p. 17; (6) Commons, History of Labor, p. 305; (7) ibid., p. 303; (8) Hunt's Mag., Aug. 1841, p. 141; (9) Pierpont, Moral Resurrection, pp. 4, 17; (10) Pierpont, Ephesian Letters, pp. 11-16; (11) Commons, History of Labor, p. 179; (12) Parrington, Romantic Revolution, p. 341; (13) Pierpont, Airs of Palestine, p. 294; (14) Pierpont, Covenant with Judas, p. 34; (15) Parkman, pp. 11-12; (16) Annual Meeting, Hollis Street Church, pp. 4-5; Documents of the Hollis Street Society, p. 1; (17) Correspondence between a Committee and the Pastor, p. 21; (18) Washburn, p. 111; (19) Ford, p. 16; Washburn, pp. 104, 120; (20) National Cyclopedia of American Biography, VI, p. 155; (21) Ware, p. 225; (22) Ford, p. 21.

CHAPTER V

(1) Clark, I, pp. 371-8; (2) Hunt's Mag., April 1857, p. 506; (3) Hoggson, p. 129; Hunt's Mag., Nov. 1844, p. 432; (4) Stevens, p. 736; (5) Hoggson, p. 140; Hunt's Mag., Nov. 1844, p. 432; (6) Bank Reformer, Dec. 1, 1841, p. 53; (7) Senate, Documents (1843), Doc. No. 104; (8) Statistical Abstract, 1928, p. 447; (9) Hunt's Mag., Jan. 1857, p. 71; Williams, pp. 13, 14; Dewey, pp. 46, 56; Hobson, p. 111; (10) Dictionary of National Biography, p. 577; (11) Hunt, II, p. 430; (12) Hanaford, pp. 240, 242; (13) Phelps, pp. 9, 10; Burr, pp. 39, 47; Moody, Masters of Capital, p. 4; (14) Hunt's Mag., Jan. 1842, p. 94; ibid., Sept. 1850, p. 348; (15) Peabody, An Address, pp. 16, 18; (16) Hunt's Mag., April 1857, pp. 8, 9; (17) Times, Dec. 4, 1869; (18) New Age, Dec. 1910, p. 503; (19) Hunt's Mag., Nov. 1844, p. 432; (20) Dewey, p. 230; Americana, Sept. 1912, pp. 860-62; (21) Tooke, II, pp. 306, 307; (22) Williams, p. 14; (23) ibid., p. 13; (24) Peabody Memorial, p. 17; (25) Duyckinck, I, p. 598; (26) Ward, p. 104; (27) Myers, II, pp. 24-5; (28) Senate Doc. No. 610 (1839-40), pp. 149-87; (29) Hungerford, p. 302; (30) Hunt's Mag., Oct. 1850, p. 487; (31) Croffutt, pp. 45-50; (32) Hanaford, p. 78; (33) Clark, I, p. 7; Hanaford, p. 79; (34) Clark, II, p. 7; (35) Hunt's Mag., Nov. 1857, p. 583; (36) Curry, p. 7; Bankers' Mag., April 1858, p. 837; (37) Hovey, p. 26; (38) McClure's, Oct. 1901, p. 509; (39) Hovey, p. 28.

CHAPTER VI

(1) Times, Aug. 19, 1864; (2) Clews, p. 664; (3) Hovey, p. 46; (4) House, Reports of Committees, 1861-62, I, p. 52; (5) Times, May 28, 1861; (6) Chase, II, p. 507; (7) U. S. Treasury Report, 1862, p. 28; (8) House Reports (1861-2), I, p. 34; (9) Cong. Globe (1862-3), p. 117; (10) House Reports (1861-2), Appendix; (11) House Reports (1861-2), I, pp. 657-8; (12) Times, Aug. 21, 1865; (13) House Reports, Appendix, LXVII; (14) ibid., LXXVI; (15) ibid., LXX; (16) House Reports (1861-2), II, LXXVII; (17) Cong. Globe (1862), p. 1851; (18) Court of Claims (1866), II, pp. 96-102; (19) Myers, III, p. 175.

CHAPTER VII

(1) Times, July 8, 11, 1865; (2) Hovey, p. 24; (3) Cornwallis, p. 8; (4) White, p. 175; Cornwallis, p. 10; Oberholtzer, I, p. 213; (5) Hovey, p. 33; (6) Times, Aug. 21, 1865; (7) ibid., July 14, 17, 1863; (8) Hovey, p. 31; (9) Times, Oct. 6, 1863; (10) ibid., Oct. 11, 1863; (11) ibid., Oct. 21, 1863; (12) ibid., Feb. 28, 1863; (13) World, June 22, 1864; (14) Bolles, p. 153; (15) Post, Oct. 1, 1862; (16) Hovey, p. 48; (17) Herald, June 23, 1864; (18) Times, June 23, 1864; (19) Cornwallis, pp. 10-11; (20) Times, Aug. 28, 1865; Sept. 2, 1865; (21) ibid., Sept. 9, 1865; (22) ibid., Dec. 31, 1865; (23) Wall Street Journal, April 1, 1913; (24) Bankers' Mag., Dec. 1864, p. 508; (25) Journal of Commerce, April 1, 1913.

CHAPTER VIII

(1) Adams, Foreign Intervention, p. 13; Schlueter, p. 10; (2) Times, Oct. 26, 1866; ibid., Oct. 31, 1866; (3) ibid., Oct. 27, 31, 1866; (4) Hanaford, p. 65; (5) Saturday Evening Post, July 12, 1930, p. 46; (6) Commons, American Industrial Society, IX, pp. 76-8; (7) ibid., p. 221; (8) Clark, II, pp. 36, 37, 40; Mitchell,

pp. 262, 388-9; (9) World, April 27, 1866; (10) Cong. Globe (1866), p. 1146; (11) Tribune, Nov. 9, 1877; (12) Pierce, p. 122.

CHAPTER IX

(1) Smith, Twenty Years, p. 411; (2) London Times, Nov. 29, 1870; (3) ibid., Sept. 20, 23, 1865; (4) Carnegie, pp. 169-70; (5) Dinner to J. S. Morgan, p. 4; (6) World, Dec. 21, 1869; (7) Times, Sept. 13, 1869; (8) Hadley, p. 131; (9) Times, June 16, Aug. 2, 1869; (10) North American Review, Jan. 1868, p. 50.

CHAPTER X

(1) Tribune, Sept. 14, 1876; (2) N. Y. State, Report on Railroads, 1879, I, p. 7; (3) North American Review, July 1869, p. 34; (4) Croffutt, p. 49; Burr, p. 57; (5) Clews, p. 629; (6) Croffutt, p. 91; (7) North American Review, July 1869, p. 53; (8) ibid., p. 60; Croffutt, p. 94; (9) ibid., p. 62; (10) Croffutt, pp. 97, 294; (11) Smith, Twenty Years, p. 110; (12) North American Review, July, 1869, p. 80; Times, Nov. 10, 1869; (13) North American Review, April 1871, pp. 247, 250; (14) Times, Aug. 12, 1869; (15) ibid., Aug. 14, 1869; Tribune, Jan. 31, 1871; (16) Smith, Twenty Years, p. 411; (17) N. Y. Supreme Court, 1869, I, p. 329; (18) Times, Aug. 5, 1869; (19) North American Review, April 1871, p. 255; (20) ibid., p. 260; (21) Times, Aug. 12, 1869; (22) North American Review, April 1871, pp. 252, 254; (23) Times, Aug. 25, 1869; (24) North American Review, April 1871, p. 259; (25) Times, Aug. 25, 1869; (26) Times, Aug. 12, 25, 1869; (27) ibid., Aug. 12, 1869; (28) N. Y. Supreme Court, I, p. 312; (29) Times, Aug. 12, 1869.

CHAPTER XI

(1) World, July 10, 1869; (2) ibid., Sept. 26, 1869; (3) Myers, II, pp. 332-4; (4) Times, Nov. 11, 1869; (5) Tribune, Nov. 10, 1869; (6) World, Nov. 11, 1869; (7) Smith, Sunshine and Shadow, pp. 204-6; (8) Times, Oct. 3, 1869; (9) ibid., Jan. 25, 1871; Croffutt, p. 294; (10) Smith, Sunshine and Shadow, p. 35; (11) World, Nov. 24, 1869; (12) ibid., Sept. 8, 9, 1869; (13) Times, Sept. 10, 1869; World, Sept. 9, 1869; (14) Times, Sept. 25, 1869; (15) World, April 9, 1871; (16) Times, Aug. 3, 1871; (17) Times, Oct. 30, 1869; (18) Times, Nov. 10, 1869; Post, Nov. 17, 1869; (19) World, April 27, 1866; (20) ibid., Sept. 8, 1869; (21) ibid., Nov. 24, 1869; (22) Times, Nov. 8, 1869; (23) ibid., Nov. 10, 1869; (24) ibid.

CHAPTER XII

(1) Times, Sept. 7, 1869; (2) Finger, p. 61; (3) Times, Sept. 7, 1869; (4) ibid., Sept. 8, 1869; (5) ibid., Nov. 30, 1869; (6) ibid., Nov. 25, 1869; (7) ibid.; (8) ibid., Nov. 26, 1869; (9) N. Y. State Report on Erie Railway, p. 72; (10) N. Y. Supreme Court, 1869, I, pp. 331, 346; (11) North American Review, April 1871, p. 291; (12) N. Y. Supreme Court, 1871, V, p. 30; (13) Report on Erie, I, p. 20, 51; (14) ibid., pp. 91, 103-6; (15) Times, Jan. 24, 1873; (16) Reports on Railroads, III, p. 2503; (17) Times, Jan. 24, 1873.

CHAPTER XIII

(1) Oberholtzer, II, p. 34; (2) ibid., p. 83; (3) ibid., p. 98; (4) ibid., pp. 157, 161; (5) ibid., pp. 32, 134, 191; (6) ibid., p. 202; (7) ibid., pp. 206, 209; (8) ibid., p. 269; (9) Times, March 4, 16, 23, 26, 1871; House Reports, 1871-2, Report No. 7, pp. 1-2; (10) Times, Jan. 17, 1873; McElroy, Levi Morton, p. 53; (11) Oberholtzer, II, p. 209; (12) Clews, p. 666; (13) Bankers' Mag., March 1872, p. 709; (14) ibid.; (15) Times, June 27, 1871; (16) Oberholtzer, II, p. 362; (17) ibid., p. 286; (18) ibid., p. 371; (19) Clews, p. 326; (20) Times, Jan. 9, 1873; (21) ibid., Jan. 17, 1873; (22) Oberholtzer, II, p. 365; (23) ibid., p. 366; (24) Times, Jan. 30, 1873; (25) ibid., Feb. 6, 1873; (26) Oberholtzer, II, p. 372; (27) Times, Feb. 10, 1873; (28) ibid., Feb. 11, 1873; (29) Oberholtzer, II, p. 369; (30) ibid., p. 372; (31) Times, Sept. 19, 1873; (32) ibid., Sept. 20, 1873; (33) ibid., Sept. 19, 1873; (34) Oberholtzer, II, 421; (35) ibid., p. 517; (36) Wells, p. 5; (37) Bankers' Mag., Sept. 1878, p. 161; (38) Nation, Oct. 23, 1873, p. 12; (39) Hibben, p. 326; (40) Tribune, April 25, 1876; (41) Tribune, July 11, 1877; (42) Sherman, II, p. 571; (43) Treasury Report, 1877, p. ix; (44) Tribune, Jan. 13, 1896; (45) Treasury Report, 1877, p. ix; (46) White, p. 162; (47) Treasury Report, 1878, p. ix; (48) Treasury Report, 1879, p. ix; (49) Noyes, Forty Years, p. 52; (50) Treasury Report, 1879, p. xv; (51) Noyes, p. 53; (52) ibid., p. 55; (53) Sherman, p. 642; (54) ibid., p. 637; (55) Bankers' Mag., Dec. 1879, p. 480.

CHAPTER XIV

(1) Tribune, May 20, 1884; (2) ibid.; (3) Times, Jan. 11, 1889; (4) Wall Street Journal, April 1, 1913; (5) Wister, p. 280.

CHAPTER XV

(1) North American Review, Jan. 1869, p. 139; (2) Depew, p. 241; Croffutt, p. 219; (3) N. Y. State, Report on Railroads, I, pp. 41, 44; (4) Railway World, Nov. 29, 1879, p. 1129; (5) Chronicle, Nov. 29, 1879, p. 554; (6) ibid., p. 564; (7) Bankers' Mag., Dec. 1879, p. 504; (8) Tribune, Nov. 21, 1879; Railway World, Nov. 29, 1879, p. 1138; (9) Chronicle, Nov. 19, 1879, p. 550; (10) Adams, Interstate Commerce Act, p. 2; (11) Ripley, pp. 37-39; (12) North American Review, Jan. 1869, p. 138; (13) Senate, Doc. No. 78 (1872-3), p. xiv; (14) Chronicle, Nov. 15, 1873, pp. 647-8; (15) Atkinson, p. 40; (16) Wells, p. 422; (17) Bankers' Mag., Feb. 1880, p. 654; (18) ibid.; (19) Chronicle, Jan. 22, 1876, p. 76; (20) Bankers' Mag., Sept. 1878, p. 189; (21) Oberholtzer, II, p. 418; (22) Hovey, p. 122.

CHAPTER XVI

(1) Hadley, p. 52; (2) Clews, p. 362; (3) Bradstreet's, April 25, 1885, pp. 274-5; (4) ibid.; Gazette, Jan. 2, 1885, p. 10; (5) Chronicle, Aug. 29, 1885, p. 242; (6) ibid.; Gazette, July 31, 1885, pp. 486, 494; (7) Gazette, July 31, 1885, p. 489; (8) Tribune, Oct. 10, 1885; (9) ibid., Oct. 14, 1885; (10) ibid.; (11) ibid., Oct. 3, 1885; (12) ibid., Oct. 14, 1885; (13) Chronicle, Aug. 29, 1885, p. 242; (14) Gazette, July 31, 1885, p. 495; (15) Tribune, Oct. 14, 1885; (16) Tarbell, p. 134; (17) Gazette, July 31, 1885, p. 495; (18) Bradstreet's, April 25, 1885, p. 274; (19) Daggett, p. 87; Tribune, Sept. 11, 1876; (20) Railway World, Feb. 20, 1886, p. 173; (21) ibid., March 20, 1886, p. 226; (22) ibid., Sept. 25, 1886, p. 926; (23)

ibid.; (24) Kennan, I, p. 65; (25) ibid., pp. 76-7; (26) ibid., p. 80; (27) Hungerford, II, pp. 165-73; Daggett, pp. 3-16; (28) Tribune, Oct. 29, 1887; ibid., Feb.
10, 1888; (29) Times, July 24, 1889; (30) Tribune, Jan. 13, 1896.

CHAPTER XVII

(1) J. A. Bliss, p. 9; (2) N. Y. State, Report on Railroads (1879), pp. 41-4; (3)
Adams, Railroads, p. 128; (4) Forum, Nov. 1889, pp. 265-6; (5) Pittsburgh Cham-
ber of Commerce, pp. 5-13; (6) Dacus, p. 477; (7) Adams, Interstate Commerce
Act, p. 4; (8) Industrial Commission, I, p. 26; (9) ibid., XIX, pp. 304-5; (10)
Railway World, April 27, 1889, p. 386; ibid., July 20, 1889, p. 675; (11) Hovey,
p. 126; Bankers' Mag., Jan. 1889, p. 482; (12) Times, Jan. 9, 1889; (13) Tribune,
Dec. 22, 1888; (14) Times, Jan. 10, 1889; (15) Hovey, p. 184; (16) ibid.; (17)
Hovey, p. 186; (18) Chronicle, Jan. 12, 1889, p. 50; (19) ibid.; (20) Tribune,
Jan. 13, 1889; (21) Times, Jan. 11, 1889; (22) ibid.; (23) Tribune, Jan. 11,
1889; (24) ibid., Jan. 12, 1889; (25) Chronicle, Jan 12, 1889, p. 49; (26) Railway
World, Jan. 19, 1889, p. 50; (27) Times, Sept. 8, 1889; (28) ibid., Dec. 14, 1890;
(29) Harper's Weekly, Dec. 27, 1890, p. 1010; (30) Times, Dec. 17, 1890; (31)
ibid., Dec. 16, 1890; (32) Tribune, Dec. 17, 1890; (33) ibid.; (34) Times, Dec.
16, 1890; (35) ibid., Dec. 17, 1890; (36) ibid., Dec. 16, 1890; (37) Tribune,
Dec. 17, 1890; (38) ibid.; (39) Chronicle, Jan. 12, 1889, p. 49.

CHAPTER XVIII

(1) Times, Nov. 1, 1896; (2) Journal, Oct. 31, 1896; (3) ibid., Nov. 2, 1896;
(4) ibid., Nov. 1, 1896; (5) ibid., Nov. 3, 1896; (6) Noyes, Forty Years, p. 180;
(7) Tribune, Feb. 14, 1893; April 26, 1893; (8) McElroy, Cleveland, II, p. 79; (9)
Chronicle, Jan. 20, 1894, p. 107; Feb. 3, 1894, p. 199; (10) Bankers' Mag., Dec.
1894, p. 92; Noyes, Forty Years, pp. 216, 231; (11) Burr, pp. 116-7; (12) Tribune,
Jan. 30, 1895; (13) Bankers' Mag., Feb. 1895, p. 315; (14) McElroy, Cleveland,
II, p. 85; (15) Times, Feb. 3, 1895; (16) Senate Doc. No. 187 (1896), p. 296;
(17) ibid., p. 294; Times, Feb. 3, 1895; (18) Senate Doc. No. 187, p. 294; (19)
McElroy, Cleveland, II, p. 86; (20) Senate Doc. No. 187, p. 294; (21) McElroy,
Cleveland, II, p. 87; (22) Bankers' Mag., March 1895, p. 582; Senate Doc. No. 187,
pp. 9-10; (23) Noyes, Forty Years, p. 234; (24) Tribune, Feb. 9, 1895; (25) Bank-
ers' Mag., March 1895, p. 477; (26) Tribune, May 11, June 27, Sept. 22, 1895;
(27) Senate Doc. No. 187, p. 297; (28) Bankers' Mag., March 1895, p. 480; (29)
Myers, III, p. 225; (30) Tribune, Feb 24, 1895; (31) ibid., Feb. 28, 1895; (32)
Noyes, Forty Years, pp. 239-50; Times, Feb. 9, 1895; (33) Senate Doc. No. 187,
p. 13; McElroy, Cleveland, II, p. 100; (34) ibid., p. 101; Senate Doc. No. 187,
p. 13; (35) Tribune, Feb. 15, 1895; (36) ibid.; (37) Tribune, Feb. 1, 1895; (38)
Noyes, Forty Years, p. 229; (39) ibid., pp. 193, 201; (40) Bankers' Mag., Aug.
1894, p. 86; (41) Beer, p. 71; Pyle, II, p. 497; (42) Noyes, Forty Years, p. 255;
Werner, p. 100; (43) ibid., p. 72.

CHAPTER XIX

(1) Tribune, June 22, 1895; (2) ibid.; (3) Railway World, July 6, p. 330; (4)
Bankers' Mag., Feb. 1900, p. 303; Industrial Commission, IV, p. 321; (5) Daggett,
p. 167; (6) ibid., p. 170; (7) ibid., p. 175; (8) ibid., p. 176; (9) Commission, XIX, p.

319; (10) Daggett, pp. 347, 373; (11) Money Trust, p. 147; (12) Daggett, p. 188; (13) Chronicle, Jan. 27, 1894, p. 167; (14) Tribune, March 4, 1894; (15) Chronicle, March 3, 1894, p. 383; (16) Kennan, I, pp. 97-103; (17) Tribune, Aug. 27, 1895; (18) Daggett, p. 69; (19) Tribune, Feb. 9, 1893; Myers, II, p. 240; (20) Hovey, p. 136; (21) Industrial Commission, XIX, p. 456; (22) Daggett, p. 124; (23) Chronicle, Oct. 28, 1893, p. 722; (24) ibid.; (25) Daggett, p. 349; (26) Tribune, Feb. 9, 1893; (27) Daggett, p. 125; (28) Myers, II, p. 240; (29) Tribune, March 25, 1893; (30) Daggett, pp. 140-3; (31) ibid., p. 249; (32) Kennan, I, p. 119; (33) ibid., p. 120; (34) ibid., p. 123; (35) ibid., pp. 125-6; (36) Daggett, pp. 256-7, 347; (37) Kennan, I, p. 121; (38) Moody, Masters, p. 56; (39) ibid., p. 66; (40) Daggett, p. 274; (41) ibid., p. 296; (42) Myers, III, pp. 357-68; (43) ibid., p. 373; (44) Daggett, p. 307; (45) Tribune, March 27, 1902; Pyle, II, p. 28; (46) Pyle, 23; (47) Moody, Masters, pp. 99-100; (48) Clews, p. 245; (49) Industrial Commission, IV, p. 298; Daggett, p. 373; (50) Industrial Commission, XIX, p. 308; ibid., XIX, pp. 305, 309, 404; (51) ibid., XIX, p. 314; Review of Reviews, Aug. 1901, p. 173; (52) Industrial Commission, IV, p. 264; (53) Jones, Coal Combination, pp. 63-4; (54) Industrial Commission, IV, p. 6; (55) ibid., XIX, p. 323; (56) Jones, Coal Combination, p. 219; (57) Industrial Commission, XIX, p. 460; (58) ibid., XIX, p. 447; (59) ibid., XIX, pp. 447-8; (60) Jones, Coal Combination, p. 75; (61) ibid., p. 78; (62) Commission, XIX, p. 459; (63) Jones, p. 84; (64) Chronicle, Dec. 5, 1900, p. 1189; (65) Jones, p. 84; (66) Commission, XIX, p. 460; (67) Quarterly Journal of Economics, Jan. 1898, p. 190; (68) Tribune, May 26, 1894; (69) ibid., May 6, 1894; (70) Glück, p. 82; (71) ibid., pp. 99, 114; (72) Tribune, Aug. 21, 1902; (73) Times, Aug. 23, 1902; (74) ibid., Aug. 27, 1902; (75) ibid., Aug. 30, 1902; (76) ibid., Sept. 11, 1902; (77) Roosevelt, p. 456; (78) ibid., p. 466; (79) Tribune, Oct. 13, 1902; (80) Times, Oct. 14, 1902; (81) Bishop, I, p. 215.

CHAPTER XX

(1) Tribune, April 12, 1901; (2) London Times, March 9, 1891; (3) ibid., March 11, 16, 1891; Chronicle, Jan. 29, 1894, p. 167; (4) Tribune, Jan. 18, 1893; (5) ibid., Feb. 16, 1893; (6) ibid., Feb. 14, 1893; (7) ibid.; (8) ibid., Feb. 16, 1893; (9) ibid.; (10) ibid.; (11) Seitz, p. 205; (12) Times, April 1, 1913; (13) Tribolet, pp. 157-8, 173-9; (14) Dunn, p. 2; (15) Nearing, p. 125; Chronicle, April 1, 1899, p. 597; ibid., Feb. 15, 1890, p. 229; Williams, p. 258; (16) Williams, p. 323; (17) ibid., p. 322; (18) Bankers' Mag., Aug. 1898, p. 171; (19) ibid., Aug. 1900, p. 175; (20) Chronicle, July 8, 1899, p. 60; (21) ibid.; (22) Chronicle, Sept. 22, 1900, p. 580; Jan. 26, 1901, p. 163; Jan. 25, 1902, p. 181; Bankers' Mag., Oct. 1900, p. 637; (23) Bankers' Mag., April 1900, p. 496; (24) Chronicle, Aug. 11, 1900, p. 258; Bankers' Mag., Sept. 1900, p. 330; May 1901, p. 748; (25) Bankers' Mag., Sept. 1900, p. 342; Oct. 1900, p. 591; (26) World, May 2, 1901; (27) Bankers' Mag., Aug. 1900, p. 160; (28) Chronicle, Dec. 24, 1898, p. 1283; (29) ibid.

CHAPTER XXI

(1) Times, Jan. 1, 1901; (2) Tribune, Jan. 1, 1901; (3) Patten, p. 1; (4) Times, Nov. 15, 1900; (5) ibid., Sept. 23, 1900; (6) World, May 26, 1901; Times, May 2, 1901; (7) ibid., Nov. 6, 1900; (8) Henry Adams, p. 305; (9) Times, Dec. 2, 1900; (10) ibid., Jan. 16, 1900; (11) ibid., Jan. 8, 1901; (12) Bankers' Mag., Jan. 1900, p. 117; (13) Times, Nov. 16, 1900; (14) ibid., Jan. 8, 1901; (15)

ibid., Dec. 2, 1900; (16) ibid., Nov. 1, 1900; (17) Clews, p. 608; (18) Henry
Adams, p. 347; (19) Croffutt, p. 152; (20) Adams, Autobiography, p. 196; (21)
Burr, p. 106; (22) Croffutt, pp. 164-6; (23) Beer, p. 43; (24) Henry Adams, p.
342; (25) Times, April 1, 1913; (26) Burr, p. 317; (27) Cortesi, p. 93; (28)
Times, Nov. 26, 1900; (29) Wall Street Journal, April 1, 1913; (30) Times, Jan.
7, 1900; (31) ibid., Nov. 8, 1900; (32) ibid., Nov. 8, 1900; (33) ibid., Jan. 6,
1901; (34) ibid., Nov. 6, 1900; (35) ibid.

CHAPTER XXII

(1) Industrial Commission, I, p. 15; (2) Chronicle, June 25, 1892, p. 1051; Feb.
13, 1892, p. 287; Bankers' Mag., March 1901, p. 438; (3) Tribune, June 22, 1895;
Dewing, pp. 112-36; (4) Chronicle, Jan. 7, 1899, p. 6; (5) ibid.; (6) Industrial
Commission, I, pp. 5, 35; (7) Report on Steel Corporation, p. 80; (8) Tarbell, p.
91; (9) ibid., pp. 82-85; (10) Industrial Commission, I, p. 986; (11) ibid., p. 969;
(12) Tribune, Oct. 14, 1898; (13) ibid.; (14) Industrial Commission, I, pp. 982-5;
(15) Report on Steel Corporation, p. 93; Jones, Trust Problem, p. 194; (16) Tarbell, p. 99; (17) Industrial Commission, I, p. 1002; (18) ibid., pp. 986, 1003;
(19) Report on Steel Corporation, p. 7; (20) ibid.; (21) Chronicle, Sept. 15, 1900,
p. 545; (22) ibid., March 27, 1901, pp. 560-1; (23) Tarbell, p. 88; (24) ibid., p.
97; (25) ibid., p. 76; (26) Tribune, March 18, 19, 1902; (27) Industrial Commission, I, pp. 5-6; (28) Burr, pp. 115-7; (29) Tribune, Nov. 11, 1894; March 14,
1900; (30) Century, July 1913, p. 461; Moody, Masters, p. 33; (31) Wall Street
Journal, April 1, 1913; (32) Tribune, Jan. 13, 1896; (33) World's Work, Nov.
1907, p. 519; (34) Bankers' Mag., May 1900, p. 718; Chronicle, Jan. 18, 1902, p.
129; (35) Chronicle, March 18, 1899, p. 502; Bankers' Mag., Sept. 1901, p. 435;
(36) Chronicle, May 19, 1900, p. 972; Jan. 25, 1902, p. 181; Bankers' Mag., Sept.
1901, p. 413; (37) Chronicle, Feb. 17, 1900, p. 306; July 28, 1900, p. 163; Bankers'
Mag., May 1900, p. 717; Nov. 1901, p. 880; (38) Bankers' Mag., March 1901, p.
438; (39) Chronicle, Feb. 8, 1902, p. 304; (40) ibid., June 24, 1899, p. 1209;
(41) Bankers' Mag., Oct. 1901, p. 694; (42) ibid., Sept. 1901, p. 440; (43) Mc-
Clure's, Oct. 1901, p. 512; (44) Tribune, March 14, 1900; (45) Jones, Trust
Problem, p. 89; (46) Clews, p. 746; (47) Chronicle, Aug. 4, 1900, p. 214; Bankers'
Mag., Oct. 1901, p. 638; (48) Bankers' Mag., Jan. 1900, p. 117; Chronicle, Feb.
11, 1900, p. 261; (49) World's Work, Nov. 1907, p. 519; (50) Burr, p. 196; (51)
ibid., p. 181; (52) Chronicle, Feb. 11, 1899, p. 261; (53) Money Trust Investigation,
pp. 1581-91; (54) Burr, p. 142; (55) Moody, Masters, p. 491.

CHAPTER XXIII

(1) Van Hise, p. 37; (2) Tribune, Jan. 19, Feb. 6, 1901; (3) Report on Steel
Corporation, p. 11; (4) ibid., p. 150; (5) Tarbell, p. 108; (6) Moody, Masters,
pp. 77-8; (7) Steel Investigation, p. 205; (8) Report on Steel Corporation, p.
103; (9) Tribune, Jan. 19, 1901; (10) Tarbell, p. 108; (11) Tribune, Jan. 19,
1901; (12) ibid., Jan. 20, 1901; (13) Moody, p. 83; (14) Money Trust Investigation, p. 1026; (15) Report on Steel Corporation, p. 152; (16) ibid., p. 163; (17)
ibid., p. 164; (18) Myers, III, p. 259; Burr, p. 159; (19) Steel Corporation, p.
174; (20) ibid., p. 175; (21) Tarbell, p. 123; (22) Report on Steel Corporation,
pp. 20, 113; (23) Tribune, May 16, 1901; (24) Report on Steel Corporation, p.
251; (25) Money Trust Investigation, p. 2131; (26) Harvey, p. 263; (27) ibid.,
p. 266; (28) Steel Investigation, p. 1857; (29) ibid., 1898; (30) ibid., p. 1899;

(31) ibid., p. 1900; (32) ibid., pp. 1854-8, 1902; (33) Report on Steel Corporation, p. 114; (34) Tribune, Aug. 21, 1901; (35) Tarbell, p. 127; (36) Report on Steel Corporation, p. 112; (37) ibid., p. 234; (38) Times, March 20, 1930; (39) Report on Steel Corporation, p. 257; (40) ibid., p. 251; (41) Noyes, Forty Years, p. 300; (42) Money Trust Investigation, p. 1025; (43) Tarbell, p. 127; (44) Report on Steel Corporation, pp. 12, 63.

CHAPTER XXIV

(1) Tribune, July 20, 1901; (2) Industrial Commission, I, p. 30; (3) Tribune, July 2, 1901; Times, April 1, 1903; (4) Tribune, July 16, 1901; Fitch, p. 89; (5) Tarbell, p. 154; (6) Tribune, July 2, 13, 14, 1901; (7) Tarbell, p. 157; (8) Tribune, Aug. 24, 1901; (9) ibid., July 20, 1901; (10) ibid., Aug. 11, 1901; (11) ibid., Aug. 1, 1901; (12) ibid., Aug. 24, 1901; (13) ibid., Aug. 3, 1901; Tarbell, p. 160; (14) Tarbell, p. 163; (15) Times, Aug. 26, 1902; (16) Fitch, p. 210; (17) ibid., p. 213; (18) Tarbell, p. 174; (19) Fitch, p. 214; (20) Tarbell, p. 176; (21) Douglas, pp. 391-2; (22) ibid., p. 271; (23) Fitch, pp. 171, 175; (24) Tarbell, p. 287; (25) Tribune, March 29, 1902.

CHAPTER XXV

(1) Post, March 20, 1902; (2) ibid.; (3) Tribune, March 27, 1902; (4) Times, June 5, 1902; (5) Moody, Trusts, p. xi; (6) Times, Oct. 21, 1907; (7) Douglas, p. 547; (8) Chronicle, Feb. 1, 1902, p. 230; (9) Tarbell, p. 143; (10) ibid.; (11) Hovey, p. 311; (12) Bankers' Mag., April 1901, p. 498.

CHAPTER XXVI

(1) Hovey, p. 139; (2) Kennan, I, p. 224; Chronicle, Feb. 2, 1901, p. 208; (3) Tribune, March 27, 1902; (4) Kennan, II, p. 292; (5) Tribune, March 27, 1902; (6) Chronicle, April 20, 1901, p. 744; Tribune, March 18, 1901; (7) Tribune, April 13, 1901; (8) Kennan, II, p. 296; (9) Pyle, II, p. 144; (10) ibid., p. 147; (11) Chronicle, May 11, 1901, p. 900; (12) Kennan, II, p. 299; (13) Tribune, March 27, 1902; (14) ibid.; (15) Chronicle, May 11, 1901, p. 900; (16) Tribune, May 10, 12, 1901; (17) ibid., May 10, 1901; (18) ibid.; World, May 12, 1901; (19) Kennan, II, p. 314; (20) Chronicle, May 11, 1901, p. 900; May 18, 1901, p. 959; (21) Clews, p. 758; Noyes, p. 301; (22) Chronicle, May 11, 1901, p. 903; (23) World, May 11, 1901; (24) Tribune, May 13, 1901; (25) ibid., May 14, 1901; (26) ibid., May 15, 1901; (27) Chronicle, July 20, 1901, p. 104; (28) ibid.; (29) Tribune, Nov. 14, 1901; (30) ibid.; (31) ibid., March 27, 1902.

CHAPTER XXVII

(1) Tribune, Dec. 13, 1901; (2) ibid., April 30, 1901; (3) ibid., Nov. 12, 1901; (4) ibid., April 22, 29, Nov. 28, 1902; (5) Chronicle, July 26, 1902; (6) Tribune, Oct. 1, 1902; (7) Noyes, Forty Years, p. 303; (8) Tribune, Nov. 20, 1902; (9) ibid., April 23, Dec. 2, 1902; (10) Chronicle, July 9, 1904, p. 126; (11) Tribune, Oct. 2, 1902; (12) World's Work, Jan. 1908, p. 9789; (13) Chronicle, July 9, 1904, p. 125; (14) Times, April 4, 15, Aug. 31, 1915; June 21, 1916; (15) Dewing, pp. 466-9; (16) Moody, Masters, p. 137; (17) Dewing, p. 486; Tribune, Oct. 8, 1903; (18) Tribune, Oct 8, 1903; (19) Post, Jan. 4, 1904; (20) Dewing, p.

499; Tribune, Oct. 8, 1903; (21) Tribune, Oct. 9, 1903; (22) Dewing, p. 491; (23) Tribune, Oct. 8, 1903; (24) Dewing, p. 420; (25) Clews, pp. 764-5; (26) Tribune, Jan. 16, 1903; (27) Chronicle, April 9, 1902, p. 800; (28) Kennan, I, p. 361; (29) ibid., p. 369; (30) Tribune, Nov. 30, 1905; (31) Kennan, I, pp. 376-7; (32) Times, March 31, 1903; (33) Tarbell, p. 171; (34) Money Trust Investigation, p. 1027; (35) Report on Steel Corporation, pp. 349-56; Chronicle, Nov. 21, 1903, p. 2001; (36) Judge, Nov. 21, 1903; (37) Wall Street Journal, April 1, 1913; Times, April 1, 1913; (38) Bishop, I, pp. 184-5; Tribune, Nov. 21, 1901; Chronicle, Nov. 23, 1901, p. 1080; ibid., Feb. 22, 1902, p. 398; (39) Supreme Court, Northern Securities Decision, pp. 19, 33; (40) ibid., p. 45; (41) ibid., p. 71; (42) Chronicle, April 11, 1902, p. 778; (43) Kennan, I, p. 388; (44) Tribune, April 5, 1904; (45) ibid., April 20, 1904; Chronicle, July 16, 1904, p. 177; Kennan, I, p. 395; (46) Tarbell, p. 189; (47) Tribune, Aug. 13, 14, 1902; (48) Jones, Trust Problem, p. 294; (49) Clark, II, p. 704; Money Trust Investigation, p. 1618; (50) Chronicle, June 30, 1903, p. 1331; Oct. 1903, p. 935; Jan. 30, 1904, p. 313; (51) ibid., Jan. 17, 1903; p. 137; (52) ibid., April 16, 1904; p. 1426; (53) ibid., March 13, 1905, p. 1889; June 24, 1905, p. 2559; (54) ibid., Oct. 18, 1904, p. 1439.

CHAPTER XXVIII

(1) Chronicle, Aug. 16, 1902, p. 321; (2) ibid., Dec. 5, 1903, p. 2132; (3) ibid., March 21, 1903, p. 622; (4) Clark, II, p. 5; Tribune, Aug. 14, 1902; Steel Investigation, p. 107; (5) Pyle, II, pp. 56-8; Pierce, p. 170; Times, June 5, 1902; (6) Tribune, Dec. 25, 1904; (7) ibid., April 12, 1901; (8) ibid., Feb. 17, 1901; June 9, 1901; (9) ibid., Oct. 22, 1902; (10) Chronicle, May 1903, p. 999; (11) Clark, II, p. 5; Nearing, p. 182; (12) Dunn, p. 240; (13) Nearing, p. 85; (14) Kennan, I, p. 256; Chronicle, May 9, 1903, p. 999; (15) Tribune, July 14, 1901; June 19, 1902; Phelps, p. 11; (16) Chronicle, March 14, 1903, p. 567; Canal Hearings, p. 1146; (17) Stuart, p. 97; Seitz, p. 297; Roosevelt, pp. 511-13; (18) Nearing, p. 83; (19) Chronicle, May 21, 1904, p. 1930; Canal Hearings, p. 1101; (20) Chronicle, Jan. 16, 1904, p. 195; Feb. 13, 1904, p. 668; World, April 1, 1913; (21) Canal Hearings, p. 1042; (22) ibid., pp. 1087, 1093; (23) Chronicle, Jan. 7, 1911, p. 4; Seitz, p. 368; (24) Chronicle, Jan. 7, 1911, p. 4; (25) Seitz, pp. 380-83; (26) Nearing, p. 97; (27) Chronicle, Jan. 25, 1902, p. 181; (28) Phelps, pp. 85, 141; (29) Chronicle, Nov. 25, 1905, p. 1519; Kennan, II, p. 14; (30) Tribune, Dec. 21, 1895; Times, Aug. 8, 1905; (31) ibid., Sept. 4, 1905; Gibson, p. 168; (32) Lichtervelde, p. 240; (33) ibid., p. 241; Gibson, p. 169; (34) Times, Aug. 8, 1905; (35) Tribune, Aug. 8, 1905; (36) Times, Aug. 8, 1905; (37) Tribune, Sept. 4, 1905; (38) Times, Aug. 8, 1905; (39) ibid.; (40) Williams, p. 30; Tribune, Aug. 30, 1905; (41) Chronicle, Aug. 12, 1905, p. 583; (42) ibid., Sept. 9, 1905, p. 800; (43) Kennan, II, pp. 22-7; (44) Dunn, p. 231; (45) Marsh, pp. 67-74; (46) ibid., p. 95; (47) Chronicle, Feb. 27, 1909, p. 528; (48) Stuart, p. 321; Paredes, p. 9; (49) Stuart, p. 321; (50) ibid.; (51) Paredes, p. 8; (52) Stuart, p. 321; (53) Nearing, p. 135; (54) ibid., p. 40; (55) Chronicle, Nov. 12, 1910, p. 1289; (56) Nearing, p. 38; (57) Chronicle, June 12, 1909, p. 1475; Times, April 20, 1913; (58) Chronicle, June 12, 1909, p. 1475; (59) Nearing, p. 43; (60) Chronicle, May 28, 1910, p. 1399; (61) ibid., p. 1390; (62) Gibson, p. 176; Nearing, pp. 46-8; (63) Chronicle, Oct. 29, 1910, p. 1134; (64) ibid., Nov. 12, 1910, p. 1289; (65) ibid., Dec. 10, 1910, p. 1544; (66) Nearing, p. 12; (67) Gibson, p. 289; (68) ibid., p. 145; (69) Times, March 19, 1913.

CHAPTER XXIX

(1) Times, Nov. 10, 1907; (2) Chronicle, March 2, 1901, p. 416; (3) Money Trust Investigation, p. 728; (4) Myers, III, p. 292; (5) Moody, Masters, p. 139; Noyes, p. 365; (6) Clews, p. 790; Times, Oct. 26, 1907; (7) Chronicle, March 16, 1907, p. 592; (8) Noyes, Forty Years, p. 360; (9) Chronicle, Aug. 24, 1907, p. 206; (10) ibid., March 16, 1907, p. 592; Times, March 13, 1907; (11) Money Trust Investigation, p. 445; World's Work, Nov. 1907, p. 9527; Chronicle, Sept. 7, 1907, p. 575; (12) Noyes, Forty Years, p. 364; (13) Chronicle, Oct. 19, 1907, p. 981; Oct. 26, 1907, p. 1059; (14) ibid., Oct. 26, 1907, p. 1060; Times, Oct. 23, 1907; (15) Burr, p. 225; Times, Oct. 20, 21, 1907; (16) Times, Oct. 23, 1907; Clews, p. 791; (17) Times, Oct. 21, 1907; (18) Money Trust Investigation, p. 443; (19) Chronicle, Oct. 26, 1907, p. 1059; (20) Times, Jan. 13, 1925; (21) ibid., Oct. 23, 24, 25, 1907; World, Oct. 24, 1907; (22) Burr, p. 235; Century, July 13, 1913, p. 459; (23) Money Trust Investigation, pp. 356-7; (24) Times, Oct. 30, 1907; (25) World, Oct. 25, 1907; (26) ibid., Oct. 24, 1907; (27) Times, Oct. 25, 26, 29, 1907; (28) Chronicle, Oct. 27, 1907, p. 1059; Burr, pp. 234-5; (29) Burr, p. 237; Times, Nov. 6, 1907; (30) Chronicle, Nov. 9, 1907, p. 1181; Steel Investigation, p. 128; (31) Steel Investigation, p. 130; (32) Times, Nov. 5, 1907; (33) Roosevelt, p. 468; (34) Steel Investigation, p. 170; (35) Report on Steel Corporation, pp. 256-9; (36) Steel Investigation, p. 125; Hovey, p. 302; (37) Times, Nov. 19, 1907; (38) ibid., Nov. 15, 1907; (39) ibid., Nov. 27, 28, 1907; (40) ibid., Dec. 29, 1907; (41) ibid., Nov. 24, 1907; (42) Chronicle, Nov. 30, 1907, p. 1373; (43) Noyes, p. 379; (44) Times, Oct. 27, 1907; Chronicle, Nov. 9, 1907, p. 1177; (45) Times, Oct 26, 1907; (46) World's Work, Nov. 1907, p. 9499.

CHAPTER XXX

(1) Chronicle, March 2, 1901, p. 416; (2) Noyes, Forty Years, p. 378; (3) Brandeis, pp. 135-48; (4) Moody, Masters, p. 118; (5) Kennan, I, p. 398; Brandeis, p. 169; (6) Kennan, II, pp. 313, 320; (7) Chronicle, June 6, 1903, p. 1221; Moody, Masters, p. 148; (8) Kennan, II, p. 334; (9) Money Trust Investigation, p. 450; (10) Moody, Masters, p. 149; (11) Brandeis, p. 93; (12) Money Trust Investigation, p. 1056; (13) ibid. (Report), p. 59; (14) ibid., p. 2129; (15) Brandeis, p. 147; (16) Money Trust Investigation (Report), p. 65; Brandeis, p. 145; (17) Noyes, Forty Years, p. 379; (18) Money Trust Investigation (Report), pp. 57, 60; (19) ibid., pp. 60-3; (20) ibid., pp. 63-5; (21) ibid., pp. 89-90; (22) ibid.; (23) Forbes, p. 11; (24) Money Trust Investigation (Report), pp. 66, 81; (25) ibid., p. 90; (26) ibid., pp. 84-5; Chronicle, March 25, 1911, p. 772; (27) Money Trust Investigation (Report), p. 89; (28) ibid., p. 90; (29) Wall Street Journal, April 1, 1913; (30) Money Trust Investigation, pp. 1423, 1433; Chronicle, July 1, 1911, p. 16.

CHAPTER XXXI

(1) Times, Dec. 31, 1903; (2) King, pp. 218, 231; (3) Douglas, p. 391; (4) Journal of Commerce, April 1, 1913; (5) Times, April 2, 1913; (6) Literary Digest, Feb. 15, 1913, p. 326; Chronicle, March 25, 1911, p. 760; (7) Seitz, p. 412; (8) Tribune, Jan. 31, 1905; (9) ibid.; (10) Chronicle, Aug. 12, 1911, p. 376; (11) Times, Nov. 14, 1907; (12) ibid., Oct. 23, 1907; (13) Tarbell, p. 183; (14) Seitz, p. 305; (15) Nation, June 30, 1926, p. 717; (16) Times, May 20, 1914; (17) Collier's, May 4, 1907, p. 14; (18) Times, Jan. 8, 1911; (19) Bishop, II, p. 110; (20) Wister, p. 212; (21) World, April 1, 1913.

CHAPTER XXXII

(1) Industrial Commission, I, pp. 122-3; (2) Steel Investigation, p. 79; (3) Jones, Coal Combination, p. 181; (4) ibid., pp. 183-202; (5) Times, July 15, 1915; (6) Seitz, p. 278; (7) Insurance Investigation (Report), p. 386; (8) ibid., pp. 11, 388-9; (9) Moody, Masters, pp. 123-5; (10) Insurance Investigation (Report), p. 388; (11) ibid., pp. 81, 122; (12) ibid. (Testimony), p. 333; (13) ibid., pp. 447, 450; (14) ibid., p. 449; (15) ibid., p. 1218; (16) Tribune, Dec. 10, 1905; (17) Insurance Investigation (Report), p. 17; (18) ibid., pp. 23, 49; (19) ibid. (Testimony), p. 1761; (20) ibid. (Report), p. 361; Chronicle, Aug. 24, 1907, p. 447; (21) Kennan, I, p. 421; (22) Money Trust, pp. 1069-70; (23) ibid., p. 1068; (24) ibid., pp. 1068-74; (25) ibid., p. 1094; (26) Times, April 20, 1911; (27) ibid., April 20, 1913; June 13, 1915; (28) Ripley, pp. 486-88; (29) ibid., pp. 201-2; (30) ibid., p. 208; (31) Tribune, Jan. 31, 1905; (32) Collier's, May 4, 1907, p. 14; (33) Tribune, Feb. 1, Oct. 12, 1905; (34) Collier's, May 4, 1907, p. 14; (35) Kennan, II, pp. 229, 306-35; (36) Times, Sept. 9, 1907; (37) Kennan, II, pp. 184, 206; (38) Moody, Masters, p. 153; (39) Chronicle, June 12, 1909, p. 1475; (40) ibid., Jan. 7, 1911, p. 8; (41) Times, Dec. 15, 1913; (42) Brandeis, pp. 179, 193; (43) Times, May 20, 1914; Nov. 10, 23, 1915; (44) Brandeis, pp. 190, 206; (45) Gazette, July 2, 1909, p. 3; Nov. 19, 1909, p. 952; (46) Times, May 20, 1914; (47) ibid., May 21, 1914; Nov. 18, 1915; (48) Everybody's, July 1914, p. 98; (49) Times, May 20, 1914; (50) ibid.; (51) ibid.; (52) ibid, May 26, 1914; (53) Everybody's, July 1914, p. 98; (54) Wall Street Journal, Dec. 24, 1912; Times, May 16, Sept. 18, 1913; (55) Brandeis, p. 133; (56) Times, July 18, Aug. 23, Sept. 12, 16, 1913; Jan. 4, 1914; (57) Forbes, p. 333; (58) Moody, Trusts, p. xi; (59) Tribune, Jan. 31, 1905; (60) Notz, p. 6; (61) Jones, Trust problem, pp. 111-13; (62) Ripley, p. 359; (63) Chronicle, Aug. 10, 1907, p. 315; (64) ibid., May 20, 1911, p. 1343; (65) ibid.; (66) ibid.; (67) Times, May 16, 17, 20, 1911; (68) Chronicle, May 20, 1911; p. 1387; June 3, 1911, p. 1460; Jones, Trust Problem, p. 449; (69) Van Hise, p. 38; (70) Chronicle, July 8, 1911, p. 74; Jones, Trust Problem, pp. 226-29; (71) Chronicle, July 8, 1911, p. 73; (72) ibid., Sept. 23, 1911, p. 754; Wall Street Journal, April 1, 1913; (73) ibid., Sept. 30, 1911; p. 843; (74) Tarbell, p. 228; (75) ibid., pp. 222-4; (76) Tribune, March 20, 1920; (77) Times, Dec. 20, 1913; (78) Brandeis, p. 1; (79) ibid.; (80) Chronicle, July 6, 1912.

CHAPTER XXXIII

(1) Money Trust Investigation, pp. 1436-7; (2) ibid., pp. 1538-9; (3) ibid., pp. 1567-8; Times, Jan. 10, 1913; (4) Money Trust Investigation (Report), p. 65; World, Dec. 18, 1910; (5) Money Trust Investigation, p. 1876; (6) ibid., p. 1855; (7) ibid., p. 1838; (8) ibid., pp. 1841, 1878; (9) World, Dec. 19, 1912; (10) ibid., Dec. 20, 1912; (11) ibid.; Tribune, Dec. 20, 1912; (12) Money Trust Investigation, p. 1053; (13) ibid., pp. 1052-3, 1061; (14) ibid., p. 1047; (15) ibid., p. 1050; (16) ibid., pp. 1087-9; (17) ibid., p. 1007; (18) ibid., p. 1062; (19) Times, Jan. 25, 1913; (20) ibid.; (21) Money Trust Investigation (Report), pp. 163-4.

CHAPTER XXXIV

(1) Wall Street Journal, April 1, 1913; (2) Times, March 31, 1913; World, April 1, 1913; (3) Cortesi, p. 101; (4) Werner, p. 225; (5) Times, April 15, 21,

1913; (6) Times, April 20, 1913; (7) ibid., April 21, 1913; (8) ibid., April 20, 1913; (9) ibid.; (10) ibid., March 6, 1913; (11) ibid., March 20, 1913; (12) ibid., March 3, 4, 7, 8, 12, 1913; (13) ibid., March 9, 1913; (14) ibid., March 3, 21, 1913; (15) ibid., March 8, 21, 1913; (16) ibid., March 4, 1913; (17) ibid., March 29, 1913; (18) ibid., March 5, 1913.

CHAPTER XXXV

(1) Times, Dec. 14, 1913; (2) Van Hise, p. 191; (3) Noyes, War Period, p. 45-6; (4) Chronicle, Dec. 27, 1913, p. 1855; (5) Times, Jan. 3, 4, July 1, 1914; (6) Saturday Evening Post, July 12, 1930, p. 46; (7) Times, Feb. 2, 1915; (8) ibid.; (9) ibid., Jan. 13, 1925; (10) ibid, Oct. 10, 1913; (11) Tarbell, p. 248; (12) Times, July 31, 1914; (13) Noyes, War Period, pp. 83, 88; (14) Times, July 1, 1914; (15) ibid., Aug. 7, 1914; (16) ibid., Aug. 14, 16, 1914; (17) ibid., Sept. 29, 1915; (18) ibid., Jan. 24, 28, 1915; (19) ibid., April 21, May 5, June 22, 1915; (20) ibid., July 5, Aug. 15, 1915; Moody, Masters, p. 166; (21) Phelps, p. 119; (22) Vauclain, p. 34; (23) Douglas, p. 391; (24) Noyes, War Period, pp. 173, 187; (25) Times, March 27, July 26, 1917; (26) Saturday Evening Post, July 12, 1930; p. 46; (27) Forbes Mag., Aug. 15, 1930, p. 14; (28) Saturday Evening Post, Aug. 9, 1930, p. 101; (29) Times, Feb. 24, 1919; (30) Forbes Mag., Aug. 15, 1930, p. 14; (31) Times, Sept. 18, 1919; (32) ibid., Nov. 13, 1919; (33) Phelps, p. 158; (34) ibid., p. 146; Dunn, p. 161; (35) Phelps, p. 119; Dunn, p. 4; (36) Times, Jan. 17, 1914; Jan. 30, 1925; (37) ibid., Nov. 25, Dec. 11, 1925; (38) ibid., Oct. 6, 1924; (39) ibid., May 24, 26, 1925; (40) ibid., July 10, 21, 1925; (41) ibid., April 29, 1925; May 5, 6, 1927; (42) ibid., April 14, 1925; May 5, 6, 1927; (43) ibid., April 14, 1925; (44) ibid., Aug. 3, 1922; (45) ibid., June 2, 1929; (46) Post, June 25, 1929; (47) Times, June 9, 1929; (48) ibid., Feb. 27, 1930; (49) ibid., June 11, 1929; (50) Journal of Commerce, July 18, 1929; (51) ibid.; (52) New Republic, Jan. 26, 1927, p. 266; (53) Journal of Commerce, July 18, 1929; (54) Times, May 18, 1928; July 14, 1929; (55) Moody's Utilities; (56) ibid., p. 1501; Journal of Commerce, May 22, 1930; (57) Moody's Utilities; (58) ibid.; (59) Moody's Utilities, pp. 1605-6; (60) Denny, p. 226; Moody's Industrials, p. 2778; (61) Times, Aug. 10, 1929; (62) ibid., July 27, 1930; (63) ibid., Aug. 10, 1929; Moody's Industrials, pp. 1885, 1931; (64) Times, Aug. 30, Sept. 3, 1928; (65) Denny, p. 332; (66) Journal of Commerce, March 26, 1928; Times, Aug. 23, 1929; (67) Forbes Mag., Aug. 15, 1930, p. 30; (68) Journal of Commerce, Feb. 5, 1929; (69) Times, Aug. 23, 1930; (70) Times, June 30, 1930; (71) ibid., July 4, 1930; (72) Denny, p. 402; (73) Journal of Commerce, May 23, 1929; (74) Census of Manufactures, 1925; (75) Statistics of Income, 1927, pp. 41-2; (76) Times, Nov. 23, 1920; (77) ibid., June 21, 1929; (78) ibid., Aug. 25, 1929; (79) Journal of Commerce, April 25, 1928; (80) Raushenbush, p. 121; (81) Times, April 17, 1930; (82) Raushenbush, pp. 66-8; (83) ibid., p. 24; (84) Times, May 1, 1929; Raushenbush, pp. 21-46; (85) Journal of Commerce, July 11, 1929; Times, May 18, 1930; (86) Times, June 19, 1929; Sept. 14, 1929; (87) ibid., Sept. 18, 1929; (88) Moody, Banks and Finance, 1930, p. a42; (89) Times, July 8, 1930; (90) data on centralization and directorships compiled from Poor's Directory of Directors and Moody's Manuals of Investment; (91) Times, July 2, 1925; May 16, 1929; (92) ibid., Oct. 25, 28, 1929; Feb. 25, 1930; Journal of Commerce, Nov. 14, 1929; Feb. 27, 1930; (93) Times, Dec. 6, 1929.

INDEX

Erie, 47, 86, 89, 91 ff., 107 ff., 144, 162, 201, 211, 310, 311, 352.
Everett, Edward, 45.

Fabbri, Egisto P., 253.
Far East Power Corporation, 436.
Farmers, 23, 27, 30, 123.
Federal Reserve System, 192, 418, 423, 426, 430, 452.
Federal Steel, 248, 250, 258, 263 ff.
Federal Trade Commission, 417.
Field, Cyrus W., 131, 222.
Finance, 39, 50, 56, 112, 157, 159, 167, 176, 196, 351, 449 f.
Finance, national, 42, 82, 85, 89, 113, 132.
Firestone interests, 436, 437.
First National Bank, 201, 209, 256, 258, 320, 337, 342, 355, 358, 419, 429, 446 ff.
Fisk, Jim, 89, 91 ff., 102, 104, 107 ff., 113, 139, 251.
Ford, Henry, 265, 436, 437.
Free lands, 36, 76.
Frémont, General J. C., 60, 62, 67.
Frick, Henry C., 150, 236, 267, 270, 278, 328, 346, 370.

Garrison, William Lloyd, 31, 33, 36, 37, 55.
Gary, Elbert H., 153, 249, 263 ff., 281, 287, 288, 319, 346, 370, 374, 394, 411, 422.
Gates, John W., 213, 248, 250, 263 ff., 278, 288, 307, 309 ff., 345.
Gates, Rev. F. T., 270.
General Electric, 247, 258, 323, 53, 354, 434, 435, 441, 447.
General Motors, 386, 435, 437, 441.
George, David Lloyd, 367, 424.
Gold, J. P. Morgan speculates in, 65 ff.
Gould, Anna, 233.

Gould, Edwin, 328.
Gould, George J., 233, 320, 370.
Gould, Jay, 56, 89, 91 ff., 102, 104, 107 ff., 113, 139, 141, 144, 148, 157, 163, 166, 169, 171, 172, 173, 201, 204, 208, 232, 260.
Grace, W. R., & Co., 223, 324, 426.
Granger movement, 123, 163.
Grant, Ulysses S., 62, 105, 119, 222, 224, 451.
Great Northern, 206, 295 ff.
Greenback Party, 123, 125, 183.
Guaranty Trust, 211, 352, 429, 446.
Guggenheim, Daniel, 320.
Guggenheim, Isaac, 328.
Guggenheim interests, 433.

Hamilton, Alexander, 29.
Hanna, Marcus A. (Mark), 182, 195, 212, 228.
Harriman, Edward H., 155 ff., 201, 205, 208, 209, 260, 293 ff., 310, 311, 314, 318, 324, 328, 331, 339, 343, 351, 353, 358, 376, 379, 382, 383, 449.
Hartford Wits, 27, 196.
Havemeyer, Henry O., 370.
Hayes, Rutherford B., 219.
Heinz, F. Augustus, 339, 340.
Hewitt, Abram S., 240, 280.
Hill, James J., 172, 195, 206, 208, 256, 257, 260, 285, 295 ff., 318, 323, 358.
Holmes, Justice Oliver Wendell, 317.
Hooker, Thomas, 27.
Hoover, Herbert, 433, 452-3.
Hopkins, Lemuel, 27.
Hughes, Charles E., 375 ff.
Huntington, Collis P., 156, 172, 223.
Hyde, Charles H., 306.

Immigrants, 15, 19, 30, 77, 101, 194, 282.

Imperialism, 48, 85, 89, 217, 222, 322 ff., 421, 428, 433.
Income tax, 193, 367.
Industrialism, 38, 39, 55, 78, 235, 369.
Insurance investigation, 380 ff.
Interlocking directors, 157, 202, 257, 258, 260, 355, 399, 407, 446 ff.
International Banking Corporation, 328, 429.
International Harvester, 319, 354, 394, 447.
International Mercantile Marine, 304 ff., 323, 377.
Interstate Commerce Commission, 165, 169, 175, 210, 417.
Intervention, 324, 438, 440.

Jackson, Andrew, 31, 39, 102.
Jacksonian Democracy, 39, 77, 196.
Jefferson, Thomas, 27, 29, 39.
Jeffersonian Democracy, 12, 77.

Kahn, Otto H., 320, 430.
Kansas Pacific, 88.
Keene, James R., 274, 345.
Kennecott Copper, 436.
Ketchum, Edward B., 66 ff., 71.
Ketchum, Morgan & Co., 25.
Ketchum, Morris, 25, 59, 61, 67.
Ketchum, Son & Co., 59, 67, 71.
Kidder, Peabody & Co., 166, 356.
King Philip's War, 16, 18.
Knox, Philander C., 272, 315, 316, 332, 334.
Kuhn, Loeb & Co., 43, 200, 204, 206, 227, 260, 295 f., 328, 331, 334, 337, 345, 356, 376.

Labor, 30, 36, 56, 77, 78, 123, 163, 172, 194, 234, 283 ff., 366, 395, 414, 420, 423, 425, 450.
La Follette, Robert M., 395.
Lake Superior Consolidated Iron Mines, 269, 272.

Lamont, Daniel S., 370.
Lamont, Thomas W., 333, 352, 355, 427, 428, 430, 437, 445, 452.
Lanier, Charles, 219.
League of Nations, 440.
Leopold, King of the Belgians, 329, 331.
Lincoln, Abraham, 58, 62, 73, 102.
Little, Jacob, 47, 91, 201.
Louisville & Nasnville, 309, 310.
Lynching, 232, 411.

Manifest Destiny, 47, 105, 223, 229.
McAllister, Ward, 193, 236.
McCall, John A., 256.
McKinley, William, 195 f., 224, 241, 248, 286, 316.
McLeod, Arthur, 202 f.
Mellen, Charles S., 321, 369, 370, 385 ff.
Mellon, A. W., 320.
Merrit, Leonidas, 270 ff.
Money Trust, 192, 275, 312, 343, 376, 392, 394 ff., 415.
Monroe Doctrine, 221, 327, 333, 428.
Moore, James H., 263, 265.
Moore, William H., 263, 265.
Morgan, Grenfell & Co., 424, 428.
Morgan, Harjes & Co., 117, 189, 309, 312, 423.
Morgan, James, 15, 20.
Morgan, J. P., & Co., 189, 191, 198, 211, 224, 227, 248, 253, 261, 264 ff., 274, 285, 300, 308, 310, 318, 322, 323 ff., 329, 342, 344, 351, 354 ff., 376 ff., 399 ff., 419 ff., 441 ff.
Morgan, J. Pierpont, Jr., 56, 189, 305, 334, 388, 413, 415, 418 ff., 427, 431, 432, 450.
Morgan, J. Pierpont, & Co., 57, 59, 61, 68, 73.
Morgan, J. S., & Co., 42, 73, 85, 87,

CPSIA information can be obtained
at www.ICGtesting.com
Printed in the USA
BVHW031818250621
610515BV00001B/7